QUESTIONS OF EVIDENCE IN THE UN HUMAN RIGHTS TREATY BODIES' INDIVIDUAL COMMUNICATIONS PROCEDURE

Eight United Nations human rights treaty bodies (UNTBs) can currently examine 'communications' (complaints) from individuals against states. This edited collection is the first in-depth analysis of the evidentiary regimes developed within this procedure. Nine case studies underscore the weak evidentiary basis of the UNTB decisions and the importance of addressing this issue, whilst the final chapter offers a set of practical recommendations. Grounded in academic research and legal practice, the volume incorporates doctrinal, critical, socio-legal and anthropological perspectives. It provides an authoritative reference on UNTBs, whilst aiming to contribute to the strengthening of their evidentiary norms and practices. The title is also available open access on Cambridge Core.

DEBORAH CASALIN was, at the time of writing, Principal Research Fellow at the Law and Development Research Group at the University of Antwerp. She is a Swiss National Science Foundation Ambizione Fellow at the Geneva Graduate Institute. Her doctoral research examined the role of the UN treaty bodies in ensuring reparation for arbitrary displacement, employing systematic case law analysis and a study of CESCR's decisions on mortgage evictions in Spain.

MARIE-BÉNÉDICTE DEMBOUR is Professor of Law and Anthropology at Ghent University, where she leads the research project 'DISSECT: Evidence in International Human Rights Adjudication' (ERC-AdG-2018-834044). Her numerous publications include a special issue on 'The Evidentiary System of the European Court of Human Rights in Critical Perspective' (2023).

CORNELIA KLOCKER is Senior Researcher at the Human Rights Centre, Faculty of Law and Criminology of Ghent University, Belgium. Her research centres on questions of non-discrimination and the intersections between human rights law and the law of armed conflict, including related evidentiary issues.

STUDIES ON INTERNATIONAL COURTS AND TRIBUNALS

General Editors
Andreas Føllesdal, University of Oslo
Geir Ulfstein, University of Oslo

Studies on International Courts and Tribunals contains theoretical and interdisciplinary scholarship on legal aspects as well as the legitimacy and effectiveness of international courts and tribunals.

Other books in the series:

Mads Andenas and Eirik Bjorge (eds.) *A Farewell to Fragmentation: Reassertion and Convergence in International Law*

Cecilia M. Bailliet and Nobuo Hayashi (eds.) *The Legitimacy of International Criminal Tribunals*

Amrei Müller with Hege Elisabeth Kjos (eds.) *Judicial Dialogue and Human Rights*

Nienke Grossman, Harlan Grant Cohen, Andreas Follesdal and Geir Ulfstein (eds.) *Legitimacy and International Courts*

Theresa Squatrito, Oran R. Young, Andreas Føllesdal, Geir Ulfstein (eds.) *The Performance of International Courts and Tribunals*

Robert Howse, Hélène Ruiz-Fabri, Geir Ulfstein and Michelle Q. Zang (eds.) *The Legitimacy of International Trade Courts and Tribunals*

Marlene Wind (ed.) *International Courts and Domestic Politics*

Christina Voigt (ed.) *International Judicial Practice on the Environment: Questions of Legitimacy*

Martin Scheinin (ed.) *Human Rights Norms in 'Other' International Courts*

Freya Baetens (ed.) *Legitimacy of Unseen Actors in International Adjudication*

Shai Dothan *International Judicial Review: When Should International Courts Intervene?*

Silje Langvatn, Mattias Kumm, Wojciech Sadurski (eds.) *Public Reason and Courts*

Daniel Behn, Szilárd Gáspár-Szilágyi, Malcolm Langford (eds.) *Adjudicating Trade and Investment Disputes: Convergence or Divergence?*

Sondre Torp Helmersen *The Application of Teachings by the International Court of Justice*

Daniel Behn, Ole Kristian Fauchald, Malcolm Langford (eds.) *The Legitimacy of Investment Arbitration: Empirical Perspectives*

Eric De Brabandere *International Procedure in Interstate Litigation and Arbitration: A Comparative Approach*

Chiara Giorgetti and Mark Pollack (eds.) *Beyond Fragmentation: Cross-Fertilization, Cooperation and Competition among International Courts and Tribunals*

Stavros Brekoulakis and Georgios Dimitropoulos (eds.) *International Commercial Courts: The Future of Transnational Adjudication*

Matthew Gillett *Prosecuting Environmental Harm before the International Criminal Court*

Sassan Gholiagha *The Humanisation of Global Politics: International Criminal Law, the Responsibility to Protect, and Drones*

Ezgi Yildiz *The European Court of Human Rights and the Norm Against Torture: Between Forbearance and Audacity*

Christina Voigt and Caroline Foster (eds.) *International Courts versus Non-Compliance Mechanisms: Comparative Advantages in Strengthening Treaty Implementation*

Luise Müller *The Right to Punish: Political Authority and International Criminal Justice*

Theresa Squatrito *Judging under Constraint: The Politics of Deference by International Courts*

Alain Zysset, *Responding to Authoritarian Populism at the European Court of Human Rights: A Calibrated Framework*

QUESTIONS OF EVIDENCE IN THE UN HUMAN RIGHTS TREATY BODIES' INDIVIDUAL COMMUNICATIONS PROCEDURE

Edited by

DEBORAH CASALIN

University of Antwerp

MARIE-BÉNÉDICTE DEMBOUR

Ghent University

CORNELIA KLOCKER

Ghent University

CAMBRIDGE
UNIVERSITY PRESS

CAMBRIDGE
UNIVERSITY PRESS

Shaftesbury Road, Cambridge CB2 8EA, United Kingdom

One Liberty Plaza, 20th Floor, New York, NY 10006, USA

477 Williamstown Road, Port Melbourne, VIC 3207, Australia

314–321, 3rd Floor, Plot 3, Splendor Forum, Jasola District Centre, New Delhi – 110025, India

Cambridge University Press is part of Cambridge University Press & Assessment, a department of the University of Cambridge.

We share the University's mission to contribute to society through the pursuit of education, learning and research at the highest international levels of excellence.

www.cambridge.org
Information on this title: www.cambridge.org/9781009639224

DOI: 10.1017/9781009639231

First published 2026

Cover image: Adult women of all ages running to vote / ivetavaicule / DigitalVision Vectors / Getty Images

A catalogue record for this publication is available from the British Library

Library of Congress Cataloging-in-Publication Data

Names: Casalin, Deborah editor | Dembour, Marie-Bénédicte, 1961- editor |
Klocker, Cornelia Angela editor
Title: Questions of evidence in the un human rights treaty bodies' individual communications procedure / edited by Deborah Casalin, University of Antwerp; Marie-Bénédicte Dembour, Ghent University; Cornelia Klocker, Ghent University.
Description: Cambridge, United Kingdom ; New York, NY : Cambridge University Press, 2026. | Series: Studies on international courts and tribunals (SICT) | Includes bibliographical references and index.
Identifiers: LCCN 2025050981 (print) | LCCN 2025050982 (ebook) | ISBN 9781009639224 hardback | ISBN 9781009639217 paperback | ISBN 9781009639231 epub
Subjects: LCSH: Burden of proof | International law and human rights | Human rights | International courts | United Nations Human Rights Council | Treaties
Classification: LCC K2263 .Q84 2026 (print) | LCC K2263 (ebook)
LC record available at https://lccn.loc.gov/2025050981
LC ebook record available at https://lccn.loc.gov/2025050982

ISBN 978-1-009-63922-4 Hardback
ISBN 978-1-009-63921-7 Paperback

To Bob, Ellis, Gregor, Karl and Tom

CONTENTS

TABLES

CONTRIBUTORS

MEGHAN CAMPBELL is Reader in International Human Rights Law at the University of Birmingham.

DEBORAH CASALIN was, at the time of writing, Principal Research Fellow at the Law and Development Research Group, Faculty of Law, at the University of Antwerp.

MARIE-BÉNÉDICTE DEMBOUR is Professor of Law and Anthropology at Ghent University and the Principal Investigator of the DISSECT: Evidence in International Human Rights Adjudication research project (ERC-ADG-2018-834044).

ELENA GHIDONI is a postdoctoral researcher at the Human Rights Institute of the University of Deusto.

MATTHEW GILLETT is Senior Lecturer at the University of Essex and a Vice-Chair of the UN Working Group on Arbitrary Detention.

HANAA HAKIKI directs the Border Justice Program at the Berlin-based European Centre for Constitutional and Human Rights (ECCHR), litigating European pushbacks and border violence in front of international adjudicative bodies.

MIIA HALME-TUOMISAARI is Associate Professor of Human Rights Studies at Lund University.

YUTAKA KARUKAYA is a PhD candidate at Aoyama Gakuin University and a member of the University of Essex's Arbitrary Detention Redress Unit.

CORNELIA KLOCKER is Senior Researcher at Ghent University and a member of the DISSECT research project.

MIA MARZOTTO is a Human Rights Advocacy Officer and a member of the University of Essex's Arbitrary Detention Redress Unit.

KASEY MCCALL-SMITH is Senior Lecturer in Public International Law at the University of Edinburgh.

VINCENT PLOTON sits on the editorial board of the *Journal of Human Rights Practice*. At the time of writing, he was Head of UN Treaty Body advocacy at the International Service for Human Rights (ISHR).

LISA REINSBERG is the founder of the International Justice Resource Center and Lecturer at the University of California, Berkeley School of Law.

CHRISTOPHER ROBERTS is Associate Professor at the Faculty of Law of the Chinese University of Hong Kong.

REETTA TOIVANEN is Full Professor in Sustainability Science (Indigenous Sustainabilities) at the University of Helsinki.

ACKNOWLEDGEMENTS

Our thanks go to the European Research Council for having made it possible for this collection of foundational research into the evidentiary regime of UN human rights treaty bodies (UNTBs) to emerge. The book is an output of the 'DISSECT: Evidence in International Human Rights Adjudication' Horizon 2020 research project (ERC-AdG-2018-834044), led by Marie-Bénédicte Dembour, and hosted by the University of Ghent.

The volume started as a symposium, held in Ghent on 15–16 May 2023. We are grateful to everyone who responded to our call for papers, and to those who accepted our invitation to come to Ghent. Besides the authors of the chapters which follow, this includes Victoria Abut, Parvana Bayramova, Adriana Bones, Wojciech Burek, Ergün Cakal, Frederick Cowell, Susan H. Farbstein, Hilary Gbedemah, Rebecca Gore, Kerem Gülay, Octavian Ichim, Özge Karsu, Louna Monaco, Sabrina Ochoa, Maithili Pai, Jimena Reyes, Diego Rodríguez-Pinzón, Carlos Leonardo Santana Bareño and Emma Várnagy. The symposium benefited from having its panels chaired and discussed by the following members of the DISSECT research team: Anne Heinisch, Ruwadzano Makumbe, Genaro Andrés Manrique Giacomán, Edward Kahuthia Murimi and Emma Várnagy. The symposium would not have been the success it was without the meticulous logistical planning provided by DISSECT's administrative support team, in the persons of Martine Dewulf and Kristien Van Ingelgem.

With participants hailing from academia and practice, including from UNTB committee membership and litigating experience, the symposium's exchanges were illuminating throughout. They were open, warm and stimulating. This congenial spirit translated in all paper-givers committing at the end of the symposium to help in shaping collective recommendations. This pledge has become Chapter 11 of this volume.

Turning the symposium into a book required further work. We thank the chapters' authors for having responded with good grace to our multiple requests for new drafts, further clarifications and additional edits. We also gratefully acknowledge the general support we received from the distinguished members of the DISSECT project's advisory board.

We are grateful to Cambridge University Press, as well as to the editors of the International Courts and Tribunals Series, for their enthusiastic reception of our book proposal and support during the publication process. We particularly wish to acknowledge the anonymous reviewers' useful comments and the helpful guidance provided by Natasha Burton and Edgar Mendez. Tiny Vandoorne from the DISSECT administrative team and Vera Wriedt lent invaluable assistance in finalising the manuscript. Finally, had it not been for Zach Woodham agreeing to prepare the index, and then doing it to his characteristically exacting standards, the manuscript would not yet have been ready to be sent to press as we were writing these words in July 2025.

NOTE ON LEGAL TECHNICAL TERMS USED BY THE UN HUMAN RIGHTS TREATY BODIES

Author: Term of art which designates the complainant in UNTB lexicon. CAT also uses the term 'complainant', CERD the term 'petitioner'.

Individual communication: Claim submitted to a UNTB by an individual, a group of persons or an organisation that their human rights have been violated; in common parlance, complaint.

View: Non-legally binding decision on the merits handed down by a UNTB; sometimes also called 'opinion'.

TABLE OF CASES

ABBREVIATIONS

ACHPR	African Court on Human and Peoples' Rights
ACmHPR	African Commission on Human and Peoples' Rights
BiH	Bosnia and Herzegovina
BRD	Beyond reasonable doubt
CAT	Convention against Torture/Committee against Torture
CCPR	Centre for Civil and Political Rights
CDE	Moldovan Council on Preventing and Eliminating Discrimination and Ensuring Equality
CED	International Convention for the Protection of All Persons from Enforced Disappearance/Committee on Enforced Disappearances
CEDAW	Convention on the Elimination of Discrimination against Women/ Committee on the Elimination of Discrimination against Women
CERD	Committee on the Elimination of Racial Discrimination
CESCR	Committee on Economic, Social and Cultural Rights
CIDT	Cruel, inhuman or degrading treatment
CMW	Committee on the Protection of the Rights of All Migrant Workers and Members of Their Families
CoE	Council of Europe
CRC	Convention on the Rights of the Child/Committee on the Rights of the Child
CRPD	Convention on the Rights of Persons with Disabilities/Committee on the Rights of Persons with Disabilities
ECCHR	European Centre for Constitutional and Human Rights
ECHR	European Convention on Human Rights
ECmHR	European Commission on Human Rights
ECtHR	European Court of Human Rights
EU	European Union
FA	Forensic Architecture
GR	General recommendation [issued by a UNTB]
HRC	Human Rights Committee
IACmHR	Inter-American Commission on Human Rights
IACtHR	Inter-American Court of Human Rights

ICCPR	International Covenant on Civil and Political Rights
ICERD	International Convention on the Elimination of Racial Discrimination
ICESCR	International Covenant on Economic, Social and Cultural Rights
ICJ	International Court of Justice
ICMW	International Convention on the Protection of the Rights of All Migrant Workers and Members of Their Families
ICPPED	International Convention for the Protection of All Persons from Enforced Disappearance
ICRC	International Committee of the Red Cross
ICSID	International Centre for Settlement of Investment Disputes
ISHR	International Service for Human Rights
NGO	Non-governmental organisation
OHCHR	Office of the High Commissioner for Human Rights
OP-. . .	Optional Protocol to . . . (affixed to the abbreviation of the relevant treaty, e.g. OP-CEDAW; OP-CRPD; OP-ICCPR; OP-ICESCR)
SAC	[Finnish] Supreme Administrative Court
SPT	Subcommittee on Prevention of Torture and other Cruel, Inhuman or Degrading Treatment or Punishment
TPI	Third-party intervention
UDHR	Universal Declaration of Human Rights
UHRI	Universal Human Rights Index
UN	United Nations
UNDRIP	United Nations Declaration on the Rights of Indigenous Peoples
UNODC	UN Office on Drugs and Crime
UN OHCHR	United Nations Office of the High Commissioner for Human Rights
UNSC	United Nations Security Council
UNTB	United Nations human rights treaty body
UNTS	United Nations Treaty Series
UPR	Universal Periodic Review
WGAD	Working Group on Arbitrary Detention
WGEID	Working Group on Enforced or Involuntary Disappearances

1

Introduction: Studying Evidence in the United Nations Treaty Bodies' Individual Communications Procedure

Why This Book, What It Offers

DEBORAH CASALIN, MARIE-BÉNÉDICTE DEMBOUR AND CORNELIA KLOCKER

1.1 Introduction

International human rights law is a circle which is not easily squared: aiming at state accountability, it nonetheless depends on state consent for its emergence and continued existence.[1] This inherent contradiction explains the unwieldy legal architecture within which it has been developed at the United Nations (UN). A multitude of treaties have come to be adopted (or not) as the tribulations of politico-historical circumstances seemed to demand and to allow (or not). No less than nine core UN human rights treaties (so qualified because their provisions entirely relate to human rights) are currently in force. Each of these treaties creates its own distinct human rights treaty body (hereafter, UNTB or committee), organised as a committee of experts tasked with supervising its implementation (see Table 1.1 for their names).[2] Eight of these nine committees currently possess the power to receive and examine

We are grateful to the contributors to this volume for having helped us to think through the field of evidence at the United Nations human rights treaty bodies (UNTBs). Special thanks go to Vincent Ploton, who diligently read and commented upon a draft of this chapter, as well as to various insiders to the procedure who kindly enlightened us on some issues.

[1] As the subtitle of Laurence Burgorgue-Larssen's book *Les Trois Cours Régionales des Droits de l'Homme in Context : La Justice qui n'allait pas de soi* (Paris: Editions Pedone, 2020) beautifully emphasises.

[2] With the exception of the ICESCR, whose associated monitoring body, CESCR, was established by the Economic and Social Council (i.e., an organ of the UN, not its 'parent' convention).

Table 1.1 *Parent treaties and associated UNTBs empowered to receive individual communications: Names and acronyms*

Parent treaty	Associated UNTB
International Covenant for Civil and Political Rights (ICCPR)	Committee on Civil and Political Rights, also known as Human Rights Committee (HRC)
International Convention on the Elimination of All Forms of Racial Discrimination (ICERD)	Committee on the Elimination of Racial Discrimination (CERD)
Convention against Torture and Other Cruel, Inhuman or Degrading Treatment (CAT)	Committee against Torture (CAT/CAT Committee)
Convention on the Elimination of Discrimination against Women (CEDAW)	Committee on the Elimination of Discrimination against Women (CEDAW/CEDAW Committee)
Convention on the Rights of Persons with Disabilities (CRPD)	Committee on the Rights of Persons with Disabilities (CRPD/CRPD Committee)
International Convention for the Protection of All Persons from Enforced Disappearance (ICPPED)	Committee on Enforced Disappearances (CED)
International Covenant on Economic, Social and Cultural Rights (ICESCR)	Committee on Economic, Social and Cultural Rights (CESCR)
Convention on the Rights of the Child (CRC)	Committee on the Rights of the Child (CRC / CRC Committee)
International Convention on the Protection of the Rights of All Migrant Workers and Members of Their Families (ICRMW)	Committee on the Protection of the Rights of All Migrant Workers and Members of Their Families (CMW)

communications by individuals who allege violations of their parent treaty by a state party.[3]

This individual communications procedure (hereafter, procedure or mechanism) is the mechanism with which this book is concerned. It is the closest to a judicial process that states could be persuaded to let emerge at the UN for the protection of human rights. The words formally

[3] The Committee on Migrant Workers will acquire this competence when ten states have both ratified its parent treaty and made the special declaration to this effect; a tenth UNTB – the Sub-Committee on the Prevention of Torture and other Cruel, Inhuman or Degrading Treatment or Punishment (SPT) – does not have this competence.

Table 1.2 *The nine UNTBs empowered to receive individual communications: Some numbers*

Parent treaty		Associated UNTB				Examination of individual communications		
Acronym	Years of adoption & entry into force	Acronym	Number of committee members	Year of first meeting	Number of sessions per year[a]	State consent is expressed through ratification (R) or special declaration (D)[b]	Year the UNTB obtained this competence	Near number of final views as of 1 June 2025[c]
ICCPR	1966/1976	HRC	18	1976	3	R of OP adopted in 1976	**1976**	1518
ICERD	1965/1969	CERD	18	1970	3	D (under Art. 14)	**1982**	60
CAT	1984/1987	CAT	10	1988	2	D (under Art. 22)	**1988**	477
CEDAW	1979/1979	CEDAW	23	1982	3	R of OP adopted in 1999	**2000**	62
CRPD	2006/2008	CRPD	18	2009	2	R of OP adopted in 2006	**2008**	45
ICPPED	2006/2010	CED	10	2011	2	D (under Art. 31)	**2011**	3
ICESCR	1966/1976	CESCR	18	1987	2	R of OP adopted in 2018	**2013**	16
CRC	1989/1990	CRC	18	1991	3	R of OP adopted in 2006	**2014**	46
ICRMW	1990/2003	CMW	14	2004	2	D (under Art. 77)	**Awaited**	N/A

[a] As indicated in each UNTB's most recent rules of procedure or, when not indicated there (as for CEDAW and CED), in the information provided on the website of the OHCHR (under treaty bodies).

[b] Ratification is of the relevant optional protocol (OP) to the parent treaty; special declaration is as provided under the relevant article (Art.) in the parent treaty.

[c] As per the information provided in the OHCHR Juris database (which is not always exhaustive and sometimes contains duplications).

used to describe it strikingly sit outside the common legal lexicon: UNTBs consist in 'committees' (not courts), made up of 'experts' (not judges), empowered to express 'final views' (not legally binding judgments) on 'communications' (not complaints) received from 'authors' (not applicants). This vocabulary intentionally emphasises the non-judicial character of the procedure, reflecting the reality that it has never been possible to create a world court of human rights.

Although UNTBs' final views are not legally binding, they carry authority. As such, they can offer some form of redress to victims of human rights violations who either are not legally entitled, or do not wish,[4] to turn to one of the three regional – African, European and Inter-American – systems of human rights protection. This is not to say that everyone around the globe has a legal avenue to complain when their human rights are violated: despite the ambition of the treaties to have a global reach, an individual can only address a communication to a UNTB regarding a state which has specifically accepted the procedure – through ratification or a special declaration to this effect, as dictated by the relevant instrument (see Table 1.2 as to which method is applicable for each body).

All UN member states have ratified or acceded to at least some core treaties.[5] The Convention on the Rights of the Child (CRC) has been almost universally adopted. Out of the 174 state parties to the International Covenant on Civil and Political Rights (ICCPR), 119 have ratified the Optional Protocol (OP) enabling individuals to bring communications to the attention of the Human Rights Committee (HRC).[6] By June 2025, the HRC had adopted some 1,500 views, representing by far the bulk of UNTB decisions on individual communications. In terms of volume of case law, the Committee against Torture (CAT) comes next with about 500 views, and then, following further behind, are the Committee on the Elimination of Discrimination against Women (CEDAW Committee, CEDAW) and the Committee on the Elimination of Racial Discrimination (CERD Committee, CERD), each with about sixty views to this day. With already more than 2,000 decisions overall, the UNTBs' quasi-judicial output is increasingly subject to academic analysis.[7]

[4] For example, M.-B. Dembour and H. Hakiki note that the ECtHR's restrictive jurisprudence is inciting at least some pushback complainants to bring their complaints before UNTBs (see Chapter 2, this volume).

[5] See OHCHR website, Status of Ratification Interactive Dashboard (under 'Indicators').

[6] OHCHR, Status of Ratification Interactive Dashboard.

[7] See, e.g., A. J. Ullman and A. von Staden, 'A Room Full of "Views": Introducing a New Dataset to Explore Compliance with the Decisions of the UN Human Rights Treaty

Partaking in this trend, this book scrutinises one essential procedural aspect of the mechanism, namely the way evidentiary questions are handled. The topic is important. Evidence can make or break cases in any judicial, or quasi-judicial, proceedings. As the studies collected in this volume demonstrate, this truism applies equally to the UNTB communications procedure. The question of what is (to be) considered appropriate evidence within the context of the procedure is therefore crucial. As one starts to reflect upon it, it does not cease acquiring additional layers of complexity. It thus transforms itself into a series of sub-questions, including, in a non-exhaustive list:

1) How much evidence can/should be considered sufficient for finding factual allegations substantiated? Is it possible to give some measure of the evidentiary level that is to be reached, and this in various circumstances and at the different stages of the proceedings? (The short answer is, yes, this can be done, with the standards of proof developed in the Common Law tradition offering a useful avenue in this respect).
2) When the evidence before the adjudicator is not convincing enough, leaving the factual basis of the complaint uncertain, should the complainant necessarily stand to lose the case? (Short answer, not necessarily; there are circumstances where the burden of proof should be shifted to the respondent state, which, as a result, should lose the case if the shifted burden remains undischarged).
3) What evidentiary position should the adjudicator adopt when a state prevents the proof of its violating practices from emerging, including by refraining from engaging in the proceedings directed against it in a

Bodies' Individual Complaints Procedures', *Journal of Conflict Resolution* 68 (2023): 534–561; L. Borlini and L. Crema, 'The Legal Status of Decisions by Human Rights Treaty Bodies: Authoritative Interpretations or mission éducatrice?', in A. A. Cançado Trindade and G. Ziccardi Capaldo (eds), *Global Community Yearbook of International Law and Jurisprudence 2019* (Oxford University Press, 2020), pp. 137–150; B. Cali, C. Costello and S. Cunningham, 'Hard Protection through Soft Courts? Non-refoulement before the United Nations Treaty Bodies', *German Law Journal* 21 (2020): 355–384; S. Liebenberg, 'Between Sovereignty and Accountability: The Emerging Jurisprudence of the United Nations Committee on Economic, Social and Cultural Rights under the Optional Protocol', *Human Rights Quarterly* 42 (2020): 48–84; K. McCall-Smith, 'Treaty Bodies: Choreographing the Customary Prohibition against Torture, *International Community Law Review* 21 (2019): 344–368; V. Shikhelman, 'Implementing Decisions of International Human Rights Institutions – Evidence from the United Nations Human Rights Committee', *European Journal of International Law* 30 (2019): 753–777.

particular case? (Short answer, the evidentiary burden on the complainant should be lightened, which can be achieved in various ways that are worth distinguishing).

The three bullet points above are offered as teasers to make it clear that evidence in international human rights (quasi-)adjudication is a field that requires reflection and clarification. They are also meant to suggest that the resolution of evidentiary issues will often be a complex exercise. Hoping merely to be able to apply common sense will not do, the more so since ostensibly objective, scientific evidence is not always available and, even where it is, it is likely to remain subject to interpretation. What is required, therefore, is the construction of a fair and clear evidentiary normative framework. This should avoid the extremes of, on the one hand, unfettered flexibility,[8] leading to lack of consistency and fairness, and, on the other hand, undue rigidity that forecloses the possibility of delivering justice.

In this overall context, the collective ambition of this volume is, first, to highlight how clarity about evidentiary norms is currently in great part lacking in UNTB quasi-jurisprudence; second, to stress through concrete examples the importance of addressing this issue; and third, to recommend the adoption of specific legal principles and/or practical ways of proceeding, which can contribute to the building of an evidentiary system fit for international human rights adjudication.

1.2 The UN Treaty Bodies: Mandate, Composition and Mode of Working

As already mentioned, there are currently nine core UN human rights treaties, each of which has an associated committee supervising its implementation. For example, the Committee on the Elimination of Racial Discrimination (CERD) monitors the implementation of the International Convention on the Elimination of All Forms of Racial Discrimination (ICERD).

The nine treaties obviously differ in the nature of their coverage. The two so-called covenants are general, aiming to cover all civil and political rights on the one hand and all economic, social and cultural rights on the

[8] Flexibility is recognised as a key feature of evidence in human rights adjudication. See, e.g., M.-B. Dembour, 'Editorial: The Evidentiary System of the European Court of Human Rights in Critical Perspectives', *European Convention on Human Rights Law Review* 4 (2023): 363–374, 365–366.

other hand. These covenants had originally been intended to follow swiftly the proclamation of the Universal *Declaration* of Human Rights (emphasis added) with legally binding provisions. However, the onset of the Cold War resulted in the covenants' negotiation taking two decades, and their entry into force a third one. Three further conventions each address a specific type of human rights violation, namely: racial discrimination; torture and other cruel, inhuman and degrading treatment or punishment; and forced disappearance. Four other instruments are framed by reference to the persons whom they seek to protect, namely: women; children; migrant workers and their families; and persons with disabilities (for these instruments' exact titles, see Table 1.1). One may imagine that additional human rights treaties may come to be adopted in the future.

In general, the core treaties not only create their supervising body but also define the latter's mandate. The central function of the committees is the examination of periodic state reports. Every state party to a treaty is expected to submit, at periodic intervals, a report detailing 'the measures they have adopted which give effect to the rights recognized herein and on the progress made in the enjoyment of those rights'.[9] Each submitted report is examined by the relevant committee, which, at the end of this process, issues 'concluding observations'. Such 'state monitoring' is the key method through which the UNTBs discharge their supervisory function. It takes an enormous amount of committee time, as well as a lot of work on the part of the participating states, which must write a periodic report for each treaty to which they are parties. This situation has resulted in calls to avoid duplications and in the adoption of 'mainstreaming' measures.[10]

UNTBs also have other functions, usually either outlined in the original text of their parent treaty or provided for in an additional protocol to the latter. The quasi-judicial competence to receive and examine communications from individuals who allege having suffered a violation of the parent treaty has become generalised across all treaty bodies. In addition, most committees are empowered to examine inter-state

[9] Art. 40 (1) ICCPR. The other core treaties contain an equivalent provision. ICCPED has the particularity that it only requires an initial report (Art. 29.1), with other reports to follow at an interval to be decided by its Committee (Art. 29.4). This has led some states parties to consider that they do not need to periodically appear before CED.

[10] See, e.g., the 2024 conclusions of the UNTB Chairs on the further advancement of a simplified reporting procedure: Report of the Chairs of the human rights treaty bodies on their thirty-sixth annual meeting, A/79/292 (6 August 2024), para. 59.

communications.[11] Admittedly, this function is almost irrelevant in practice due to states' overall reluctance to institute proceedings against their peers.[12] Under the condition that the state party has agreed to the relevant provisions, most committees are granted the power to investigate a situation through an inquiry procedure,[13] early warning mechanisms[14] and/or urgent actions.[15] The Subcommittee on Prevention of Torture and other Cruel, Inhuman or Degrading Treatment or Punishment (SPT), created in 2002 by the Optional Protocol to the Convention Against Torture, has a specific mandate to visit places where people are deprived of their liberty (states willing).[16] Finally, all UNTBs have developed a practice of writing 'general comments' which interpret the rights guaranteed by their parent treaty.

It is not only each committee's mandate but also the number of experts sitting on it, their conditions of eligibility and the broad terms of reference for their work which are set out in the relevant parent treaty. In a range going from ten (CAT and CED) to twenty-five (SPT) members, the majority of committees are made up of eighteen members, as indicated in Table 1.2.

The ICCPR mandates that the members of its committee be 'persons of high moral character and recognized competence in the field of human rights, consideration being given to the usefulness of the participation of some persons having legal experience'.[17] Without being exactly reproduced, this formulation has a broad equivalent in the parent treaties that followed. The Addis Ababa Guidelines represent the most elaborate attempt so far to ensure that candidates for UNTBs have the required skills to qualify for membership, and importantly, that they are independent. In particular, the Guidelines provide that 'Members [shall] avoid functions or activities which are … incompatible with the

[11] Art. 41 ICCPR; Art. 11 ICERD; Art. 21 CAT; Art. 76 ICRMW; Art. 10 OP-ICESCR; Art. 12 OP-CRC; Art. 32 ICPPED.

[12] Only three inter-state communications have been received so far, all by CERD, with only one examined and concluded to this day. See Chapter 4, this volume.

[13] CESCR, CEDAW, CAT, CRPD and CRC.

[14] CERD and CRPD.

[15] CERD, CRPD and CED.

[16] The Optional Protocol to the Convention against Torture was adopted in 2002 and entered into force in 2006. The SPT, which does not have an individual communications procedure, started operating in 2007.

[17] Art. 28 (2) ICCPR.

obligations and responsibilities of independent experts under the relevant treaties'.[18]

There is no requirement for members to be legally trained, let alone to have legal or judicial experience. This arguably presents both advantages and disadvantages. For example, the Committee Against Torture has reportedly benefited from being able to rely on medical or psychological expertise within its membership.[19] On the minus side, those members who are not legally trained are dependent on others (such as the administrative staff who support the UNTBs' work) to explain to them the significance of the legal intricacies that their quasi-judicial function inevitably generates.

The members of any given committee are elected by the states parties to the parent treaty. They serve in a personal capacity for four years, with elections staggered every two years. Members are elected in line with the principle of equitable geographical distribution, and two treaties (ICRPD and ICPPED) also explicitly mention balanced gender representation.[20]

[18] Addis Ababa Guidelines on the independence and impartiality of members of the human rights treaty bodies: UN Doc A/67/222, 2012.

[19] See E. Cakal, 'Evidence between Expertise and Expedience: Reflections on the Symposium "Evidentiary Regimes of UN Treaty Bodies: Perspectives from Research and Practice" (Ghent, 15–16 May 2023)', *DISSECT* (blogpost dated 29 May 2023).

[20] Art. 31 (2) ICCPR: '. . . equitable geographical distribution of membership and to the representation of the different forms of civilization and of the principal legal systems'; Art. 8 (1) ICERD: '. . . equitable geographical distribution and to the representation of the different forms of civilization as well as of the principal legal systems'; Art. 17 (1) CEDAW: 'consideration being given to equitable geographical distribution and to the representation of the different forms of civilization as well as the principal legal systems'; ECOSOC Resolution 1985/17, para. b: '. . . due consideration being given to equitable geographical distribution and to the representation of different forms of social and legal systems'; Art. 17 (1) CAT: 'consideration being given to equitable geographical distribution and to the usefulness of the participation of some persons having legal experience'; Art. 43 (2) CRC: '. . . consideration being given to equitable geographical distribution, as well as to the principal legal systems'; Art. 72 (2) (a): '. . . due consideration being given to equitable geographical distribution, including both States of origin and States of employment, and to the representation of the principal legal systems'; Art. 34 (4) ICRPD: '. . . consideration being given to equitable geographical distribution, representation of the different forms of civilization and of the principal legal systems, balanced gender representation and participation of experts with disabilities'; Art. 26 (1) ICPPED: 'The members of the Committee shall be elected by the States Parties according to equitable geographical distribution. Due account shall be taken of the usefulness of the participation in the work of the Committee of persons having relevant legal experience and of balanced gender representation.'

In practice, political considerations enter this electoral process, with a generalised practice of vote trading among states reported by some observers.[21] Despite this context, 'the overall level of independent expertise possessed by committees [remains] surprisingly high'.[22]

The rules of procedure of each committee outline the general conduct of sessions. For example, the Rules of Procedure for the HRC state that the Committee 'shall hold sessions as may be required for the satisfactory performance of its functions' and 'normally hold[s] three regular sessions each year'.[23] It has become the norm for a committee to meet in Geneva two or three times a year for between two to four weeks, depending on the number of state reports received and communications registered. Some committees hold pre-sessional preparatory meetings.[24] Due to a number of UN member states not paying their financial contributions, funding for the organisation of these meetings has been under pressure.[25]

Committee members are not remunerated for the time they devote to fulfilling their UNTB functions. They perform these functions on the side of their regular professional occupation. Only their expenses directly related to their obligatory attendance at in-person meetings are compensated by the UN through a daily subsistence allowance, with travel costs also borne by the UN.

Given their restrictive mandates and their composition of unremunerated independent experts meeting for limited periods, UNTBs were not expected to make much of a difference. It is precisely because of this predicted insignificance that states had originally agreed to their creation. In practice, however, UNTBs have grown to play an important role, including as quasi-judicial bodies. It is to this procedure, which is the focus of this book, which we now turn.

[21] See, e.g., V. Ploton, 'NGOs, China and the UN Treaty Bodies', in B. Ramcharan, R. Brett, A. M. Clark and P. Parker (eds), *The Protection Roles of Human Rights NGOs: Essays in Honour of Adrien-Claude Zoller* (Brill, 2023) pp. 955–981, 956, 959; V. Carraro, 'Electing the Experts: Expertise and Independence in the UN Human Rights Treaty Bodies', *European Journal of International Relations* 25 (2019): 826–851.

[22] Carraro, 'Electing the Experts', 826.

[23] HRC, Rules of Procedure, Rules 1 and 2 (1), CCPR/C/3/Rev.12 (4 January 2021).

[24] The HRC holds a one-week working group meeting before the session on individual communications; CEDAW as well as the CRC and CESCR (since 2021) hold pre-sessional working groups for between one and three days (UN staff, personal communication).

[25] See, e.g., the following news item: 'Human Rights Committee Holds Thirteenth Informal Meeting with States Parties', 21 March 2024, on ungeneva.org.

1.3 The UNTB Individual Communications Procedure: General Features

In addition to the eight UNTBs that currently fall within the purview of this book, we have decided to include a chapter in this book on a ninth body: the Working Group on Arbitrary Detention (WGAD). The WGAD is a special procedure created by the former Commission on Human Rights (predecessor of the Human Rights Council), with competence to examine individual communications related to a particular right – the right to be free from arbitrary detention. Although the WGAD is not attached to a specific treaty, it is concerned with an issue that cuts across the scope of a number of core human rights treaties. The procedure it follows is also akin to how the UNTBs proceed, with the difference that the respondent state does not need to have specifically accepted the WGAD's competence. Many of the features outlined below may therefore also be shared by the WGAD, albeit with necessary nuances to be taken into account.

The UNTB individual communications procedure starts with one or more individuals sending a communication alleging they have suffered a violation of their rights, due to a particular action or omission by a state, under the parent treaty of the UNTB addressed. Nowadays, this communication is done online.[26]

Instead of going directly to the UNTB concerned, this communication is first looked at by the Petitions Section, which fulfils the secretariat function on behalf of the Office of the UN High Commissioner for Human Rights (OHCHR). This small section, of which all members are currently legally trained, lends UNTBs the administrative support they need for their functioning. As such, it handles all cases that enter the individual communications procedure, whichever particular UNTB is addressed.

As is the case for the three regional human rights courts, the procedure is comprised of four distinct stages: (1) registration, (2) admissibility, (3) merits and (4) follow-up. Registration[27] is to take place on the simple verification that elementary conditions are fulfilled. Although the successful passing of this initial stage requires some facts to have been stated

[26] OHCHR, 'Form and guidance for submitting an individual communication to treaty bodies', updated 31 October 2025.

[27] The founding treaties do not speak of 'registration', but the term appears in the UNTBs' Rules of Procedure. See Chapter 11, this volume.

(such as the name of the complainant and the object of the complaint),[28] registration does not involve a thorough examination of evidence; at this stage, statements are meant to be taken at face value. This does not prevent, however, over eighty per cent of complaints from already being rejected at this stage,[29] and this without public trace (as there has been no registration of the case).

After registration comes the admissibility stage. Each UNTB sets its admissibility conditions in its rules of procedure. Whatever the exact phrasing under which they appear, these conditions are typical of international human rights adjudication. They may include that the complaint must be directed against a state which has specifically accepted the procedure; it must not be anonymous; it cannot have been submitted to the adjudication of another international body; domestic remedies must have been exhausted (with exceptions discussed in Chapter 6 of this volume); and it must be sufficiently substantiated (the normative meaning that this phrase should receive is explored in Chapter 3 of this volume).[30] The state is obviously the party that has an interest in claiming that one or more of the admissibility conditions are not fulfilled. It often does this. To determine whether such a claim is legitimate, the adjudicating committee may have to assess related evidence which has been submitted by the parties. Especially in regard to the last two conditions, this may give rise to complex issues and/or controversial decisions.[31]

If a committee decides that the complaint is admissible, it goes on to address its merits. In such a case, the admissibility and merits of the communication are usually addressed within the same written decision. Until recently, a state could request proceedings to be 'split' between these two phases. However, this possibility disappeared in May 2024, when all eight committees with the power to examine individual communications announced that in the interests of efficiency, they would address admissibility and merits at the same time.[32]

[28] For the registration requirements before each UNTB, see Table 11.3.

[29] See Chapter 11, this volume; see also Chapter 3, this volume.

[30] See Table 11.3 for the list of admissibility requirements which apply to each UNTB.

[31] See Chapters 2 and 7, this volume.

[32] Notice of 8 May 2025 on suspension of split requests, reproduced on the OHCHR website (under Treaty bodies, Complaints about human rights violations). The Committees nonetheless retain the power, in line with their rules of procedure, to split a case which raises specific admissibility issues ex officio, at registration.

Unless the committee is persuaded that the facts underlying the complaint have been properly established by the domestic authorities prior to having been communicated, consideration of the merits inherently requires a determination of the facts. In turn, this almost inevitably involves the resolution of evidentiary questions, and therefore the application of evidentiary principles. As repeatedly observed in the chapters that follow, these are often and regrettably left implicit in UNTBs' decisions.

The follow-up stage does not feature much in this book, but the few chapters addressing this nonetheless indicate that evidentiary issues can arise at this stage too.[33]

The reader interested in learning more about the procedural aspects outlined above is invited to turn immediately to Chapter 11, which not only systematises the recommendations which the contributors to this volume have individually and collectively identified, but also puts these recommendations in the context of the procedure, thereby giving slightly greater detail on the latter than provided in this introduction.

Within the confines of the present chapter, we shall content ourselves with highlighting four major characteristics of the procedure. The first is that the procedure, usually conducted in English,[34] is typically written from beginning to end. The parties take it in turn to submit their arguments, including the evidence upon which they wish to rely. Whilst UNTBs' rules of procedures tend to provide for how many rounds of exchange can take place before a decision is to be adopted, little regard seems to be given to these precepts in practice, putting especially the less resourced complainant under strain.[35] Importantly

[33] See Chapter 4, this volume.

[34] With likely impact on evidentiary assessments when original documents are not in English: see Chapter 11, this volume.

[35] 'CEDAW, CESCR and CCPR's Rules provide that parties have two rounds of exchange of submissions, after which the facts should be settled (thus resembling the exchange of pleadings in a civil suit). The Rules of CRC, CRPD and CED provide for one round only, but without limiting additional rounds. CAT and CERD's Rules mention no limit. Whilst the rules are one thing, practice can be another. For example, CEDAW hardly adheres to its prescribed rounds, and there are often as many as four or five rounds of exchanges, repeating and rebutting facts previously canvassed, and containing extraneous facts not relevant to the determination of the matter. Such a process places burdens on the parties, especially the less resourced author': Hilary Gbedemah, personal communication. Indeed, Hanaa Hakiki's litigating experience before three UNTBs (CAT, CRC and HRC) has also been that the state tends to send subsequent submissions, which then puts the complainant under an obligation to respond, even when every argument has already been put forward: Hakiki, personal communication.

given the subject of this book, at least some committees may hold oral hearings. However, the avenues that exist to make this possible are rarely, if ever, applied.[36] In practice then, bar the occasional exception, only the information submitted in writing by the parties is before the committee. This may include third-party interventions (TPIs). (Although only twenty-six TPIs had been referenced in UNTB views up until 2021,[37] their number is increasing).[38]

The second point we wish to stress is that the procedure relies heavily on the secretariat work accomplished by OHCHR through the Petitions Section. The fact that each committee meets for a limited period each year and that its members have other main professional activities means that the support provided by the secretariat is crucial. Committees generally base their deliberations in individual cases on, inter alia, summaries of the parties' submissions and a draft decision which the committee's rapporteur has prepared with the secretariat's support. Draft decisions being confidential, it cannot be gauged how often committees (do not) follow them. Committee members have always been entitled to receive the parties' submissions (including those regarding evidence) in full.[39] This, however, used to require proactivity on their part, in that this was subject to their specific request. This is no longer the case: members are now able to access case files directly on the intranet (with the possible exception, e.g., of documents that were not submitted electronically).

[36] 'The practice of holding hearings when deciding [on individual communications] is rare for UNTBs; only three UNTBs have ever done so: CRC, HRCHRC and CAT. Out of these three, only the CRC explicitly allows for the possibility of allowing oral interventions from third parties as well': V. Ploton and J. Urizar Montes de Oca, '"Friends of the Court": Making the Most of Amicus Curiae with UN Treaty Bodies', *EJIL: Talk!* (blogpost dated 18 April 2022). See more generally G. Ulfstein, 'Individual Complaints', in H. Keller and G. Ulfstein (eds), *United Nations Human Rights Treaty Bodies: Law and Legitimacy* (Cambridge: Cambridge University Press, 2012), pp. 73–115, 90–92.

[37] Ploton and Urizar, '"Friends of the Court"', also reporting that by 2021, CAT – the sole committee without a procedure dedicated to TPIs – had referred to a TPI only once in its comparatively large set of views.

[38] UN staff, personal communication.

[39] See, e.g.: Rules of Procedure of the Human Rights Committee, 2021, CCPR/C/3/Rev.12, Rule 89 (3); Rules of Procedure of the Committee on the Elimination of Racial Discrimination, 1986, CERD/C/35/Rev.3, Rule 85 (4). Anne Heinisch has documented a very different practice in respect of the ECtHR: 'The Evidentiary Practice of the European Court of Human Rights: Critical Reflections on its Historical, Institutional and Political Underpinnings' (PhD thesis, Ghent University, 2024–2025), section 6.4.2, entitled 'This Is a Court Where the Judge Cannot Read the [Case] File', pp. 159–161.

Our third point relates to the general under-resourcing of the procedure. The under-funding from which UNTBs have chronically suffered is getting worse as member states are increasingly refraining from paying (all of) their contributions to the UN. Anthropologists Niezen and Sapignoli have poignantly described how dependence on unforthcoming financial state support is 'the most significant peril faced by international organizations'.[40] This conclusion applies in particular to the UNTBs, as may be illustrated by the superficially mundane but ultimately significant example of the time and word space within which they are expected to process individual communications. In 2014, the UN General Assembly decided that, in view of the need for greater efficiency, a committee would be allocated 1.3 hours of discussion time for each individual communication; a word limit of 10,700 words was imposed for the drafting of all UNTB documents, including final views on individual communications.[41] The time limit was expressly reaffirmed in 2022.[42] The aforementioned suspension of the consideration of 'split requests', announced in May 2024, is another example of a measure adopted to increase efficiency amid chronic budget shortfalls. Worst of all, in autumn 2024, the deepening funding crisis led to a shortening of UNTBs' ordinary sessions, with uncertainty lingering as to whether they might be able to hold their next session.[43]

These logistical conditions do not leave UNTBs' functioning unscathed. They cannot but have knock-on effects all around UNTB work, including on the evidentiary examination in the individual communications procedure. Whilst we are not in a position to document this exact impact in this book, this is an important dimension which cannot be ignored.

[40] R. Niezen and M. Sapignoli, 'Introduction', in R. Niezen and M. Sapignoli (eds.), *Palaces of Hope: The Anthropology of Global Organizations* (Cambridge: Cambridge University Press, 2017), pp. 1–30, 16.

[41] A/RES/68/268 Strengthening and Enhancing the Effective Functioning of the Human Rights Treaty Body System, 9 April 2014, paras. 15, 26 (b).

[42] A/RES/77/210 Human Rights Treaty Body System, 15 December 2022, para. 5.

[43] The budget shortfall was predicted at 2.4 billion US dollars in 2025: 'UN faces deepening financial crisis, urges members to pay up', *UN News*, 19 May 2025. A 'Secretariat-wide regular budget recruitment freeze and liquidity crisis' was previously reported: A/77/279 Status of the human rights treaty body system, 8 August 2022, para. 44. This has also affected the committees. See, e.g., 'Human Rights Committee Holds Thirteenth Informal Meeting with States Parties', 21 March 2024, on ungeneva.org.

1.4 Research Challenges and How This Volume Met Them

This collection is an output of the DISSECT research project devoted to the study of evidence in international human rights adjudication, and more specifically, of the work package within this project devoted to the UNTBs' individual communications procedure.[44] This work package required eight institutions to be studied (with the addition of WGAD raising this to nine) – a number prone to daunt even the most experienced comparatist. An additional difficulty arose due to the difficulty of accessing data. Although the JURIS database was created by the OHCHR in 2022, the search results it generates are not comprehensive. These sometimes contain duplications, and other times miss some relevant cases due to keywords not always being consistently tagged. Furthermore, the database seems to suffer delays in its updating. Taking the HRC as example, the latest searchable views in June 2025 dated back to March 2024, thus excluding the views adopted over the then last three sessions.[45] Yet another issue exacerbated by funding constraints is the lack of translation, with decisions and guidance material not made available in all six official UN languages.[46]

Whilst the UNTB work package of the DISSECT project was never going to be easy to complete, a fortunate serendipitous series of events led to the idea of completing it through the organisation of a symposium, followed by the publication of an edited collection. Of course, this way of proceeding did not make the research challenges of this study evaporate. Two elements nonetheless rendered them more manageable. The first is that it no longer fell upon one individual researcher to ensure sufficient mastery of a case law dispersed across a large number of bodies. Instead, each contributor could take advantage of the expertise which they had acquired prior to joining the project, in respect of either a particular UNTB or a jurisprudential issue. The second is that both our call for papers and the symposium generated a wide range of contributions of high quality, from which we were able to select studies that would collectively offer a remarkable breadth and depth of research.

The majority of our contributors hail from legal academia; many are (also) involved in legal practice, or straddle two academic disciplines. The

44 See the DISSECT website hosted at UGent.

45 Being its 141st to 143rd sessions, as listed on the OHCHR website (UN Treaty Body Database).

46 As becomes clear when consulting, e.g., the JURIS database.

chapters are geared towards providing a sustained case analysis, except for Chapter 8, of which the central argument is built normatively, and Chapter 11, which systematises the recommendations. The number of cases reviewed in the other eight chapters is explicitly communicated each time. It varies from over four hundred cases (Chapter 3) to just two cases arising from the same situation (Chapter 10). The ten chapters address evidence in the UNTB procedure from different angles: four studies analyse the evidentiary approach of one particular body; four studies consider how one specific evidentiary question is/should be addressed across the committees; and two case studies fall outside this categorisation.

Citing them in the order in which they appear in this volume, the four studies focusing on a particular body relate to:

- CERD's persistently weak evidentiary framework – even after four decades of adjudicatory practice (Chapter 4 by academic lawyer Klocker).
- WGAD's increasingly systematic evidentiary approach over time, traced through three successive phases (Chapter 5 by academic lawyer and WGAD member Gillett, together with Karukaya and Marzotto, two legal practitioners who had previously studied with Gillett).
- HRC's readiness to reverse the burden of proof when the state refrains from participating in proceedings against it, in an analysis based on the adjudication of torture complaints (Chapter 7 by academic lawyer McCall-Smith).
- CEDAW's pioneering willingness to identify and denounce stereotypes which could otherwise be mistaken for evidence (Chapter 9 by legal academic Ghidoni).

The four cross-body studies analyse how one particular evidentiary issue is and/or should be dealt with across the UNTBs, as follows:

- How prima facie, the standard of proof that should apply at the admissibility stage, is often distorted in practice, to the complainant's detriment (Chapter 3 by legal practitioner and lecturer Reinsberg).
- How a complainant should not be expected to exhaust domestic remedies which are not accessible (thereby also ineffective), and how to best address the evidentiary questions which arise in this particular respect (Chapter 6 by academic lawyer Campbell).
- The importance of the adjudicator identifying when a seemingly isolated violation of human rights actually reflects a general practice,

therefore needing to be treated differently (Chapter 8 by academic lawyer and legal practitioner Roberts).

- Which practical recommendations derive from the various studies collected in this volume, to be offered to the UNTBs for their consideration (Chapter 11 by human rights practitioners Hakiki, Ploton and Reinsberg).

In addition, two case studies open and close the collection:

- The first, on pushback complaints, calls for the human rights adjudicator to defeat state-created evidentiary voids through adjusted, clear and fair, evidentiary principles (Chapter 2 by law/anthropology academic Dembour and border litigator Hakiki).
- The second can be seen as a cautionary tale against the impulse for the adjudicator (*in casu*, the HRC) to accept the allegations of a complainant without properly reflecting upon the (im)plausibility of the evidence submitted (Chapter 10 by anthropologists Halme-Tuomissaari and Toivanen).

In Section 1.5, we provide a longer summary of each chapter, this time within the context of the part in which we have located it in the volume.

1.5 The Book's Overall Structure

Following a logic which helps us to start exposing what we consider to be the volume's main findings, the book is divided into five substantive parts. Part I highlights the lack of clarity that characterises UNTBs' evidentiary norms and practices across the board. Part II contrasts the long-term evidentiary trajectories of two particular bodies. Part III proposes solutions to the perennial problem of the most powerful party in proceedings, that is, the state, often trying to evade accountability. Part IV provides crucial socio-legal insights about how evidence 'really' works (or not). Part V systematises our collective recommendations for evidentiary clarity, fairness and transparency.

1.5.1 Part I: Standards and Burdens of Proof in Need of Clarification

Part I starts by highlighting the lack of clarity in the evidentiary practice of the UNTBs. This weakness, present across the whole field of international human rights adjudication, is no doubt encouraged by the flexibility which is said to characterise the consideration of evidence in this field, thereby discouraging the 'fixing' of the principles that are applied.[47] The result, however, is that evidentiary concepts and principles (including their exceptions) are not clearly enunciated, let alone consistently applied. Vagueness ensues. Worse still, the wrong understanding and/or incorrect application of appropriate evidentiary principles mean that justice is not attained. Two studies have been selected to illustrate this point.

Chapter 2 by Dembour and Hakiki notes the acute evidentiary challenges which pushback complaints raise, due to states actively striving to suppress any evidence of their pushback operations. The authors of the chapter argue that, despite state denials, the four pushback cases so far decided by UNTBs see the adjudicating committees (HRC, CAT and CRC) invariably reaching the right conclusion about the facts. However, these findings are not accompanied by clear evidentiary reasoning. This produces two risks. The first is that a procedural establishment of the facts, achieved through a reversal of the burden of proof onto the respondent state which then fails to discharge this burden, does not get distinguished from a substantive establishment of the facts (which is preferable when it can take place). The second risk is that vagueness surrounding the standard of proof applied may create the impression that stronger evidence needs to be presented than is actually normatively required.

Chapter 3, by Reinsberg, concerns the requirement for complainants to have demonstrated that their allegations are 'sufficiently substantiated' or 'not manifestly unfounded' to pass the admissibility stage. Reinsberg argues that these expressions equate to a prima facie threshold, which is commonly understood – throughout all types of international adjudication – as requiring the complainant to make a *plausible* claim. Having reviewed over four hundred decisions, Reinsberg advances that UNTBs neither apply the prima facie standard consistently nor even seem to have a clear understanding of what it requires. She demonstrates that the UNTB case law often ends up distorting the widely accepted meaning of prima facie by (1) requiring the complainant to present not only plausible but actually convincing allegations; (2) taking into account the state's arguments and evidence for deciding admissibility; and (3) even sometimes appearing to expect the complainant to have already at

[47] Dembour, 'Editorial', p. 363.

this stage pre-emptively responded to defences which the state might consider raising in the future. In short, Reinsberg shows the 'sufficiently substantiated' requirement to be a bundle of confusions.

1.5.2 *Part II: Overall Trajectories of Evidentiary Systems in the Making*

Part II consists of two chapters, each of which looks at the evidentiary approach of one single body over its entire lifetime. The two histories recounted could not offer a more striking contrast. On the one hand, CERD is shown in Chapter 4 to remain to this day without an evidentiary system worthy of the name, despite having exercised the procedure for four decades. On the other hand, Chapter 5 praises WGAD for having refined its evidentiary system throughout its short existence, to the point of constituting an example that the UNTBs should emulate.

Her familiarity with CERD allows Chapter 4's author, Klocker, to observe that CERD rarely discusses evidence. She offers, as an extreme example of this, the case of *Dawas and Shava* v. *Denmark* (2012, concerning mob violence against refugees) in which evidentiary questions were left completely unaddressed by the Committee at the merits stage. These questions were then brought back to the table by the respondent state during the follow-up phase, at a time when they no longer could be properly dealt with, in an attempt to justify the state's strong resistance to implementing the decision. Klocker identifies a case at the other end of the spectrum, *Zapescu* v. *Moldova* (2021, about discriminatory employment practices), where both the standard of proof for procedural violations and the submitted evidence were comprehensively and convincingly discussed. Her hopeful conclusion is that subsequent elaborations of the same kind in its case law will lead CERD to develop a clear evidentiary pathway.

Chapter 5 argues that the more recently established WGAD is already there. Benefiting from insider knowledge, Gillett and his co-authors identify three distinct phases of establishment, expansion and consolidation in the development of the evidentiary approach of the Working Group. Throughout these phases, the WGAD's evidentiary approach was progressively formalised and standardised, improving its appropriateness and consistency. In the authors' view, this process reflects the entrenchment of the Working Group in the ecosystem of human rights bodies, rendering the WGAD an appropriate point of comparison for the UNTBs.

1.5.3 *Part III: Developing Evidentiary Techniques Capable of Holding States Accountable*

The book opens by planting the theme, in Part I, that a lack of evidentiary clarity mars much of the UNTB case law, and that this is problematic. Part II follows, highlighting that lack of clarity can be remedied by bringing . . . clarity. Its message is that evidentiary clarity can be achieved, since both WGAD and CERD (the latter admittedly not yet consistently) have managed this. Part III moves to another attribute which high-quality adjudication must also exhibit, namely that it actually delivers on its intended aims, and does so in a way that is fair to all parties.

The core aim of human rights adjudication is to hold states accountable for human rights violations. Within the focus of this book, the greatest obstacle to achieving such accountability is possibly the inequality of evidentiary arms which exists between the parties. If human rights adjudication is not to fail in its core mission, this inequality must deliberately and effectively be redressed by the adjudicator. Part III accordingly sheds light on evidentiary principles which are not yet (widely) accepted, but whose universal recognition and application would help in ensuring that states do not wriggle themselves off the hook of human rights accountability.

Chapter 6, by Campbell, is concerned with the admissibility of complaints: more specifically, with the rule that domestic remedies must have been exhausted before bringing a case internationally. Campbell accepts that the rule exists for good reasons, having to do with the subsidiarity of international human rights mechanisms and the importance of recognising domestic justice systems' crucial role in remedying human rights wrongs. She is concerned, however, that exemptions to this rule must be recognised in respect of remedies that lack effectiveness owing to their inaccessibility. Reviewing a large body of case law, Campbell detects a return by the UNTBs to a more formalistic application of the exhaustion rule. Taking an opposite stand, she pleads for an expansive consideration of the variety of barriers that prevent access to domestic justice. She also reflects upon how specific barriers may realistically be evidenced by a complainant. She argues that both the identification of barriers and their evidencing would be best achieved through the adoption of an individual-centred, contextual approach.

Chapter 7 addresses a question pertaining to the merits phase – namely how the adjudicator should proceed when a state chooses not to defend itself against a complaint. Shifting the evidentiary burden from the author to the state appears to be the appropriate response in such a case. How exactly should this happen, however? McCall-Smith's analysis of the HRC's case law dealing with torture allegations reveals an increasingly consistent approach over time. Whether the shift is operated depends on the nature of the allegations, the evidence used to corroborate the allegations, and the extent of the state's (non-) engagement. The HRC now seems to proceed in three logical steps before finding a violation of the prohibition of torture: (1) it verifies that there is at least some evidence corroborating the allegations; if so, (2) it presumes that the author's factual allegations are true; (3) it upholds this presumption, which is rebuttable, only if the state has not offered evidence counteracting the author's allegations.

Part III's last chapter (Chapter 8) has a more systemic and contextual outlook. Authored by Roberts, its underlying premise is that even though human rights violations often form part of a pattern or practice of violations, the nature of the individual communications procedure often leads the adjudicator to treat them as if they were isolated incidents. Roberts explores how awareness of contexts of violations could and should inform UNTB practice, and this at four different levels: the way UNTBs receive information and the types of sources they recognise in their decisions; their approaches to the exhaustion of domestic remedies and the burden of proof; their case structuring; and their findings, recommendations and follow-up procedures. Roberts ends by observing that UNTBs are not only receivers but also key disseminators of information, and suggests ways in which their findings on patterns and practices of violations could be more effectively disseminated.

1.5.4 Part IV: What 'Evidence' May Leave Unseen

The first three parts of the book are mainly written from a legal perspective. Their chapters grapple with aspects of which most lawyers would instantly recognise the importance, but to which non-lawyers may find it difficult to relate due to their legal technicality. Part IV continues to scrutinise case law and to engage with the law. However, it does so in order to bring to light elements which are beyond the legal horizon, in that they would not immediately catch a typical lawyer's attention. One chapter addresses the polluting effect of stereotypes on evidence; the next, the dangers of what its authors call 'distant evidence'.

Chapter 9 explains that stereotypes are generalisations about the behaviour or characteristics of a group's members. Presuming how certain individuals will act or present themselves, they provide ready-made narratives as to why and how events unfold. When operating 'undetected', they hamper the capacity to objectively analyse a factual situation. In the courtroom, they may lead to relevant pieces of evidence being ignored, irrelevant circumstances being given weight and unduly high standards of proof being imposed. Ghidoni notes that the CEDAW Committee deserves praise for having been a pioneer in recognising the polluting effect of stereotypes on the assessment of evidence. She observes, however, that the Committee does not invariably detect the impact of gender stereotypes on the evaluation of evidence performed by domestic courts. Her in-depth analysis of the views adopted by the Committee in selected individual communications reveals a mixed record. Ghidoni concludes by calling on the Committee members to become yet more attuned to the effects and harms of stereotypes, so that they are in a better position to 'see' discrimination.

Chapter 10 is a fascinating study of just two cases decided by the HRC. It highlights the multiple processes of translation of evidence which are involved in the processing of a complaint before a UNTB: from human event to legal case, from original language to the English UN lingua franca, from the parties' original submissions to summaries prepared by the Petitions Section for Committee members. In the process, evidence becomes ever more distanced from its original texture and meaning. The analysed communication emanated from a Sámi leader in Finland who alleged that ninety-three persons had been unduly added to the Sámi Parliament's electoral roll by a domestic court, and that another half a million could well follow suit. The Committee accepted these allegations, which the authors of the chapter, Halme-Tuomisaari and Toivanen, argue were utterly implausible. They conclude that, far from protecting human rights, the Committee's decision had the opposite effect, including on the Sámi. This prompts them to reflect on the way an evidentiary regime shapes and supports certain narratives whilst marginalising others.

1.5.5 Part V: Going Forward: Practical Recommendations

Finally, Part V, consisting of just one chapter, brings together the recommendations that both the discussions at the symposium and the preparation of this book generated. Written by three practitioners from the civil society sector, with experience of the procedure – namely Hakiki, Ploton and Reinsberg – Chapter 11 acts as a very good introduction to the procedure. It addresses technical aspects (e.g., which standard of proof should be applied in which circumstances and at which moment of the proceedings; how and when the burden of proof should be shifted) with great precision. It also brings forth general organisational issues, including the importance of proper resourcing to create a transparent and accessible system.

1.6 Cross-Cutting Themes

The chapters collected in this book can be read independently of each other. However, they constitute more than a mere collection of distinct elements. Together, they offer an encompassing and multi-layered analysis of how UNTBs have been/are/should be (in our view) engaging with evidentiary issues in the procedure. Not surprisingly, then, the ten chapters echo each other at multiple levels. To appreciate this, the reader may wish to consult the index, which has been carefully compiled to make it possible to follow up on particular interests but also to discover themes which run across various chapters. As for this introductory chapter, we end it by identifying three points which have come up again and again in discussions with our contributors.

The first is that having a good evidentiary system is an aspect of access to justice. A rather mundane observation, this nevertheless needs to be stated in a context where evidentiary issues often escape academic attention. This book keeps returning to the fact that a lack of conceptual clarity characterises UNTB evidentiary practice, be it on basic concepts (e.g., 'prima facie' and the other standards of proof), more complex operations (e.g., the conditions under which the burden of proof should be reversed), or through a multitude of statements which appear in the evidentiary reasoning (e.g., the pronouncement that an evidentiary submission must be given 'due weight' – an expression which appears in our index). If the various standards of proof applicable at different stages of the proceedings are not properly distinguished, this is likely to lead to individual communications being declared inadmissible which should have had their merits examined (as Chapter 3 so eloquently highlights). At a more general level, if facts are not found to be established, this will foreclose any possibility that the human rights violations which they constitute will be recognised. Even if other violations are found in the case in question, this cannot but weaken the impact of the decision (as Chapters 2 and 9 especially note). There are, of course, multiple ways in which justice ends up being denied due to evidence-related factors.

Chapter 4, for example, recounts a case where the state refused to implement a UNTB decision by rejecting the factual findings, which rested on poor evidentiary reasoning.

The OHCHR webpage on 'Individual communications' starts by stating: 'Anyone may bring a human rights problem to the attention of the United Nations and thousands of people around the world do so every year.'[48] The same page concludes its introduction to the procedure with the following words: 'The complaint mechanisms are designed to be accessible to the layperson. It is not necessary to be a lawyer or even familiar with legal and technical terms to bring a complaint under the treaties concerned.'[49] Whilst such accessibility may well be the procedure's honourable intention, the reality of its practice belies this. Firstly, there are many people who are under the jurisdiction of a state which has not agreed to the procedure, and who therefore cannot avail themselves of it. Secondly, the rule of the exhaustion of domestic remedies, in force in respect of the eight UNTBs empowered to examine communications, considerably restricts the procedure's practical reach. Obstacles to domestic justice which are not recognised by a committee translate into an insurmountable barrier to UNTB justice (Chapter 6). Thirdly, this book amply demonstrates that, in contrast to the case of WGAD (Chapter 5), the evidentiary requirements laid down by UNTBs are difficult to ascertain even by practicing and/or academic lawyers, let alone the general public. It therefore appears unduly optimistic to think that a victim of human rights violations could routinely, without the benefit of legal advice, manage to identify the type and level of evidence they should submit in support of their substantive claim (which itself will also need to be couched in legal terms). Indeed, the general opacity of the evidentiary system is the reason why the recommendations chapter, which concludes this book (Chapter 11), puts a lot of emphasis not only on the need for the applicable evidentiary principles to be clearly enunciated, but also on their effective communication, including on the currently rather difficult-to-navigate OHCHR website.[50]

We now turn to our second cross-cutting point, which seeks to amplify the message at the core of Part III of the book. Simply put, there are many ways in which the respondent state may (seek to) torpedo the proceedings. Some state strategies are transparent, such as a complete disengagement

[48] See the OHCHR website, under 'Treaty bodies' and then 'Individual communications'.
[49] Appearing before the listing of shortcuts to further information.
[50] See Chapter 11, this volume, n 65.

from the proceedings, or utter denials that the facts at the basis of the complaint ever took place. To the extent that these manoeuvres are obvious, they may be relatively easy for a determined adjudicative committee to counteract, for example, by shifting the burden of proof or drawing adverse inferences (as in the torture case law examined in Chapter 8). However, it is important to bear in mind that the state's evidentiary conduct may compromise the fair adjudication of a complaint in more subtle or inadvertent ways, as per the case study offered in Chapter 10.

This chapter is concerned with the *Näkkäläjärvi* case, where Finland was found by the HRC to be in violation of the ICCPR for having included certain individuals on the Sámi electoral register.[51] The chapter explains that the individuals in the case had actually been rightfully registered. This is to say that any human rights violations which arose in connection with this case were due not to the impugned actions of the State, but to the HRC's decision itself, as it provoked Finland to deregister the individuals concerned. This is an extraordinary upending of human rights adjudication.[52] Going beyond the reflections offered in the Chapter, it can be observed that it is the failure of the respondent state – which neither defended the decisions of its Court of Appeal before the Committee, nor pointed to the absurd character of the 'mathematical' evidence submitted by the complainants – which led the HRC astray. The core problem, then, is that Finland erred in leaving certain facts undisputed; HRC therefore accepted the complainant's factual allegations as established, as per the relevant legal principle.[53] Had Finland fulfilled its role of enlightening the Committee properly, another conclusion may likely have been reached. As it is, the decision deprived a number of Sámi of their right to vote, at the same time as putting the UNTB procedure, if not the human rights system more broadly, in a questionable light.

The third and final point we wish to make is that our critiques are not intended to beleaguer the UNTBs. This is the more so since we recognise the value of the human rights work accomplished by the committees,

[51] *Klemetti Näkkäläjärvi et al.* v. *Finland*, CCPR/C/124/D/2950/2017, 2 November 2018.

[52] C. Roberts has noted that, in cases of reversals of the burden of proof, 'the cost' of ending up with a false presumption of violation by the state can be assumed to be lower than 'the cost' of failing to find existing human rights violations: 'Reversing the Burden of Proof Before Human Rights Bodies', *The International Journal of Human Rights* 25 (2021): 1682–1703, 1687. *Näkkäläjärvi et al.* is an example of a *specific* individual case where this assumption clearly failed to hold.

[53] See Chapter 2, this volume, p. 47.

under logistical conditions which can only be described as sub-optimal. We particularly commend the development of case law that manages to denounce human rights violations, even in the face of serious evidentiary obstacles. Still, it is important that the case law achieves legal precision, consistency and fairness, and this requires reflection and conceptualisation. During the Symposium from which this volume emerged, CEDAW's former Chair Hilary Gbedemah recounted how she had been in the habit of instructing new committee members to read the academic 'bible' on gender stereotypes[54] (also cited in Chapter 9). Our hope is that the present volume may emulate this experience, and encourage both UNTBs and committee members to recognise the importance of dealing with evidentiary issues in a systematic way, with constant reference to sound normative principles. The technical character of the field may appear forbidding at first sight, especially to the non-legally trained expert. Evidence, however, is an essential part of the task of delivering justice to victims of human rights violations.

Grappling with evidence cannot and should not be avoided. On the positive side, as the book hopefully also testifies, many of its complications tend to dissipate once it is given proper attention, allowing its rationale and requirements to become increasingly obvious.

Select Bibliography

Borlini, L. and Crema, L., 'The Legal Status of Decisions by Human Rights Treaty Bodies: Authoritative Interpretations or mission éducatrice?', in Cançado Trindade, A. A. and Ziccardi Capaldo, G. (eds.), *Global Community Yearbook of International Law and Jurisprudence 2019* (Oxford: Oxford University Press, 2020), pp. 137–150.

Cali, B., Costello, C., and Cunningham, S., 'Hard Protection through Soft Courts? Non-refoulement before the United Nations Treaty Bodies', *German Law Journal* 21 (2020): 355–384.

Carraro, V. 'Electing the Experts: Expertise and Independence in the UN Human Rights Treaty Bodies', *European Journal of International Relations* 25 (2019): 826–851.

Dembour, M.-B., 'The Evidentiary System of the European Court of Human Rights in Critical Perspective', *European Convention on Human Rights Law Review* 4 (2023): 363–374.

[54] Cook, R. J. and Cusack, S., *Gender Stereotyping: Transnational Legal Perspectives* (Philadelphia: University of Pennsylvania Press, 2010).

Liebenberg, S., 'Between Sovereignty and Accountability: The Emerging Jurisprudence of the United Nations Committee on Economic, Social and Cultural Rights under the Optional Protocol', *Human Rights Quarterly* 42 (2020): 48–84

McCall-Smith, K., 'Treaty Bodies: Choreographing the Customary Prohibition against Torture', *International Community Law Review* 21 (2019): 344–368.

Niezen, R. and Sapignoli, M. (eds.), *Palaces of Hope: The Anthropology of Global Organizations* (Cambridge: Cambridge University Press, 2017).

Ploton, V., 'NGOs, China and the UN Treaty Bodies' in Ramcharan, B., Brett, R., Clark, A. M. and Parker, P. (eds.), *The Protection Roles of Human Rights NGOs: Essays in Honour of Adrien-Claude Zoller* (Leiden: Brill Nijhoff, 2023), pp. 955–981.

Shikhelman, V., 'Implementing Decisions of International Human Rights Institutions: Evidence from the United Nations Human Rights Committee', *European Journal of International Law* 30 (2019): 753–777.

Ulfstein, G., 'Individual Complaints', in Keller, H. and Ulfstein, G. (eds.), *United Nations Human Rights Treaty Bodies: Law and Legitimacy* (Cambridge: Cambridge University Press, 2012), pp. 73–115.

Ullman, J. and von Staden, A., 'A Room Full of "Views": Introducing a New Dataset to Explore Compliance with the Decisions of the UN Human Rights Treaty Bodies' Individual Complaints Procedures', *Journal of Conflict Resolution* 68 (2023): 534–561.

PART I

Standards and Burdens of Proof in Need of Clarification

2

Evidencing Pushbacks?

Why Fair, Clear and Consistently Applied Burdens and Standards of Proof are Essential to Human Rights Adjudication

MARIE-BÉNÉDICTE DEMBOUR AND HANAA HAKIKI*

2.1 Introduction

States violate human rights. If this were not the case, a multi-layered human rights framework aiming at accounting for states' human rights violations would not have been created. States may be participating in this accountability system in good faith, by which we mean they are willing – at least to some extent – to acknowledge their behaviour and change their ways. In other situations, however, human rights violations are deliberate and entrenched, having become part and parcel of state policy. Examples include systematic practices of torture, forcible disappearance, assassination of political opponents or, coming to the subject of our chapter, recklessly and often violently pushing people on the move back over the state border. A state which intentionally commits serious violations of human rights is unlikely to own up to its actions. Its tendency will be to deny the violations – ensuring at the same time that as little evidence of them as possible emerges. The resulting evidentiary gaps then make it difficult for accountability mechanisms to operate as intended.

Successful litigation should be possible even in these circumstances. However, it depends on the adjudicator accepting a complaint's factual

* This chapter is the result of a most fruitful collaboration between an analytical academic (Dembour) and an experienced litigator (Hakiki). Sections 2.2 and 2.3 owe more to Hakiki, Sections 2.4 and 2.6 to Dembour. The chapter is an output of the ERC project DISSECT and of the iBOF project 'Future-proofing human rights. Towards a thicker understanding of accountability', coordinated by Prof Tine Destrooper. Thanks are due to Isabel Kienzle, Cornelia Klocker, Bob Morton and Vera Wriedt for comments on an earlier draft.

basis. If states suppress evidence of their deeds, conclusive evidence that a complainant was treated as alleged will be lacking. Still a bedrock in evidentiary law today, the Latin adage *actori incumbit probatio* ('it is for the claimant to prove their claim') is often taken to mean that a complaint left without the proof of its factual allegations stands to be rejected. Such an outcome is problematic and requires a corrective when the complainant's evidentiary incapacity stems from actions or omissions purposefully instigated by the perpetrating state precisely in order to avoid human rights accountability.

One solution is to have the adjudicator shift the burden of proof from the complainant to the respondent state.[1] Although such a shift is often referred to in legal scholarship, the question of its exact conditions of operation is not settled. Surprisingly human rights jurisprudence tends not to address it head-on. In-depth academic analyses are conspicuous mostly by their absence.[2] We shall propose that the shift be conditioned on two sets of circumstances being established, each attracting a different standard of proof. We shall further argue that the shift-based evidentiary route must be distinguished from the 'normal' evidentiary route whereby, against the odds of state-created holes, the facts can get established on the substantive strength of the evidence submitted.

To make these arguments, we use the adjudication of pushback complaints by UN treaty bodies (UNTBs) as a case study. Pushbacks are expulsions designed to circumvent the law, by the state, of people on the move. (We favour this expression over other terms such as 'migrants', due to its bypassing the problematic migrant/refugee binary at the heart of most legal frameworks and migration discourses).[3] When the state

[1] Baranowska has persuasively argued that such a shift, now widely accepted to *have to* take place in forced disappearance cases, should equally be operated in pushback cases: G. Baranowska, 'Exposing Covert Border Enforcement: Why Failing to Shift the Burden of Proof in Pushback Cases Is Wrong', *European Convention on Human Rights Law Review*, 4 (2023): 473–494.

[2] But see C. Roberts, 'Reversing the Burden of Proof before Human Rights Bodies', *The International Journal of Human Rights*, 25 (2021): 1682–1703.

[3] 'The term "people on the move" is used to capture the diverse populations and circumstances of individuals and communities that find themselves in new locations. Sometimes movement has been voluntary, in search of new economic opportunities or new social horizons; at other times, movement has been forced as a result of armed conflict, discrimination or human rights violations. In reality, the distinction between voluntary and forced movement is blurred and challenged by the multiplicity of reasons for movement. Groups and communities of people on the move are further complicated by a variety of protection profiles, their reasons for moving and needs.' Human Rights

'pushes' people 'back', it forces them out of its jurisdiction, in such a way that they cannot access procedural and/or other legal safeguards.[4] Such evasion of legal frameworks may concern international instruments, such as the Refugee Convention or the protection granted to a person who is, for example, a victim of torture, a trafficked victim or an unaccompanied minor. It may also concern provisions found in domestic and international law for the benefit of the whole population, such as those adopted in order to guard against arbitrary detention or excessive state violence.

The evasion of legal guarantees is what makes an expulsion a 'pushback' (without the latter word being a legal term). This means that a pushback *always* entails expulsion-related human rights violations, including the denial of the expelled's right-holding status.[5] In addition, between the moment of their apprehension by state agents and their expulsion, people may have been beaten, secretly detained, tortured, left to die, disappeared or refouled to a place where their life or integrity is at risk – in short, subjected to serious human rights violations.[6]

In Europe, one would hope the European Court of Human Rights (ECtHR or Court) to be the go-to body for individuals seeking redress for the violations of human rights they have suffered. However, as Dembour has extensively documented,[7] the Court has shown itself reluctant to

Council, 'Report of the Special Rapporteur on the Situation of Human Rights Defenders' (A/HRC/37/51), 16 January 2018, para. 9.

4 See, e.g., Council of Europe's Commissioner for Human Rights, 'Pushed Beyond the Limits: Four Areas for Urgent Action to End Human Rights Violations at Europe's Borders', April 2022, p. 16.

5 D. Rodrik, 'Rights Not Recognized: Applying the Right to Recognition as a Person before the Law to Pushbacks at International Borders', *International Journal of Refugee Law* 33 (2021): 541–580. For a lived-experience perspective, D. Yambio, 'EU Law and Life of Us the Black Migrants', *Refugees in Libya* (15 May 2025), www.refugeesinlibya.org/post/eu-law-and-life-of-us-the-black-migrants.

6 Keady-Tabbal and Mann have warned against the danger of not recognising the serious violations that pushbacks entail: N. Keady-Tabbal and I. Mann, '"Pushbacks" as euphemism', *EJIL: Talk!* (blogpost dated 14 April 2021), www.ejiltalk.org/pushbacks-as-euphem ism/; UN Committee on Enforced Disappearances, General Comment No 1 on Enforced Disappearances in the Context of Migration (CED/C/GC/21), 26 October 2023, para. 6; Council of Europe's Committee for the Prevention of Torture and Inhuman or Degrading Treatment or Punishment, '32nd General Report of the CPT', March 2023, pp. 23ff.

7 M.-B. Dembour, *When Humans Become Migrants: Study of the European Court of Human Rights with an Inter-American Counterpoint* (Oxford: Oxford University Press, 2015); M.-B. Dembour 'The Migrant Case Law of the European Court of Human Rights: Critique and Way Forward' in B. Çalı, L. Bianku and I. Motoc (eds.), *Migration and the European Convention on Human Rights* (Oxford: Oxford University Press, 2021), pp. 19–40; M.-B.

defend the human rights of people on the move. This observation also holds for pushbacks: the Court has hardly ever found a 'no-paper pushback'[8] – that is one that leaves no trace of their occurrence in state records, as explained below – to have breached the European Convention on Human Rights.[9] The orientation of its jurisprudence is inciting litigators, including the European Centre for Constitutional and Human Rights (ECCHR), for which Hakiki works, to address pushback complaints to UNTBs, a telling change of forum since these bodies are not empowered to deliver legally binding judgments.

UNTBs' final views are nonetheless precious: carrying some authority, they offer some redress to victims as well as contribute to the development of human rights international law. In respect to our topic, they provide an official confirmation, against state denials, that pushbacks *are* a reality. Our analysis of the four final views UNTBs have so far adopted in pushback cases[10] concludes that the correct factual determinations were reached, with the UNTBs willing to see through the state-instigated evidentiary holes, but on a weak legal reasoning. In response, we identify evidentiary principles which we argue can contribute to the building of a fair, clear and coherent evidentiary framework.

Our chapter proceeds as follows. Section 2.2 classifies pushbacks into 'no-paper' and 'paper' categories, with each type giving rise to particular

Dembour and M. Rota, 'Le rôle des Cours européenne et interaméricaine des droits de l'homme face à l'enjeu migratoire', *Questions of International Law* 85 (2021): 47–63.

8 After the ECCHR coined the expression 'paper pushback', Alpes and Fehr started to talk of 'non-paper pushback', a label we find useful: I. Fehr and J. Alpes, 'Pushing states to evidence pushbacks: Lessons from MH v. Croatia for intersecting domestic criminal law and international human rights'. *DISSECT* blog (11 June 2023). See also J. Alpes and G. Baranowska, 'The Politics of Legal Facts: The Erasure of Pushback Evidence from the European Court of Human Rights', *Law and Social Inquiry* (2024): 1–24.

9 D. Rodrik and H. Hakiki, 'Accessing Borders, Accessing Justice? The European Court of Human Rights' Jurisprudence on Pushbacks at Land Borders', *Asyl, Schweizerische Zeitschrift für Asylrecht und praxis | Revue Suisse pour la pratique et le droit d'asile*, 1 (2023): 3–17.

10 More cases are pending, including six litigated by ECCHR. *Parvin A* v. *Greece* (HRC 4632/2024, pending), see www.ecchr.eu/en/case/bringing-greek-push-backs-to-justice/; *SM* v. *Croatia* (HRC 3857/2020, pending), see www.ecchr.eu/en/case/push-backs-croatia-complaint-un-human-rights-council/; *IM* v. *Slovenia and Croatia* (HRC 4574/2024 and 4573/2024, pending), see www.ecchr.eu/en/case/bildmaterial-beweist-gewaltsame-pushback-praxis/; *UF* v. *Slovenia and Croatia* (CRC 195/2022 and 196/2022, pending), see www.ecchr.eu/en/case/pushbacks-un-child-rights-croatia-slovenia/; *Ludovic N* v. *Spain* (CAT, pending), see https://www.ecchr.eu/es/caso/cuando-habra-justicia-para-las-victimas-de-el-tarajal/. See also *Fady* v. *Greece* (HRC, pending), see https://theintercept.com/2021/02/28/enforced-disappearances-asylum-migrant-abuse/.

forms of state denials. Section 2.3 reviews the limited evidentiary elements which, in a context of state-created evidentiary holes, may nonetheless potentially remain accessible to a pushback survivor. The chapter then moves to a legal analysis. Section 2.4 starts by mapping out the four logical outcomes which the adjudicator can reach regarding the disputed facts of a complaint: these can be upheld or rejected, procedurally or substantively so, following a number of evidentiary principles. This conceptual exercise provides the basis for critically analysing, in Section 2.5, the four pushback cases which have been decided by UNTBs to this day. Section 2.6 identifies what we regard as the two major risks of a loose evidentiary reasoning: the adjudicator's failure to demarcate the procedural (shift-based) and substantive (evidence-based) evidentiary routes; the upscaling of applicable standards of proof (e.g., due to the higher-than-legally-required standard met in some extraordinary cases becoming expected in subsequent cases, even where the shift is called for). Section 2.7 concludes.

2.2 State Denials: Typical Forms in 'No-Paper' and 'Paper' Pushback Cases

The stronger the secrecy surrounding a pushback operation, the less effective the legal safeguards against abuse, the more serious the human rights violations tend to become. This spiral then provokes states to want to deny their actions and in turn to dispense huge efforts in suppressing evidence. The following measures have been reported[11] to have been taken by states with regard to pushbacks: systematically failing to record people's presence, handling and custody; using unmarked vehicles for transportation, unofficial means for communication and unofficial detention sites; redirecting border cameras to 'unwitness'[12] human rights violations or refusing to share border cameras' footage;[13] criminalising audiovisual recording by third parties; seizing and destroying people's mobile phones; and expelling victims and witnesses, thus making them inaccessible to investigations.[14]

[11] See, e.g., ECCHR, 'Analyzing Greek Pushbacks: Over 20 Years of Concealed State Policy Without Accountability', February 2022; ECCHR, 'Croatia's Pushback Policy: A System of Unlawful, Covert, and Perpetuated Expulsions', February 2023.

[12] G. Reder, 'Unwitnessing the Border', *Oxford Border Criminologies* (blogpost dated 17 June 2024).

[13] As in *M.H. and Others* v. *Croatia*, ECtHR, 15670/18 and 43115/18, Judgment, 18 November 2021, paras. 11 and 271.

[14] As in *Doumbe Nnabuchi* v. *Spain*, ECtHR, 19420/15, Inadmissibility Decision, 1 June 2021, para. 18.

In the course of litigating cases, the ECCHR has come to distinguish between two broad types of pushbacks. No-paper pushbacks leave no trail in official records, such that even the most minutious examination of state records would give no hint whatsoever that they ever took place. By contrast, paper pushbacks leave an official trace, for example a refusal-of-entry decision or a readmission under a bilateral agreement, both of which qualify as pushbacks if the authorities ignored the protection needs and rights of the person refused or 'readmitted'.

The ECCHR has observed that when a person complains to have been no-paper pushbacked, their apprehension by state agents – of which there is by definition no official record – is often the centrally disputed fact. The situation presents itself differently in paper pushbacks, where the core problem is that the state record typically fails to mention protection claims. The factual issue most saliently disputed in this type of complaint is not whether the person was expelled (this is clearly documented) but whether they had expressed, or could have expressed, protection needs at the time of their expulsion. In paper pushbacks, the state typically claims to have respected all relevant applicable legal frameworks.

2.3 Which Types of Evidence Are Accessible to a Pushback Survivor?

Whilst the complainant is generally expected to bring the proof of their factual allegations, state-created evidentiary holes make this difficult, if not impossible. Based on Hakiki's litigating experience, this section identifies nine types of evidentiary material a pushback victim may nonetheless potentially be able to submit, as follows: (1) the complainant's own account; (2) identity documents; (3) digital messages and pictures/videos; (4) medical records; (5) fellow survivors' testimonies; (6) technological analysis of digital material; (7) legal correspondence; (8) state documents; (9) general reports. This section briefly discusses each element, highlighting their challenges and potential value. Elements (7) and (8) are especially relevant to paper pushbacks, whilst the others are addressed having mostly no-paper pushbacks in mind.

2.3.1 The Complainant's Own Account of the Events

With rare exceptions, pushback complainants have little to no external, stand-alone conclusive evidence of their factual claims. In this context, their own account of what happened to them often becomes the central piece of evidence they submit to the adjudicator. Few survivors, however, are ready to go through the process of recounting their pushback, as this tends to be a lengthy and retraumatising experience, often affecting a person for days and even weeks.

If a survivor wants to enter this process – which they should be encouraged to do only if they are already in a stable environment, ideally with access to psycho-social services – they cannot be expected to write their account alone. That they will need assistance is recognised in adversarial legal systems, which, leaving it to the parties to produce evidence,[15] devote a substantial part of the training of lawyers-to-be to the taking of truthful, non-leading and clarifying statements. When the witness is a survivor, additional specialised training is required so as to minimise the re-traumatisation which occurs when a person is brought back to their original ordeal.[16]

A 'detailed and credible' account (to cite qualificatives found in the jurisprudence) should attract high probative value, given it is virtually impossible for a person who has not directly lived a situation to recount it without getting into 'twists' and introducing incoherences within their previous inventions. When such an account is submitted, the evidentiary elements discussed below mainly serve to corroborate it. By contrast, these elements have to become the main evidence when a victim cannot recall their pushback in detail, possibly due to memory loss provoked by the trauma of the pushback.

2.3.2 *Identification Documentation*

States commonly object in pushback litigation that the complainant is not who they say they are. Even though they most likely will have travelled undocumented and with their presence in most of the countries they crossed left unregistered, the complainant will typically have in their possession some documents bearing their identity, which they can submit to the adjudicator. These papers, however, will often have been

[15] As opposed to investigatory systems which task a judge with the collection and submission of evidence.

[16] Internationally agreed best practices are gathered in the Istanbul Protocol, which aims to guide legal and health professionals working with torture survivors, as well as state authorities investigating torture allegations. OHCHR, *Istanbul Protocol: Manual on the Effective Investigation and Documentation of Torture and Other Cruel, Inhuman or Degrading Treatment or Punishment*, 2022.

hastily drawn by the authorities, without respecting specific spelling or transcription in the Latin alphabet. The state then commonly relies on orthographic variances to argue that the complainant is not the same person as, for instance, the person whose readmission from one state to another was registered. Proving the basic fact of one's identity becomes a challenging evidentiary matter for the complainant, necessitating corroboration and/or proof of credibility.

2.3.3 Digital Messages and Pictures/Videos Sent Around the Time of the Pushback

People often lose their belongings or have them destroyed, including by the police, during their journeys. This is particularly true of mobile phones, as already mentioned. Thus, original footage with metadata – including geolocation of where it was recorded – will rarely be available.[17] However, important evidence may be retrieved from messaging services and social media platforms, which remain accessible even after losing access to the mobile phone that was originally used. Proofs are also created from keeping supportive contacts (kin, activists, lawyers, journalists, non-governmental organisations [NGOs]) informed of one's whereabouts and state of health through sending messages, including videos and/or pictures. These may serve during litigation to prove that the complainant was at the place they say in their submissions and are not inventing the treatment their complaint alleges they have suffered. In awareness that states are prone to subsequently deny the abusive treatment they inflict, a victim occasionally seeks to record what is being done to them as it is being done, in which case they are likely to then ask trusted contacts to safeguard electronically sent information (see examples in Section 2.3.6).

A technical note is in order. Posts and messages on social media platforms such as Facebook, Instagram or TikTok theoretically remain accessible even after phones are lost or destroyed. By contrast, messages sent through messaging services such as WhatsApp, Telegram or Signal tend to get lost on the sender's end, but may be accessible if receivers safekept them (for instance in the home country). The metadata of a file shared through either technology is automatically erased and replaced by a new time-record indicating the day the file was last shared. However,

[17] For an example when such metadata remained available, see S. Lüdke and N. Vögele, 'Video Documents Illegal Refugee Pushbacks in Croatia', *Der Spiegel* (18 January 2020).

the evidentiary significance of the absence of original metadata should not be overestimated, in light of the limited probative value of metadata, especially given the possibility to attribute later dates to pictures (for instance by taking a picture of a picture). In extremely rare circumstances, applicants may be able to safekeep original pictures or videos, with the original metadata, sometimes even including the GPS location of the taking of the picture or video. However, because of the routine seizure and destruction of phones, this is rare.

2.3.4 (Absent) Medical Records

In instances of violence and injury, medical records will rarely exist, since people on the move have little to no access to medical assistance. Some victims may photograph their injuries, though the resulting pictures will rarely be dated, as addressed above, let alone comply with forensic requirements. For example, they may show the injured body parts but not the complainant's face, or may lack scale references to understand the extent of the injury, potentially requiring additional expert analysis.

2.3.5 Fellow Survivors' Testimonies

Whilst on the move, people form temporary communities whose members are, like them, undocumented and vulnerable. As people tend to travel and be pushed back in groups, a complainant should theoretically be able to rely on the testimony of fellow survivors. This could be extremely precious in the (often state-instigated) absence of local civilian witnesses. However, most complainants will have lost contact with their travel companions by the time they submit a claim. Further, even if an erstwhile companion can be located, they may not wish to provide a statement.

Where a willing survivor is identified, the collection of their testimony is logistically demanding. People who are pushed back together rarely form a homogenous group: they generally come from a mixture of countries, speak different languages and end up in various places. Obtaining a testimony therefore typically necessitates transnational travel and translation into several languages. The task is also emotionally demanding: it is as painful, intense and laborious a process, and requires as much training, experience, empathy and resources, as taking a statement from a complainant. This is because 'witnesses' (in the proceedings) are themselves victims/survivors, often of several pushbacks. In particular, it would be wrong to ask them to focus strictly on the elements relevant to the complaint being litigated, as preventing them from recounting what is important to them could aggravate their trauma.[18]

Procedurally, a statement from a witness presents the advantage that adjudicative bodies are familiar with this type of evidence.[19] What is more, the circumstances of its production may make it immediately clear to the adjudicator that the complainant and the witness have had no recent interaction, thereby eliminating the possibility of them having 'concocted' the statement, thereby enhancing the probative value of the submitted testimony.

2.3.6 Technological Analysis of Digital Materials by Organisations Such as Forensic Architecture

When an exceptional level of evidence is gathered in support of the victim's account, this may provide the opportunity for its evidential value to be further enhanced through technological operations. This section recounts two examples drawn from the ECCHR case work where this happened.

Our first example is the case of Parvin A., an Iranian refugee who was pushed back from Greece to Turkey no less than six times.[20] Despite the risks, Parvin A. had resolved to hide and use her phone for recording the circumstances of her apprehensions and detentions during the first push-backs she suffered. Through messaging services, she sent out over forty pieces of audio and/or visual material to trusted contacts. Forensic Architecture (FA), the University of London-based research group famous for its pioneering use of cutting-edge techniques for the investigation of state and corporate violence, worked on this material. It reconstructed the events complained of in a platform specifically designed to this effect, even creating a 3D model of the detention sites where Parvin A. had been placed during her first pushback.[21] Images FA

[18] For a description of the same effect due to judicial interventions, see M.-B. Dembour and E. Haslam, 'Silencing Hearings? Victim-Witnesses at War Crimes Trials', *European Journal of International Law*, 15 (2004): 151–177.

[19] See, e.g., *Kimouche* v. *Algeria*, CCPR/C/90/D/1328/2004, 10 July 2007, para. 7.4.

[20] *Parvin A.* v. *Greece* (HRC), pending, on which see, e.g., www.ecchr.eu/en/case/bringing-greek-push-backs-to-justice/.

[21] Forensic Architecture, 'Pushbacks across the Evros/Meriç River: The Case of Parvin', 2022, https://forensic-architecture.org/investigation/pushbacks-across-the-evros-meric-river-the-case-of-parvin.

subsequently obtained through open sources led to the identification of the police stations in which she had been secretly detained. They corroborated her account regarding inter alia the way people were handled. The similarities between her and other pushback cases involving the same police stations and similar forces revealed the scope of coordination and infrastructure deployed by the state for pushback operations, confirming her treatment was not an 'isolated event' but part of a 'pattern' or 'practice' by the Greek authorities.[22]

Our second example is the case of I. M., a refugee from the Pakistani-controlled side of Kashmir, who was pushed back from Slovenia to Croatia, and severely ill-treated in Croatia before being pushed back to Bosnia and Herzegovina (BiH). A courageous travel companion had taken a video recording after I.M.'s ill-treatment and expulsion to BiH, showing him in great pain. The video was analysed and verified by the NGOs No Name Kitchen/Border Violence Monitoring Network, and the case was investigated again by journalists from Lighthouse Reports and German media outlet *Der Spiegel*.[23] Its originally fuzzy imagery was stabilised, leading to the identification of (1) the location of the incident through GPS metadata and corroboration from a close examination of the landscape; (2) the affiliation of the officers appearing in the footage through an analysis of the details of their uniforms; and (3) the identification of the perpetration of similar acts of violence and expulsions in the background of the footage.

The afore-described technological feats are evidentiary gold. However, they are extremely costly and unavailable to most pushback victims, the overwhelming majority of whom do not even have access to legal representation. Three or more organisations belonging to the not-for-profit and/or journalistic worlds worked on each case for months. The dispensation of such a level of resources clearly cannot set the bar for what an adjudicator may expect to see evidenced in any given case.

2.3.7 Legal Correspondence

Rarely, people on the move may be in contact with lawyers as they are literally facing pushback risks at the border. These lawyers may represent

22 See the ECCHR and Forensic Architecture websites for details.

23 Lüdke and Vögele, 'Video Documents Illegal Refugee Pushbacks'; No Name Kitchen/Border Violence Monitoring Network, 'Reconstructing a Violent Pushback of Asylum Seekers from Croatia to BiH | BVMN Border Investigations' (18 November 2020), www.youtube.com/watch?v=rtEDbuDbqzU.

them before the authorities, for example faxing international protection claims to national border authorities to put the latter on notice of their clients' asylum-seeking status, or seeking interim measures from regional and/or international adjudicative bodies such as UNTBs, despite risks of criminalisation, for example, for facilitating irregular movement. Correspondence which has arisen between lawyer, state and international body may later be submitted to defeat the state's claim that the complainant had never expressed or intended to make a protection claim at the border.[24]

2.3.8 State Documents on the Complainant's Case

In paper pushbacks, the state will per definition have documented the supposedly legitimate measure through which it has pushbacked the complainant. These state documents may constitute the sole evidence the complainant is able to submit to prove their interaction with state authorities. Needless to say, the state will have had exclusive control of what they record. Their content, therefore, including the absence of any protection claim, should be approached with caution by the adjudicator when assessing the content of said interaction.

2.3.9 External Reports Documenting State Practice

Published reports documenting a state practice of pushbacks are an essential part of the complainant's submissions. They make sense of the evidentiary difficulties which mar the complaint. Moreover, they usually confirm some of the details provided in the complainant and/or the witnesses' accounts, strengthening their credibility. The gathering and submission of reports from as authoritative sources as possible is also a highly time-consuming task.[25]

2.3.10 Conclusion

This section has identified the types of evidentiary materials that a pushback complainant may be able to submit to an adjudicatory body

[24] For an example, see Section 2.5.4.

[25] Although adjudicators prefer reports emanating from inter-state organisations, such as the UN, the Council of Europe or the European Union, reports from NGOs and the media should also be considered authoritative.

in support of their factual allegations. Our review has made clear that for a complainant to submit strong evidence necessitates the deployment of resources to which most people on the move – and their lawyers – do not have access. Expecting pushback complainants to routinely submit strong evidence would defeat human rights accountability and justice. In a context where the state is likely to dispute whatever weak or strong evidentiary submissions the complainant is able to make, an in-depth reflection as to how the evidentiary system should work is needed. Section 2.4 starts this work by abstractly mapping out the possible end forms of a factual dispute.

2.4 Disputed Facts: Four Logically Possible Adjudicatory Outcomes

Pushback litigation sees the word of the complainant pitted against state denials: the facts are thus 'in dispute' between the parties. Such a situation is not one that international human rights law relishes; it prefers when the facts of a case arrive before the international adjudicator already established by the domestic authorities. Pushback victims, however, by definition have no opportunity to challenge their expulsion prior to being pushed back, and they also usually face a system of utter impunity with regard to any ill-treatment or arbitrary detention, with no possibility of having their claims effectively investigated and dealt with within the national criminal system.[26] In short, no domestic court will have properly considered their case, if at all. The admissibility requirement of exhaustion of domestic remedies, amply discussed elsewhere in this volume, should consequently be waived,[27] leaving it to the international judge to determine the facts of the complaint.

Abstractly thinking about how a disputed fact can present at the end of the adjudicatory process, two outcomes are logically possible: either it remains disputed and unclear, or it has been resolved – each time in favour of either the complainant or the respondent state.[28] This results in four logical possible factual outcomes, as per Table 2.1:

[26] On the inexistence of effective investigations into pushbacks in Europe, see Fundamental Rights Agency, *Guidance on Investigating Alleged Ill-Treatment at Borders*, 20 July 2024.

[27] See especially Chapter 7, this volume.

[28] We do not have the space here to go into how the law–facts distinction is not as sharp as often imagined.

Table 2.1 *Four logically possible adjudicatory outcomes for disputed facts*

Facts remain unclear	To the benefit of the state	Outcome 1
	To the benefit of the complainant	Outcome 2
Facts are resolved	In favour of the complainant	Outcome 3
	In favour of the state	Outcome 4

In practice, things are unlikely to be as clear-cut as Table 2.1 makes out. For example, one disputed point may be resolved in favour of the complainant, another in favour of the respondent, whilst others remain unresolved. Importantly, it is not because one party's factual allegations are accepted as established that this party will win the case – they may lose on legal arguments. Finally, whether a particular judicial decision would best be categorised as supporting one or the other party's account is not always obvious. Table 2.1 must be approached as a heuristic device.

Outcome 1 arises when a complainant fails to establish the factual basis of their complaint. It can thus be conceptualised as an application of the *actori incumbit probatio* principle. It is important to underscore, however, that the Latin term *actor* (used in its dative form *actori*') is really meant to designate *any* party who is making a factual claim in the proceedings so that the adage does not so much allocate the burden of proof to the complainant as distribute it between the parties (even if in practice the initial burden rests on the complainant). Outcome 1, therefore, need not be the end point for all the cases whose facts remain uncertain by the end of the adjudicatory process – even under the adage.

Outcome 2 arises when, despite the continual lack of factual clarity, the adjudicator eventually considers the complainant's factual allegations established, due to having shifted the burden of proof from the complainant to the state, and the latter not having then discharged it. Although the shift (also known as 'reversal') in the burden of proof is much talked about in international human rights adjudication, its exact conditions of operation have not been clarified. We submit that the shift should be subject to two conditions, which we propose to call the context condition and the linkage condition. We further submit that each of these conditions should be proven to a different standard of proof, as we explain after having introduced this concept.

One need not be a lawyer to understand that a fact can be established to a higher or lesser degree of certainty – in the same way that one can either very strongly or more circumspectly believe that something has happened. The Common Law recognises four such degrees: a finding can be so secure as being 'beyond reasonable doubt'; it can be made on evidence which is 'clear and compelling' (less than virtually certain, but more than probable); it may be adopted 'on the balance of probabilities' (being 'more likely than not', that is, having at least fifty-one per cent chances of being correct); and, at the bottom of this descending scale, it may be no more than just plausible – prima facie. Evidentiary rules refer to these various bands of persuasion to indicate the level – in legal language, 'threshold' or 'standard of proof' – to which a disputed factual allegation must be proven for the adjudicator to accept to be persuaded to uphold it. These are (in phrasings which in practice may be expressed under slightly different formulations):

1) Beyond reasonable doubt (BRD)
2) Clear and compelling
3) More probable than not
4) Prima facie (meaning 'at first sight' in Latin, and evoking a standard which is also sometimes expressed as requiring no more than a 'beginning of proof')[29]

This Common Law classification has no equivalent in the Civil Law tradition, which contents itself with speaking of the *intime conviction du juge* ('inner conviction of the judge'), without attempting to differentiate the degree or depth of the judge's conviction. This stark difference in evidentiary approaches may well explain the rarity of references to specific standards of proof in international human rights adjudication: many international judges have not been trained in them. This, however, is a great pity. Alongside the other contributors to this volume, we have come to the conclusion that the notion of the standard of proof is an indispensable evidentiary tool to achieve fairness and justice in human rights adjudication – as the operation of the shift, to which we now return, may serve to illustrate.

The shift's first condition commands that there exists a context which indicates that the respondent state may well have acted in the way claimed by the complainant. Roberts distinguishes two such broad contextual situations: (1) the state is known to have previously been acting in

[29] E. Murimi, 'Fluctuating Standards of Proof at the African Court: A Case for Principled Flexibility', *African Human Rights Yearbook* 7 (2023): 158–182; see Chapter 11, this volume.

the way described by the complainant (state practice or pattern), or (2) the state is refraining from sharing evidence which it either possesses (due, e.g., to the events having occurred under state surveillance) or should possess (due, e.g., to a legal duty on the state either to record the contested event, as for any detention, or to investigate, as in the case of serious injury, death or disappearance, the more so when the latter occurs under its custody).

We concur with Roberts that the context condition should neither have to be established beyond reasonable doubt nor be found established merely on prima facie evidence. Roberts proposes that the general standard applicable in human rights adjudication, namely more probable than not, should be applied here too. We believe some adjudicators may be more comfortable to impose the clear and compelling standard in this instance. Of course, in practice, whether the clear and compelling or the probable standard is reached is a judgment call. Whatever standard is adopted, the important thing is that, in case of hesitations, the adjudicator favours finding the condition established rather than rigidly insisting that the complainant submits a level of evidence which is beyond their reach.[30] One would expect the context condition to be established in respect to virtually every pushback complaint. If it is not, it may indicate that the adjudicator expected an unreasonably high level of evidence or, alternatively, that the complainant did not have sufficient resources to gather the documentation that could have established that it was *not unreasonable to presume* (no more than that) that the state acted in the way alleged.

The shifting of the burden of proof depends on the linkage condition also being met. This condition requires the applicant to establish that it is *plausible* that they were *personally* affected by the presumed events, in other words, that they were one of the people (in our selected topic) pushed back. Importantly, this only needs to be established prima facie, a 'beginning of proof' thus being sufficient for the condition to be found established. Accordingly, just one of the following pieces of evidence next to the applicant's statement should be enough for the adjudicator to consider the linkage condition fulfilled:

1) A detailed account from the applicant of what happened to them
2) A picture of the pushback operation taken despite the obstacles, where the applicant appears

[30] Hesitations of this kind are a feature of bands, as academics experience when having to grade a student's assessment (e.g., as a lower or an upper 2.1 in the British scale).

3) A witness statement emanating from a fellow migrant who testifies having seen the applicant being pushed back
4) A social media message recounting the event and the presence of the applicant in it, sent shortly after the pushback in question occurred
5) Confirmation by whatever means of the applicant's location during, immediately before or immediately after the pushback[31]

If these two conditions are met, the adjudicator *must* shift the burden of proof onto the state. It therefore now falls on the state to rebut the presumption of veracity of the complainant's factual allegations. In the absence of said rebuttal, the adjudicator *must* uphold the complainant's factual account, even if the facts remain uncertain. Were this outcome not reached, it would defeat the purpose of having introduced the mechanism of the shift as a corrective to the application of the normal evidentiary rules.[32] To be noted that the standard of proof which the state's rebuttal must meet for it to be accepted by the adjudicator is hardly ever discussed in the literature[33] or spelt out in the case law. Our opinion is that it should be at least clear and compelling and, in some circumstances, even BRD.

In the last analysis, Outcomes 1 and 2 are procedural in nature: under Outcome 1, the complaint is 'automatically' rejected when the adjudicator assesses its factual basis has not been evidenced; under Outcome 2, the factual basis of the complaint *must* be upheld once it is seen that the state has not rebutted the presumption which has arisen that it acted in the way alleged by the complainant.

By contrast, Outcomes 3 and 4 are substantive. Like Outcome 2, Outcome 3 ends up upholding the complainant's factual allegation, but here it is because the adjudicator finds for the complainant's version of the facts upon the substantive consideration of all the circumstances of the case – including any presumption which arises against the state's

[31] This list is lifted from the third party intervention submitted to the ECtHR in March 2025 in the case of *A.A.N. and Others* v. *Greece* by G. Baranowska, M.-B. Dembour and I. Kienzle, 2025, https://hrc.ugent.be/wp-content/uploads/2025/03/TPI-evidence.pdf.

[32] The use of the subjunctive in the last sentence nonetheless indicates that this normative framework, although commonly accepted in theory, is not consistently applied throughout international human rights adjudication practice. For a shocking example of disrespect by the ECtHR, see M.-B. Dembour 'The Escape of the State: No Shift in the Burden of the Proof and No Anti-Roma Discrimination by the Police in P.H. v Slovakia', *DISSECT* (blogpost dated 31 October 2022), https://dissect.ugent.be/the-escape-of-the-state-no-shift-in-the-burden-of-the-proof-and-no-anti-roma-discrimination-by-the-police-in-p-h-v-slovakia/

[33] For an exception, see Roberts, 'Reversing the Burden of Proof'.

factual allegations/denials. The taking into account of presumptions is entirely appropriate since, under the Latin adage quoted above, the state is one of the parties to the proceedings expected to bring the proof of *all* their factual claims. This important consideration is too often neglected.

There is no requirement before the UNTBs for the complainant to prove their case beyond reasonable doubt.[34] Although hardly ever explicitly stated, the default standard of proof applied in international human rights adjudication at the merits stage seems to be the balance of probabilities (i.e., something being 'more probable than not'), also sometimes expressed as 'preponderance of evidence' (more evidence leans on one side as opposed to the other). Consequently, whenever the adjudicator is able to find that the complainant's version of the facts is, on balance, more persuasive than the state's, the corrective of the shift is not needed and should not be applied. Even if the conditions for such a shift, as identified above, appear to be met, in reality they are not since the second condition is proven to a higher degree than required. In such a scenario, the adjudicator should find the facts established on their own probative basis, resulting in a *substantive* finding – an outcome which is preferable to a *procedural* finding obtained through the shift. We come back to this point later.

Finally, it is of course theoretically possible that the adjudicator comes to the conclusion that the facts are as described by the state rather than by the complainant. Outcome 4 captures this scenario in our table. As with all other outcomes, the adjudicator should explain why they reach this conclusion.

A new table (Table 2.2) can be produced which incorporates the normative discussion above.

Two remarks are in order. The first is an important legal point: the discussion offered above exclusively concerns scenarios which involve disputed facts. When facts are uncontested, the principle is that the adjudicator is to consider them established. The second is a reminder that neither Table 2.1 nor Table 2.2 intends to capture the complexities of the potentially multiple evidentiary processes and decisions which arise in any one case. Whilst the Tables are drawn as if one single and clear

[34] The ECtHR is the only international human rights adjudicatory body who has chosen to adopt beyond reasonable doubt as its default standard of proof. In her discussion of the origin and implications of this adoption, Dembour concludes that BRD can be an acceptable standard for the ECtHR to apply as long as presumptions and inferences are considered within it. M-B. Dembour, 'Beyond Reasonable Doubt at Its Worst – But Also at Its Potential Best: Dissecting Ireland v the United Kingdom's No-Torture Finding', *European Convention on Human Rights Law Review* 4 (2023): 375–425.

Table 2.2 *The four outcomes, with legal bases and consequences*

The facts	Outcome	Legal basis
Remain unclear	**1** Procedural rejection	The complainant has not established the factual basis of their complaint. The latter is therefore rejected as per the Latin adage.
	2 Procedural upholding	The complainant having established a suspicious state context and brought a beginning of proof that their case relates to this context, the adjudicator has shifted the burden of proof onto the state, which has failed to discharge it. The factual basis of the complaint must therefore be considered established, generally leading to violation finding(s).
Are resolved	**3** Substantive upholding	The adjudicator finds the complainant's version of the facts established on the balance of probabilities (or to a higher standard of proof). Although this factual outcome does not guarantee the complaint will be upheld on legal grounds, this will generally follow.
	4 Substantive rejection	The adjudicator finds the state's version of the facts established. This factual outcome does not automatically lead to the complaint being rejected on legal grounds.

factual conclusion was reached in any given case, which would nicely encompass any and all more specific factual 'sub-claims', things do not necessarily work like this.

2.5 How UNTBs Have Navigated the Challenge of Pushbacks' Disputed Facts: Case-by-Case Analysis

To our knowledge,[35] so far UNTBs have only decided four pushback complaints.[36] This small number gives us the opportunity to review each final view in detail. We do this in the chronological order of their

[35] Our cautious formulation is due to the difficulties of researching the UNTB case law, as explained in Chapter 1, this volume.

[36] Cases concerning border issues but without presenting an over-the-border pushback element, such as failures to rescue (*A.S.* v. *Malta*, CCPR/C/128/D/3043/2017, 13 March 2020; *A.S. et al* v. *Italy*, CCPR/C/130/D/3042/2017, 4 November 2020)

adoption. For each case, we start by offering a summary of the complainant's factual account and the response it attracted from the respondent state (often, denials following the patterns identified in Section 2.2), before analysing the reasoning provided by the committee on the facts. We conclude that the UNTBs have reached the correct determinations, but following an evidentiary reasoning lacking in clarity and sharpness.

2.5.1 Sonko *v.* Spain

Sonko, the first case to be reviewed, was decided by the Committee against Torture (CAT) in 2011.[37] Both parties agreed on the following facts: Mr Sonko and three other persons had been in Moroccan waters, each floating on a dinghy and trying to reach the Spanish enclave of Ceuta. The group of four was pulled up into a boat by the Spanish Guardia Civil (a paramilitary force) and taken to Moroccan waters, and then thrown back into the sea at a place where they could not stand up. As Mr Sonko started drowning, a Spanish officer swam to him, dragged his body onto the shore and tried to reanimate him, but to no avail – Mr Sonko had died. The parties disagreed on one crucial fact: whether the officers had pierced Mr Sonko's dinghy before throwing him back into water.

Atypically for a no-paper pushback, Spain opened a domestic judicial investigation of the incident. Whether the complainant (the deceased's sister) was informed of these proceedings was disputed between the parties. Spain would only have needed to produce a copy of its alleged notification for this issue to be settled. Without remarking upon this, let alone requesting the State to produce said copy, CAT stated that the domestic remedies had been exhausted (a bewildering determination since it was not the complainant who had pursued the domestic investigation, which the Committee had moreover specifically recognised to have been flawed).[38]

In yet more atypical submissions in a 'no-paper' case, Spain neither denied before CAT that the pushback had taken place (on the contrary, it confirmed its occurrence by saying it had been carried out 'in accordance

and detention (*J.H.A.* v. *Spain*, CAT 323/207, 11 November 2008), are outside the purview of this chapter.

[37] *Sonko* v. *Spain*, CAT/C/47/D/368/2008, 25 November 2011.

[38] *Sonko*, para 3.5. On exhaustion of domestic remedies before UNTBs, see Chapter 7, this volume.

with the procedures for dealing with immigration by sea'),[39] nor that Mr Sonko had encountered its officers. We hypothesise that the State refrained from totally denying the pushback due to the victim's very public death in the presence of its agents and on foreign territory, which would likely have produced local knowledge and thus potential witnesses.

CAT upheld the complaint, having observed that

> it [fell] to the State party to explain the circumstances surrounding Mr. Sonko's death, considering that he was alive when he was pulled out of the water. [R]egardless of whether or not the Civil Guard officers punctured Mr. Sonko's dinghy or at what distance from the shore he was expelled from the boat, he was placed [by the authorities] in a situation that caused his death.[40]

This reasoning resonates with the principle according to which a presumption of state responsibility arises (which the state must rebut) when a person comes under its custody or control in good health, and then leaves it injured or dead. Whilst its gist is to be approved, the reasoning falls short in two respects.

Firstly, the Committee does not explicitly state that the State had failed to provide a convincing explanation for the death of Mr Sonko. This conclusion, albeit congruent with the finding that the State had breached its obligation to investigate, is left implicit.[41] Secondly, the evidentiary basis upon which the violation is found is not exactly identified. In evidentiary terms, this could have been *either* because the State had failed to discharge the burden of proof which the Committee had shifted onto its shoulders (Outcome 2), *or* because the Committee was convinced of the accuracy of the complainant's version of the events (Outcome 3). Whatever the route followed, the violation outcome stood. The one does not exactly amount to the other, however. A procedural shift-based violation seems weaker than one reached substantively, thus with the facts at issue being positively established to have taken place.

The Committee may purposefully have avoided clarifying the basis of its decision. This could explain why, before coming to the passage quoted above, it 'recalls' (a word which wrongly suggests that the pronouncement which follows is a staple of its jurisprudence) that 'it is not its task to weigh the evidence or to reassess the statements made regarding the

[39] *Sonko*, para. 4.3.
[40] *Sonko*, para 10.4.
[41] *Sonko*, para. 10.7.

facts or the credibility of the relevant national authorities'.[42] Such a limited interpretation of its task gestures to the no-fourth-instance principle, according to which international bodies should not (gratuitously) review domestic findings reached after possibly three sets (first instance, appeal, final instance) of proceedings. This principle, however, should be of no import when the domestic authorities have failed to (properly) investigate and establish the facts. One Committee member, Ms Gaer, vehemently objected to the words quoted above, which she described as a 'shocking pronouncement',[43] which went against both the Committee's own jurisprudence[44] and reason. To quote:

> The State party [has confirmed] that its Civil Guard officers did in fact take Mr. Sonko and his companions on board their vessel and subsequently 'released them,' but argues that they did so 'in an area very close to the shore,' and did not puncture the dinghies. Thus, the State party alleges, the death of Mr. Sonko was 'an unfortunate accident' rather than an act of cruel, inhuman, or degrading treatment or punishment.[45]

She continued:

> For the Committee to reach a decision that a violation of article 16 of the Convention [prohibition of ill-treatment] occurred, it must reject the version of the facts articulated by the State party in this case. [. . .] It is not the case that every death that occurs in custody constitutes a violation of the Convention [. . .] In [a] case [such as this one], the Committee is called upon [. . .] to resolve [the] tensions between the accounts offered by the author and the State party, such as whether the State's agents left Mr. Sonko in possession of his dinghy when they expelled him from the patrol vessel [. . .]. The Committee has apparently determined that the State's version of the events is not credible. It is well within its power to do so and should have stated so plainly.[46]

The last three lines suggest that the Committee found in fact for the complainant rather than simply considering that the State had failed to discharge its burden of proof. However, the route followed was not made clear.

42 *Sonko*, para 10.2.

43 *Sonko*, 'Individual opinion of Committee member Ms. Felice Gaer (partially dissenting)', para 3.

44 Ms Gaer refers to General Comment no 1 (*Sonko*, para 4) as well as some individual decisions (*Sonko*, para 5).

45 *Sonko*, para. 6.4.

46 *Sonko*, para. 6 of Ms Gaer's dissenting opinion. This was more so in the absence of proper domestic proceedings, and thus irrelevance of the no-fourth-instance principle.

This lack of transparency in reasoning is to be lamented on two important grounds. First, it risks raising the evidentiary standard which the Committee applies in future cases, since its decision suggests that it felt that the evidence before it was not sufficient for a straightforward substantive finding of violation to be reached – despite the fact that in this case its members were apparently more convinced by the version of the complainant than by that of the state. The Committee's hesitation may influence future jurisprudence, which would implicitly, perhaps even unconsciously, expect a standard of proof higher than the balance of probabilities to be met.

Second, whether or not the dinghy had been pierced was a crucial question – not only factually but also legally. Admittedly, on paper, failing to protect life and intentionally endangering it both amount to the violation of the same state obligation (here Article 16 CAT). However, the former is an omission, the latter a positive action, so that the two are different in nature and gravity. By not having come to a determination that the dinghy must have been (presumed to have been) pierced, but having simply found that the State had failed to protect life, the Committee's decision has less of a legal import than it otherwise would have had. This illustrates the obvious point that evidentiary reasoning impacts material obligation findings. Otherwise said, express factual findings are central to the very implementation of human rights. It is therefore essential that a fair and clear evidentiary framework be defined and applied.

2.5.2 Diory Barry *v.* Morocco

The second case, *Diory Barry (or Diodory Barry)*[47] v. *Morocco*, was decided in 2014, again by CAT.[48] The complainant explained he had set from Mauritania for the Canary Islands by pirogue in a perilous journey in which some thirty of his companions had died. Two weeks after departure, the forty or so remaining survivors were intercepted by the Moroccan authorities, taken to a detention camp in Morocco, kept there for roughly ten days, at which point the Moroccan gendarmerie took them to the desert in the border area separating Morocco and

[47] This official denomination of the complainant illustrates our earlier point about complainants commonly being known by more than one name (as is also the first author of this chapter).

[48] *Barry* v. *Morocco*, CAT/C/52/D/372/2009, 19 May 2014.

Mauritania. There they were told to walk to the closest Mauritanian town, approximately fifty kilometres away, each having been given a pair of plastic flip-flops, a bottle of water and a few sandwiches – no additional food or water, no protection against the sun and no blankets. Their itinerary crossed a minefield, causing the death of a person the day before the group was found, some of its members seriously wounded – including from the time they were adrift at sea. The complainant argued his expulsion had happened 'in a flagrantly illegal manner' with 'no official record of his detention or expulsion',[49] and had resulted in inhumane treatment.

The State admitted the interception of a vessel by the Moroccan Royal Navy in the area referred to by the complainant, and the detention and expulsion to Mauritania of the people found on this vessel. In a typical line of paper pushback defence, it stated that this expulsion had been executed 'in accordance with the legislation in force', which 'guarantees the right of aliens to access to a lawyer, an interpreter and a doctor, to communicate with their consulate or a person of their choice and to appeal a decision to escort them to the border within 48 hours of being notified of the decision'.[50] The admitted interception, however, had not occurred on the date given by the complainant, and had concerned a larger group than the one he had described. This led CAT to observe (in a paragraph which we shall quote in its entirety, although doing so little by little rather than in one go):

> The State party has partially confirmed the facts as submitted by the complainant, although confusion regarding dates and the number of migrants on board the intercepted boat means that *it cannot be proven beyond doubt* that the State party and the complainant are referring to the same boat and group of migrants.[51]

This convoluted formulation (which resembles – without fully adopting it – the Common Law standard of 'proven beyond *reasonable* doubt') appears to want to convey that the two parties could not have been referring to the same event. Despite this, CAT took it that the State had 'confirmed the facts as submitted by the complainant', but without specifying which of these facts exactly.[52]

[49] *Barry*, para. 3.1.
[50] *Barry*, para. 4.3.
[51] *Barry*, para. 7.1, emphasis added.
[52] *Barry*, . para 7.1.

The paragraph we have started to quote continues as follows:

> Given that the State party has not provided any observations on the treatment of the complainant while the decision to expel him to Mauritania was being implemented,[53] due weight must be given to the complainant's allegations.[54]

With this the State is implicitly castigated for having failed to address in its submissions the way the complainant had been treated during the expulsion. This criticism does not lead CAT to apply the principle according to which a fact alleged by one party and left undisputed by the other is accepted as established, however. Instead, CAT merely derives from the absence of refutal by the State that 'due weight must be given to the complainant's allegations'. This formulation, routinely found in CAT's case law when the state has failed to address the core of the complaint,[55] is regrettably ambiguous. It can mean at least three things: (1) that in the absence of refutal by the respondent state, CAT is simply to accept the complainants' allegations (which it indeed does in some cases);[56] (2) that it has given these allegations significant weight; or (3) that it has been mindful to carefully assess which weight to grant them before finding them established.

In *Barry*, the 'due weight' formulation cannot be used in the first sense, since CAT carries on its reasoning by stating:

> The Committee also refers to its concluding observations,[57] adopted following consideration of the fourth periodic report submitted by the State party, in which it expressed its concern regarding information received that, in practice, 'undocumented migrants [had] been escorted to the border or otherwise expelled in violation of Moroccan law without having been given the opportunity to exercise their rights. Several allegations have been made that hundreds of migrants have been abandoned in the desert without food or water.' The facts reported by the complainant are therefore not isolated.[58]

Such referencing of a periodic monitoring report is permitted under CAT's Rule 3 (2), which rightly allows use of knowledge obtained outside the particular case at hand, including as to the existence of 'a consistent

[53] See *Barry*, para 6.2 on the fact that no information was provided by the State.

[54] *Barry*, para 7.1.

[55] For further discussion of this formulation in this volume, see Chapters 6 and 7.

[56] See, e.g., *Dragan Dimitrijevic* v. *Serbia and Montenegro*, CAT/C/33/D/207/2002, 24 November 2004; *B.N. and S.R* v. *Burundi*, CAT/C/71/D/858/2018, 19 July 2021.

[57] Reference omitted in our quotation.

[58] *Barry*, para. 7.1.

pattern of gross, flagrant or mass violations of human rights'.[59] This knowledge can potentially play a crucial evidentiary role, contributing to the factual basis of a complaint being upheld, whether procedurally (Outcome 2) or substantively (Outcome 3).

The periodic report could have been sufficient evidence for establishing that the first context condition towards operating the shift was fulfilled. *Barry*, however, never mentions the burden of proof or its shift. In this particular case, we suggest it is because the decision actually constitutes a substantive finding, as confirmed by the last quoted sentence referring to 'the facts *reported* by the complainant',[60] a choice of words which puts at a distance the idea that the complainant would have offered mere allegations that were upheld only because they were not rebutted by the State. If deliberately chosen (which of course we cannot know for sure), the word 'reported' suggests that CAT had no doubts about the facts of the case. Putting it in a positive light, the Committee would have felt certain about them.

Whilst we approve of a substantive finding having been made in this case, we regret the appearance earlier in the reasoning of the 'due weight' phrasing, which may suggest a procedural upholding (Outcome 2), therefore muddying the waters. If a procedural upholding, then the decision should have expressly stated that the respondent state had failed to rebut the presumption of responsibility which had arisen against it. If a substantive upholding, the decision should have spelt out that its factual findings rested on the *substantive* strength of the evidentiary material before it – including their alignment with what the Committee knew about Morocco's pushback practices. Due to the lack of clarity in the reasoning, we propose to classify *Barry* as an 'Outcome 5', which ambiguously sits between Outcomes 2 and 3, as per Figure 2.1.

2.5.3 D.D. *v.* Spain

The third case to be reviewed is *D.D.* v. *Spain*, decided by the Committee on the Rights of the Child (CRC) in 2019.[61] With support from ECCHR,

[59] As C. Roberts explains (Chapter 8, this volume), it is important for a UNTB acting in its quasi-judicial function not to disregard the knowledge it has acquired through another of its functions, enabling it to appreciate that the violation complained of may be participating of a pattern, thus being a more serious matter than an isolated event would have been.

[60] *Barry*, para 7.1, emphasis added.

[61] *D.D.* v. *Spain*, CRC/C/80/D/4/2016, 01 February 2019.

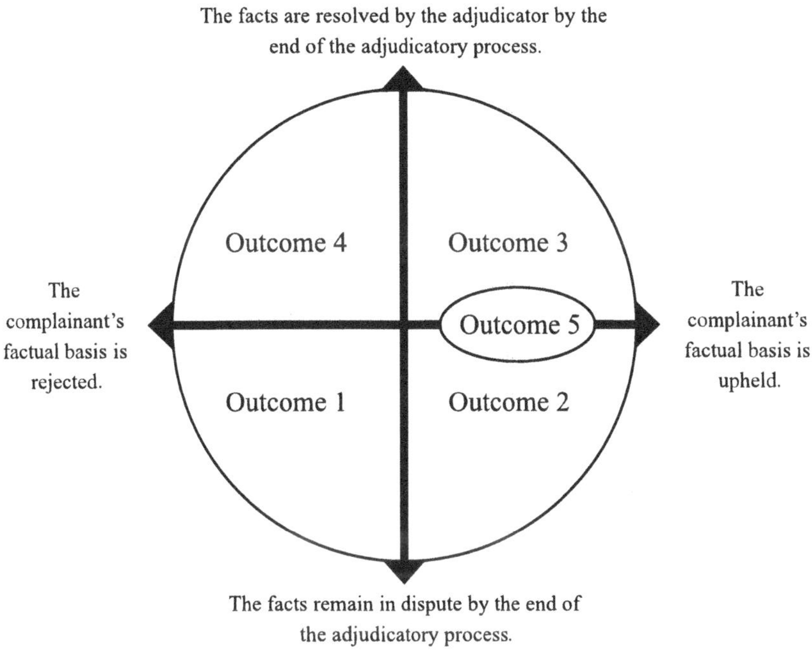

Figure 2.1 Adding a fifth outcome (ambiguous upholding) to our matrix.

D.D. complained to have been no-paper pushed back to Morocco on 2 December 2014 from the top of a border fence located on the Melilla enclave (which is Spanish territory), directly into Morocco in the custody of Moroccan officers. Even though he was 15 years old and unaccompanied, D.D. did not benefit from any process or identification in Spain. He was simply expelled, despite ill-treatment risks in Morocco.[62]

The State initially disputed only his minor status and the alleged illegality of his handling.[63] Subsequently, it started to make submissions classically found in no-paper pushback cases. For example, it disputed D.D.'s identity. It stated that 'the author ha[d] not proved that he [had taken] part in an assault on the border fence in Melilla and that there [was] no record of how he [had] entered Spain'.[64] It additionally relied on a lack of correspondence in the names that appeared on two

[62] As he had himself previously experienced.

[63] *D.D.*, paras. 4.1 and 4.3.

[64] *D.D.*, para. 6.1.

documents D.D. produced (records of his registration in Melilla submitted to CRC to prove his presence at the border around the time of the contested pushback on the one hand; ID documents from when the Spanish State later registered him in Madrid as a minor on the basis of his Malian documentation on the other hand).[65] The State finally alleged that the complainant did not appear in the photographs he submitted, which a journalist had taken of the 2 December pushback.[66]

That the state would deny at the admissibility stage that a complainant has victim status is nothing unusual in no-paper pushback litigation. Such a submission is nonetheless rare in international human rights adjudication: the facts having normally been established by their domestic courts, states do not commonly argue that an international complaint is manifestly ill-founded by disputing its facts. When a state does this, this may well in itself signal that the case deserves a full assessment, i.e., an examination that takes place at the merits stage.

At admissibility, the only thing which can be decided is whether the case is admissible, that is, whether it deserves full consideration later – nothing else. In *D.D.*, however, the Committee proceeded to resolve the question of the disputed identity already in the part of its decision addressing admissibility. This was not the right place to do this. When a state contends that a claim is inadmissible as ill-founded on its legal substance, UNTBs routinely start by briefly addressing this point in the admissibility section, confirming that the substance of the claim is not ill-founded, before delving into a more in-depth analysis of the legal claims in the merits section. The same should happen when the facts are in dispute. They should first be assessed at admissibility and then again at the merits stage.

At admissibility, the standard of proof to be applied when assessing the facts should be prima facie. In practice, as Lisa Reinsberg explains in Chapter 3,[67] this means that the alleged facts' plausibility (nothing more) must be verified without the adjudicator paying any attention to any state submission. At the merits stage, the applicable standard is higher, namely, more probable than not, as noted above. Not systematically going through one and then the other stage risks the two thresholds becoming somewhat amalgamated, possibly resulting in an upsliding of

[65] *D.D.*, para. 13.1.
[66] *D.D.*, para. 6.1.
[67] Chapter 3, this volume.

the prima facie standard, thus a negation of the raison d'être of the admissibility stage, and the wrong dismissal of cases as inadmissible.

Leaving aside the question of the stage of the proceedings at which factual determination should have occurred, we now turn to analysing *D.D.*'s evidentiary reasoning. CRC found in favour of the complainant regarding his identity, due to the State having been in the unique position to compare fingerprints but having failed to do so. For the first time in its own case law, but citing decisions by the Human Rights Committee (HRC) on secret detention, torture and enforced disappearances,[68] the Committee stated:

> The Committee considers that the burden of proof cannot rest solely on the author of the communication, especially given that the author and the State party do not always have equal access to the evidence and that frequently the State party alone has access to the relevant information.[69]

This formulation could have indicated that the context condition for operating the shift was fulfilled. Such an interpretation would appear supported by the references which CRC included (but which our quotation omits) to jurisprudence commonly described by legal scholars as exemplars of the shift. However, there was no shift being operated in *D.D.* as no presumption was identified which it would have been for the State to rebut. Instead, what the Committee operated was an explicit *distribution* of the burden.

This burden, CRC said, '[could not] rest solely' on the complainant. The Committee weighed the arguments and evidence provided by both parties to arrive at its conclusion – a substantive upholding of the complainant's factual allegation (Outcome 3). It is regrettable that the reasoning did not make clear that the outcome was in no way procedural. As formulated, the last quoted sentence is reminiscent of the shift, at the same time as the State's failure to compare fingerprints is emphasised. The latter element could be mistaken to indicate that a higher level of evidence (i.e., actual knowledge that the State refrained from comparing fingerprints in its possession) than is legally necessary is required for the shift to be operated.

Spain had also disputed whether the complainant was on Spanish territory. In this regard, the Committee stated: '*according to the author*, he was arrested by Spanish security forces at the third fence of the Melilla

[68] *D.D.*, fn. 38.
[69] *D.D.*, para. 13.3.

border crossing'.[70] The italicised qualification is regrettable since, beyond the identity question, Spain had accepted that its agents had handled someone on 2 December, whom they had taken from the third Spanish border fence to Moroccan authorities. What Spain disputed was the qualification of this handling as an expulsion.[71]

The complainant had advanced the existence of a risk of ill-treatment and further refoulement upon expulsion to Morocco.[72] Spain addressed this point factually, neither accepting nor rebutting it.[73] Without noting this, the Committee upheld it, neither as an undisputed fact, nor within the mechanism of the shift, but relying on its own reporting.[74] This reporting – as Hakiki knows for having been part of the team litigating the case – had been specifically submitted by the complainant, alongside other reports by the UN Special Rapporteur on Torture, the BBC, Human Rights Watch and Médecins Sans Frontières. The latter reports are mentioned in the decision in relation to the factual issue of the content of Spanish policy[75], but regrettably not in relation to the risk of ill-treatment upon expulsion. It would have been better for the Committee to acknowledge these reports' probative value in corroborating its own reporting.

Section 2.5.1, we have observed in relation to *Sonko* that a vague assessment of the evidence may lead to material state obligations being left undetermined. The same phenomenon is visible in *D.D.* Here the Committee did not assess whether the evidence showed the existence of 'substantial grounds for believing that there is a real risk of irreparable harm to the child' if the child were to be expelled (Article 37 of the Convention for the Rights of the Child). The Committee restricted itself to concluding that the evidence showed that the State had not assessed whether such substantial grounds existed. A violation of procedural obligations under Article 37 was confirmed,[76] but the related *substantive* human right was not addressed.

In conclusion, although the Committee's evidentiary conclusions in *D.D.* deserve to be broadly applauded, explicit and precise reasoning is

[70] *D.D.*, para 13.4, emphasis added.
[71] *D.D.*, para. 4.1.
[72] *D.D.*, para 14.2.
[73] *D.D.*, para 14.6.
[74] *D.D.*, fn. 6 and para. 14.6.
[75] *D.D.*, fn. 6.
[76] *D.D.* v. *Spain*, CRC, para 14.6.

lacking. Not only does it leave practitioners in the dark as to which evidentiary rules apply, but it also weakens human rights accountability.

2.5.4 A.B and B.D. *v.* Poland

The last case to be considered is *A.B. and B.D.* v. *Poland*, decided by the HRC in 2023.[77] It concerns a paper pushback, here of a Chechen family who had presented themselves over twenty times to the Polish authorities at the border crossing from Belarus to Poland, and had each time been issued with a refusal of entry.[78] The complainants eventually gained access to the Polish asylum framework: after HRC itself granted them interim measures for Poland to register their asylum claims and to refrain from removing them from the territory until its own decision on the merits of their complaint.[79]

As typical of paper pushbacks, the key disputed point between the parties was whether, in their previous interactions with the Polish officers, the family had attempted to claim asylum. The complainants claimed this,[80] referring to national judgments confirming the existence of a state practice of denying access to asylum procedures, findings by various UNTBs and other human rights institutions and organisations as to systematic pushbacks taking place at the Polish borders, and governmental public declarations confirming the same.[81] In contrast, the State submitted that the complainants had been interviewed as to their reasons to seek entry into Poland and had only ever expressed economic or personal reasons, as per 'reports of the Border Guard officers'.[82]

The first remarkable feature of this decision holds in its opening. Usually, a decision starts by simply recording the identity of the complainant, the legal provisions relied upon in the complaint, and the name of the representative(s). In this case, however, the decision begins as follows:

> The authors fled the Russian Federation and arrived in Belarus in January 2017, with the intention of applying for asylum in Poland at the border between Belarus and Poland, in Terespol. The authors made more than 20

[77] *A.B. and B.D.* v. *Poland*, CCPR/C/135/D/3017/2017, 21 July 2022.
[78] *A.B. and B.D.* para. 1.1.
[79] *A.B. and B.D.*, paras. 1.2, 9.4.
[80] *A.B. and B.D.* , paras. 2.5–2.8, 5.1, 7.1.
[81] *A.B. and B.D.*, paras. 7.1–7.2, 7.12.
[82] *A.B. and B.D.*, paras. 4.2, 4.4, 6.2.

> attempts, in the period from January to August 2017, to request asylum at the border. On each of those occasions, however, their claim for asylum was not recognized as such by Border Guards with the result that the claim was not passed on to the competent authorities for consideration. As a result of their not having valid travel documents and not being acknowledged as having claimed asylum, the authors were issued decisions by which they were denied entry into Poland and were immediately expelled and sent back to Belarus.[83]

What is extraordinary in this quotation is that the Committee adopts the complainant's version of the events from the very start.

Whilst there is no explicit explanation as to why these events were not reported in the section of the decision entitled 'Facts as presented by the author', the seasoned observer can later guess what led the Committee to proceed in the way it did. The next paragraph records that the Committee had examined and granted an application for interim measures upon submission of the complaint on 24 and 25 August 2017.[84] The section entitled 'Facts as presented by the authors' subsequently reports that the complainants were again denied access to asylum at the border post on 29 August 2017. (This would normally have been mentioned in the introductory paragraph summarising the procedure). In the section dealing with admissibility, the Committee notes that whether the complainants had claimed asylum was disputed by the parties,[85] but resolves it simply by stating: 'the authors have sufficiently substantiated their claims that they presented information to authorities at the Terespol border checkpoint'.[86] In the section devoted to the merits, the Committee yet again notes the State had brought up this issue.[87] This time it does not address it itself, presumably because it considers it was resolved at admissibility.

Given the State's non-compliance with the interim measures, followed by its shameless denial that the complainants had ever wished to claim asylum, against the Committee's own finding that they had had such a wish, as confirmed by its very request to the State that they be given access to asylum procedures, the Committee could not but be entirely confident about the facts. A substantive upholding of the factual basis of the complaint was therefore the right outcome in this case. However, the

83 *A.B. and B.D.*, para. 1.1.
84 *A.B. and B.D..*, para. 1.2.
85 *A.B. and B.D.*, para. 2.7.
86 *A.B. and B.D.*, para. 8.4.
87 *A.B. and B.D.*, para. 9.3.

Committee should have expressly explained this, as well as recorded that the standards of proof applicable at the admissibility and merits stages differ.

2.5.5 *Conclusion*

The analysis offered in this section can be summarised as follows: UNTBs are to be commended for having, to this day, seen through the state denials and for having invariably accepted the factual allegations of the complainants in pushback cases, despite the evidentiary challenges these cases raise; however, their evidentiary reasoning would gain in being sharper. What is needed, then, is not only clarity regarding the identification of applicable principles but also appreciation of the negative impact of lack of clarity. Section 2.6 starts this conceptual work by highlighting the pitfalls that arise when the evidentiary framework is loose.

2.6 The Risks of a Vague Evidentiary Reasoning

Having demonstrated in Section 2.5 that UNTB jurisprudence suffers from a lack of evidentiary clarity,[88] this section seeks to highlight the risks which this weakness generates for human rights accountability by analysing in further depth two 'clouding' elements. We argue that the absence of specification of the standard of proof applied by the adjudicator, commonly lamented in the literature, risks producing an inadvertent raising of the standard of proof to the detriment of the complainant. The second element we have selected for discussion relates to our recommendation that the either procedural or substantive manner in which the factual basis of a complaint is upheld be distinguished. Confusing these two routes, we argue, risks obliterating the obligation for the adjudicator to uphold the complainant's factual allegations when the circumstances for reversing the burden of proof are present.

Table 2.3 helps visualise these two risks. Its vertical axis lists the evidentiary standards of proof that can be reached when seeking to substantiate a complaint's factual basis. The horizontal axis lists the three outcomes discussed above.[89] The table's top three circled areas indicate where the two axes normatively intersect, that is, which standard of proof is applied that triggers a particular outcome.

[88] This weakness also affects the jurisprudence of the human rights regional courts.
[89] Table 2.2's fourth logical outcome need not retain our attention here.

Table 2.3 *Matching evidentiary thresholds and outcomes (merits stage)*

Outcome / Standard of proof (SoP) reached	Procedural rejection	Procedural (shift-based) upholding[90]	Substantive (evidence-based) upholding
Prima facie	Outcome 1 (*except if* the burden of proof is to be shifted onto the state)	Outcome 2's linkage condition (SoP near-universally recognised)	
More probable than not		Context condition (Roberts)	Outcome 3 (SoP widely recognised)
Clear and compelling		Context condition (Dembour and Hakiki)	Outcome 3 (even more warranted than in box above)
Beyond reasonable doubt (BRD)			Outcome 3 (even more warranted than in two boxes above)
Absolutely certain			Outcome 3 'infinitely' more warranted than in three boxes above

The 'more-probable-than-not' standard, also known as preponderance of evidence, is the standard of proof generally accepted to be of application in international human rights adjudication at the merits stage.[90] By definition this standard is respected when higher standards are met, as Table 2.3's last column's three bottom light grey boxes capture.

These same three boxes indirectly suggest how the standard of proof imposed on the complainant could inadvertently be raised. For the sake of this discussion, let us assume that a couple of pushback cases were

[90] An outlier, the European Court of Human Rights professes to have adopted the BRD standard, but in a sui generis manner which differs from the one the Common Law applies in criminal matters, notably by (theoretically) admitting it can be met through presumptions and inferences. See Dembour, 'Beyond Reasonable Doubt'.

decided by a committee on unusually strong evidence, possibly enhanced by technological operations (as in *Parvin A* and *I.M.* discussed above). If this is done without appreciating that the submitted evidence was stronger than legally required, committee members may come to expect the same level of evidence to be reached in subsequent cases. In the absence of clearly set and understood standards of proof, previous adjudicating experience risks becoming the adjudicator's point of reference. Academic studies have observed that the *prima facie* standard of proof commonly gets distorted in human rights adjudication in a way that disadvantages the complainant victim. The Strasbourg BRD standard is similarly affected.[91] We speculate that an upward slippage could also affect the 'more probable than not' standard.

Table 2.3's two dark-shaded encircled boxes help visualise the risk of an incorrect application of the shift. They show that a violation finding can only be reached *procedurally* – through the operation of the shift – if the evidence linking the complainant's complaint to the problematic human rights contextual situation is *no stronger than* prima facie. Additionally, they show that when there is plausible evidence of this link (and the underlying problematic context has been proven to a higher standard, and the state has failed to rebut the presumption which has arisen against it), then the adjudicator *must* find in favour of the complainant factually. If this were not an automatic outcome, there would be no point in envisaging the shift as a corrective mechanism in the evidentiary framework when states for example suppress evidence of their violating practices. If the standard which is met is the balance of probabilities, then the case is a standard one, represented in Table 2.3 by the darkest-shaded box (substantive upholding).

2.7 Conclusion

It is crucial that human rights adjudication takes place in evidentiary normative fairness, clarity and consistency. Three points in particular have emerged for special attention in the course of our analysis of the UNTB pushback case law. Firstly, in international human rights adjudication, disputed factual allegations must be examined first at admissibility – under the prima facie standard of proof, and again at the merits stage – under the preponderance of evidence standard. Secondly, whilst a

[91] Dembour, 'Beyond Reasonable Doubt'.

complainant will not suddenly stop their submissions when they think they have achieved the minimum standard of proof legally required, the adjudicator must, for its part, recognise when the submitted evidence has gone beyond the set minimum legal standard so as to avoid the understanding of the requirements of relatively low standards being skewed and slipping upwards. Thirdly, for the shifting of the burden of proof to remain a meaningful corrective to the application of the normal evidentiary principles when the state attempts to escape human rights accountability, its operation must take place in strict adherence to the conditions and mechanisms of its application. This requires, amongst other elements, that the adjudicator identify the cases where the shift is not appropriate, due to a substantive upholding of the factual basis of the complaint actually being indicated.

Select Bibliography

Azarova, V. and N. Magugliani, 'EU Border Violence at the European Court of Human Rights: Reflections on G.R.J. v Greece', *de:border collective* (10 February 2025), https://debordercollective.org/updates/border-violence-ecthr-reflections-grj-greece/.

Baranowska, G. 'Exposing Covert Border Enforcement: Why Failing to Shift the Burden of Proof in Pushback Cases Is Wrong', *European Convention on Human Rights Law Review*, 4 (2023), 473–494.

Dembour, M.-B. 'The Migrant Case Law of the European Court of Human Rights: Critique and Way Forward' in B. Çalı, L. Bianku and I. Motoc (eds.), *Migration and the European Convention on Human Rights* (Oxford: Oxford University Press, 2021), pp. 19–40.

'The Escape of the State: No Shift in the Burden of the Proof and No Anti-Roma Discrimination by the Police in P.H. v Slovakia', *DISSECT Blog* (31 October 2022), https://dissect.ugent.be/the-escape-of-the-state-no-shift-in-the-burden-of-the-proof-and-no-anti-roma-discrimination-by-the-police-in-p-h-v-slovakia/.

'Beyond Reasonable Doubt at Its Worst – But Also at Its Potential Best: Dissecting Ireland v the United Kingdom's No-Torture Finding', *European Convention on Human Rights Law Review*, 4 (2023): 375–425.

Keady-Tabbal, N. and I. Mann, '"Pushbacks" as Euphemism', *EJIL: Talk!*, (14 April 2021), www.ejiltalk.org/pushbacks-as-euphemism/.

Murimi, E. 'Fluctuating Standards of Proof at the African Court: A Case for Principled Flexibility', *African Human Rights Yearbook*, 7 (2023): 158–182.

Roberts, C. 'Reversing the Burden of Proof Before Human Rights Bodies', *The International Journal of Human Rights*, 25 (2021): 1682–1703.

Rodrik, D. and H. Hakiki, 'Accessing Borders, Accessing Justice? The European Court of Human Rights' Jurisprudence on Pushbacks at Land Borders', *Asyl, Schweizerische Zeitschrift für Asylrecht und-praxis | Revue Suisse pour la pratique et le droit d'asile*, 1 (2023): 3–17.

Yambio, D. 'EU Law and Life of Us the Black Migrants', *Refugees in Libya* (15 May 2025), www.refugeesinlibya.org/post/eu-law-and-life-of-us-the-black-migrants.

3

UN Treaty Bodies' 'Sufficiently Substantiated' Admissibility Requirement

Endorsement or Distortion of the Prima Facie Threshold?

LISA REINSBERG*

3.1 Introduction

Each of the eight United Nations human rights treaty bodies (UNTBs) currently authorised to receive individual complaints[1] requires that such complaints be 'sufficiently substantiated', 'not manifestly unfounded' or 'not manifestly ill-founded', to be deemed admissible.[2] In this chapter,

* I am profoundly grateful to Marie-Bénédicte Dembour for her thought-provoking suggestions, questions and partnership in developing this chapter, which has benefited enormously in substance and structure as a result. My sincere thanks to Deborah Casalin, Cornelia Klocker, Meghan Campbell and Grażyna Baranowska for their detailed feedback on early drafts. Thank you, as well, to the Centre for Fundamental Rights at the Hertie School for hosting me as a visiting fellow and providing an early opportunity to workshop this piece, and to Başak Çalı, Cathryn Costello, Joseph Finnerty, Francesca Palmiotto, Nino Tsereteli and others for their helpful comments.

[1] See Table 1.2.

[2] Human Rights Committee (HRC), Rules of Procedure (CCPR/C/3/Rev.12), 4 January 2021, Rule 99; Committee against Torture, Rules of Procedure (CAT/C/3/Rev.6), 1 September 2014, Rule 113; Optional Protocol to the Convention on the Elimination of All Forms of Discrimination against Women (CEDAW-OP), New York, 10 December 1999, in force 22 December 2000, 2131 UNTS 83, Art. 4; International Convention for the Protection of All Persons from Enforced Disappearance (CED), New York, 6 February 2007, in force 23 December 2010, 2716 UNTS 3, Art. 31; Optional Protocol to the Convention on the Rights of Persons with Disabilities (CRPD-OP), New York, 30 March 2007, in force 3 May 2008, 2518 UNTS 283, Art. 2 (e); Optional Protocol to the International Covenant on Economic, Social and Cultural Rights (ICESCR-OP), New York, 24 September 2009, in force 5 May 2013, 2922 UNTS 29, Art. 3; Optional Protocol to the Convention on the Rights of the Child on a communications procedure (CRC-OP3), New York, 28 February 2012, in force 14 April 2014, 2983 UNTS 135, Art. 7 (f). The Committee on the Rights of Migrant Workers has not adopted rules on its individual complaint procedure, which has not yet entered into force, but its founding instrument

I refer to these admissibility criteria, together, as the substantiation requirement. This requirement contributes to the high rate of rejection due to inadmissibility, which is the final outcome for as many as 65 per cent of registered complaints.[3] Despite its enormous impact, the substantiation requirement is clouded in confusion: the UNTBs have neither clearly nor consistently defined the criterion. In any human rights complaint proceedings, a lower standard of proof necessarily applies at admissibility, when the complainant is merely introducing the complaint that they will later be required to prove in the merits stage. The UNTB complaint procedures were envisioned as directly accessible to all individuals, without the need for legal counsel, and although time and practicalities have prompted increased formality and rigidity, the admissibility criteria should not be interpreted to improperly impede access to justice at the United Nations. This chapter accordingly aims at reviewing and making sense of the enduringly amorphous substantiation requirement,[4] thereby hopefully helping complainants to navigate it and UNTBs to uniformly implement it.

The analysis offered in this chapter is based on an extensive review of admissibility decisions published between 1977 and 2023 by the eight treaty bodies referred to above. The general difficulties in searching UNTB case law have inevitably complicated the research.[5] Understanding decisions concerning substantiation is additionally challenging because UNTBs

does not contain a substantiation requirement. The Committee on the Elimination of Racial Discrimination, which has not revised its relevant rules of procedure since 1986, has asserted a substantiation requirement in its decisions, although none appears in its founding instrument or rules. See, e.g., *Jallow* v. *Denmark*, CERD/C/108/D/62/2018, 1 December 2022, paras. 6.3–6.5.

[3] See Report of the Human Rights Committee (A/76/40), 2021, para. 21.

See also C. P. R. Romano, 'The Rule of Prior Exhaustion of Domestic Remedies: Theory and Practice in International Human Rights Procedures', in N. Boschiero, T. Scovazzi, C. Pitea and C. Ragni (eds.), *International Courts and the Development of International Law: Essays in Honour of Tullio Treves* (The Hague: Springer, 2013) pp. 555–566, 574, 579 (citing Y. Tyagi, *The UN Human Rights Committee: Practice and Procedure* (Cambridge: Cambridge University Press, 2011), p. 498; J. Th. Möller and A. M. De Zayas, *The United Nations Human Rights Committee Case Law 1977–2008: A Handbook* (Kehl am Rhein: Engel, 2009) p. 91.

[4] See, e.g., *Morael* v. *France*, CCPR/C/OP/3, 10 July 1987; *Loor Chila* v. *Spain*, E/C.12/70/D/102/2019, 12 October 2021, para. 6.6; *Aden and Hassan* v. *Denmark*, CCPR/C/126/D/2531/2015, 25 July 2019, para. 9.8.

[5] As highlighted in both Chapters 1 and 11 of this volume. For example, the WorldCourts database contains decisions from seven UN human rights treaty bodies, but the most recent cases in the database are from between 2016 and 2019. As of 20 November 2023, the JURIS database of the OHCHR contains 460 decisions tagged as concerning

publish neither the parties' submissions nor any explanation of their rejection of complaints in the registration stage (including for lack of substantiation).[6] Their admissibility decisions often merely conclude that the complainant has or has not adequately supported their factual or legal claims, without explaining why.[7] All in all, I have read more than 400 admissibility decisions concerning substantiation.[8] My analysis of these decisions reveals that, although UNTBs frequently invoke the prima facie evidentiary threshold, they often require complainants' claims to be probable or even convincing – when weighed against the state's submissions – to satisfy the substantiation requirement at admissibility.

The text is organised as follows: having clarified when the substantiation requirement applies, Section 3.2 reviews the evolution and status of the corresponding treaty body rules. Section 3.3 compares descriptions of the substantiation requirement to the commonly accepted legal meaning of the prima facie threshold. Section 3.4 examines the first distortion of prima facie by identifying five reasons UNTBs often find claims insufficiently substantiated, which appear reasonable but have allowed UNTBs to reject claims for lacking convincing (rather than plausible) legal or evidentiary support. Section 3.5 addresses prima facie's second distortion, which arises when treaty bodies weigh states' arguments and evidence against those of the complainant in their assessment of substantiation. This often results in a claim being declared inadmissible because the state's official determinations and documentation are presumed to be credible, while the complainant does not benefit from the same presumption. Section 3.6 outlines six scenarios when treaty bodies may apply a low standard of proof or partially shift the burden of proof onto the state, thereby making it easier for the complainant to satisfy the substantiation requirement. UNTBs' occasional and exceptional use of a lower evidentiary standard further throws into relief the elevated

'substantiation of claims', but only one from prior to 2002 and many that do not actually involve substantiation.

6 See, e.g., HRC, Rules 89 (3), 111.

7 See, e.g., OHCHR, UN Human Rights Report 2021, 2 June 2022, p. 441 (indicating 86% of complaints are rejected at registration); I. Jelić and L. Mührel, 'The Human Rights Committee: Challenges and Prospects for Enhanced Effectiveness and Integration', *Journal of Human Rights Practice* 14 (2022): 17–43.

8 In addition to using the databases mentioned above, I have reviewed decisions available in the UN Treaty Body Database, Bayefsky.com, University of Minnesota Human Rights Library and the UNTBs' compilations of select decisions not included in the UN Treaty Body Database.

requirement more typically applied and constitutes a third distortion of the prima facie threshold, as commonly understood. In its final section (3.7), the chapter urges the treaty bodies to harmonise their approach to the substantiation requirement in a way that respects prima facie's etymological meaning.

3.2 Origins and Formalisation of the Substantiation Requirement

Before discussing the meaning of the substantiation requirement, it is important to clarify when it applies. In short, substantiation is assessed both at the registration stage and, if the complaint is registered, again at the admissibility stage. At the registration stage, treaty bodies weed out more than eighty percent of incoming complaints based on an initial assessment of admissibility, without a reasoned decision.[9] At admissibility, UNTBs again assess substantiation, alongside other criteria that require at least some evaluation of the substance of the complaint. These include whether the named victim has been personally affected by the alleged violation or has been 'clear[ly]' disadvantaged[10] and whether the kind of violation alleged falls within the UNTB's jurisdiction *ratione materiae*.[11]

Over time, UNTBs have rejected an increasing number of complaints for lack of substantiation.[12] This may be partly explained by the constant

[9] See, e.g., United Nations Human Rights Report 2021, p. 441. Treaty bodies' practices vary, with some delegating registration decisions to the Secretariat staff and others assigning a Rapporteur or Working Group to make registration decisions.

[10] *Sacchi et al.* v. *Argentina*, CRC/C/88/D/104/2019, 22 September 2021, paras. 10.1ff (discussing jurisdiction and victim status); *A.W.P.* v. *Denmark*, CCPR/C/109/D/1879/2009, 1 November 2013 (Individual opinion of Yuval Shany, Fabian Omar Salvioli and Victor Manuel Rodriguez-Rescia), para. 2; Art. 4 OP-ICESCR (allowing rejection of a complaint if it does not show 'the author has suffered a clear disadvantage').

[11] Secretary-General, Comparative Summary of Existing Communications and Inquiry Procedures and Practices under International Human Rights Instruments and under the Charter of the United Nations (E/CN.6/1997/4), 21 January 1997, para. 24. See also OHCHR, Reporting under the International Covenant on Civil and Political Rights: Training Guide (New York and Geneva: United Nations Publications, 2021), p. 108; *Wasitha Ranawaka* v. *Australia*, CAT/C/68/D/855/2017, 5 December 2019, para. 8.3 (distinguishing jurisdiction *ratione materiae* from substantiation); *H.S.* v. *Australia*, CCPR/C/113/D/2015/2010, 30 March 2015, paras. 8.3–8.12; Y. Shany, *Questions of Jurisdiction and Admissibility before International Courts* (Cambridge: Cambridge University Press, 2016), p. 1.

[12] As of 18 January 2023, the JURIS Database contained 382 decisions tagged as pertaining to 'substantiation of claims'. Of these, 16 (4%) were decided between 2002 and 2008; 32

growth of their case load which,[13] coupled with their generally inadequate resourcing, has prompted a search for efficiency in the treaty bodies' operations.[14] That the admissibility requirements have become more demanding through the years is confirmed by an analysis of the governing texts.[15]

The Human Rights Committee (HRC or Committee) was the first treaty body to consider how to interpret and apply the admissibility requirements. When it discussed its initial draft rules of procedure in 1977, there was apparently no mention of substantiation or well-foundedness with respect to admissibility.[16] However, the HRC began assessing the evidentiary support for individuals' claims at the admissibility stage as early as 1978.[17] It soon explicitly asserted a 'sufficiently substantiated' admissibility criterion, based on the requirement found in the Optional Protocol that authors 'claim' that a state party to the ICCPR has violated their rights.[18] For example, in its 1985 views concerning *J.H. v. Canada*, the Committee stated that an author 'must himself claim, in a substantiated manner, that he is or has been a victim of a violation'.[19] In a private meeting in 1989, the HRC formally revised its Rules to add this admissibility requirement.[20]

(8%) were decided between 2009 and 2013; 124 (32%) were decided between 2014 and 2018; and 209 (55%) were decided between January 2019 and December 2022.

[13] See, e.g., Secretary-General, Status of the UN Human Rights Treaty Body System (A/71/118), 18 July 2016, paras. 4, 20, 21; P. Alston, Effective Implementation of International Instruments on Human Rights, Including Reporting Obligations under International Instruments on Human Rights (A/ 44/ 668), 8 November 1989, paras. 13, 19; United Nations Human Rights Report 2021, p. 441.

[14] See, e.g., Secretary-General, Report on the Process of the Consideration of the State of the United Nations Human Rights Treaty Body System (A/75/601, Annex), 17 November 2020, para. 21. See also Jelić and Mührel, 'The Human Rights Committee', 17.

[15] See, e.g., M. Langford, B. Porter, R. Brown and J. Rossi (eds.), *The Optional Protocol to the International Covenant on Economic, Social and Cultural Rights: A Commentary* (Pretoria: Pretoria University Law Press, 2016), pp. 7–8, 75.

[16] Report of the Human Rights Committee (A/32/44), 30 September 1977.

[17] *Z.Z.* v. *Canada*, 18 July 1978, in United Nations, Human Rights Committee: Selected Decisions under the Optional Protocol (2nd to 16th Session) (1985), p. 19.

[18] Arts. 1, 2 of the Optional Protocol to the ICCPR; Report of the Human Rights Committee (A/39/40/SUPP), 20 September 1984, para. 588.

[19] *J.H.* v. *Canada*, CCPR/C/24/D/187/1985, 12 April 1985, para. 4.1.

[20] Rules of Procedure of the Human Rights Committee, CCPR/C/3/Rev.2 (1989), Rule 90 (b), cited in K. A. Young, *The Law and Process of the U.N. Human Rights Committee* (Ardsley: Transnational Publishers, 2002), p. 156, n. 81.

The HRC's two closest contemporaries took different approaches. By the late 1990s, both the Committee on the Elimination of Racial Discrimination (CERD) and the Committee against Torture (CAT) had begun to expressly require substantiation in the admissibility analysis they provided in their decisions.[21] However, CERD, whose complaint process became operational in 1982,[22] has never included a substantiation requirement in its Rules.[23] By contrast, when CAT revised its Rules in 2002, it added an admissibility requirement to the effect that communications not be 'manifestly unfounded'.[24]

In 1999, states began to include a substantiation requirement when creating new individual complaint processes. That year, states adopted the Optional Protocol to the Convention on the Elimination of All Forms of Discrimination against Women (CEDAW), which became the first UN human rights instrument to include a substantiation requirement – namely that complaints not be 'manifestly ill-founded'.[25] The four UN treaty-based individual complaint processes created since 2006 – those of the Committee on Economic, Social and Cultural Rights (CESCR); Committee on the Rights of the Child (CRC); Committee on the Rights of Persons with Disabilities (CRPD); and the Committee on Enforced Disappearances (CED) – each reference one or both standards (not manifestly unfounded or ill-founded, and sufficiently substantiated) in their respective treaties or optional protocols, as well as in their rules.[26] While each treaty body is unique in whether and how its founding instrument or rules explicitly require substantiation, treaty bodies and their secretariat staff in the Office of the High Commissioner for Human Rights (OHCHR) have generally treated this as a uniform requirement for all UNTB individual complaint processes, albeit without having consistently defined it.[27]

[21] See, e.g., *S and Y* v. *Netherlands*, CAT/C/15/D/31/1995, 20 November 1995, para. 4.2; *Barbaro* v. *Australia*, CERD/C/51/D/7/1995, 14 August 1997, para. 10.2.

[22] UN Treaty Collection, 'ICERD'. Website, n. 35. https://treaties.un.org/Pages/ViewDetails.aspx?src=TREATY&mtdsg_no=IV-2&chapter=4&clang=_en#35.

[23] CERD, Rules of Procedure (CERD/C/35/Rev.3), 23 May 2025.

[24] CAT, Rules of Procedure, Rule 107 (b). *See also* CAT, Report of the Committee against Torture (A/57/44/SUPP), 2002, para. 199. *Compare* United Nations, Compilation of Rules of Procedure Adopted by the Human Rights Treaty Bodies (HRI/GEN/3), 6 June 2001. At the time, four treaty bodies – the HRC, CERD, CAT and CEDAW Committee – had active individual complaint processes.

[25] Arts 2, 4, CEDAW-OP.

[26] Art. 31 CED; Arts. 1, 2 CRPD-OP; Art. 3 ICESCR-OP; Arts. 5, 7 CRC-OP3.

[27] See, e.g., OHCHR. 'Individual Communications'. www.ohchr.org/en/treaty-bodies/individual-communications. ('Is the complaint sufficiently substantiated? If the relevant

3.3 Behind a Confusing Variety of Labels: Understanding the Prima Facie Threshold

In their decisions, the treaty bodies have offered differing explanations of the nature and stringency of the standard of proof by which they assess the substantiation or foundedness of the complainant's allegation at the admissibility stage. They have varyingly stated that the complainant must 'establish' the relevant facts, provide 'convincing arguments' of a violation or 'adequately explain' the allegations, but also, merely, 'raise the possibility of a violation'.[28]

Nonetheless treaty bodies, states and scholars have identified a common legal standard for assessing substantiation at admissibility: prima facie.[29] The Latin term prima facie is commonly translated as 'at first appearance' or 'on the face of it'.[30] In UNTB decisions and scholarship, it appears repeatedly as a stand-in for 'not manifestly unfounded' and 'sufficiently substantiated'. Rather than bringing clarity, however, invoking this legal term poses two primary problems: first, the different

Committee considers, in the light of the information before it, that the complainant has not sufficiently presented/ described the facts and arguments for a violation of the Covenant, it may reject the case as insufficiently substantiated, and thus inadmissible').

28 *B.M.* v. *Switzerland*, CEDAW/C/83/D/132/2018, 17 October 2022, para. 12.8 ('establish'); *Alger* v. *Australia*, CCPR/C/120/D/2237/2013, 13 July 2017, para. 6.5 ('convincing arguments'); *P.T.* v. *Denmark*, CCPR/C/113/D/2272/2013, 1 April 2015, para. 6.4 ('adequately explained ... with plausible arguments'); *P.S.B.* v. *Canada*, CAT/C/55/D/505/2012, 18 August 2015, para. 7.2 ('sufficiently detailed'); *I.D.G.* v. *Spain*, E/C.12/55/D/2/2014, 17 June 2015, para. 9.7 ('raises the possibility of a violation'); *A.B.H.* v. *Denmark*, CCPR/C/126/D/2603/2015, 8 July 2019, para. 8.4 ('adequately explain').

29 See, e.g., *S.M.* v. *Denmark*, CRPD/C/29/D/61/2019, 25 August 2023, para. 6.5 (State's argument); *Acosta Martínez and Amaghnouge* v. *Spain*, E/C.12/73/D/213/2021, 27 February 2023, para. 6.2; *Jallow* v. *Denmark*, CERD/C/108/D/62/2018, paras. 4.4, 6.2; *K.Y.M.* v. *Denmark*, CRC/C/77/D/3/2016, 25 January 2018, para. 4.7 (State's argument); *S.O.* v. *Canada*, CEDAW/C/59/D/49/2013, 27 October 2014, para. 9.5; *H.J.H.* v. *Netherlands*, CCPR/C/43/D/448/1991, 7 November 1991, para. 4.2. See also letter on individual communications from 42 states to high commissioner Michelle Bachelet, 30 May 2022, www.ohchr.org/sites/default/files/2022-05/EN_Treaty-Body-Letter-on-Individual-Communications-30May2022.pdf (describing the substantiation criterion as requiring 'sufficient documentation to substantiate the case on a *prima facie* basis'); M. Gillett, Y. Karukaya and M. Marzotto, 'Reconciling the Dual-Faceted Mandates of Quasi-Judicial Human Rights Bodies: The Working Group on Arbitrary Detention's Prima Facie Approach to Evidence', *Human Rights Law Review* 24 (2024) 1–25.

30 Prima facie, J. Law and E. A. Martin (eds.), *A Dictionary of Law* (Oxford: Oxford University Press, 2009); Prima facie, *Black's Law Dictionary*, 2nd ed. (West Publishing, 1910).

formulations of the substantiation requirement do not necessarily share the same meaning; and second, prima facie itself is a debated term.

The criterion of 'not manifestly ill-founded' (or 'not manifestly unfounded') and 'not insufficiently substantiated' appear as separate and distinct grounds of inadmissibility in treaty body rules. The two conditions are not synonymous. Potentially, there is a vast difference between making a claim that is *clearly* false or *obviously* unsupported and making one that is not *fully* convincing. It follows that, even if either 'sufficiently substantiated' *or* 'not manifestly ill-founded' could be understood to be interchangeable with the term 'prima facie', both cannot be. Yet, CAT, for example, has 'found claims to be manifestly unfounded where the author of the communication has failed to present an arguable case, that is, to submit substantiated arguments . . . in such a way that they establish a prima facie case for the purpose of admissibility of the complaint'.[31] This statement seems to conflate the two distinct terms and to equate them with the prima facie threshold.

Separately, there appears to be confusion around the meaning of prima facie itself. The CESCR recently noted that 'even where a communication appears prima facie to be admissible because the initial submission is sufficiently substantiated for purposes of registration, nothing prevents the Committee from concluding, after further examination and on the basis of the information on admissibility provided by both parties, that the communication is inadmissible for want of sufficient substantiation'.[32] This implies that at least some of the CESCR members believe the purportedly prima facie threshold applied at registration is lower than the (unspecified) standard applied at admissibility. Scholars' explanations reflect the UNTBs' various interpretations of these terms. Tom Zwart has proposed that the prima facie standard means that '[f]or purposes of admissibility, the author of a complaint . . . has only to make a reasonable effort to adequately substantiate his allegations' before a UNTB.[33] Taking a slightly different view, Thomas Buergenthal asserted that the prima facie standard means 'that the communication must contain allegations which, if proved, would amount to a violation'.[34]

[31] *S.B.M.* v. *Sweden*, CAT /C/77/D/1011/2020, 10 July 2023, para. 8.8.

[32] *Stitou and Ben Hmdou* v. *Spain*, CE/C.12/72/D/86/2018, 10 October 2022, para. 6.5.

[33] T. Zwart, *The Admissibility of Human Rights Petitions: The Case Law of the European Commission of Human Rights and the Human Rights Committee* (Dordrecht: Martinus Nijhoff Publishers, 1994), p. 11.

[34] T. Buergenthal, 'The U.N. Human Rights Committee', in J. A. Frowein and R. Wolfrum (eds.), *Max Planck Yearbook of United Nations Law* 5 (2001): 341–98, 380.

For Kirsten Young, however, 'even if the facts alleged by the author would, if proved to be true, amount to a violation of the Covenant, the claim will still be inadmissible . . . if the [treaty body] finds that the facts have not been 'sufficiently substantiated'.[35] Each of these explanations describes a different conception of the substantiation requirement and of the term prima facie. Indeed, Frans Viljoen has observed that the substantiation requirement has not always been interpreted in the same way by UNTBs: 'In some instances this has been set as a prima facie standard, in others merely as providing some substantiation.'[36]

Other international tribunals have grappled with contradictory interpretations of prima facie, as well. For example, the International Criminal Tribunal for the former Yugoslavia has asserted, on different occasions, that the prima facie threshold requires either the presentation of evidence that would be sufficient for a conviction if not contradicted, or – merely – a pleading that sets out a credible case.[37] The European Court of Human Rights' not 'manifestly ill-founded' admissibility requirement has commonly been described as 'tantamount' or 'analogous' to the minimal prima facie substantiation threshold found in the UNTB procedural rules.[38] However, scholars and practitioners have criticised the Court for applying a higher standard in practice.[39] Regarding World Trade Organization dispute settlement processes, it has been observed that prima facie is incoherently and unsatisfactorily used in at least three different ways,[40] namely as: (1) an evidentiary threshold that the complainant, alone, must satisfy in order for the dispute to be considered; (2) a rebuttable presumption of truth, whereby the complainant's coherent complaint is taken as true unless and until rebutted by the other party; or

[35] K. A. Young, *The Law and Process of the U.N. Human Rights Committee*, p. 157.

[36] F. Viljoen, 'Fact-Finding by UN Human Rights Complaints Bodies: Analysis and Suggested Reforms', in A. von Bogdandy and R. Wolfrum (eds.), *Max Planck Yearbook of United Nations Law* 8 (2004): 49–100, 65 (internal citations omitted).

[37] *Prosecutor* v. *Slobodan Milosevic*, ICTY, Decision on Review of Indictment, 22 November 2001, paras. 11–15.

[38] M. O'Boyle, 'Proof: European Court of Human Rights', *Max Planck Encyclopedia of International Procedural Law* (last updated August 2018); OHCHR. 'Complaints Procedures under the Human Rights Treaties'.

[39] *Ukraine and Netherlands* v. *Russia*, ECtHR, 8019/16, 43800/14 and 28525/20, Decision, 25 January 2023, paras. 449–451. M.-B. Dembour, 'Introduction: The Evidentiary System of the European Court of Human Rights in Critical Perspective', *European Convention on Human Rights Law Review* 4.4 (2023): 363–374, 367.

[40] J. G. Devaney, *Fact-Finding before the International Court of Justice* (Cambridge: Cambridge University Press, 2016), p. 161.

(3) the evidentiary standard that the complainant must satisfy on the merits, based on consideration of all the available evidence.[41] This diversity of approaches at the international level mirrors the various interpretations found in national legal systems, where, for example, prima facie can refer either to a minimal standard of proof (meaning, evidence sufficient, at first sight, to avoid summary dismissal so that the case can proceed to the merits), or as a threshold which impacts the burden of proof (by requiring a decision on the merits in the complainant's favour unless the other party presents stronger evidence).[42]

Despite these differing explanations, there does appear to be a prevailing understanding of prima facie in international law. In line with its colloquial meaning, prima facie is most commonly understood as a low standard of proof – a requirement to present an initial claim that is cognizable, but that need not (yet) be convincing nor more persuasive than the other party's submissions. Case law from international tribunals often suggests that the prima facie threshold requires, first, that the complainant's submissions alone be examined (without attention given to the submissions of the other party) and, second, that the alleged treaty violation appear to be plausible at the preliminary stage.[43] Thus, the Inter-American Commission on Human Rights describes its assessment of whether a petitioner's claim is 'colorable' and therefore not manifestly groundless, for purposes of admissibility, as 'a prima facie analysis of the substance ("*caracterización*") of the allegations' 'to determine whether the petition establishes the legal grounds for a possible or potential violation of a right'.[44] The European Court of Human Rights most often equates the prima facie burden with a plausibility standard when deciding requests for interim measures.[45] The African Commission on Human and Peoples' Rights has described the prima facie threshold as requiring

[41] J. G. Devaney, *Fact-Finding before the International Court of Justice*, p. 161.

[42] See, e.g., G. N. Herlitz, 'The Meaning of the Term Prima Facie', *Louisiana Law Review* 55 (1994–1995): 391–408.

[43] R. Wolfrum and M. Möldner, 'International Courts and Tribunals, Evidence', *Max Planck Encyclopedia of International Law*, para. 79 (last updated August 2013). In addition to the examples given below, see WTO Panel Report, 'China: Countervailing and Anti-Dumping Duties on Gran Oriented Flat-Rolled Electrical Steel from the United States' (WT/DS414/R), 15 June 2012, para. 7.637.

[44] IACHR, 'Digest of the IACHR on Its Admissibility and Competence Criteria' (2020), paras. 2, 242.

[45] H. Keller and C. Marti, 'Interim Relief Compared: Use of Interim Measures by the UN Human Rights Committee and the European Court of Human Rights', *Heidelberg Journal of International Law* 73 (2013): 325–372, 334.

'preliminary evidence indicative of a violation', implying that only the complainant's submissions are considered.[46] Its counterpart Court has specified that a prima facie finding of jurisdiction is based on a factual assessment 'at a glance'.[47] Moving away from the human rights field, the International Centre for Settlement of Investment Disputes (ICSID) tribunal has stated that its responsibility under a prima facie standard is to assess whether the 'the facts alleged *by the Claimants* . . . are capable of coming within . . . the Treaty's provisions, [and] the Claimants' allegations [are not] incoherent and conclusory'.[48] In these contexts, the tribunals may accept the complainant's factual allegations as true – unless manifestly untrue – and do not attempt to ascertain whether the complainant will be able to conclusively prove them to be true.[49] Thus, on the basis of the most persuasive discussions, I view the proper normative understanding of prima facie to be consistent with a plausibility standard of proof, assessed on the basis of the complainant's submissions alone.

The UN treaty bodies' interpretation of the substantiation requirement appears – at least at times – to be at odds with the prevailing understanding of the prima facie threshold. In light of the dominant legal interpretation of prima facie, and the preliminary procedural stage when the substantiation requirement applies, such an understanding is regrettable. Plausibility at first glance is all that should be required for the purpose of admissibility (even if the UNTBs are admittedly not alone in invoking the

[46] *Al-Asad* v. *Djibouti*, ACmHPR, 383/10, Decision, May 2014, para. 143. See also *Southern Africa Human Rights NGO Network and Others* v. *Tanzania*, ACmHPR, 333/06, Decision, May 2010, para. 51.

[47] *Michelot Yogogombaye* v. *Senegal*, ACtHPR, 001/2008, Judgment, 15 December 2009, para. 40.

[48] *Strabag SE et al.* v. *Poland*, ICSID Case No. ADHOC/15/1, Partial Award on Jurisdiction, 2 March 2020, para. 3.2. But see *SGS* v. *Paraguay*, ICSID Case No. ARB/07/29, Decision on Jurisdiction, 12 February 2010, paras. 47–58 (indicating prima facie is a higher standard).

[49] See, e.g., *Ramiro Ibarra Rubi* (United States of America), IACHR, 13.829, Admissibility and Merits, 31 December 2021, para. 43. See also C. Miles, 'Provisional Measures and the "New" Plausibility in the Jurisprudence of the International Court of Justice', *British Yearbook of International Law* 34 (2018), https://academic.oup.com/bybil/advance-article/doi/10.1093/bybil/bry011/5066610. But see M. Potestà and M. Sobat, 'Frivolous Claims in International Adjudication: A Study of ICSID Rule 41(5) and of Procedures of Other Courts and Tribunals to Dismiss Claims Summarily', *Journal of International Dispute Settlement* 3 (2012): 137–168, 155–158.

prima facie threshold and then requiring that the allegation be convincing, rather than merely plausible).[50]

3.4 The First Distortion of Prima Facie: The Application of Too High a Standard

Turning from abstract descriptions of the substantiation requirement and its relationship to the prima facie standard, this section analyses how the UNTBs interpret and apply the evidentiary standard in the particular circumstances of actual admissibility decisions. UNTBs may find a complaint insufficiently substantiated for lack of detailed factual explanation, legal argument, or supporting documentation. The cases discussed indicate that treaty bodies sometimes require the complainant's claim to be convincing, however, suggesting a distortion of the prima facie standard. More specifically, rejections for insufficient substantiation tend to fall into one the following five categories: (1) the complainant provides evidence which is deemed not to sufficiently support their factual allegations; (2) the complainant fails to provide evidence pertaining to each element of the applicable legal standard or test; (3) the complainant provides inadequate proof of the individual harm the alleged violation caused them; (4) the complainant fails to provide official documentation – or, alternatively, the state has provided official documentation that contradicts their claim; and (5) the treaty body is unconvinced of the legal existence of the right allegedly violated. Each of these categories will be briefly described in turn, along with examples of how the application of seemingly straightforward grounds for rejection can result in an evidentiary standard that is higher than prima facie.

3.4.1 Unsupported Factual Allegations

First, when a complaint asserts a violation of the relevant treaty without describing the factual circumstances in detail or without providing

[50] See, e.g., *R.S.* v. *Denmark*, CAT/C/32/D/225/2003, 19 May 2004, paras. 6.2, 6.3; M.-B. Dembour, 'Beyond Reasonable Doubt at Its Worst – But Also at Its Potential Best: Dissecting Ireland v the United Kingdom's No-Torture Finding', *European Convention on Human Rights Law Review* 4.4 (2023): 375–425, Part 4.1.2; M. A. Jimoh, 'A Critique of the Seizure of the African Commission on Human and Peoples' Rights', *African Human Rights Law Journal* 22 (2022): 362–378; J. Gerards, 'Inadmissibility Decisions of the European Court of Human Rights: A Critique of the Lack of Reasoning', *Human Rights Law Review* 14 (2014): 148–158.

evidentiary support for the factual claims, a treaty body will likely find a lack of substantiation.[51] However, UNTBs have rejected allegations for these reasons even when the only evidence available to the complainant is their own memory of events. For example, the HRC '[took] into account the absence of further information and supporting evidence' when rejecting an author's claim that he had not been provided with legal assistance after having been charged with a crime; his narrative recitation was considered insufficient to satisfy the substantiation requirement.[52] The Committee seemed to have wanted the author to prove a negative (that he was not informed of his right to counsel), and to provide documentary evidence of an oral exchange between himself and the authorities. Similarly, the HRC rejected a protester's allegations that Uzbek authorities had denied her legal counsel, not provided her with Russian translations of police reports, and held court hearings in her absence. This was on the grounds that she had 'provided no specific arguments', apparently indicating the HRC required additional details, possibly dates.[53] Given that the summary of the author's allegations was arguably quite detailed, one nonetheless wonders what exactly the Committee expected her to submit.

3.4.2 *Inadequately Supported Legal Claim*

Second, complainants must provide substantiation for each legal conclusion necessary to find a violation, for every claim within the complaint.[54] In one case, the HRC rejected an alleged violation of the right to freedom of assembly as insufficiently substantiated because the complainant was the only person who had participated in the protest and 'one-person protests normally do not fall under. . .the right of peaceful assembly', but are rather analysed under the right to freedom of expression.[55] In other instances, treaty bodies have drawn unfavourable legal conclusions when

[51] See, e.g., *Werenbeck* v. *Australia*, 27 March 1997, para. 9.6, in Report of the Human Rights Committee (Vol. II), A/52/40[VOL.II](SUPP), Annex VII, p. 256.

[52] See, e.g., *Tikhonov* v. *Kazakhstan*, CCPR/C/130/D/2551/2015, 5 November 2020, paras. 5.4, 9.4.

[53] *Kim* v. *Uzbekistan*, CCPR/C/122/D/2175/2012, 4 April 2018, para. 12.6.

[54] See, e.g., *al-Sayed and Mangisto* v. *Palestine*, CRPD/C/28/D/67/2019, paras. 7.8, 7.9 (rejecting some alleged violations where the complainant did not provide separate support specific to those claims).

[55] *Baydildayeva* v. *Kazakhstan*, CCPR/C/137/D/2545/2015, 10 March 2023, para. 7.4.

they considered a complainant to have 'made no link between the alleged facts and the violation'.[56]

When a complainant asserts a legal claim that requires the UNTB to apply a specific test or a particular standard of proof on the merits, treaty bodies have sometimes interpreted the substantiation requirement to require evidentiary support that satisfies the elements of that particular legal claim, sometimes seeming to address the merits fully and directly.[57] For example, in cases involving allegedly unfair domestic proceedings, complainants must show that the domestic process was manifestly or clearly unfair or arbitrary, and treaty bodies have required specific – and convincing – evidence as to these points.[58] In such a case, the HRC seemed to demand *conclusive* evidence when it found the individual's claim unsubstantiated, stating that it '[could not] conclude, on the basis of the materials at its disposal, that in deciding the author's case the domestic courts [had] acted in a clearly arbitrary or manifestly erroneous manner'.[59] The individual alleged that the state had violated his privacy rights by, inter alia, using evidence against him obtained through covert surveillance. He alleged that this did not satisfy the requirements of international human rights law as it lacked safeguards and its parameters were secret or vague.[60] A faithful application of the prima facie standard would have assessed the plausibility of his claim (whether as to the conventionality of the surveillance or the domestic courts' conduct), rather than requiring convincing evidence that domestic courts clearly erred.

UNTBs have also sometimes conflated the substantiation requirement with the standard of proof on the merits in discrimination cases, when the complainant must (only) make a prima facie showing in order for the

[56] *M.C.* v. *Denmark*, CEDAW/C/62/D/56/2013, para. 9.4. See also *K.Y.M.* v. *Denmark*, CRC/C/77/D/3/2016, 25 January 2018, para. 10.

[57] See, e.g., *Alger* v. *Australia*, CCPR/C/120/D/2237/2013, 13 July 2017, para. 6.5; *A.M.* v. *Switzerland*, CAT/C/25/D/144/1999, 14 November 2000, para. 6.7; *H.S.V.* v. *Sweden*, CAT/C/32/D/229/2003, 12 May 2004, para. 8.3; *R.T.* v. *Switzerland*, CAT/C/35/D/242/2003, 24 November 2005, para. 6.2.

[58] See, e.g., *L.O. et al.* v. *Switzerland*, CEDAW/C/76/D/124/2018, 6 July 2020, para. 6.8; *G.I.* v. *Denmark*, CAT/C/61/D/625/2014, 10 August 2017, para. 8.4. See also *S* v. *Australia*, CCPR/C/137/D/2999/2017, 21 March 2023, joint opinion of Committee members Farid Ahmadov, Carlos Gómez Martínez, Laurence R. Helfer, Marcia V. J. Kran, Kobauyah Tchamdja Kpatcha and Teraya Koji (dissenting)), para. 4.

[59] *G.A.P.* v. *Romania*, CCPR/C/137/D/3662/2019, 23 March 2023, para. 8.5.

[60] *G.A.P.* (HRC), paras. 3.2, 3.3.

state to be required to provide an acceptable explanation.[61] In a 2015 dissent concerning an allegedly discriminatory compensation regime, three HRC members called the majority to task for their apparent 'confusion [regarding the difference] between the absence of a prima facie violation and manifestly ill-founded nature of the claim'[62] when rejecting a complaint for insufficient substantiation. They wrote, '[w]hile the existence of a violation might not be clearly apparent at first sight, that does not mean that the lack of a violation itself is clear or that the evidence provided by the author to substantiate his claim is so unconvincing that the claim must be declared manifestly ill-founded. However, in this case, the Committee is basing itself on this prima facie assessment to put a stop to the proceedings.'[63] These objections imply that in this particular case, the HRC majority interpreted the substantiation requirement to mean the alleged violation must be 'clearly apparent' rather than plausible, and required the complainant to meet the standard of proof applicable to the merits of the claim.[64] Expecting the complainant to conclusively prove the merits of the claim in order to survive admissibility appears to conflate these two procedural phases and their evidentiary standards.

3.4.3 No Demonstration of Specific Personal Disadvantage

Third, a treaty body may find a complaint insufficiently substantiated if the author does not demonstrate how they have been affected individually. For example, when a complainant alleged the state violated its positive obligation to prosecute hate speech, but 'failed to establish that [public officials' Islamophobic] statements had specific consequences for him or that the specific consequences of the statements were imminent and would personally affect him', the HRC declared his complaint inadmissible for lack of substantiation.[65] The HRC also found his

[61] Non-refoulement cases present a similar problem. See CAT, General Comment No. 4 on the implementation of Article 3 of the Convention in the context of Article 22 (CAT/C/GC/4), 4 September 2018, para. 31.

[62] *X* v. *Czech Republic*, CCPR/C/113/D/1961/2010, 2 April 2015, partly dissenting opinion of Olivier de Frouville, Mauro Politi and Víctor Manuel Rodríguez-Rescia, para. 4.

[63] *X* v. *Czech Republic* (HRC).

[64] Interestingly, the HRC's Rules refer only to a requirement that the complaint be sufficiently substantiated, but the dissenting Committee members refer to 'not manifestly unfounded' as the relevant standard.

[65] *A.W.P.* (HRC), paras. 6.4, 6.5. See also *V.B.* v. *Czech Republic*, CCPR/C/108/D/1809/2008, 24 July 2013, para. 7.4.

claim regarding lack of an effective remedy insufficiently substantiated because he 'has not been able to prove that he was a direct victim of such violations'.[66]

Some cases in this category illustrate the difficulty of distinguishing between general conditions and individualised harm.[67] In a case concerning conditions in a labour camp in Turkmenistan, which the HRC had previously found to be incompatible with the ICCPR, member Hélène Tigroudja dissented from the Committee's inadmissibility determination, pointing out that the Committee already knew of the conditions in this particular camp and the difficulties for detainees to present complaints to authorities.[68] She asserted: 'It is therefore reasonable to infer from this previously established jurisprudence of the Committee that the objective conditions of detention in the labour camp are incompatible with the Covenant,' making it 'odd to require the authors to demonstrate having been "personally" subjected to such conditions, given that this extreme and unhealthy environment is imposed on all the detainees'.[69] Even leaving aside the HRC's own prior findings, one could argue that the detainees' claim that the camp conditions violated their rights would easily pass a prima facie or plausibility standard based on their individual accounts of beatings in addition to their description of the general conditions documented in independent reports.[70] Yet, the HRC referred to 'the absence of detailed explanations' in rejecting the claim as insufficiently substantiated.[71]

3.4.4 *Supportive Official Documentation Not Provided*

Fourth, when an event would ordinarily generate official documentation, treaty bodies appear to expect the applicant to provide this documentation in order to satisfy the substantiation requirement. For example, when a complainant alleged he had been convicted twice for the same crime, but 'failed to provide any documents, such as copies of arrest warrants, court decisions or imprisonment records', the HRC found his

[66] *A.W.P.* (HRC), para. 6.5.

[67] *A.W.P.* (HRC), individual opinion by Committee members Mr. Yuval Shany, Mr. Fabian Omar Salvioli and Mr. Victor Manuel Rodríguez-Rescia (concurring).

[68] *Nazarov* v. *Turkmenistan*, CCPR/C/126/D/2302/2013, 25 July 2019, dissenting opinion of Hélène Tigroudja.

[69] *Nazarov* (HRC).

[70] *Nazarov* (HRC), paras. 3.3, 3.4, 3.5.

[71] *Nazarov* (HRC), para. 6.4.

allegation insufficiently substantiated.[72] This practice is related to treaty bodies' general view that 'official documentation' provided by the state should be treated as credible,[73] and their deference to national authorities' fact-finding.[74] In an interesting contrast, though, treaty bodies typically do not appear to take official notice of relevant documents that are publicly available or generated by the UN treaty bodies themselves, unless those are submitted by the parties themselves.[75] Relatedly, where a state contests the complainant's allegations, the treaty body may not consider a complaint sufficiently substantiated unless the complainant can provide relevant official documentation. For example, in a case where a migrant alleged he had been subjected to inhumane treatment by Italian immigration authorities, but Italy claimed to have no record of his detention, the CAT did not accept the complainant's allegations alone. CAT required that he present 'documentary evidence of his travel, his stay at the detention facility in Lampedusa or on a boat in Palermo, or his return to Tunisia', or that he satisfactorily explain why he could not produce that evidence.[76] This approach diverges from the prevailing understanding of prima facie by requiring that the complainant's allegations be convincing, rather than merely plausible or credible.

3.4.5 Unclear Existence of the Claimed Right

Fifth, in arguably more legally nuanced or novel cases, treaty bodies have sometimes rejected complaints as insufficiently substantiated when the committee members find the legal argument (rather than the factual allegations) to be unconvincing.[77] For example, the CEDAW Committee

[72] *Nazarov* (HRC), para. 6.5.

[73] See, e.g., *D.K.N.* v. *Spain*, CRC/C/80/D/15/2017, 1 February 2019, para. 11.5. See also *Y.M.* v. *Spain*, CRC/C/78/D/8/2016, 31 May 2018, para. 8.2.

[74] *E.W.* v. *Denmark*, CEDAW/C/66/D/54/2013, 28 February 2017, paras. 11.2–12.

[75] See, e.g., *S* v. *Australia*, joint opinion (dissenting), para. 4. In contrast, the CAT does sometimes take notice of material not submitted by the parties, at least on the merits. See *J.L.L.* v. *Switzerland*, CAT/C/48/D/364/2008, 18 May 2012, para. 8.5; *Aemei and His Family* v. *Switzerland*, CAT/C/18/D/34/1995, 9 May 1997, para. 9.9. See also B. Çalı, C. Costello and S. Cunningham, 'Hard Protection through Soft Courts?: Non-refoulement before the United Nations Treaty Bodies', *German Law Journal* 21 (2020): 355–384, 378–379 (discussing CAT's varying approach to fact-finding and review of the state's findings of fact).

[76] *B.R.* v. *Italy*, CAT/C/57/D/598/2014, 29 April 2016, para. 6.2. See also *T.N.* v. *Denmark*, CEDAW/C/59/D/37/2012, 3 November 2014, para. 12.7.

[77] See, e.g., *M.S.* v. *Philippines*, CEDAW/C/58/D/30/2011, 16 July 2014, para. 6.5. See also *A.P.* v. *Russia*, CCPR/C/107/D/1857/2008, 28 March 2013; *J.A.B.S.* v. *Costa Rica*, CRC/C/

rejected, on substantiation grounds, a woman's complaint that the Philippines violated its CEDAW obligations when the Supreme Court repeatedly relied on discriminatory gender stereotypes in deciding her sexual harassment complaint.[78] The Committee noted that 'even if it could be argued that some aspects of gender-based stereotypes may appear to be indicated in the Court's decision, they do not suffice, per se, to demonstrate that they have negatively affected the Court's assessment of the facts and the outcome of the trial, or to corroborate the author's claims of a violation of ... the Convention for purposes of admissibility'.[79] CEDAW Committee member Patricia Schulz wrote in dissent: 'for admissibility purposes, the author has brought sufficient elements to substantiate her claim' based on the text of the judgment and other information, which the state failed to address in its submissions.[80] In declaring the author's claim unsubstantiated, the CEDAW Committee majority seemed to reject the argument that judicial reliance on gender stereotypes, in and of itself, could constitute a violation of CEDAW, rather than concluding that the allegations were unclear or unsupported.

Similarly, in a case concerning an alleged violation of the right of unconditional access to shelter, the HRC found the claim unsubstantiated because the complainant could have chosen to stay in a shelter if he had cooperated in his own deportation. Hélène Tigroudja again dissented, arguing that the Committee 'ignored the regional and universal criticisms' of the shelter available to irregular migrants in the country and failed to explain its conclusion concerning what she considered to be a clear and substantiated 'breach of the enjoyment and exercise of a right that is supposed to be absolute'.[81]

In another instance, the HRC rejected a challenge to Moldova's restrictions on foreign nationals' practice of law, ostensibly because the complainant had failed 'to substantiate, for purposes of admissibility, that the differentiation in treatment based on nationality was not based on

74/D/5/2016, 17 January 2017, para. 4.2. Cf. *Pérez Guartambel* v. *Ecuador*, CERD/C/100/D/61/2017, 4 December 2019, para. 6.7.

78 *M.S.* (CEDAW) .

79 *M.S.* (CEDAW), para. 6.5.

80 *M.S.* (CEDAW), individual opinion of Committee member Patricia Shulz (dissenting), para. 2.

81 *A.D.-N.* v. *Netherlands*, CCPR/C/137/D/2894/2016, 22 March 2023, individual opinion of Committee member Hélène Tigroudja (dissenting)).

reasonable and objective criteria and in pursuit of a legitimate aim'.[82] However, the complainant had presented arguments as to the illegitimacy of the state's aim and, rather than addressing these, the HRC grounded its decision in the complainant's failure to factually demonstrate that he could not overcome the restrictions by meeting the additional requirements imposed on non-nationals. In each of these examples, the UNTB appeared to be questioning the legal significance of the factual allegations, rather than finding those allegations to be implausible or lacking evidentiary support. In addition to directly and decisively engaging in the legal merits of the claim in their admissibility analysis, in these cases UNTBs required the complainant's (legal and factual) claim to be persuasive at this preliminary procedural stage.

While the above review suggests that treaty bodies have identified some seemingly straightforward criteria for assessing substantiation, these same criteria can be invoked to set a high evidentiary bar. Sometimes, beyond requiring detailed allegations, UNTBs require a reliable and convincing account of the facts and wholly persuasive legal arguments. They sometimes expect documentary evidence to support the complainant's allegation, and will find a lack of substantiation in its absence. In these ways, UNTBs have demanded more than a colourable claim or plausible allegation, diverging from the prima facie standard.

3.5 The Second Distortion of Prima Facie: UNTBs' Premature Regard for State Submissions

In addition to sometimes requiring that complainants present claims that are convincing on their own, UNTBs have often raised the evidentiary bar even higher by critically assessing those claims, including in light of the state's submissions. For purposes of substantiation, UNTBs do not generally accept complainants' allegations as true even when the state has not refuted them and they are not implausible.[83] Going further, while UNTBs will accept some inconsistencies in the complainant's allegations or evidence,[84] they often require the complainant to explain discrepancies that arise out of the state's presentation of a different version of events or contradicting evidence, already at the admissibility

[82] *S.T.* v. *Moldova*, CCPR/C/135/D/3050/2017, 24 July 2017, para. 6.7.

[83] *Nazarov* (HRC), para. 6.4.

[84] *N.P.* v. *Australia*, CAT/C/22/D/106/1998, 6 May 1999, para. 6.6.

stage.[85] For example, in the covert surveillance case mentioned in Section 3.4, the HRC seemed to accept the state's assertion that the surveillance regime satisfied the treaty requirements, therefore expecting the complainant to present a more convincing rebuttal.[86] This is all rather incongruent with what prima facie is classically understood to entail. As explained in Section 3.3, the prima facie threshold is defined as a preliminary assessment of the plausibility of the allegations based on the complainants' submissions alone.

In contrast, treaty bodies routinely consider *all* the information submitted by *both* parties when evaluating substantiation for purposes of admissibility. This is not following any explicit legal prescription, but may be the unintended consequence of three types of procedural rules and practices. First, some treaty body rules require that the state's views on admissibility be considered before a treaty body can declare a complaint admissible (as opposed to inadmissible),[87] or allow treaty bodies to revoke an admissibility decision made before receiving the state's submissions.[88] Second, some rules require treaty bodies to consider 'all the information before [them]' when deciding on the merits.[89] Despite the reference to the merits stage, treaty bodies have sometimes interpreted this as an obligation to consider both parties' submissions even when assessing admissibility, and to do so with regard to each admissibility criterion.[90] For example, in 2013, the HRC asserted that the substantiation requirement means 'authors must provide sufficiently detailed information to allow the Committee to make a well-founded decision

[85] *Tikhonov* v. *Kazakhstan*, CCPR/C/130/D/2551/2015, para. 9.4. See also *Loor Chila* v. *Spain*, E/C.12/70/D/102/2019, para. 6.6; *J.S.* v. *Netherlands*, CCPR/C/137/D/3210/2018, 22 March 2023, para. 7.6.

[86] *G.A.P.* v. *Romania* (HRC), paras. 8.5, 6.7.

[87] For example, the CAT's Rule 115 (8) states, 'A complaint may not be declared admissible unless the State party concerned has received its text and has been given an opportunity to furnish information or observations . . .'

[88] CEDAW Committee, Rules of Procedure, Rule 71 (2).

[89] See, e.g., CEDAW Committee, Rule 72 (1); HRC, Rule 102 (1).

[90] Compare Secretary-General, Comparative Summary of Existing Communications and Inquiry Procedures and Practices under International Human Rights Instruments and under the Charter of the United Nations (E/CN.6/1997/4), 21 January 1997 with *A.P.* v. *Russia* (HRC), para. 10.7 and *N.U.* v. *Finland*, CAT /C/76/D/1044/2020, 21 April 2023, para. 7.3. See also *S.S.R.* v. *Spain*, E/C.12/66/D/51/2018, 11 October 2019, para. 8; *T.N.* v. *Denmark*, CEDAW/C/59/D/37/2012, para. 12.8; *Goekce* v. *Austria*, CEDAW/C/39/D/5/2005, 6 August 2007, para. 11.1.

on the merits of the claim'[91] Third, treaty bodies increasingly decide on admissibility and merits simultaneously, in the interest of efficiency.[92]

Consequently, treaty bodies' practice is to give equal consideration to the state's arguments and evidence when deciding substantiation, a practice that is difficult to reconcile with their obligation to ascertain whether 'the *individual claims*, in a manner sufficiently substantiated, to be a victim of a violation'.[93] In other words, by considering the state's arguments and evidence at this stage, the treaty body is no longer simply determining whether the individual has provided support for their allegations; instead, it ventures into assessing the *relative* credibility and persuasiveness of their evidence. This approach risks improperly simplifying the analysis treaty bodies would have undertaken if only they had weighed the evidence at the merits stage, with the possible result of prematurely rejecting a complaint that could have been successful on the merits. It also may entail a potentially unfair allocation of the burden of proof, as we shall now see.

3.6 The Third Distortion of Prima Facie: Inconsistent Allocation of Burden of Proof

As observed above, the substantiation requirement in practice often entails more than minimal support for a claim. This is problematic not only as a possibly erroneous interpretation of the procedural requirements, but also as a potentially unfair allocation of the burden of proof. There are, however, cases in which treaty bodies may excuse the complainant from having to substantiate a claim for purposes of admissibility to the generally expected (if arguably too high) degree. UNTBs have come closer to applying a prima facie standard in a handful of the many cases that fall into the following six categories: (1) the complainant lacks legal representation; (2) the complainant is in detention; (3) relevant documentation is in the state's sole possession or control; (4) the complainant faces difficulty obtaining documentation because of prevailing conditions; (5) the complainant is suffering from trauma related to the

[91] *A.P.* v. *Russia* (HRC), para. 10.7. See also *S.O.* v. *Canada*, CEDAW/C/59/D/49/2013, 27 October 2014, para. 9.5. Cf. Report of the Human Rights Committee, Volume I (A767/40), 2012, para. 137: '[A]lthough an author does not need to prove the alleged violation at the admissibility stage, he or she must submit sufficient material substantiating the allegation for purposes of admissibility'.

[92] See, e.g., OHCHR, Individual Complaint Procedures, Fact Sheet No.7/Rev.2 (2013), p. 10.

[93] See, e.g., HRC, Rules of Procedure, Rule 99 (b).

alleged rights violations; and (6) the merits and admissibility of the claim are closely linked. Each situation will be reviewed in turn, with a view to identifying what these exceptions may reveal about the general rule. While these exceptional decisions hint at a path toward a lower evidentiary standard, they also underscore the current lack of an approach that is consistent and that aligns with the accepted understanding of prima facie. More significantly, some of these decisions indicate that (beyond imposing too high a standard of proof and prematurely assessing the state's submissions) UNTBs are sometimes expecting complainants to provide arguments or evidence – at admissibility – to pre-emptively counter the state's possible defences on the merits.

3.6.1 Complainant Lacking Legal Representation

Treaty bodies have suggested that they expect more substantiation from a complainant who is represented by counsel than from one who is not.[94] For example, the CESCR has noted that it 'understands that communications are sometimes submitted by persons who are not represented by lawyers or jurists trained in international human rights law. The CESCR must therefore, in accordance with the victim-centred approach, refrain from imposing any unnecessary formalities in order to avoid creating obstacles to the submission of communications for its consideration.'[95] By contrast, when a complainant is represented by counsel, the Committee may be less forgiving of a lack of substantiation, including because 'legal representatives have a procedural due diligence obligation in the submission and processing of communications before the Committee'.[96] The CEDAW Committee has similarly indicated that it expects greater clarity and responsiveness from complainants when they are represented by counsel.[97] This is notable because the majority of complainants before UNTBs now have legal representation.[98] Accordingly, UNTBs' consideration

[94] See, e.g., *Loor Chila* v. *Spain*, E/C.12/70/D/102/2019, para. 6.6 ('although the author is represented by counsel . . . the discrepancy as to her income has not been explained'); *H.D.* v. *Denmark*, CEDAW/C/70/D/76/2014, 9 July 2018, para. 7.4.

[95] *S.S.R.* (CESCR), para. 6.4. *See also S.C. and G.P.* v. *Italy*, E/C.12/65/D/22/2017, 7 March 2019, para. 6.15.

[96] *S.S.R.* (CESCR), para. 6.4; *Acosta Martínez and Amaghnouge* v. *Spain*, E/C.12/73/D/213/2021, 27 February 2023, para. 6.2.

[97] See, e.g., *H.D.* (CEDAW), para. 7.4.

[98] For example, in cases before the CAT, authors had legal representation in 88 out of 107 decisions (82%) published between 2010 and 2015. This research was conducted by

of whether an individual has legal representation may more often serve to raise the standard of proof, rather than lower it.

3.6.2 Complainant in Detention

If a complainant is in detention at the time of presenting their complaint, the treaty body may be persuaded to lighten the burden of proof. For example, the HRC has noted 'the difficulties that living in detention entails' and assessed substantiation in view of the author's 'individual circumstances'.[99] Nonetheless, UNTBs have not consistently adopted this approach in complaints presented by individuals in detention, nor have they uniformly embraced consideration of individual circumstances, more broadly, in assessing substantiation.

3.6.3 State Controls Access to Relevant Documentation

When a complainant's ability to substantiate their allegations depends on information or documentation in the state's sole control or possession, a treaty body may admit the complaint so long as the complainant's claim is credible in light of the limited information available. The HRC has explained, '[i]n cases where the allegations are corroborated by credible evidence submitted by the author and where further clarification depends on information exclusively in the hands of the State party, the Committee may consider the author's allegations substantiated in the absence of satisfactory evidence or explanations to the contrary presented by the State party'.[100] The CRC has similarly noted in another admissibility decision that 'the burden of proof cannot rest solely on the author of the communication, especially given that the author and the State party do not always have equal access to the evidence and that frequently the State party alone has access to the relevant information'.[101]

Nonetheless, while treaty bodies have sporadically referenced states' duty to participate in the proceedings and furnish relevant information,

the Yale Lowenstein Human Rights Project and International Justice Resource Center in 2015 (on file with author). Review of the 35 views published by the HRC in 2022 reveals that the authors had legal representation in 24 cases (69%). See OHCHR, Jurisprudence Database (search conducted 18 January 2023).

99 *F.K.A.G. et al.* v. *Australia*, CCPR/C/108/D/2094/2011, 26 July 2013, para. 8.7

100 *Turaeva and Kodirov* v. *Uzbekistan*, CCPR/C/97/D/1284/2004, 20 October 2009, para. 8.4. See also Çalı et alia, 'Hard Protection through Soft Courts?', p. 376.

101 *D.D.* v. *Spain*, CRC/C/80/D/4/2016, 1 February 2019, para. 13.3.

there is not a consistent, clear expectation that a state must provide the evidence that it has an obligation to generate; at least, there are no automatic procedural repercussions for its failure to do so.[102] The complainant will not always be excused from sufficiently substantiating their claims even when it is the state that has possession over relevant documentation or an ex officio obligation to collect it. Moreover, by allowing for the possibility that a complaint will be deemed insufficiently substantiated if the state presents contrary evidence or explanations, UNTBs again make clear that the complainant's allegations alone may be inadequate to satisfy the substantiation requirement even when 'corroborated by credible evidence'.[103]

3.6.4 *Evidentiary Inconsistencies Related to the Alleged Violation's Impact*

Treaty bodies, and particularly the CAT, may demand less substantiation from complainants who are suffering from trauma related to the alleged violations.[104] For example, the CAT has '[taken] note of the authors' assertion that [factual] inconsistencies were due in part to the trauma that they had endured' and '[concluded] that, for the purposes of admissibility, the authors have sufficiently substantiated their allegations'.[105] UNTB decisions do not, however, illustrate a broader pattern of considering the effects of trauma on fulfilment of the substantiation requirement.

3.6.5 *Country Conditions Impeding Complainant's Access to Documentation*

Similarly, when country conditions complicate a complainant's access to supporting documentation, a treaty body may lower the substantiation standard. For example, the CEDAW Committee 'consider[ed] that, even if many of the author's statements were contradictory, the threshold for

[102] Cf. *S.R.* v. *Netherlands*, CAT/C/71/D/834/2017, 22 July 2021, para. 7.5. See also K. McCall-Smith, 'Reversing the Burden of Proof in Response to States' Non-Participation: the Human Rights Committee's Evolving Case Law on Torture', Chapter 6, this volume.

[103] *Turaeva and Kodirov* (HRC), para. 8.4.

[104] See, e.g., *Alan* v. *Switzerland*, CAT/C/16/D/21/1995, 8 May 1996, para. 11.3; *J.K.* v. *Canada*, CAT/C/56/D/562/2013, 23 November 2015, para. 10.4. See also *E.T.B.* v. *Denmark*, CAT/C/28/D/146/1999, 30 April 2002, paras. 5.3, 6, 10, 11.

[105] *F. and G.* v. *Denmark*, CCPR/C/119/D/2530/2015, 16 March 2017, para. 7.5.

admissibility should not be set too high in view of the situation in the author's country, which makes it difficult, if not impossible, for a woman to obtain documentation attesting to gender-based violence from the police, courts or medical facilities'.[106] Likewise, the CRC considered the complainants' relationship to the alleged victims sufficiently substantiated, in part, due to 'the difficulty in obtaining [identity documents and family record books] given the children's current situation [in refugee camps in a conflict zone]'.[107] These kinds of cases combine challenges related to both individual circumstances and to the accessibility of information that is, or should be, in a state's possession. As in each of those categories, UNTB decisions in this combined category are also limited and do not demonstrate a consistent practice of requiring the complainant to merely make a plausible claim for purposes of substantiation.

3.6.6 Closely Linked Merits and Admissibility

When the questions of substantiation and determination of the merits are very closely linked, the treaty body will sometimes defer scrutiny of the facts and admit the complaint.[108] This has occurred when the complaint raises alleged due process or judicial protection violations. For instance, when a woman alleged that domestic courts failed to appropriately consider her claim of gender-based employment discrimination, the CEDAW Committee concluded that 'the issues of admissibility of the author's claims ... and the level of their substantiation in the present communication are so closely linked to the merits of the case that it would be more appropriate to determine that at the merits stage of the proceedings' and, therefore, declared the complaint sufficiently substantiated and admissible.[109] Essentially, when the treaty body must decide whether the alleged facts constitute a possible treaty violation, and the answer is unclear or depends on a nuanced legal analysis, the treaty body may decide to resolve that question on the merits.

[106] *A.M.* v. *Denmark*, CEDAW/C/67/D/77/2014, 21 July 2017, para. 7.5. See also *Abdi-Osman* v. *Switzerland*, CEDAW/C/76/D/122/2017, 6 July 2020, para. 6.7.

[107] *F.B. et al.* v. *France*, CRC/C/86/D/R.77/2019, 4 February 2021, para. 8.4.

[108] See, e.g., *R.K.B.* v. *Turkey*, CEDAW/C/51/D/28/2010, 24 February 2012, para. 7.8. See Chapter 4, this volume.

[109] *R.K.B.* (CEDAW), para. 7.8. See also, e.g., *W.K.* v. *Canada*, CCPR/C/122/D/2292/2013, 27 March 2018, para. 9.5.

One may observe, however, that other cases illustrate a contrary practice.[110] For example, where a complainant presented information showing that national law and political realities made it very difficult for him to meet the requirements for seeking election to public office, the HRC rejected his complaint as unsubstantiated rather than proceeding to the merits. HRC members Yuval Shany and Konstantine Vardzelashvili argued that the individual's detailed allegation of an interference with the right to political participation satisfied the substantiation requirement. They found that the majority erroneously expected the complainant to prove the unreasonableness of the law rather than properly requiring the state to 'justify the restrictions found in the legal framework of the federal law' once the complainant demonstrated their prima facie incompatibility with the treaty.[111] Similarly, in *S.T.* v. *Moldova*, the HRC found the claim of discrimination based on nationality unsubstantiated because the complainant did not prove the difference in treatment was unreasonable, rather than requiring the state, on the merits, to prove that it was reasonable.[112] This inadmissibility determination stands in contrast to the HRC's merits decisions, indicating that it will find a violation of the right to non-discrimination if the state fails to meet its 'heavy burden … to explain the reason for the differentiation' shown by the complainant.[113]

These six scenarios indicate some overlap in the reasons why a treaty body may sometimes come closer to applying a prima facie standard when assessing substantiation, particularly where the power differential between the complainant and the state is exacerbated or the state is responsible for the difficulties the complainant is experiencing in obtaining supporting documentation. Nonetheless, this small body of exceptional decisions also serves to highlight the stringency of the evidentiary standard more often imposed, including in factually similar cases. Moreover, it bears repeating that treaty bodies have not established consistent policies or lines of jurisprudence addressing the standard or burden of proof at admissibility. Outside these six scenarios (or in cases when a UNTB does not lighten the evidentiary burden even though one of these exceptions could apply), complainants must often do more than

[110] See, e.g., Chapter 7, this volume.

[111] *A.P.* (HRC), individual opinion by Committee members Mr. Yuval Shany and Mr. Konstantine Vardzelashvili (dissenting).

[112] *S.T.* v. *Moldova*, CCPR/C/135/D/3050/2017, para. 6.7.

[113] See, e.g., *Müller and Engelhard* v. *Namibia*, CCPR/C/74/D/919/2000, 26 March 2002, para. 6.7. See also, e.g., *Kavanagh* v. *Ireland*, CCRP/C/71/819/1998, 4 April 2001, para. 10.3.

present a plausible claim supported by credible evidence. They must make out a claim that is *more* probable than the state's as to the existence of an alleged violation or, in some cases, pre-emptively counter the state's possible defence that a restriction was reasonable. In other instances, UNTBs may declare a complaint inadmissible because the complainant does not produce evidence that is within the state's control or possession. The individual's inferior access to evidence may not be considered reason enough to require only a plausible claim. The UNTBs could decide that conflicting versions of events or the complainant's lack of access to state-held evidence means there is enough to take up the merits, but they do not always do so. While UNTBs have frequently repeated the principle that the complainant should not bear the burden of proof alone, especially when the state is in possession or control of relevant information, they do not consistently apply this principle in practice.

3.7 Implications and Conclusion

This chapter has reviewed the origins, description and application of the requirement that individual complainants sufficiently substantiate their complaints for purposes of admissibility. As we have seen, the requirement originates from the HRC's practice, rather than treaty text. The term *sufficiently substantiated* is not found in other human rights systems and, perhaps because of this, has developed in a sui generis manner, despite its sporadic conflation with the terms *prima facie* and *not manifestly ill-founded*, which are used by other international tribunals. While treaty body rules of procedure have formalised the substantiation requirement – for all but the CERD – its contours remain blurry in practice. Several other takeaways are worth emphasising.

First, the variations in both the description of the substantiation requirement and its application in practice present significant challenges to a coherent explanation of this standard and, therefore, to access to justice. While at least five common grounds of insufficient substantiation can be identified, treaty bodies themselves have never specified *any* categories or common grounds of unfoundedness. Moreover, some of these categories and corresponding analysis are premised on somewhat subjective and vague concepts, such as what constitutes *specific* detail, leaving room for stringent interpretation. Most problematically, the treaty bodies have sometimes rejected a claim as unsubstantiated when they are not fully convinced of the legal existence of the asserted right, which appears to go beyond the question of whether the complaint provides sufficient information to allow a determination of its admissibility or, even, discussion of its merits. Similarly, while treaty bodies have sometimes expressed a willingness to lighten the evidentiary burden based on the nature of the alleged violation or the circumstances of the complainant, they do not do so in a consistent manner. Complainants have little clear guidance to help them understand the evidentiary requirements or to anticipate how a treaty body will assess the substantiation of their complaint.

Second, and relatedly, equating the substantiation requirement with a prima facie threshold is likely to be unhelpful to complainants (and to treaty body members), given the lack of a universally shared understanding of this term among UNTB members. As Stirner writes, '[the Human Rights] Committee's reference to a *prima-facie* case in the admissibility context is unnecessarily confusing. The reference to a *prima-facie* case does not provide any additional insights as to the requirements to meet the 'substantiation' threshold'.[114] In practice, UNTBs typically refer to a prima facie standard 'without indicating the procedural relevance of the *prima-facie* case or why it is referred to in this case'.[115] Fundamentally, the variations in UNTB decisions concerning substantiation illustrate that they are not applying the commonly accepted definition of this term, as requiring that the claim be plausible, without regard for the other party's submissions.

To improve access to justice before the treaty bodies, and in addition to other recommendations made in Chapter 11, the treaty bodies could: (1) adopt clear, accessible, shared definitions of the terms 'sufficiently substantiated', 'not manifestly unfounded' and 'not manifestly ill-founded'; (2) interpret the substantiation requirement to impose an evidentiary threshold that is considerably lower than the standard of proof that must be satisfied on the merits, and consistent with a plausibility standard; (3) synthesise their practice with regard to the kind of documentation required in order for a complaint to be considered sufficiently substantiated for purposes of registration and admissibility; (4) reconsider the practice of evaluating both parties' submissions on admissibility and merits when deciding on substantiation and revise their rules of procedure as necessary; and (5) remove references to a prima facie standard in OHCHR guidance and similar materials, unless accompanied by a clear definition of what this term is understood to mean.

[114] Stirner, *Procedural Law Governing Facts and Evidence*, p. 406.
[115] Stirner, *Procedural Law Governing Facts and Evidence*, p. 404.

The UNTBs play a vital role in interpreting international human rights law, guiding states in its implementation and ensuring that individuals have access to an independent and respected process for the determination and vindication of their rights. Treaty bodies can improve both the appearance and the reality of access to justice at the UN level by clarifying the evidentiary requirements relevant to the admissibility of individual complaints. Doing so may bring an added benefit of increased efficiency by reducing the time spent on complaints that cannot be, or have not been, adequately substantiated.

Select Bibliography

Alston, P., *Effective Implementation of International Instruments on Human Rights, Including Reporting Obligations under International Instruments on Human Rights* (A/ 44/ 668), 8 November 1989.

Çalı, B., Costello, C. and Cunningham, S., 'Hard Protection through Soft Courts? Non-refoulement before the United Nations Treaty Bodies', *German Law Journal* 21 (2020): 355–384.

Jelić, I. and Mührel, L., 'The Human Rights Committee: Challenges and Prospects for Enhanced Effectiveness and Integration', *Journal of Human Rights Practice* 14 (2022): 17–43.

OHCHR, *Individual Complaint Procedures under the United Nations Human Rights Treaties*, Fact Sheet No.7/Rev.2 (2013).

Secretary-General, *Comparative Summary of Existing Communications and Inquiry Procedures and Practices under International Human Rights Instruments and under the Charter of the United Nations* (E/CN.6/1997/4), 21 January 1997.

Shany, Y., *Questions of Jurisdiction and Admissibility before International Courts* (Cambridge: Cambridge University Press, 2016).

Stirner, T., *The Procedural Law Governing Facts and Evidence in International Human Rights Proceedings: Developing a Contextualized Approach to Address Recurring Problems in the Context of Facts and Evidence* (Leiden: Koninklijke Brill NV, 2021).

Young, K. A., *The Law and Process of the U.N. Human Rights Committee* (Ardsley: Transnational Publishers, 2002).

Viljoen, F., 'Fact-Finding by UN Human Rights Complaints Bodies: Analysis and Suggested Reforms', in A. von Bogdandy and R. Wolfrum (eds.), *Max Planck Yearbook of United Nations Law*, Volume 8 (2004): 49–100.

Zwart, T., *The Admissibility of Human Rights Petitions: The Case Law of the European Commission of Human Rights and the Human Rights Committee* (Dordrecht: Martinus Nijhoff Publishers, 1994).

PART II

Overall Trajectories of Evidentiary Systems in the Making

4

Forty Years and Counting

CERD's Ongoing Search for a Clear Evidentiary Path

CORNELIA KLOCKER*

4.1 Introduction

The International Convention on the Elimination of All Forms of Racial Discrimination (ICERD) was adopted by the United Nations (UN) General Assembly in 1965 and entered into force in 1969.[1] Almost all states have acceded to the treaty, making its coverage nearly universal.[2] ICERD was the first UN human rights treaty, and the Committee on the Elimination of Racial Discrimination (CERD, the Committee) was the first UN treaty monitoring body.[3] As Keane and Waughray rightly hold, the Committee 'pioneered' the different monitoring mechanisms for all the UN human rights treaty bodies (UNTBs) that were to follow.[4] Given this longstanding history, one might expect that CERD would by now have had the chance to consolidate its evidentiary regime; such consolidation, however, has not materialised yet. This chapter traces CERD's development in this area by drawing the contours of its evidentiary

* The author would like to thank Marie-Bénédicte Dembour and Deborah Casalin for their thoughtful comments, feedback and suggestions on many early drafts and their tremendous support. The author would also like to thank all Symposium participants and the DISSECT team for their valuable comments.

1 International Convention on the Elimination of All Forms of Racial Discrimination, New York, 21 December 1965, in force 4 January 1969, 660 UNTS 195.

2 In June 2025, ICERD counted 182 states parties: UN Treaty Collection, 'ICERD', https://treaties.un.org/pages/ViewDetails.aspx?src=IND&mtdsg_no=IV-2&chapter=4&clang=_en.

3 D. Keane and A. Waughray, 'Introduction' in D. Keane and A. Waughray (eds.), *Fifty Years of the International Convention on the Elimination of All Forms of Racial Discrimination: A Living Instrument* (Manchester: Manchester University Press, 2017), pp. 1–31, 1.

4 Keane and Waughray, 'Introduction', p. 2.

regime through an assessment of its overall case law, before offering a closer analysis of two cases that can be considered exemplary of its approach.

It is important to start by locating the Convention in its broader political context, which arguably impacts the way the Committee assesses evidence to this day. Racial discrimination was on the UN General Assembly's agenda from early on, often in connection with discrimination based on religion.[5] Following a global wave of anti-Semitic incidents in 1959/1960, the UN Sub-Commission on the Prevention of Discrimination and Protection of Minorities issued a resolution condemning these 'manifestations of anti-Semitism and other forms of racial and national hatred and religious and racial prejudices of a similar nature'.[6] In the 1960s, the two issues – discrimination based on race and discrimination based on religion – were split and separate conventions proposed. This split was partly triggered by political opposition to the inclusion of anti-Semitism in ICERD, due to some states' perception of potential implications for the recognition of the State of Israel. In addition, ICERD's intended focus, establishing an explicit link between racism, colonialism and apartheid, moved the Convention's scope away from discrimination based on religion. After this split, ICERD was dealt with as a matter of priority. This was preferred by especially Soviet and Eastern European states, which considered tackling racial discrimination to be more urgent than religious discrimination.[7] Although ICERD's origins were shaped by the Second World War and *anti*-Semitism, its realisation was strongly influenced by African and Asian states and their fight against apartheid and colonialism. Yet, due to the Global North–dominated composition of the drafting Sub-Commission, Southern states and actors such as liberation movements could only comment on the process from the sidelines, such as through

[5] Keane and Waughray, 'Introduction', p. 2; UN General Assembly, Persecution and Discrimination (A/RES/103(I)), 19 November 1946.

[6] Keane and Waughray, 'Introduction', p. 3; Report of the 12th session of the Sub-Commission on Prevention of Discrimination and Protection of Minorities to the Commission on Human Rights (E/CN.4/Sub.2/206), 1960, p. 69 (Resolution 3 (XII)); P. Thornberry, *The International Convention on the Elimination of All Forms of Racial Discrimination: A Commentary* (Oxford: Oxford University Press, 2016), pp. 24ff.

[7] Keane and Waughray, 'Introduction', p. 3; Thornberry, *Commentary*, p. 27; UN General Assembly, Preparation of a draft declaration and a draft convention on the elimination of all forms of racial discrimination (A/RES/1780 (XVII)), 7 December 1962; UN General Assembly, Preparation of a draft declaration and a draft convention on the elimination of all forms of religious intolerance (A/RES/1781 (XVII)), 7 December 1962.

UN General Assembly debates.[8] While ICERD was adopted in 1965, efforts to combat religious discrimination resulted only in a non-binding declaration adopted by the UN General Assembly in 1981.[9]

As this brief historical account illustrates, the application of the Convention is prone to generating political tensions – and even CERD's role was controversial. Initially, CERD's membership was dominated by diplomats. This had the effect of the Committee and its tasks being considered as more of a diplomatic rather than a legal platform. Stronger engagement with and criticism of state reports only made its way into CERD's practice once it began to include members from less government-bound and more independent backgrounds, and the number of members with legal expertise increased.[10] While the perception of the Committee as a primarily diplomatic forum has thankfully changed, some underlying constraints remain. These are grounded in CERD's (and indeed any UNTB's) dependence on support, cooperation and funding from the states that it might criticise for racist behaviour in the context of monitoring or views on individual communications. This dependence can lead to a fragility within UNTBs, which, crucially, can also affect their ability to ascertain facts and evaluate evidence. This can be seen in a chronic lack of resources – in particular, trained staff – to deal with incoming individual communications. Furthermore, Committee members frequently lack time to discuss individual communications due to insufficient funding or the refusal of states to cooperate and deliver relevant evidence that is solely within their control.[11]

These general complexities may contribute to explaining why CERD's evidentiary path is not as well settled as one might have expected after more than forty years of activity. Assessing CERD's journey so far, this chapter starts by outlining ICERD's key concepts and the Committee's evidentiary framework (Section 4.2), before examining how the latter has

[8] Keane and Waughray, 'Introduction', pp. 5–6.

[9] Keane and Waughray, 'Introduction', p. 4; UN General Assembly, Declaration on the Elimination of All Forms of Intolerance and of Discrimination Based on Religion or Belief (A/RES/36/55), 25 November 1981.

[10] Keane and Waughray, 'Introduction', p. 10.

[11] R. Niezen and M. Sapignoli, 'Introduction' in R. Niezen and M. Sapignoli (eds.), *Palaces of Hope: The Anthropology of Global Organizations* (Cambridge: Cambridge University Press, 2017), pp. 1–30, 12ff; R. A. Wilson, 'Propaganda on Trial: Structural Fragility and the Epistemology of International Legal Institutions' in R. Niezen and M. Sapignoli (eds.), *Palaces of Hope: The Anthropology of Global Organizations* (Cambridge: Cambridge University Press, 2017), pp. 266–293, at 270ff; see also Chapter 1, this volume; on uncooperative states, see Chapter 6, this volume.

been applied in merits decisions (Section 4.3). The findings indicate the use of a lower standard of proof for racial discrimination in the application of procedural rights, but the Committee has not taken a discernible stance on evidentiary questions regarding substantive rights yet.[12] The chapter then proceeds with a more detailed discussion of two cases that illustrate the importance of CERD taking a clearer position: *Dawas and Shava* v. *Denmark* (2012) in Section 4.4 and *Zapescu* v. *Moldova* (2021) in Section 4.5. In *Dawas*, the Committee did not engage with the unclear factual situation and the underlying evidence as it was examining the case, resulting in heated debates during the follow-up process. In *Zapescu*, however, CERD was more transparent on the evidence required from the parties and its relevance for its own decision-making process. This not only provided more direct engagement with evidence but also greater clarity for the handling of future individual communications. Section 4.6 offers concluding reflections on CERD's continuing efforts to consolidate its evidentiary approach and the need for greater consistency.

4.2 CERD's Evidentiary Framework

Racial discrimination is difficult to prove due to a number of compounding factors. One is that petitioners[13] need to prove the causal link between the violation and either the motivation for or effects of racial discrimination (corresponding to direct and indirect discrimination, respectively).[14] Generating proof of such motivation or effect is often

[12] The difference between the substantive and procedural dimensions of discrimination can be explained (and is understood here) as follows: 'the first being the prohibition to engage in discriminatory violence and the second concerning duties to properly investigate incidents of possible discriminatory violence': K. Henrard, 'The European Court of Human Rights and the "Special" Distribution of the Burden of Proof in Racial Discrimination Cases: The Search for Fairness Continues', *European Convention on Human Rights Law Review* 4 (2023): 426–446, 439.

[13] While most UNTBs refer to the complainant as *author*, CERD more frequently uses the term *petitioner*.

[14] These two concepts are defined in EU legislation (featuring later in this chapter) as follows: '(a) direct discrimination shall be taken to occur where one person is treated less favourably than another is, has been or would be treated in a comparable situation on grounds of racial or ethnic origin; (b) indirect discrimination shall be taken to occur where an apparently neutral provision, criterion or practice would put persons of a racial or ethnic origin at a particular disadvantage compared with other persons, unless that provision, criterion or practice is objectively justified by a legitimate aim and the means of achieving that aim are appropriate and necessary': Article 2 (2) of Council Directive 2000/43/CE of 29 June 2000 on implementing the principle of equal treatment between persons irrespective of racial or ethnic origin (Race Equality Directive).

more difficult than proving the act itself. Furthermore, discrimination describes differential treatment in comparable situations – requiring evidence of how the situation would have unfolded if there had been no discrimination. This presupposes that an appropriate comparator has been selected to assess whether a difference in treatment has occurred. In order to take these complexities into account, Section 4.3 starts with some introductory remarks on CERD and ICERD before diving into CERD's evidentiary framework.[15]

CERD consists of eighteen experts who are elected by states parties but serve in their personal capacity.[16] The Committee monitors the implementation of ICERD through issuing general and country-specific recommendations; an early warning procedure and urgent action procedure; and – most importantly in the context of this chapter – the handling of communications, which can be brought by individuals or states.[17] The individual communications procedure under Article 14 is optional and has been recognised by fifty-nine states parties so far.[18] The decisions on the merits adopted by CERD in individual communications are called views and have an advisory character.[19]

ICERD defines racial discrimination in Article 1 (1) as 'any distinction, exclusion, restriction or preference based on race, colour, descent, or national or ethnic origin which has the purpose or effect of nullifying or impairing the recognition, enjoyment or exercise, on an equal footing, of human rights and fundamental freedoms in the political, economic, social, cultural or any other field of public life'. This definition makes

[15] Unless otherwise indicated, all mentioned articles refer to ICERD.

[16] Art. 8 ICERD; Thornberry, *Commentary*, pp. 43–44.

[17] Arts. 9, 11–13, 14 ICERD; Annex III: Prevention of racial discrimination, including early warning and urgent procedures (A/48/18), 15 September 1993; Report of the Committee on the Elimination of Racial Discrimination, Annex III: Guidelines for the early warning and urgent action procedures (A/62/18), 70th and 71st Session, 2007; Thornberry, *Commentary*, pp. 45ff.

[18] Thornberry, *Commentary*, pp. 56ff; Declarations under Article 14 ICERD as 1 June 2025: UN Treaty Collection, 'ICERD', https://treaties.un.org/pages/ViewDetails.aspx?src=IND&mtdsg_no=IV-2&chapter=4&clang=_en#35.

[19] M. Banton, 'Extending the Rule of Law' in D. Keane and A. Waughray (eds.), *Fifty Years of the International Convention on the Elimination of All Forms of Racial Discrimination: A Living Instrument* (Manchester: Manchester University Press, 2017), pp. 35–50, 44; note how the terminology has changed from 'opinion' to 'view' with the most recent revision of the Rules of Procedure: CERD, Rules of Procedure (CERD/C/35/Rev.4), 23 May 2025, Rule 113 (3); previous version: CERD, Rules of Procedure (CERD/C/35/Rev.3), 1986, Rule 95 (3). Unless otherwise indicated, all mentioned Rules refer to the 2025 CERD Rules of Procedure).

clear that ICERD covers both direct and indirect discrimination (as reflected in the 'purpose or effect' phrasing).[20] In line with the principles set out in General Recommendation 32, ICERD addresses unequal treatment in comparable situations and equal treatment in non-comparable situations.[21] Differential treatment can only be justified if it pursues a legitimate aim and achieves this through proportionate means.[22] The special measures under Article 1 (4) aimed at advancing effective equality are an explicit example of justified differential treatment. Other kinds of differential treatment will be assessed based on whether they have an 'unjustifiable disparate impact'.[23] However, discussion of such justifications has not been very explicit in CERD's opinions on individual communications.[24] While notions such as the *comparator* and *comparable situation* do feature in a few opinions, it is not standard for the Committee to have an introductory paragraph in opinions setting out these general principles. Rather, these notions tend to come up in CERD's references to party submissions.[25]

Paragraphs 2 and 3 of Article 1, which limit the scope of the prohibition of racial discrimination regarding distinctions based on citizenship and nationality, contain a note on evidentiary principles in their supplementary material. Any distinctions falling under these two paragraphs 'must be construed so as to avoid undermining the basic prohibition of discrimination'.[26] In this context, there is an explicit statement regarding

[20] Thornberry, *Commentary*, p. 115; W. Vandenhole, *Non-discrimination and Equality in the View of the UN Human Rights Treaty Bodies* (Antwerp: Intersentia, 2005), p. 6; CERD, General Recommendation No. 32, The meaning and scope of special measures in the International Convention on the Elimination of All Forms Racial Discrimination (CERD/C/GC/32), 2009, paras. 7–8.

[21] CERD, General Recommendation No. 32, para. 8; Thornberry, *Commentary*, p. 129.

[22] CERD, General Recommendation No. 30, Discrimination Against Non-Citizens (CERD/C/64/Misc.11/rev.3), 2004, para. 4; for a general overview of the features of discrimination and further references see: Henrard, 'The European Court of Human Rights'.

[23] CERD, General Recommendation No. 14, Article 1, paragraph 1, of the Convention, (A/48/18), 1993.

[24] According to Thornberry, CERD has not yet developed a clear mode of review in this regard, pointing to the ECtHR as contrasting example: Thornberry, *Commentary*, p. 133.

[25] *V.S.* v. *Slovakia*, CERD/C/88/D/56/2014, 4 December 2015, ('comparator'); *Breleur* v. *France*, CERD/C/107/D/66/2018, 30 August 2022, ('comparable situation'); *Kotor* v. *France*, CERD/C/105/D/65/2018, 25 November 2021, ('comparable situation'); *D.R.* v. *Australia*, CERD/C/75/D/42/2008, 14 August 2009, ('unjustified or disproportionate distinctions'); *Habassi* v. *Denmark*, CERD/C/54/D/10/1997, 17 March 1999, ('objectively justified').

[26] CERD, General Recommendation No. 30, para. 2.

evidence, as General Recommendation 30 calls on states parties to enact legislation providing for a shift in the burden of proof applied in civil proceedings once a non-citizen has established a prima facie case of discrimination.[27]

Having set out these general principles, we can turn to the question of which evidentiary principles guide the practical assessment of racial discrimination. The one explicit reference in General Recommendation 30 has already been mentioned. In addition, Article 14 contains an evidentiary hint by providing that CERD will consider individual communications 'in the light of all information made available to it by the State Party concerned and by the petitioner', indicating a shared burden of production of evidence.[28] Beyond this, no other ICERD provisions expressly address evidentiary issues.

Continuing the search for evidentiary principles, it is worth looking into CERD's Rules of Procedure, which were adopted in 1970 and have been amended several times since then.[29] In the first edition, no rules were laid out for individual communications as the system was not yet operational – the required number of ten states parties was reached only in 1982.[30] In the following years, close to thirty rules (Rules 91 to 117) pertaining to this procedure were adopted. Already at the admissibility stage, there is an option for CERD to request additional information from the parties (Rule 107). The parties can also submit further information at the merits stage and respond to each other's submissions within a given time limit (Rule 111). Furthermore, the Committee has the option to invite both parties to provide information in person. While this has been considered an exceptional measure in the past, the fact that the 2025 Rules of Procedure contain a new rule on the conduct of hearings, even through videoconferencing, might make this avenue more

[27] CERD, General Recommendation No. 30, para. 24; see also: *L.G.* v. *Korea*, CERD/C/86/D/51/2012, 1 May 2015.

[28] Art. 14 (7) (a); Rule 113; P. Thornberry, 'The Committee on the Elimination of Racial Discrimination (CERD)' in Frédéric Mégret and Philip Alston (eds.), *The United Nations and Human Rights: A Critical Appraisal*, 2nd edn. (Oxford: Oxford University Press, 2020), pp. 309–338, 318ff.

[29] Report of the Committee on the Elimination of Racial Discrimination, 25th Session, Supplement No. 27, Annex II (A/8027), 1970; the version most frequently cited and referred to in the following unless, otherwise indicated, is: Rules of Procedure of the Committee on the Elimination of Racial Discrimination, 1986, CERD/C/35/Rev.3.

[30] The tenth declaration was received on 3 December 1982: UN Treaty Collection, 'ICERD', https://treaties.un.org/Pages/ViewDetails.aspx?src=TREATY&mtdsg_no=IV-2&chapter=4&clang=_en#35.

accessible in future.[31] The rather brief rules for the actual phase of considering a communication on its merits include just one provision related to evidence – regarding the ability of CERD to obtain additional information from other UN bodies.[32]

In addition to individual communications, states can submit interstate communications to CERD. Although interstate communications are not the focus of this chapter, they are briefly mentioned to take note of evidentiary issues in this area of CERD activity. The interstate communications procedure is designed as a friendly settlement process where CERD deals with jurisdiction and admissibility. The merits decision is then adopted by an ad hoc Conciliation Commission, which is established for each case anew.[33] In 2018, the first three cases were brought under this procedure. While two of them were discontinued per request of the applicant State,[34] the third case – *Palestine* v. *Israel* – has been decided on the merits.[35] CERD has issued new Rules of Procedure relating to interstate communications, but there are no specific rules on evidence, apart from the possibility of an information request.[36] Furthermore, ad hoc Conciliation Commissions adopt their own rules of procedure, which means that the procedure for interstate communications is even more flexible than for individual communications.[37]

[31] Rule 103; OHCHR, Individual Complaint Procedures, Fact Sheet No.7/Rev.2 (2013), p. 16.

[32] Rule 113.

[33] D. Angst and E. Lantschner, 'Artikel 11 – 13' in D. Angst and E. Lantschner (eds.), *ICERD: Internationales Übereinkommen zur Beseitigung jeder Form von Rassendiskrimi nierung: Handkommentar* (Baden-Baden: Nomos, 2020), pp. 473–488, 476ff.

[34] *Qatar* v. *Kingdom of Saudi Arabia,* ICERD-ISC 2018/1, 8 March 2018; *Qatar* v. *The United Arab Emirates,* ICERD-ISC 2018/2, 8 March 2018.

[35] *Palestine* v. *Israel,* ICERD-ISC 2018/3, 23 April 2018; Report of the Ad Hoc Conciliation Commission (case *State of Palestine* v. *Israel*), CERD/C/113/3, 22 August 2024; for further analysis, see C. Klocker and D. Casalin, 'Discriminatory Practices in Armed Conflict Contexts: Exploring (Parallel) Proceedings Under the European Convention on Human Rights and the International Convention on the Elimination of All Forms of Racial Discrimination', *The International Journal of Human Rights* 27 (2023): 896–924; D. Keane, 'A Missed Opportunity: The Decision in Palestine v Israel', *EJIL:Talk!* (blogpost dated 5 September 2024).

[36] Report of the Committee on the Elimination of Racial Discrimination, Annex II: Rules of Procedure specific to the hearings held pursuant to Article 11 of the International Convention on the Elimination of All Forms of Racial Discrimination, 96th and 97th Session (A/74/18), 2018; J. Eiken and D. Keane, 'New Rules of Procedure of the Ad Hoc Conciliation Commission in Palestine v Israel', *EJIL:Talk!* (blogpost dated 23 May 2022).

[37] Rules of Procedure of the ad hoc Conciliation Commission on the interstate communication submitted by the State of Palestine against Israel under Article 11: OHCHR.

This brief outline already shows that discussions on a general level about the treatment of evidence under ICERD are rare, and the structural framework leaves many questions unanswered. The Committee's approach towards evidence is thus characterised by flexibility – or, to put it less positively, by uncertainty or a lack of clarity.[38] With general rules and principles barely being defined, a look at the individual communications procedure and the handling of evidence in practice becomes all the more important.

4.3 CERD's Approach to Evidence in Practice

Before turning to the two selected case studies, some general remarks are in order about the way CERD handles evidence in its examination of individual communications. This is based on a study of the Committee's opinions up to November 2024 (excluding the text of petitioners' communications or potential internal minutes of Committee meetings, neither of which is publicly available).[39] In this period, the Committee handed down forty-six opinions on the merits.[40] The majority do not directly engage with questions of evidence. The few that do (sometimes only tangentially) confirm that the evidentiary norms are far from clear. It appears that in several cases, evidentiary matters have been discussed by the parties but not so much by the Committee itself.[41] One example is

CERD, 'Inter-state communications', www.ohchr.org/en/treaty-bodies/cerd/inter-state-communications.

[38] K. Henrard, The Impact of International Non-discrimination Norms in Combination with General Human Rights for the Protection of National Minorities (DH-MIN(2006) 021), 2006, p. 16; on flexible approaches towards evidence, E. K. Murimi, 'Fluctuating Standards of Proof at the African Court: A Case for Principled Flexibility', *African Human Rights Yearbook* 7 (2023): 158–182; T. Stirner, *The Procedural Law Governing Facts and Evidence in International Human Rights Proceedings* (Leiden: Brill Nijhoff, 2021); C. Roberts, 'Reversing the Burden of Proof Before Human Rights Bodies', *The International Journal of Human Rights* 25 (2021): 1682–1703; A. Riddell, 'Evidence, Fact-Finding, and Experts' in C. P. R. Romano, K. J. Alter and Y. Shany (eds.), *The Oxford Handbook of International Adjudication* (Oxford: Oxford University Press, 2013), pp. 848–870.

[39] There are exceptions; see, e.g., the full submission of the State of Palestine of its interstate communication: https://tbinternet.ohchr.org/_layouts/15/treatybodyexternal/Download.aspx?symbolno=INT%2fCERD%2fISC%2f9325&Lang=en.

[40] A search effected on the OHCHR JURIS Database (OHCHR, Jurisprudence Database, https://juris.ohchr.org/) on 1 June 2025 for CERD opinions on individual communications returned 60 hits. However, this list comprised several duplications.

[41] See, e.g., *B.M.S.* v. *Australia*, CERD/C/54/D/8/1996, 12 March 1999; *Durmic* v. *Serbia and Montenegro*, CERD/C/68/D/29/2003, 6 March 2006; *Er* v. *Denmark*, CERD/C/71/D/40/

the case of *Er* v. *Denmark*, concerning a carpentry student who was denied a traineeship based on a company's discriminatory policies.[42] Here, the petitioner and the State advanced different concepts of the burden of proof, including with reference to Danish legislation that specifically shares this burden. In addition, the State noted the need for the petitioner to present a prima facie case before CERD.[43] The Committee's assessment, however, did not engage directly with these arguments. It was observed that one aspect of the petitioner's claim had not been 'sufficiently substantiated', indicating the threshold for the standard of proof (see further down below in Section 4.3).[44] It did not mention the burden of proof specifically, but simply noted that the existence of racial discrimination in the case was an 'uncontroversial fact', before finding a violation of the petitioner's right to education.[45]

In a similar fashion, the Committee made short work of a few cases dealing with hate speech (Article 4), where neither the petitioners nor the States seemed to have directly taken issue with evidence: the racist statements in question were uttered at a public event, printed in newspapers and even featured in resolutions adopted by public authorities.[46] Being readily available, they could be assessed as to their potentially racist content. In those cases, the Committee found not only procedural (investigative failure) but also substantive (actual racist motivation) violations of ICERD. Another example where evidence was not discussed is *Habassi* v. *Denmark*, where a Tunisian citizen was denied a bank loan because he was not Danish. The petitioner submitted proof of his nationality as well as the bank's loan form asking whether he was a Danish national, without discussing evidence further; the Committee also did not mention evidence at either the admissibility or the merits stage while confirming a violation of his right to an effective remedy under ICERD.[47]

2007, 8 August 2007; *Jama* v. *Denmark*, CERD/C/75/D/41/2008, 21 August 2009; *L.G.* v. *Korea*, CERD; *Adan* v. *Denmark*, CERD/C/77/D/43/2008, 13 August 2010.

42 *Er* (CERD), para. 2.1.

43 *Er* (CERD), paras. 2.5, 3.3, 4.7, 4.9.

44 *Er* (CERD), para. 7.2.; see also Chapter 3, this volume.

45 *Er* (CERD), para. 7.3.

46 *Jewish Community of Oslo et al.* v. *Norway*, CERD/C/67/D/30/2003, 15 August 2015; *Gelle* v. *Denmark*, CERD/C/68/D/34/2004, 6 March 2006; *TBB-Turkish Union in Berlin/Brandenburg* v. *Germany*, CERD/C/82/D/48/2010, 26 February 2013; *Koptova* v. *Slovakia*, CERD/C/57/D/13/1998, 8 August 2000; *L.R. et al.* v. *Slovakia*, CERD/C/66/D/31/2003, 7 March 2005.

47 *Habassi* v. *Denmark*, CERD.

One element that CERD generally does not expect petitioners to prove is discriminatory intent. A good example of this is *Gabaroum* v. *France*, concerning a black employee who was not given the same opportunities for career advancement as other employees in a comparable position in the car company at which he worked.[48] The Committee referred to the reversal of the burden of proof which domestic legislation commanded to take place in such a case. In so doing, it endorsed the view that the petitioner could not be expected to prove discriminatory intent.[49] However, instead of then setting out its own evidentiary principles regarding the burden of proof, it contented itself with observing that the national legislation requiring the burden to be shifted had not been applied properly. The way CERD relies on the resulting domestic legislation, however, can have the effect of leaving out any recognition of a substantive violation by limiting itself to a discussion of procedural matters in the light of domestic law. In the context of individual communications brought against member states of the European Union (EU), this recurring reference to domestic legislation can be explained by an EU directive requiring the shift of the burden of proof once a prima facie case of discrimination has been established.[50]

Given that UNTBs have a smaller caseload and therefore also a smaller pool of their own case law to draw from compared to other legal fora, it makes sense for CERD to look beyond the UN context for inspiration, such as the example based on EU legislation just mentioned. Yet what is missing still is the Committee's explicit engagement with information on the way in which standards and burdens of proof are handled by other bodies in cases that are brought before it. This can be observed in several cases, potentially suggesting the Committee does not wish to pronounce itself on the allocation of the burden of proof explicitly, while

48 *Gabaroum* v. *France*, CERD/C/89/D/52/2012, 10 May 2016, paras. 2.1ff.

49 *Gabaroum* (CERD), para. 7.2; *V.S.* (CERD), para. 7.4.

50 Race Equality Directive (2000/43/CE); Council Directive 2000/78/CE of 27 November 2000 establishing a general framework for equal treatment in employment and occupation; Directive 2006/54/EC of the European Parliament and of the Council of 5 July 2006 on the implementation of the principle of equal opportunities and equal treatment of men and women in matters of employment and occupation. All these directives contain a reaffirmation of a shift of the burden of proof in their preambles and articles requiring a shift of the burden of proof after a prima facie case has been presented (2000/43, Art. 8; 2000/78, Art. 10; 2006/54, Art. 19); on this point, see also Henrard, 'The European Court of Human Rights', pp. 428–429.

the reversal enshrined in domestic legislation might reflect its own preferred stance.[51]

Terminologies such as *prima facie*, *sufficiently substantiated* or *arguable*, which hint at the Committee's implicit application of evidentiary standards and burdens, can be found in its decision-making practice.[52] For instance, the Committee has found cases were admissible after having qualified them as *sufficiently substantiated*, due to the petitioner having made their case *prima facie*.[53] However, the Committee did not explain why and how it was reaching the conclusion that the petitioner had managed to sufficiently substantiate their claim. In *Hagan* v. *Australia*, a case concerning a racist term appearing within the name of a sports ground, the Committee described the petitioner's claim at the admissibility stage as having been *sufficiently substantiated*. However, the phrase was used without further elaboration on its meaning, apart from CERD stating that the petitioner's claim fell within the scope of the Convention and that the details would be discussed at the merits stage – which they were not.[54]

The terms *prima facie* and *sufficiently substantiated* appear most often at the admissibility stage.[55] At the merits stage, reference is made to the case being *arguable*, although only in relation to the procedural right to effective remedies under Article 6.[56] The Committee explained its rationale in the case *Durmic* v. *Serbia and Montenegro*, which concerned a Roma individual who had been denied access to a public place (a discotheque):

> the State party must provide for the determination of this right ... a guarantee which would be void were it unavailable in circumstances where a violation had not yet been established. While a State party cannot be reasonably required to provide for the determination of rights under the Convention no matter how unmeritorious such claims may be, article 6, provides protection to alleged victims if their claims are *arguable* under the Convention.[57]

[51] See, e.g., *V.S.* (CERD); *Gabaroum* (CERD); *Breleur* (CERD); *Zapescu* v. *Moldova*, CERD/C/103/D/60/2016, 22 April 2021.

[52] For a penetrating analysis of the use of these terms across the UNTB, see Chapter 3, this volume.

[53] See, e.g., *Jallow* (CERD), paras. 6.3–6.4; *Jama* (CERD), para. 6.2.

[54] *Hagan* v. *Australia*, CERD/C/62/D/26/2002, 20 March 2003, para. 6.2.

[55] Exceptions are *Er* (CERD), para. 7.2 and *Ågren et al.* (CERD), para. 6.24, where the Committee had found a part of the petitioner's claim not *sufficiently substantiated* at the merits stage of its opinion, which rather read like a delayed admissibility decision.

[56] *Pjetri* (CERD); *Durmic* (CERD); *Ågren et al.* (CERD); *Zapescu* (CERD).

[57] *Durmic* (CERD), para. 9.6 (emphasis by the author).

CERD found that by not investigating the petitioner's substantive claim under Article 5 (f) (equal access to services), the State had violated Article 6.[58] The quoted passage indicates that the Committee applies a specific threshold to cases related to procedural rights. However, it is unclear how the petitioner can prove their case is *arguable*. Apart from the qualifier at the lower end of the spectrum – *unmeritorious* – there is not much information on the evidence that the parties need to provide. In circumstances where procedural violations barred the Committee from examining the substantive part of a claim (such as where it had no access to the information pertaining to the case due to a flawed investigation), the standard for the merits assessment seems lower, but there is no determination of its exact degree. However, evidentiary matters are even less discussed in relation to substantive violations, and the case examples mentioned above read more as if CERD would be inclined to take an approach that tends to favour the petitioner.[59] It could therefore be inferred that the *arguable case* standard is to be understood as lower than other standards, such as *preponderance of evidence* or *more probable than not*, and thus more akin to prima facie.

This brief overview indicates that CERD has not yet developed a clear evidentiary path. While there are evidentiary hints in the form of recurrent terminology here and there, these have not been incorporated by the Committee into a fully fledged system for the treatment of evidence. Furthermore, discussions of evidence mostly arise in respect of complaints concerning procedural rights under Article 6. Evidence is rarely discussed when substantive violations are assessed, in which case CERD seems to be inclined to take a generous stance towards petitioners' narratives, simply adopting them unless disputed. This lack of a clear evidentiary path creates uncertainty for all parties involved. In addition, the absence of direction may leave the Committee to produce contradictory decisions and/or outliers, as arguably happened in the two cases discussed below.

4.4 *Dawas and Shava* v. *Denmark*: The Late Resurfacing of Unresolved Evidentiary Questions

At first sight, the *Dawas* case, decided in 2012 and dealing with direct discrimination in the form of racist violence, may appear to be like many

[58] *Durmic* (CERD), para. 10.

[59] A similar phenomenon (on the impact of the HRC's too quick acceptance of complainants' factual allegations regarding the addition of persons on the Sami electoral roll in Finland) is highlighted in Chapter 10, this volume.

other cases decided by the Committee. Usual points were made: for example, the government argued that the petitioners had failed to present a prima facie case, while the Committee found their claims sufficiently substantiated without further elaboration. Uncommonly, however, both the facts of the case and the relevant evidence were hotly disputed between the parties. Not only does the opinion start with a section entitled 'facts as submitted by the petitioner' instead of 'factual background' (which would indicate a general agreement about the facts), but these facts are subsequently the main point of argument between the State and the petitioners, as is laid out in a response and counter-response in the opinion. As we shall see, the Committee failed to engage with these factual disputes appropriately, showing that CERD's use of a few recurring phrases is not enough to establish a clear evidentiary path that securely guides its decision-making. In *Dawas*, unanswered evidentiary questions lingered and ended up being debated even after the Committee had handed down its opinion. What makes the case stand out, then, is not so much the Committee's lack of engagement with evidence as the reaction of the respondent State to the Committee's opinion.[60] The follow-up procedure saw an exchange emerging between the petitioners and the State regarding core facts of the case, which still had not been established at the merits stage.

4.4.1 Overview

The two petitioners were Iraqi citizens living as recognised refugees in Denmark. In June 2004, a group of young people (numbering thirty-five at the highest point) attacked the petitioners' home. One of the attackers managed to break into the house and physically assaulted the petitioners. These acts were accompanied by chants exhorting the petitioners to 'go home' and referring to foreigners in offensive language. This led the petitioners and their family to relocate.[61] In the criminal trial that followed the attack, four perpetrators (aged between fifteen and seventeen) were convicted on counts of violence, vandalism and weapon possession, but the question of a racist motive was not discussed.[62] The petitioners claimed that the Danish authorities had failed to investigate the racist motive behind the attack and did not provide them with

[60] Thornberry, *Commentary*, p. 62.
[61] *Dawas and Shava* (CERD), para. 2.1.
[62] *Dawas and Shava* (CERD), paras. 2.2ff.

effective remedies for the violations they had suffered (Articles 2 (1)(d) and 6). In addition, they claimed that the racist motive, in combination with the demand that the petitioners leave the municipality, amounted to a violation of Article 3 on racial segregation and apartheid and Article 4 on hate speech.[63]

The summary of Denmark's submission, as reproduced in the Committee's opinion, concluded that there was no evidence of a racist motive and called on CERD to dismiss the communication.[64] The racist language used during the attack, and the 'no blacks allowed' sign on the door of two offenders in the same neighbourhood, were not investigated – the domestic court merely noted that it was unclear who had put up the sign.[65] In addition, the police had referred the case to the Security and Intelligence Service, as required for potentially racially or religiously motivated criminal incidents, meaning that it had been aware of the potentially racist nature of the attack.[66] The State claimed that none of this was sufficient to prove a racist motive;[67] it further stressed that the police, having interviewed witnesses and undertaken an investigation, had found 'no possible inference' of a racist motive.[68]

The Committee declared the communication admissible on all counts except Article 3, about which it said that the petitioners had not substantiated how the attackers' intent to make them leave the municipality amounted to an act of racial segregation or apartheid.[69] With regard to the remainder of the communication, CERD held that the petitioners had 'sufficiently substantiated' their claim for purposes of admissibility. It deferred any further discussion of whether or not the assault constituted racial discrimination to the merits stage (where this was ultimately not further addressed).[70] On the merits, the Committee first noted 'that it is not its role to review the interpretation of facts . . ., unless the [domestic] decisions were manifestly arbitrary, or otherwise amounted to a denial of justice'.[71] The Committee nonetheless moved to criticise the summary

63 *Dawas and Shava* (CERD), paras. 3.1–3.2.
64 *Dawas and Shava* (CERD), para. 4.1.
65 *Dawas and Shava* (CERD), para. 4.14.
66 *Dawas and Shava* (CERD), para. 5.1.
67 *Dawas and Shava* (CERD), para. 4.14.
68 *Dawas and Shava* (CERD), para. 4.17.
69 *Dawas and Shava* (CERD), para. 6.2.
70 *Dawas and Shava* (CERD), para. 6.3.
71 *Dawas and Shava* (CERD), para. 7.2. This is otherwise known as the no-fourth-instance principle; see Chapter 2, this volume.

nature of the domestic proceedings, the shift from a more severe to a more lenient sentence, and the lack of adjudication on the racist motive.[72] As a result, the Committee found that the State party had failed to carry out an effective investigation into the possible racist nature of the attack. It confirmed that this obligation is held by the State and cannot be passed on to the petitioners – who shouldered the burden of proof in the civil proceedings.[73] Nevertheless, as the investigation into the attack was 'incomplete' and the facts of the case remained in dispute, the Committee held that it was unable to find a violation of Article 4 on hate speech; it only declared a violation of the right to an effective remedy, which it based on the ineffective investigation.[74] CERD recommended that the petitioners be adequately compensated and that Denmark undertake a review of its policies regarding investigating racial discrimination.[75]

During the merits assessment, the Committee stayed away from assessing the original facts of the incident. Its observations were mainly directed at the domestic proceedings rather than at the claims in dispute between the parties, such as whether the racist door sign was relevant to the case. In *Hagan* v. *Australia*, the Committee had called upon the State to ensure the removal of a racist sign.[76] Yet in *Dawas*, the Committee did not explore this potential avenue and failed to assess whether there had been a substantive violation of the prohibition of hate speech. Its only constructive evidentiary engagement was noting that the State had not submitted any information on the outcome of the referral to the Security and Intelligence Service. However, the Committee did not specifically request this information from the State, but simply mentioned at the merits stage that this piece of information was missing, without elaborating on its relevance.[77] It is important to add that the Committee held that some facts were 'undisputed' between the parties, such as the number of assailants and that the petitioners were exposed to racist language. Yet, these points were challenged by the State in the follow-up procedure, and it is unclear how the Committee came to the conclusion that they were settled.[78]

[72] *Dawas and Shava* (CERD), para. 7.2.
[73] *Dawas and Shava* (CERD), para. 7.4.
[74] *Dawas and Shava* (CERD), para. 7.5.
[75] *Dawas and Shava* (CERD), paras. 9, 10.
[76] *Hagan* (CERD), para. 8.
[77] *Dawas and Shava* (CERD), para. 7.3.
[78] *Dawas and Shava* (CERD), para. 7.3.

4.4.2 *The Afterlife of Evidence*

As seen above, the facts of the *Dawas* case were contested right from the start of the proceedings, which put the Committee in a difficult position. Yet, apart from the remark that the petitioners were left with the burden of proof in civil proceedings and the relatively low threshold at the admissibility stage, the Committee did not go into further detail about what principles would properly guide its treatment of evidence and what kind of evidence it expected the parties to present in order to prove their claims. Having addressed these points might perhaps have prevented what was to come in the follow-up procedure, where evidence seems to have led some kind of afterlife after having been sidelined by the Committee when it would have mattered most.

In 2018, what had happened in the follow-up procedure was laid out in two CERD reports to the UN General Assembly.[79] The first of these reported that Denmark had requested outright that the Committee reconsider its opinion and objected to its obligation to disseminate the Committee's findings. CERD's Rapporteur on Communications had met with a Danish official in 2013 and reaffirmed that CERD would not reconsider its opinion, that the findings had to be disseminated widely and that the petitioners should be adequately compensated. In December 2013, Denmark had responded that it 'did not wish to make further comments'.[80]

The second report revealed another layer to the discussion, revolving around evidence. Denmark had claimed that CERD's opinion was 'based on number [sic] of misunderstandings regarding the facts of the case and the legal provisions applicable to the case'.[81] Regarding the assessment of evidence, Denmark had argued that the Committee had been wrong to find that Danish authorities had not investigated the racist motive, as 'it would not be possible during the trial to prove that the assault was indeed racially motivated'.[82] With reference to a video recording of parts of the attack and to witness statements, Denmark submitted that there were no indications of a racist motive.[83] Furthermore, Denmark disputed the

[79] Report of the Committee on the Elimination of Racial Discrimination, 81st and 82nd Session (A/68/18), 2012/2013, pp. 160ff; Report of the Committee on the Elimination of Racial Discrimination, 83rd and 84th Session (A/69/18), 2013/2014, pp. 159–160.

[80] CERD Report, A/69/18, p. 160.

[81] CERD Report, A/68/18, p. 161; Report of the Committee on the Elimination of Racial Discrimination, 85th and 86th Session (A/70/18), 2014/2015, Annex II.

[82] CERD Report, A/68/18, p. 162.

[83] CERD Report, A/68/18, pp. 162–163.

number of assailants and the use of offensive language. According to the State, witness statements rather indicated a smaller group, possibly only the four individuals who were eventually charged, while others had merely been 'spectators'.[84] In addition, Denmark argued that the petitioners had not made any reference to a racist motive in their initial statements, therefore diminishing the credibility of their allegations. Reading Denmark's comments, one could assume that the only potential indicator of a racist motive would have been the racist sign on the offenders' door,[85] regarding which the State asserted that it was unclear who had put it up and whether it was directed at the petitioners.[86]

The petitioners had responded to the State's comments. As to the number of people involved in the attack, the petitioners stated that the police had not made any effort to establish a complete account of everyone present and their reasons for being there. Furthermore, their arrival by invitation spoke against the idea that those present at the scene would have been mere spectators, but rather bolstered their characterisation as 'supporters'.[87] According to the petitioners, these additional persons had never been interviewed by the police. Regarding the video recording, the petitioners noted that in addition to documenting only parts of the attack, its quality was not very good, and it did not include offensive language shouted at the petitioners. This led them to dispute that the recording should even have been considered admissible evidence. Furthermore, they pointed out that the racist sign was only taken down after their complaint to local authorities.[88] Another round of exchanges had followed, which had seen Denmark and the petitioners restating their positions. In 2014, Denmark provided additional information regarding legislative changes that had occurred since the attack in 2004, but remained insistent that it would not consider paying compensation in the case at hand. The Committee then decided to close the follow-up procedure, with the outcome defined as 'partly satisfactory'.[89]

As highlighted above in the case law overview, it is rare for the Committee to address evidence in its discussion of the merits of a case. In *Dawas*, general principles were nonetheless mentioned both by the

[84] CERD Report, A/68/18, p. 162.
[85] CERD Report, A/68/18, p. 163.
[86] CERD Report, A/68/18, p. 163.
[87] CERD Report, A/68/18, pp. 163–164.
[88] CERD Report, A/68/18, p. 164.
[89] CERD Report, A/70/18, Annex II.

State and the Committee. However, there was no effort to link these principles specifically and coherently to the concrete evidentiary issues which arose in the case. The facts were disputed by the parties, but the Committee did not spell out what proof each side would have been expected to provide for them to be considered established. Addressing only the ineffective domestic investigation, it failed to engage with the substantive hate speech complaint. It contented itself with noting that some aspects were contested between the parties and others 'undisputed', without either explaining the reasons for its conclusions or identifying which was which. Its factual findings were not received well by the State, which strongly opposed them in the follow-up. In other words, questions of evidence left unaddressed at the right time came back to haunt the Committee. A conscious engagement with the facts and with evidence at the merits stage would have been preferable, as illustrated in the second case selected for review (Section 4.5).

4.5 *Zapescu* v. *Moldova*: Towards Direct Engagement With Evidence

Whether or not Committee members had *Dawas* in mind as they were examining *Zapescu* in 2021, they did not make the same mistakes as nine years earlier. *Zapescu*, another direct discrimination case, saw the Committee take a clearer stance on the evidence the parties should have provided to substantiate their claim. It also offered direct reasoning on several pieces of evidence, as well as on the role that this evidence played in the Committee's decision-making.

4.5.1 Overview

In 2012, the petitioner and his friend simultaneously applied for a position as a waiter at a pizza restaurant. On the questionnaire, the petitioner stated that Romani was his mother tongue, and he allegedly confirmed his Roma ethnicity during the interview.[90] He and his friend were interviewed for the job on the same day. The petitioner's friend was offered the position, but he himself never heard back from the restaurant. The only manifest difference he could see between him and his friend was his ethnicity, with their language skills and work experience otherwise

[90] *Zapescu* (CERD), paras. 2.1, 3.4.

being similar. He initiated civil proceedings on grounds of discrimination, but to no avail, whether at first instance or on appeal.[91]

Before CERD, the petitioner claimed violations of Article 5 (e)(i) (right to work) and Articles 6 (right to a remedy) and 7 (measures in education to combat racial discrimination), read in conjunction with Article 2 (1) (d) (state obligation to prohibit discrimination and bring it to an end).[92] The petitioner argued that although Moldovan legislation prohibited racial discrimination, the implementation of some of the laws relevant to his case was insufficient (an argument which could also have counteracted the State defence in *Dawas* that legal provisions had been changed – on paper).[93] Referencing cases from the European Court of Human Rights, the Court of Justice of the European Union and the UN Human Rights Committee, the petitioner argued for the burden of proof to be shifted since he had established a prima facie case.[94] This argument first appears in the complaint section of the text of the opinion, but is then reiterated when the petitioner's comments on the merits are reported (rather than featuring only when admissibility is discussed). This indicates the relevance of this point for the merits of the case.[95] As noted above in the general discussion as well as regarding *Dawas*, at admissibility, the Committee has at times deferred its examination of whether the claim had been sufficiently substantiated to the merits stage but had then failed to return to this issue later. Such a deferral (as long as it is properly taken up again), however, can make sense in the context of an Article 6 complaint. This is because the substance of Article 6 is precisely procedural issues, including the reversal of the burden of proof after a prima facie case has been submitted.[96] Read together with the arguable case standard, this indicates that the standard of proof required from the petitioner in support of allegations related to Article 6 is relatively low.

The State party's submission contained several statements from governmental authorities, some of which will now be discussed. First, the State seemed to have taken for granted that the recruitment process of the restaurant chain had been non-discriminatory. To quote the

[91] *Zapescu* (CERD), paras. 2.1–2.2, 3.1.
[92] *Zapescu* (CERD), para. 3.1.
[93] *Zapescu* (CERD), para. 3.2.
[94] *Zapescu* (CERD), para. 3.4.
[95] *Zapescu* (CERD), para. 5.3.
[96] *Zapescu* (CERD), para. 8.5; for a similar approach, see: *V.S.* (CERD).

Moldovan Ministry of Health, Labour and Social Protection, 'the selection process was governed by a regulation, adopted at the company level, that establishes clear and non-discriminatory recruitment criteria. Consequently, the outcome of the selection process should be considered to have been based on legitimate grounds.'[97] However, how the Ministry arrived at this conclusion is not discussed, and no evidence is provided in support of the statement. Indeed, the lack of any information detailing the 'clear and non-discriminatory' criteria was criticised by the petitioner and the Committee.[98]

The Ombudsman's Office had contributed to the State's submission. It noted that the Moldovan Council on Preventing and Eliminating Discrimination and Ensuring Equality (CDE) had issued an advisory opinion on the case, in which it drew the domestic courts' attention to the need to reverse the burden of proof in cases dealing with discrimination.[99] The Ombudsman's Office also held that while the petitioner had proven a prima facie case of discrimination, the Court of Appeal of Chisinau had noted that several employees of the company with different ethnicities had 'confirmed the friendly and tolerant attitude of the company's administration toward its employees'.[100] This, however, is not convincing. Such general statements offered by other employees cannot outweigh the petitioner's individual prima facie case, the more so since it is questionable how much credibility can be given to feedback gathered from active employees, especially when it is unclear how they were questioned and by whom. Indeed, as will be shown below, the Committee took issue with this part of the State's submission as well.

In their refutation of the State's arguments, both the petitioner and a third-party intervention by the Legal Resources Centre from Moldova referenced international case law.[101] They also backed their submissions with information regarding the Moldovan judicial system and its specific shortcomings, including a 'systemic failure regarding the understanding

[97] *Zapescu* (CERD), para. 4.2.

[98] *Zapescu* (CERD), paras. 5.3, 8.3.

[99] *Zapescu* (CERD), paras. 4.3, 5.1.

[100] *Zapescu* (CERD), para. 4.3.

[101] Including: *D.H. and Others* v. *Czech Republic*, ECtHR, 57325/00, Judgment, 13 November 2007; *Handels- og Kontorfunktionrerernes Forbund I Denmark* v. *Dansk Arhejdsgiverforening, acting on behalf of Danfoss*, CJEU, C-109/88, 17 October 1989; *Dr. Pamela Mary Enderby v. Frenchay Health Authority and Secretary of State for Health*, CJEU, C-127/92, 27 October 1993.

of how the burden of proof should apply in discrimination cases'.[102] The Legal Resources Centre highlighted the failure of the courts to draw inferences from the company's refusal to submit the petitioner's application form as evidence. It also criticised the domestic courts' readiness to draw inferences, by contrast, from the petitioner's actions, including his decision not to seek a court order compelling the company to hire him.[103]

Presented with these claims and arguments, how did CERD decide the case? Regarding admissibility, it did not discuss whether the petitioner had substantiated his case. Instead, the focus was on points brought forward by the State, such as the non-exhaustion of domestic remedies, which it refuted one by one.[104] At the merits stage, the two pertinent provisions became Article 5 (e)(i) addressing the right to work and Article 6 on effective remedies.[105] As to the former, the Committee held that simply enacting legislation prohibiting discriminatory employment practices was insufficient, as effective implementation in practice also needed to be ensured. The Committee further noted 'with concern' that the State party seemingly took for granted that the recruitment criteria adopted by the restaurant chain were non-discriminatory, without this being supported by any further information.[106] Having adopted these findings, the Committee decided not to rule on the right to work or on Article 7 (education measures), but only to examine the merits related to Article 6, as most claims were about effective protection and remedies rather than access to work.[107]

With regard to the standard of proof required for Article 6, meaning procedural violations, the Committee noted that the petitioner only needs to present an arguable case.[108] CERD also noted that the State 'did not provide any specific arguments' regarding the effectiveness of the available domestic remedies, including on whether and how the burden

[102] *Zapescu* (CERD), para. 6.2.

[103] *Zapescu* (CERD), paras. 5.1ff, 6.2; on drawing presumptions and a useful discussion of decision-making in situations of uncertainty see, T. Altwicker and A. E. Hansen, 'Presumptions as Secondary Rules in the Judicial Interpretation of International Human Rights' in G. Kajtár, B. Çalı and M. Milanovic (eds.), *Secondary Rules of Primary Importance in International Law* (Oxford: Oxford University Press, 2022), pp. 167–182.

[104] *Zapescu* (CERD), paras. 7.1–7.5.

[105] *Zapescu* (CERD), para. 8.3.

[106] *Zapescu* (CERD), para. 8.3.

[107] *Zapescu* (CERD), para. 8.3.

[108] *Zapescu* (CERD), para. 8.4.

of proof is reversed in discrimination cases.[109] Following this, CERD restated its general position that petitioners should not be required to prove discriminatory intent and held that, despite the reversal of the burden of proof being enshrined in domestic legislation, it was not applied in the petitioner's case. Instead, the domestic courts held it against the petitioner that he had not provided further evidence of his ethnic origin apart from his own statement – thus contradicting the generally accepted principle of self-identification.[110] Furthermore, the Committee rightly confirmed that the domestic courts had placed too much emphasis on the fact that the petitioner had asked for compensation instead of employment by the restaurant.[111] In response to the domestic courts' view that the petitioner's decision not to approach the CDE confirmed 'the absence of a "real situation of discrimination"',[112] the Committee persuasively noted that the petitioner's choice to seek a judicial remedy instead of a CDE decision, which had only declaratory effect, could not be taken to diminish the credibility of his claim.

The Committee further criticised the domestic courts for not requiring the company to detail the specific reasons why the petitioner had not been hired, and for putting the emphasis on witness testimonies and general statements collected from other employees instead. In other words, the Committee put the burden of producing relevant evidence on the State (meaning on the domestic courts to have requested this information from the company in the course of the proceedings). In the context of any future similar individual communication, this logically should mean that the state party would be expected to produce evidence as to whether the domestic courts actually did request information from the company, as well as on the results of this request. Furthermore, CERD criticised the courts for ignoring the guidance submitted by the CDE on reversing the burden of proof. Regarding the statements of other employees, the Committee made the important point that these statements were not only general in nature, but were also made by persons 'of a different age, gender and ethnicity than the petitioner and who are employed in other positions'. This could 'not guarantee that these persons were in an identical situation to the petitioner', thus questioning the

109 *Zapescu* (CERD), para. 8.5.
110 *Zapescu* (CERD), para. 8.6.
111 *Zapescu* (CERD), para. 8.7.
112 *Zapescu* (CERD), para. 8.8.

choice of comparator group.[113] In the Committee's opinion, this also led to a failure to appreciate the potential effects of intersectionality and 'ethnic hierarchies' on access to the labour market.[114]

Concluding on Article 6, the Committee found that the petitioner had presented an 'arguable case', but 'that he was nonetheless left with a disproportionate burden to prove the respondent company's discriminatory intent'.[115] While domestic legislation did call for the reversal of the burden of proof, this had not been applied here, leaving the petitioner without effective protection from discrimination. Consequently, the Committee found a violation of Article 6 caused by the failure of domestic courts to properly shift the burden of proof.[116] The Committee recommended that the State party convey an apology to the petitioner, as well as provide adequate compensation and undertake measures to ensure the proper enforcement of anti-discrimination legislation. The latter included a recommendation on the training of judges to make sure 'that the principle of shifting the burden of proof is fully observed'.[117]

4.5.2 Breathing New Life Into Evidentiary Practices

As can readily be seen, in *Zapescu*, the Committee specified at length the kind of evidence that would be required to prove or disprove a claim, and from whom. It also provided more direct information on its own assessment of particular pieces of evidence. By doing so, the Committee brought abstract principles to life and made them more tangible. This is an important step, as this clarification of the Committee's approach will both help future parties to prepare their cases and support Committee members in their decision-making.

Zapescu is part of an ongoing line of cases where the Committee has found that the failure to shift the burden of proof amounts to a violation of Article 6.[118] However, this finding is generally linked to a failure by the

113 *Zapescu* (CERD), para. 8.9.

114 *Zapescu* (CERD), para. 8.9; CERD, Concluding observations on the combined tenth and eleventh periodic reports of the Republic of Moldova (CERD/C/MDA/CO/10-11), 8 May 2017; CERD, Concluding observations of the Committee on the Elimination of Racial Discrimination: Republic of Moldova (CERD/C/MDA/CO/8-9), 10 March 2011.

115 *Zapescu* (CERD), para. 8.10.

116 *Zapescu* (CERD), para. 8.10.

117 *Zapescu* (CERD), para. 10; see also: *Gabaroum* (CERD), para. 9; *V.S.* (CERD), para. 9.

118 See, e.g., *Breleur* (CERD); *Kotor* (CERD); *Gabaroum* (CERD); *V.S.* (CERD).

state to respect its own domestic legislation requiring this shift. The Committee has not gone as far as holding that *under the Convention*, the failure to reverse the burden of proof would amount to such a violation. Still, this is an important recurring finding that could at least be indicative of the Committee's own stance in this regard. What was new in *Zapescu* is that CERD took more time to address the evidence than in previous cases. A good counter-example here is *V.S.* v. *Slovakia*. This case, decided in 2015, concerned discriminatory recruitment practices by a public elementary school. The school did not hire the petitioner, a qualified teacher of Roma origin, but instead a non-Roma individual who was less qualified.[119] Here, the Committee did not address the evidence presented by the parties in any detail. How relevant were: general reports on the situation of Roma in Slovakia; the statement by the head of school that the petitioner should not look for a job but instead have children like other Roma women; or the point made by the State that the school had employed Roma before?[120] In its assessment of the right to work, the Committee simply found that the State had 'not satisfactorily replied to the petitioner's allegations' and that it had failed to provide 'persuasive arguments to justify the differential treatment'. There is no further mention of these points in the assessment of Article 6.[121] While in *V.S.*, CERD did not comment further on the evidence that the State would have needed to provide to comply with the burden of production imposed on it after a shift, it did so in *Zapescu*. This gave the parties a better idea of the Committee's understanding of what shifting the burden of proof would entail in practice. The Committee commented on the burden of production of evidence regarding the company's recruitment criteria, on the relevance of testimonies by other employees, on the inferences (not) drawn by domestic courts, and on the relevance it attributed to this information. This made the decision-making process of the Committee more transparent. While it is regrettable that CERD only had discussed but not ruled on the substantive violations in *Zapescu*, its more direct guidance on what amounts to relevant evidence is a welcome step towards greater clarity for future parties and Committee members alike.[122]

[119] *V.S.* (CERD), paras. 2.1ff.

[120] *V.S.* (CERD), paras. 5.8, 2.2, 4.10.

[121] *V.S.* (CERD), para. 7.3.

[122] This trend seems to be continuing, as CERD was more direct regarding the evidence required in *U.I. and G.I.* v. *Switzerland*, CERD/C/112/D/74/2021, 26 April 2024, as well.

4.6 CERD and Evidence: Still Trying to Find Its Feet

After more than forty years of practice, the Committee is still clearly trying to find its evidentiary feet. The cases discussed above show that there is no clear stance on the assessment of evidence yet, and that this uncertainty has resulted in some outlier cases. In *Dawas*, the facts of the case were disputed, and the Committee struggled to engage with them, leading to a fierce debate about the core issues of the case even after the Committee had adopted its opinion. *Zapescu*, by contrast, may be considered as a case that indicates a way forward, as the Committee strived to spell out which evidence it would expect from the parties to prove their claim. The Committee could nonetheless be more forthcoming in its use of information requests (also through hearings as laid out in its new Rules of Procedure), instead of later informing the parties, as it discusses the merits, that some information that it considered relevant was missing. Such information requests would be a good opportunity to trigger a reaction by the respective party, who then would have the chance to deliver the evidence requested before their claim fails.

Procedural violations under Article 6 seem to be at the centre of the evidentiary debate. There are indications that the standard of proof is lower in this context and that the failure to shift the burden of proof after presenting a prima facie case amounts to a violation. Regarding substantive violations, there is little to no discussion of evidence, and the Committee either simply finds a violation or focuses on procedural aspects under Article 6 instead. Given that the opinions the Committee has adopted so far offer several diverging scenarios, it is not possible to discern a clear line of decision-making practice (even implicitly) in this regard just yet.

Although CERD is a longstanding actor in the UNTB system, there is still a lot of uncertainty regarding key questions of evidence and their treatment in principle and in practice. The complexities in proving racial discrimination or indeed any form of discrimination do not make the Committee's task any easier. Yet developing a clearer approach to the handling of evidence and the guiding principles behind it could help the Committee in doing its work, at the same time as making the individual communications procedure more accessible and predictable. Beyond these practical considerations, a clearer stance on evidentiary principles would also have broader benefits as it would enhance the Committee's credibility and legitimacy and ultimately, the fairness of the individual communications procedure as a whole.

Select Bibliography

Angst, D. and Lantschner, E. (eds.), *ICERD: Internationales Übereinkommen zur Beseitigung jeder Form von Rassendiskriminierung: Handkommentar* (Baden-Baden: Nomos, 2020).

Henrard, K., 'The European Court of Human Rights and the "Special" Distribution of the Burden of Proof in Racial Discrimination Cases: The Search for Fairness Continues', *European Convention on Human Rights Law Review*, 4 (2023): 426–446.

Keane, D. and Waughray, A. (eds.), *Fifty Years of the International Convention on the Elimination of All Forms of Racial Discrimination: A Living Instrument* (Manchester: Manchester University Press, 2017).

Niezen, R. and Sapignoli, M. (eds.), *Palaces of Hope: The Anthropology of Global Organizations* (Cambridge: Cambridge University Press, 2017).

Riddell, A., 'Evidence, Fact-Finding, and Experts', in Romano, C. P. R., Alter, K. J. and Shany, Y. (eds.), *The Oxford Handbook of International Adjudication* (Oxford: Oxford University Press, 2013), pp. 848–870.

Roberts, C., 'Reversing the Burden of Proof Before Human Rights Bodies', *The International Journal of Human Rights*, 25 (2021): 1682–1703.

Stirner, T., *The Procedural Law Governing Facts and Evidence in International Human Rights Proceedings* (Leiden: Brill Nijhoff, 2021).

Thornberry, P., *The International Convention on the Elimination of All Forms of Racial Discrimination: A Commentary* (Oxford: Oxford University Press, 2016).

'The Committee on the Elimination of Racial Discrimination (CERD)', in Mégret, F. and Alston, P. (eds.), *The United Nations and Human Rights: A Critical Appraisal*, 2nd edn. (Oxford: Oxford University Press, 2020), pp. 309–338.

Vandenhole, W., *Non-discrimination and Equality in the View of the UN Human Rights Treaty Bodies* (Antwerp: Intersentia, 2005).

5

The Working Group on Arbitrary Detention's Treatment of Evidence

A Three-Phase History of Increasing Sophistication

MATTHEW GILLETT, YUTAKA KARUKAYA AND MIA MARZOTTO[*]

5.1 Introduction

Redressing arbitrary detention is imperative, as this practice violates a peremptory norm of international law. It is often a gateway to further violations, including extrajudicial killings, torture and other cruel, inhuman or degrading treatment or punishment, enforced disappearances and sexual- and gender-based violence.[1] In confronting these human rights violations, several human rights monitoring mechanisms within the United Nations (UN) system are able to hear individual cases. Among these, the United Nations human rights treaty bodies (UNTBs), such as the Human Rights Committee (HRC), the Committee against Torture and the Committee on the Rights of the Child, are particularly prominent and share a quasi-judicial character with the Working Group on Arbitrary Detention (Working Group). While there are differences between the Working Group and UNTBs – including the formalised admissibility procedures at the UNTBs – one feature common to all these mechanisms is that they must deal with evidence in order to reach

[*] The views herein are those of the authors alone and do not necessarily reflect those of the United Nations Working Group on Arbitrary Detention or any other entity. The views are made without prejudice to the veracity of any claim concerning a particular incident, situation or case. The authors thank the editors of the present volume for the helpful feedback; any errors remain those of the authors.

[1] Human Rights Council, *Resolution on Arbitrary Detention* (A/HRC/RES/51/8), 6 October 2022, para. 2.

their conclusions on violations of international human rights law.[2] Reviewing the Working Group's approach to evidence provides useful points of comparison regarding the UNTBs and their evidentiary procedures.

The Working Group on Arbitrary Detention, which has operated since 1991, has heard over 1,600 individual cases based on information submitted by persons or organisations alleging arbitrary arrest or detention. The increasing sophistication of the Working Group's approach to evidence demonstrates the maturing of its work over the decades from a focus on substantive developments, which have largely been established in its jurisprudence, to cementing its procedural practices. This is also reflected in the Working Group's gradual shift to examining the secondary level legal standards that it applies, such as by formalising the burden of proof.[3] As a mechanism which has been described as enforcing human rights law through recommendations,[4] the Working Group's impact is heavily conditional on the quality of its fact-finding procedures and the accuracy of its assessments.[5] As it heightens the rigour of its approach, the Working Group provides strong incentives for rules-based bodies at the domestic and international levels to take up its conclusions and procedures.

In this way the Working Group's approach to evidence provides a model from which UNTBs may draw inspiration.[6] Just like the Working Group, UNTBs rely on material submitted to them to reach their views. This raises questions as to how evidence is submitted and assessed, what standards and burdens are applied to evidentiary questions and what

[2] See F. Viljoen, 'Fact-Finding by UN Human Rights Complaints Bodies – Analysis and Suggested Reforms', *Max Planck Yearbook of United Nations Law* 8 (2004): 49–100, 63 and 77–80.

[3] On 'secondary law', see H. L. A. Hart, *The Concept of Law* (Oxford: Oxford University Press, 1961).

[4] J. Cohen and C. Sabel, 'Global Democracy?', *New York University Journal of International Law and Politics* 37 (2005): 763–797, 773.

[5] See J. Genser and M. Winterkorn-Meikle, 'The Intersection of Politics and International Law: The United Nations Working Group on Arbitrary Detention in Theory and in Practice', *Columbia Human Rights Law Review* 39 (2008): 159-162.

[6] See generally J. Connors and S. Shah, 'United Nations' in D. Moeckli, S. Shah and S. Sivakumaran (eds.), *International Human Rights Law* (4th edn., Oxford: Oxford University Press, 2022), pp. 393–418. See further M. Gillett, Y. Karukaya and M. Marzotto, 'Reconciling the Dual-Faceted Mandates of Quasi-Judicial Human Rights Bodies: The Working Group on Arbitrary Detention's Prima Facie Approach to Evidence', *Human Rights Law Review* 24 (2024): 1–25; Viljoen, 'Fact-Finding', pp. 77–80.

evidentiary challenges are emerging in the practice of these human rights bodies.

This chapter provides a unique point of comparison[7] for UNTBs by reviewing the phases of the Working Group's jurisprudential development and arguing that (1) the Working Group's increasingly formalised and standardised approach to evidence reflects the maturing of the Working Group and its entrenchment in the ecosystem of human rights bodies; (2) such a considered evidentiary approach on its part can serve to enhance its credibility with States (and claimants, who are called 'sources'), which in turn can prompt higher rates of compliance; and (3) its detailed approaches to evidentiary standards and challenges could inspire UNTBs with individual claims mandates to follow a similar approach. These arguments fit into the theoretical framework of effective supranational adjudication proposed by Helfer and Slaughter for transposing practices from the European Court of Human Rights (ECtHR) onto the HRC.[8] In particular, it prioritises legitimacy, in the sense of principled decision-making, coherent processes, impartiality and consistency, as the fulcrum for effectiveness for bodies with limited enforcement tools such as the Working Group.[9]

The arguments set out above stem from a detailed retrospective and prospective analysis of the evidentiary approach adopted by the Working Group in the conduct of its individual complaints mandate and associated activities. Following this introduction (Section 5.1), Section 5.2 situates the Working Group's evidentiary approach within its mandate to rely on credible and reliable information. Section 5.3 then outlines the development of this approach across three phases of the Working

[7] The detailed review of the Working Group's developmental phases and emerging challenges, along with the insights to be drawn from this trajectory for UNTBs, combine to make this a novel contribution to the scholarship on quasi-judicial human rights bodies. Other works have reviewed the Working Group's jurisprudence without examining in detail how its burdens and standards have developed over the phases of its existence and without applying those findings in relation to the emerging challenges of digital materials, external evidence and country visits as discussed below. See, e.g., J. Genser, *The United Nations Working Group on Arbitrary Detention* (Cambridge: Cambridge University Press, 2019); Viljoen, 'Fact-Finding'; D. Weissbrodt and B. Mitchell, 'The United Nations Working Group on Arbitrary Detention: Procedures and Summary of Jurisprudence', *Human Rights Quarterly* 38 (2016): 655–705; Gillett et al., 'Reconciling the Dual-Faceted Mandates'.

[8] L. Helfer and A. Slaughter, 'Toward a Theory of Effective Supranational Adjudication', *Yale Law Journal* 107 (1997): 273–391, 318–29.

[9] Helfer and Slaughter 'Toward a Theory of Effective Supranational Adjudication', p. 284.

Group's operations, namely its establishment (Section 5.3.1), expansion (Section 5.3.2) and consolidation (Section 5.3.3). Section 5.4 proceeds to address emerging evidentiary issues in the Working Group's practice, namely the heightened standard of review in certain cases (Section 5.4.1), the use of digital evidence (Section 5.4.2), the use of external evidence beyond that submitted by the parties (Section 5.4.3) and the Working Group's own gathering of relevant information while on mission (Section 5.4.4). Each of these challenges has potential ramifications for UNTBs, whose evidentiary approaches and standards may come to be scrutinised. Moreover, because the Working Group is not a consent-based body like the UNTBs, its acceptance is particularly contingent on the quality and robust evidentiary findings of its decisions. In this light, Section 5.5 examines three indicia through which the impact of the Working Group's evidentiary approach can be observed, namely compliance (Section 5.5.1), state responses (Section 5.5.2) and the responses of third parties such as regional human rights courts and UNTBs (Section 5.5.3). Section 5.6 concludes with recommendations for the Working Group's approach to evidence, which may also prove valuable for UNTBs facing similar issues.

5.2 Encouraging Credible and Reliable Information: The Working Group's Overall Evidentiary Mandate

The Working Group was established by the former Commission on Human Rights, under Resolution 1991/42.[10] Its mandate has been renewed periodically, most recently in 2025 under Human Rights Council Resolution 51/8. Regarding the Working Group's core task, the Commission on Human Rights reiterated that this is to 'investigate cases of detention imposed arbitrarily or otherwise inconsistently with the relevant international standards set forth in the Universal Declaration of Human Rights or in the relevant international legal instruments accepted by the States concerned'.[11] To carry out its mandate, the Working Group should 'seek and gather information from Governments and inter-governmental and non-governmental organizations, as well as from the individuals concerned, their families or their legal representatives'. The Working Group must carry out its task with 'discretion, objectivity, impartiality

[10] UN Commission on Human Rights, Resolution 91/42 (Question of Arbitrary Detention) (E/CN.4/RES/1991/42), 5 March 1991.

[11] UN Commission on Human Rights, Resolution 1997/50 (E/CN.4/1997/50), 15 April 1997.

and independence, within the framework of its mandate', and the experts should 'perform their task with rigour, having regard to the very specific nature of their mandate, and to respond effectively to credible and reliable information that comes before them'.[12]

The reference to a threshold of credible and reliable information relates directly to the approach and standards that the Working Group applies to evidence. Indeed, the Working Group's evidentiary procedures are the vehicle by which it can filter out unreliable and incredible information in a fair, transparent and consistent manner. As will be mapped in the following sections, the Working Group has developed its approach to evidence over time through its jurisprudence and its other normative instruments. Examining this developmental arc reveals how the Working Group's approach has coalesced on a specific sequenced method, which shares burdens between the complainant and the respondent government. A clearer articulation of this method may help to encourage consistency across quasi-judicial human rights bodies, including UNTBs, when determining disputed cases of alleged violations.

5.3 Developing a Standardised Approach to Evidentiary Assessments

From the outset of its operations, the Working Group's core task has involved the collection of information regarding potential cases of arbitrary detention.[13] Relevant governments and individuals, as well as intergovernmental and non-governmental organisations (NGOs), are required to provide information to the Working Group to this end.[14]

Quantitatively, from 1991 to the end of 2022, the Working Group has generated at least 1,600 judgments (called opinions) as a result of its adversarial process.[15] Qualitatively, the Working Group's opinions now have a relatively settled structure, based on five categories of arbitrary detention, covering: detention for which it is impossible to invoke a legal

[12] UN Commission on Human Rights, Resolution 1997/50.

[13] UN Commission on Human Rights, Resolution 91/42.

[14] UN Commission on Human Rights, Resolution 91/42; Resolution 1997/50.

[15] See L. Toomey, 'Detention on Discriminatory Grounds: An Analysis of the Jurisprudence of the United Nations Working Group on Arbitrary Detention', *Columbia Human Rights Law Review* 50 (2018–2019): 185–282, fn. 26 (noting that the Working Group had issued 1199 opinions by December 2017). The Working Group's annual reports indicate the following number of adopted opinions: 90 (2018); 85 (2019); 92 (2020); 85 (2021); 88 (2022).

basis (category I); detention resulting from the exercise of certain human rights (category II); detention following serious violations of fair trial rights (category III); immigration and asylum related detention (category IV); and discriminatory detention (category V).

A survey of the Working Group's activities during its three decades of operations indicates that it has undergone three major phases: (1) an initial 'establishment' phase; (2) an 'expansion' phase; and (3) its current 'consolidation' phase.[16] As set out in Sections 5.3.1–5.3.3, in relation to evidentiary standards and burdens, the Working Group has employed increasing precision and consistency as it has progressed through these phases, to the point where its current jurisprudence has a uniform expression of its approach. However, that explicit uniformity does not comprehensively address all evidentiary issues, and in some respects raises further questions, as subsequently addressed in Section 5.4.

5.3.1 Phase 1: Establishment (1991–2011)

In the first phase of its operation after its creation in 1991, the Working Group set up its procedures and developed its major lines of jurisprudence in its opinions, including its three initial categories of arbitrary detention (i.e. detention with no legal basis, detention resulting from an exercise of rights and detention following serious violations of fair trial rights).[17] Opinions during this period were relatively short, listing the three categories, a brief summary of the parties' main arguments and the Working Group's conclusions.[18] Alongside its opinions in individual cases, the Working Group also expressed views on relevant human rights standards in its deliberations, legal opinions, country visit reports, urgent appeals and joint reports with other mandates of the special procedures on legality and arbitrariness in human rights treaties and customary international law.[19] On 1 May 2000, the Working Group issued its Fact Sheet No. 26, which explicitly set out its working methodology in a

[16] These phases are the authors' own interpretation and do not reflect any official designation on the part of the Working Group.

[17] See, e.g., *Ali Ardalan and others* v. *Islamic Republic of Iran*, WGAD opinion 1/1992, 14 October 1991.

[18] See, e.g., *Colonel Bertrand Mamour* v. *Central African Republic*, WGAD opinion 15/2007, 13 September 2007.

[19] WGAD, Report of the Working Group on Arbitrary Detention (A/HRC/19/57), 26 December 2011, para. 65.

codified manner.[20] A revised version, issued in advanced format in 2019 and formally issued in 2024, sets out the relevant procedures applied by the Working Group.[21] However, the fact sheet does not elaborate on evidentiary burdens and standards, which are instead addressed in various opinions of the Working Group that it references.

With regard to evidence and burdens, the Working Group's opinions during its establishment phase exhibited a variety of approaches. They variously suggested an overarching burden on the source or on the Government, or sometimes did not mention the burden at all. The latter was the tendency in the early years, when the Working Group frequently pointed to the lack of a response from the government before reaching its factual determination, without explaining the impact on its assessment of the source's claims.[22] However, various indirect references gave a mixed picture as to the evidentiary approach being taken. When the Working Group noted a lack of material on the record, this led in some cases to findings against the government – for example, that '[t]here is no material on record to lead the Working Group to draw an inference that the expression of [the claimant's] opinions endangered in any way national security or public order'.[23] In other such cases, findings were made against the source, for example, that '[w]ith regard to the use of a statement obtained under torture, there is no evidence to justify a finding by the Working Group that this allegation has been proved'.[24] Conversely, the absence of sufficient evidence sometimes led the Working Group to decide to take no further action, stating for example that: 'if [the Working Group] does not have enough information to take a decision, the case remains pending for further investigation and if the Working Group considers that it does not have enough information to warrant keeping the case pending, the case is filed without further action'.[25]

20 OHCHR, Fact Sheet No. 26, The Working Group on Arbitrary Detention, 2000.

21 OHCHR, Working Group on Arbitrary Detention – Fact Sheet No. 26 Rev. 1, 2024.

22 See, e.g., *Ali Ardalan* (WGAD); *Latsami Khamphoui and others* v. *Lao People's Democratic Republic*, WGAD opinion 2/1992, 14 October 1991; *Al-Ajili Muhammad Abdul Rahman al-Azhari and others* v. *Libyan Arab Jamahiriya*, WGAD opinion 3/1992, 14 October 1991; *Goodluck Mhango and others* v. *Malawi*, WGAD opinion 4/1992, 14 October 1991.

23 *Ali Ardalan* (WGAD) (unopposed).

24 *Wilfredo Estanislao Saavedra Marreros* v. *Peru*, WGAD opinion 7/1992 (opposed), 14 October 1991.

25 *U Nu and Aung San Suu Kyi* v. *Myanmar*, WGAD opinion 9/1992 (opposed), 14 October 1991.

On one occasion, the Working Group referred to a lack of convincing evidence as excluding the possibility of reaching a finding that detention was arbitrary or otherwise.[26] However, it also made 'reasonable' assumptions due to government silence on an issue, for example, that:

> [i]n its reply, the Government does not maintain having complied with this provision and the Working Group must consequently presume that the Government did not order any investigation. It is therefore at least reasonable to assume that Mr. Kakoun may well have been subjected to acts of torture and that his confession could well be the result of such acts, in which case, pursuant to article 15 of the Convention against Torture, the confession in question should not have served as evidence, as it did.[27]

In another case, the Working Group referred to the need for justification by the government, stating that 'the Working Group has not been provided with clear reasons to question the allegation of the source'.[28]

Despite its indirect references to evidentiary burdens, the Working Group's approach in this respect was still not presented in a settled or uniform way after two decades of its operations. However, this establishment phase came to a close in 2011, when the Working Group took several significant steps towards the expansion of its operations, including a more explicit codification of its approach to evidence and burdens.

5.3.2 Phase 2: Expansion (2011–2019)

The year 2011 saw three major developments which reflected a discernible change in the operations and outputs of the Working Group.

First, in the Working Group's annual report of 19 January 2011,[29] the Working Group expanded the range of categories of arbitrary detention it dealt with from three to five, adding category IV on immigration-related detention and category V on discriminatory detention. The expanded categories have been repeated in Working Group reports and

[26] *Juan Enrique García Cruz and Ramón Obregón Sarduy* v. *Cuba*, WGAD opinion 10/1992 (opposed), 14 October 1991.

[27] *Assem Kakoun* v. *Lebanon*, WGAD opinion 17/2008 (opposed), 9 September 2008; *Pastor Gong Shengliang* v. *China*, WGAD opinion 21/2008 (opposed), 9 September 2008.

[28] *Abdel Hakim Abdel Raouf Hassan Soliman* v. *Egypt*, WGAD opinion 22/2010 (opposed), 2 September 2010.

[29] A/HRC/16/47 and Corr.1, annex.

opinions over the ensuing years,[30] and have been extremely important facets of its work.[31]

Second, the Working Group launched a database to facilitate access of victims, states and civil society to its opinions and other materials.[32] This was followed by a steady increase in the number of individual complaints submitted to the Working Group and a corresponding rise in its output of opinions. At the time of writing, these numbered around 70–90 per year, up from 60–70 per year around 2011.[33]

Third, and most significantly for present purposes, 2011 saw the Working Group explicitly set out how it deals with burdens and evidentiary issues in its 2011 Annual Report, after years of developing jurisprudence.[34] In this report, the Working Group noted that its evidentiary approach, established through practice, was in line with the International Court of Justice (ICJ)'s position on evidentiary burdens in the case of *Ahmadou Sadio Diallo*.[35] The Working Group articulated this approach as such:

> In general the burden rests with the Government: it is for the Government to produce the necessary proof. More generally, the matter of the evidentiary burden arises where the source has established a prima facie case for breach of international requirements constituting arbitrary detention.[36]

This statement reflects two separate but related points: (1) the overall burden which typically falls on a source (also known as the claimant or initiator) of a judicial process to establish a case (*onus probandi incumbit actori*);[37] (2) the evidentiary burden of providing materials that a victim

[30] See, e.g., HRC, Methods of work of the Working Group on Arbitrary Detention (A/HRC/30/69), 4 August 2015; HRC, Methods of work of the Working Group on Arbitrary Detention (A/HRC/33/66), 12 July 2016; HRC Methods of work of the Working Group on Arbitrary Detention (A/HRC/36/38), 13 July 2017.

[31] See, e.g., Opinions 69/2021, 69/2022 (both concerning, inter alia, immigration detention under category IV).

[32] WGAD, Report 2011, summary and para. 5.

[33] See WGAD, Report of the Working Group on Arbitrary Detention (A/HRC/51/29), 21 July 2022, para 14 for the number of cases in 2021, and WGAD 'Report 2011', para 8 for the number of cases in 2011.

[34] A/HRC/19/57, para. 68.

[35] *Ahmadou Sadio Diallo (Republic of Guinea v. Democratic Republic of the Congo)*, ICJ, Judgment, 30 November 2010, paras. 53–57.

[36] A/HRC/19/57, para. 68.

[37] See M. Kazazi, *Burden of Proof and Related Issues: A Study on Evidence Before International Tribunals* (The Hague: Kluwer Law International, 1996), p. 369. See also C. E. Foster, *Science and the Precautionary Principle in International Courts and Tribunals: Expert*

could not reasonably be expected to access. Both principles are important, but the conceptual distinction between them becomes significant in terms of the sequencing of the burdens in the Working Group's usual approach to evidence, which will be discussed in Section 5.3.3. Whereas the Working Group had referred to this approach in prior opinions,[38] its adoption of this formulation in its 2011 report marked a clear shift towards formalising it. Since then, the Working Group has referred to this statement and clarified it in several of its opinions,[39] and has more or less uniformly applied this approach since 2019.[40]

With regard to evidence, this expansion phase saw the Working Group elaborate on its approach with statements that were often repeated in subsequent opinions. In relation to the source's allegations, it explained that submission is considered 'consistent' or 'detailed' when the source provides corroborating evidence;[41] when co-claimants share similar accounts that are nearly the same in all material aspects;[42] when the

Evidence, Burden of Proof and Finality (Cambridge: Cambridge University Press, 2011), p. 185, referring to the principle as *actori incumbit probatio*.

38 *Thamki Gyatso and others* v. *China*, WGAD opinion 29/2010, 24 November 2010, para. 25.

39 For example, see *Nasrin Sotoudeh* v. *Islamic Republic of Iran*, WGAD opinion 21/2011, 6 May 2011, para. 31; *Saif Al-Islam Gaddafi* v. *Libya*, WGAD opinion 41/2013, 7 April 2014; *Reza Raeesi* v. *Australia and Papua New Guinea*, WGAD opinion 52/2014, 13 February 2015; *Nazanin Zaghari-Ratcliffe* v. *Islamic Republic of Iran*, WGAD opinion 28/2016, 7 September 2016; *Adilur Rahman Khan* v. *Malaysia*, WGAD opinion 67/2017, 7 December 2017; *Can Thi Theu* v. *Viet Nam*, WGAD opinion 79/2017, 12 December 2017; *Yamashiro Hiroji* v. *Japan*, WGAD opinion 55/2018, 27 December 2018; *Abbas Haiji Al-Hassan* v. *Saudi Arabia*, WGAD opinion 56/2019, 10 October 2019; *Walid El Batal* v. *Morocco*, WGAD opinion 68/2020, 2 February 2021; and *Said Said* v. *Australia and Nauru*, WGAD opinion 68/2021, 22 February 2022.

40 See, e.g., *José de la Paz Ferman Cruz and Aren Boyazhyan* v. *Mexico*, WGAD opinion 54/2019, 18 February 2020, para. 146; *Abbas Haiji Al-Hassan* v. *Saudi Arabia*, WGAD opinion, para. 73; *Gokarakonda Naga Saibaba* v. *India*, WGAD opinion 21/2021, 17 June 2021, para. 60; *Ahmed Samir Santawy* v. *Egypt*, WGAD opinion 83/2021, 28 January 2022, para. 60; *Alexey Gorinov* v. *Russian Federation*, WGAD opinion 78/2022, 20 March 2023, para. 77; *Naji Fateel* v. *Bahrain*, WGAD opinion No. 65/2022, 16 March 2023, para. 89; *Zara Mohammadi v. Islamic Republic of Iran*, WGAD opinion 82/2022, 6 March 2023, para. 32; *George Nyakpo* v. *Ghana*, WGAD opinion 47/2022, 31 January 2023, para. 42; *Sharofiddin Gadoev* v. *Russian Federation and Tajikistan*, WGAD opinion 48/2021, 15 December 2021, para. 48 (all referring to the 2011 Annual Report A/HRC/19/57, para. 68).

41 See, e.g., *A and others* v. *Saudi Arabia*, WGAD opinion 61/2016, 6 February 2017, paras. 50 and 53. See also *Walid El Batal* (WGAD), paras. 72–73.

42 See, e.g., *Abdullah Ahmed Mohammed Ismail Alfakharany and others* v. *Egypt*, WGAD opinion 7/2016, 14 June 2016, para. 47 and *Mi Sook Kang and Ho Seok Kim* v. *Democratic*

source's claims are supported with external documentation such as credible news reports and findings by other international human rights bodies;[43] and when the source's claims are supported by the Working Group's own prior findings that detention was arbitrary under similar conditions.[44] If a source has presented a prima facie case of arbitrary detention, the implicated government can meet its burden by producing a detailed and substantiated account of the actions that were carried out.[45] However, in an oft-repeated refrain, the Working Group has held that 'mere assertions by the Government that lawful procedures have been followed are not sufficient to rebut the source's allegations'.[46] Consequently, where the government disputes credible allegations by the source but fails to address specific points or provide details that it should know, the Working Group will typically accept the source's factual submissions.[47]

Alongside the increase in the number of categories of detention to include immigration-related detention and discriminatory detention, the expansion phase saw the Working Group explicitly express its approach to burdens and evidence and increasingly apply this in opinions. Nonetheless, questions of evidence continued to arise throughout this period, and became particularly prominent during the subsequent consolidation phase.

5.3.3 Phase 3: Consolidation (2019 Onwards)

Having engaged in an expansion phase from 2011, the Working Group has since 2019 entered what could be seen as a phase of consolidation.

People's Republic of Korea and China, WGAD opinion 81/2017, 26 December 2017, para. 23.

43 See, e.g., *Ramón Nsé Esono Ebalé* v. *Equatorial Guinea*, WGAD opinion 15/2018, 24 September 2018, para. 29; *Han and Young-joo Lee* v. *Republic of Korea*, WGAD opinion 22/2017, 30 May 2017, para. 74; *Musallam Mohamed Hamad alBarrak v. Kuwait*, WGAD opinion 20/2017, 18 July 2017, paras. 33 and 40; *Pongsak Sriboonpeng* v. *Thailand*, WGAD opinion 44/2016, 21 November 2016, paras. 25–27.

44 See, e.g., *Arash Sadeghi* v. *Islamic Republic of Iran*, WGAD opinion 19/2018, 24 May 2018, para. 27; *Nguyen Van Dai* v. *Viet Nam*, WGAD opinion 26/2017, 8 June 2017, para. 50; *Pongsak Sriboonpeng* v. *Thailand*, WGAD, para. 25; *Yu Shiwen* v. *China*, WGAD opinion 11/2016, 16 June 2016, para. 27 and *Befekadu Hailu and others* v. *Ethiopia*, WGAD opinion 10/2016, 14 June 2016, para. 41.

45 See further at Section 5.2.

46 WGAD, Report 2011, para 68.

47 See, e.g., *Issam Mohamed Tahar Al Barqaoui Al Uteibi* v. *Jordan*, WGAD opinion 18/2007, 22 November 2007.

This was marked by the issuance of revised Fact Sheet No. 26. It provides more details about the procedures followed by the Working Group and, significantly, adds an important new reference to discrimination as one of the major causes of arbitrary detention.[48] The Working Group's adversarial process has also progressed to the point where many states engage with this on a relatively regular basis, although not always in a timely or comprehensive manner.

During this consolidation phase, the major legal lines in the jurisprudence have been relatively settled and clear. For example, the Working Group has found detentions to be arbitrary when persons are placed incommunicado and/or without access to legal advice during significant periods of their detention;[49] or when the authorities detain a person participating in a peaceful protest and fail to demonstrate that the person was engaged in violence or any other activity falling under a permissible exception to the rights to freedom of expression and assembly.[50] These are instances which could be incorporated into UNTBs' approaches where relevant.

While a reasonably consistent substantive jurisprudence has developed, the Working Group's approach to evidence has received increasing focus in this phase. The Working Group has now largely settled its approach to evidence, particularly in terms of the burden, but has not definitively settled the standard it applies to weighing evidence. These and other issues that continue to arise during this current phase are analysed in detail in the following section.

5.4 Emerging Evidentiary Issues

With the Working Group having firmly established its approach to evidence over these three phases of its existence, several questions arise regarding associated tests, such as the heightened standard of review in certain cases, the use of digital and external materials as evidence and the evidentiary standards applied by the Working Group in its other functions beyond considering individual cases. Responses to these issues could be instructive for other human rights bodies, particularly UNTBs with adjudicative functions.

48 On 14 February 2024, the Revised Factsheet was officially published: OHCHR, Fact Sheet No. 26, Rev. 1: Working Group on Arbitrary Detention, 14 February 2024.

49 See, e.g., *Pham Doan Trang* v. *Viet Nam*, WGAD opinion 40/2021, 4 November 2021; *Mehmet Ali Öztürk* v. *United Arab Emirates*, WGAD opinion 51/2021, 8 February 2022.

50 See, e.g., *Ros Sokhet* v. *Cambodia,* WGAD opinion 75/2021, 27 January 2022; *Sharofiddin Gadoev* v. *Russian Federation and Tajikistan* (WGAD).

5.4.1 The Heightened Standard of Review

When claims involve certain rights or victims, the Working Group has often reiterated that it applies a 'heightened standard of review'.[51] This includes cases when the deprivation of liberty results from the exercise of fundamental rights and freedoms (category II)[52] or involves a discriminatory aspect or targeting of certain individuals, such as human rights defenders (category V).[53] Concerning the cases of human rights defenders, in particular, the Working Group has held that restrictions on their expression would be subject to 'particularly intense review'[54] and 'strict scrutiny',[55] adding that to detain a human rights defender because of their work would violate their rights to equality under the law.[56] The Working Group has also stated that this heightened review by international bodies is especially appropriate where there is a 'pattern of harassment' by national authorities targeting such individuals.[57]

In its 2017 Annual Report, the Working Group laid out how it determines whether a source has demonstrated a case of arbitrary

[51] The justification for this heightened standard of review is apparently derived from article 9, paragraph 3, of the Declaration on the Right and Responsibility of Individuals, Groups and Organs of Society to Promote and Protect Universally Recognized Human Rights and Fundamental Freedoms adopted by the General Assembly. It clarifies that it requires State parties to provide information that *directly* rebuts claims that human rights guarantees have been violated. For example, see *Nasrin Sotoudeh* (WGAD), para. 31, noting that '[a] mere listing up of the judgements and other decisions is not sufficient in this respect'. See also J. Genser, *Working Group on Arbitrary Detention*, pp. 153 and 177.

[52] See, e.g., *Aleksandr Viktorovich Bialatski* v. *Belarus*, WGAD opinion 39/2012, 23 November 2012, para. 45; *Thirumurugan Gandhi* v. *India*, WGAD opinion 88/2017, 23 January 2018, para. 25; *Chayapha Chokepornbudsri* v. *Thailand*, WGAD opinion 3/2018, 9 July 2018, para. 40; *Yamashiro Hiroji* (WGAD), para. 62.

[53] See, e.g., *Aleksandr Viktorovich Bialatski* (WGAD), para. 45; *Yamashiro Hiroji* (WGAD), para. 62; *Eskinder Nega* v. *Ethiopia*, WGAD opinion 62/2012, 9 August 2013, para. 39; *Nasrin Sotoudeh* (WGAD) para. 29; and *Đinh Thị Thu Thuỷ* v. *Viet Nam*, WGAD opinion 82/2021, 9 September 2022, para. 69. See also Genser, *Working Group on Arbitrary Detention*, p. 177.

[54] See, e.g., *Tran Duc Thach* v. *Viet Nam*, WGAD opinion 40/2022, 4 November 2022, para. 76; *Nguyen Ngoc Anh* v. *Viet Nam*, WGAD opinion 43/2022, 10 November 2022, para. 97; *Le Huu Minh Tuan* v. *Viet Nam*, WGAD opinion 11/2021, 7 June 2021, para. 79; *Pham Doan Trang* (WGAD), paras. 78–79.

[55] See *Haytham Fawzy Mohamden* v. *Egypt*, WGAD opinion 53/2022, 5 October 2022, para. 78; *Jagtar Singh Johal* v. *India*, WGAD opinion 80/2021, 4 May 2022, para. 105.

[56] See, e.g., *Muhammad Ismail* v. *Pakistan*, WGAD opinion 37/2021, 1 October 2021, para. 82.

[57] *Aleksandr Viktorovich Bialatski* (WGAD), para. 43; and *Nasrin Sotoudeh* (WGAD), para. 29.

deprivation of liberty on discriminatory grounds to the requisite prima facie standard.[58] In such cases, governments have the obligation to demonstrate that the detention is proportional and absolutely necessary and no other alternative measure is feasible on the basis of a legitimate state interest. Governments are also under the obligation to prove that the length and the overall conditions of custody are in full respect of international guarantees. In a similar vein, the Working Group has held that when individuals are detained under preventative detention, the government's burden of proof increases the longer the person is detained, which aligns with the HRC's position on the issue.[59] Given the synchrony between the Working Group and the HRC on this issue, it could be taken up by other UNTBs as a guide for their application of the law to the facts concerning potentially discriminatory detention (or any similar type of human rights violation).

However, based on its category V jurisprudence, it is not yet clear how the Working Group might take into account multiple, intersecting forms of discrimination, and whether this requires the government to rebut each alleged ground with evidence[60] or to demonstrate that the cumulative effect of multiple forms of discrimination did not result in arbitrary detention.[61] The Working Group could be more explicit in its analysis of what constitutes intersectional discrimination under international law and add significant value to its jurisprudence, as well as to the broader understanding of detention on discriminatory grounds.[62]

5.4.2 Digital Evidence and Digital Submissions

Another emerging issue is that of the Working Group's receipt and assessment of digital evidence. The Working Group requires information to be submitted digitally under its communications procedure but has not explicitly stated how it deals with the use and management of digital

[58] WGAD, Report of the Working Group on Arbitrary Detention (A/HRC/36/37), 19 July 2017, para. 48.

[59] See, e.g., *Salem Badi Dardasawi* v. *Israel*, WGAD opinion 86/2017, 18 December 2017, para. 31.

[60] The Working Group took a similar approach in *Ammar al Baluchi* v. *United States of America*, WGAD opinion No. 89/2017, 24 January 2018, para. 62.

[61] See Toomey, 'Detention on Discriminatory Grounds', p. 185.

[62] A. Traldi, 'The Recent Free Expression Jurisprudence of the Working Group on Arbitrary Detention', *Chicago Journal of International Law* 24.1 (2023): pp. 160–161.

evidence.[63] The Working Group's Model Questionnaire refers to the submission of documents but does not explicitly address the types of evidence formats that the Working Group may accept or how it uses and manages digital evidence.[64] In its practice, the Working Group has dealt with evidence and information in digital formats, including both scanned documents and originally electronic documents. However, questions that may arise concern how the Working Group evaluates and stores such evidence, in line with principles of data integrity, authenticity, confidentiality and quality, as well as the source's privacy where applicable.

In this respect, the Council of Europe's guidelines on electronic evidence in civil and administrative proceedings provide examples of good practices, including those aimed at assuring authenticity and avoiding falsification.[65] The Office of the High Commissioner for Human Rights (OHCHR's) submission form for other UN human rights special procedures also accepts digital evidence, and does not limit this to printable materials.[66] Furthermore, the Working Group on Enforced or Involuntary Disappearances (WGEID) is currently studying the use of new digital technologies, including digital evidence, in prosecutions.[67] It is expected that WGEID's study will contribute to developing the position of other UN human rights mechanisms in relation to the use of digital evidence in proceedings.

On the other hand, the UNTB online submission portal for individual communications only accepts certain file formats and is limited to printable materials.[68] Although this is a technical matter, it can result in restricting the ability of sources (claimants) to provide cogent evidence regarding human rights violations, such as contemporary videos and photos.

Substantively, digital evidence – such as video footage and social media posts – features frequently and with increasing significance in

[63] Digital evidence is understood here to mean 'any evidence derived from data contained in or produced by any device, the functioning of which depends on a software program or data stored on or transmitted over a computer system or network'. Council of Europe, 'Electronic Evidence in Civil and Administrative Procedures', 30 January 2019, https://rm.coe.int/guidelines-on-electronic-evidence-and-explanatory-memorandum/1680968ab5, 6.

[64] WGAD, Model Questionnaire, www.ohchr.org/en/special-procedures/wg-arbitrary-detention/complaints-and-urgent-appeals.

[65] Council of Europe, Electronic Evidence in Civil and Administrative Procedures.

[66] OHCHR, Submission of Information to Special Procedures.

[67] UNWGEID, Report of the Working Group on Enforced or Involuntary Disappearances (A/HRC/51/31), 2022, para 37.

[68] OHCHR, Submission of an individual communication to a UN Treaty Body.

international criminal trials and international human rights investigations.[69] The Working Group is increasingly confronted with such materials, particularly in the context of protests, where footage can help provide insights which written materials may not capture or effectively convey. However, the Working Group has not adopted a specific approach regarding digital materials to date. Other UNTBs have also not yet adapted their formal procedures in this respect. As digital evidence becomes more ubiquitous, the UNTBs and the Working Group will have to become more accustomed in practice and procedure to accommodating their use.

5.4.3 Use of External Materials in Determining Cases

The Working Group engages in independent fact-checking under its regular communications procedure. Though it has repeated that its role is not to substitute itself for a domestic fact-finder, it does consider various reputable sources in its evaluation of factual narratives by parties.[70] Beyond referencing its jurisprudence and findings from country visits, the Working Group appears to increasingly reference third-party information for both procedural and substantive purposes.

Technically, there are no explicit limitations in this respect. The Working Group may reference reports by other UN bodies engaging on the same or similar cases, or other credible sources about relevant developments on a specific case.[71] This may include referencing any joint communications from UN special procedure mandate holders and related press coverage to highlight the urgency of the situation, as in the case concerning the Government of Malaysia's treatment of Mr. Khan.[72] For substantive reasons, the Working Group may reference authoritative sources evidencing historic discrimination and emerging patterns of human rights violations involving arbitrary deprivation of

[69] M. Gillett and W. Fan, 'Expert Evidence and Digital Open Source Information: Bringing Online Evidence to the Courtroom', *Journal of International Criminal Justice* 21. 4 (2023): 661–693. Even the International Court of Justice has seen posts from social media used as key items of evidence, in its recent provisional measures order in *South Africa* v. *Israel*, ICJ, pending.

[70] Genser, *Working Group on Arbitrary Detention*, Part III.

[71] See, e.g., *Adilur Rahman Khan* (WGAD); *Thirumurugan Gandhi* (WGAD); *Walid El Batal* (WGAD); *Hamid Soudad* (WGAD), Avis 4/2023, 10 May 2023.

[72] *Adilur Rahman Khan* (WGAD), para. 29.

liberty.[73] As a case in point, the Working Group has identified an emerging pattern involving the arbitrary deprivation of liberty of dual nationals in Iran, referencing the findings and reasoning of the Special Rapporteur on the situation of human rights in the Islamic Republic of Iran.[74] More recently, the Working Group cited the latest findings from the Human Rights Council's Universal Periodic Review and other reports related to Algeria to support its reasoning on the discriminatory detention of Mr Soudad.[75]

This use of external materials in determining cases is consistent with the Working Group's flexible approach to evidence, based on assessing the 'totality of the circumstances'.[76] It also demonstrates that despite its specific mandate, the Working Group sees its work as essentially complementary to other international justice-seeking efforts, both within the UN system and beyond.

UNTBs could adhere to the same approach. Beyond enhancing fact-finding, this has the potential to contribute to the Working Group and UNTBs' efforts to better coordinate within the UN system. Furthermore, it can foster cohesion and consistency across the law, institutions, and practice of the contemporary human rights regime. Finally, this can lead to significant advances in specific cases and help serve the broader goal of harmonious jurisprudential development in the field of human rights.

5.4.4 Standards Applied During the Working Group's Own Fact-Finding

As with its opinions, the Working Group has not yet fully addressed what standard of proof it applies during country visits for fact-finding. The Working Group's Methods of Work and Terms of Reference for Country Visits are both silent in this sense. However, the Code of Conduct for Special Procedures Mandate holders of the Human Rights Council states that mandate holders shall 'always seek to establish the facts, based on

[73] See, e.g., *Nazanin Zaghari-Ratcliffe* (WGAD); *Tashi Wangchuk* v. *China*, WGAD opinion 69/2017, 7 December 2017; *Thirumurugan Gandhi* (WGAD); *Bakri Mohammed Abdul Latif and others* v. *Egypt*, WGAD opinion 28/2018, 30 May 2018 and *Abbas Haiji Al-Hassan* (WGAD). See also C. Roberts, 'Reversing the Burden of Proof Before Human Rights Bodies', *The International Journal of Human Rights* 25 (2021): 1682–1703, 1682.

[74] *Nazanin Zaghari-Ratcliffe* (WGAD), para. 48.

[75] *Hamid Soudad* (WGAD), para. 98.

[76] See, e.g., *Julian Assange* v. *Sweden and the United Kingdom of Great Britain and Northern Ireland*, WGAD opinion 54/2015, 6 April 2016, para. 91.

objective, reliable information emanating from relevant credible sources, that they have duly cross-checked to the best extent possible'.[77] It further states that mandate holders shall 'rely on objective and dependable facts based on evidentiary standards that are appropriate to the non-judicial character of the reports and conclusions they are called upon to draw up'.[78] A similar provision is included in the Manual of Operations of the Special Procedures of the Human Rights Council.[79] The Manual further requires mandate holders to assess the reliability of the information and of the person(s) providing the information collected during interviews with victims and witnesses of human rights violations.[80] Overall, this may suggest that the Working Group should apply a standard of proof that is deemed appropriate on a case-by-case basis.

A review of recent country visit reports indicates that the Working Group issues its conclusions on the basis of having more evidence supporting findings than contradicting them.[81] For example, when concluding that there are discrepancies between domestic legal provisions in principle and practice, the Working Group relies on its own observations and the testimonies collected during a visit, sometimes corroborated by third-party reports, as reason enough to disprove information shared by official authorities in the country under consideration.[82] Yet, in some cases, the Working Group appears to apply a higher standard of proof by looking for clear and convincing evidence – that is, significantly more evidence supporting a finding and limited information suggesting the contrary. For example, the Working Group has concluded that some facilities visited were not places of deprivation of liberty on the basis of its interviews with both the officials in charge and the residents in such

[77] Human Rights Council, Code of Conduct for Special Procedures Mandate holders of the Human Rights Council (A/HRC/RES/5/2), Article 6(a).

[78] Human Rights Council, Code of Conduct for Special Procedures Mandate holders of the Human Rights Council, Article 6(a) and Article 8(c).

[79] OHCHR, Manual of Operations of the Special Procedures of the Human Rights Council, August 2008, para. 24.

[80] OHCHR, Manual of Operations of the Special Procedures of the Human Rights Council, para. 73.

[81] The review included reports from country visits to the following countries (in chronological order): Azerbaijan, the United States of America, Argentina, Sri Lanka, Hungary, Bhutan, Qatar, Greece and Maldives.

[82] See, e.g., reports of visits to the USA (A/HRC/36/37/Add.2), Sri Lanka (A/HRC/39/45/Add.2) and Greece (A/HRC/45/16/Add.1).

facilities.[83] In other cases, the Working Group has concluded that it was 'not clear' whether the information gathered amounted to arbitrary deprivation of liberty and invited stakeholders to submit further information.[84] This may impact the uptake of the Working Group's findings.[85] Therefore, the Working Group should consider the application of a set standard of proof and clarify its evidentiary considerations for country visits. It should also address its standard of proof at the outset of its country visit reports, following its general remarks about the visits' programmes.

In this regard, it should be noted that a balance of probabilities standard (often expressed as 'reasonable to conclude' and equivalent to a 'preponderance of evidence', or 'convincing evidence' standard) charts a careful course for human rights monitoring and litigation. This standard is likely to be the most coherent standard of proof to apply in most circumstances, because of the inherent limitations of fact-finding mechanisms coupled with the interests at stake.[86]

The balance of probabilities standard fits well, as it must naturally be higher than the preliminary prima facie threshold but lower than a criminal standard of beyond reasonable doubt. Regarding the latter, victims and complainants should not be held to the same level of proof as police and prosecution services, as they do not have the same access to investigative materials and techniques.[87] The balance of probabilities standard matches that applicable in many types of civil claims. It is achievable for complainants, particularly if evidentiary presumptions are adopted, such as not requiring the complainant to produce a document or piece of information to which they would not reasonably have access. It is nevertheless also a robust standard capable of providing some insulation against reaching incorrect and ill-founded conclusions,

[83] See, e.g., reports of visits to Qatar (A/HRC/45/16/Add.2) and Bhutan (A/HRC/42/39/Add.1).

[84] See, e.g., report of visit to Qatar (A/HRC/45/16/Add.2), Argentina (A/HRC/39/45/Add.1) and Sri Lanka (A/HRC/39/45/Add.2).

[85] S. Wilkinson, *Standards of Proof in International Humanitarian and Human Rights Fact-Finding and Inquiry Missions* (Geneva: Geneva Academy of International Humanitarian Law and Human Rights, 2014).

[86] Wilkinson, *Standards of Proof*, 4.

[87] For similar observations, M.-B. Dembour, 'Beyond Reasonable Doubt at Its Worst but Also at its Potential Best: Dissecting *Ireland v the United Kingdom*'s No-Torture Finding', *European Convention on Human Rights Law Review* 4 (2024): 375–425, 381.

which would open human rights bodies up to claims of inconsistency, selectivity, opacity and unconscious biases.[88]

Hence, explicitly adopting the balance of probabilities standard would place the Working Group on a defensible footing, while ensuring that its approach is transparent. Similarly, other human rights bodies, such as UNTBs, could benefit from the combination of reliability and flexibility provided by this evidentiary standard.

5.5 Impact of the Working Group's Changing Approach to Evidence

There are a number of indicia to gauge the impact of the Working Group's approach to evidence, namely compliance with decisions, state responses and the responses of other third parties such as UNTBs and regional human rights courts. These indicia will be examined in the subsections below.

5.5.1 Compliance

In the context of the Working Group, compliance is primarily an issue of releases of arbitrarily detained persons, though the Working Group also typically calls for compensation to be afforded to them. Fundamentally, it is the release of persons found to have been arbitrarily detained which signals States' commitment to redressing arbitrary detention. Historically, compliance has been hard to measure. However, a rough evaluation can be made from the fact that in the 2022 Annual Report, the Working Group noted that it had learned of approximately 22 individuals subject to its opinions being released in the reporting period, during which it had issued 88 opinions.[89] In 2023, there were 38 releases and 77 opinions issued, a significant increase on the year before.[90] In preceding years, that rate appears relatively stable. This only gives an approximate assessment of compliance, as there are also forms of implementation which

[88] See Viljoen, 'Fact-Finding', pp. 55–56 and 77–78 (referring to examples where the Working Group was (incorrectly) accused of including 'inaccuracies' and 'false facts' in its reports).

[89] See WGAD, Report of the Working Group on Arbitrary Detention (A/HRC/54/51), 2023, para.12. Note that many of the releasees were subjects of opinions issued prior to 2022, and so only an approximate estimate of compliance can be ascertained.

[90] See WGAD, Report of the Working Group on Arbitrary Detention (A/HRC/57/44), 2024, para. 11.

are less easily quantifiable, such as adhering to Working Group recommendations to bring domestic laws into line with international human rights law.[91] Nonetheless, broadly speaking, the rate of implementation of the Working Group's findings could be roughly seen as hovering somewhere around 20–40 per cent. In that light, the Working Group's compliance rate falls broadly within the range of UNTBs with individual complaint mandates, which Ullman and von Staden have measured as between nineteen and thirty-nine percent.[92]

By comparison, for regional bodies, there appears to be great variation in the rate of compliance: around 50–60 per cent for the (ECtHR) but only 6–14 per cent for judgments of the Inter-American Court of Human Rights.[93] More broadly, at the ICJ, which is increasingly being confronted with human rights-related claims, the compliance rate has been 49 per cent for provisional measures orders, but seems to have fallen in recent years as it takes on more contentious cases.[94]

[91] See, e.g.,, Letter on Opinion 40/2018 from the Republic of Korea, 22 February 2019 (indicating in response to the Working Group's recommendations of Opinion 40/2018, that the Korean courts had since changed their interpretation of the governing legislation regarding detention of conscientious objectors).

[92] A. J. Ullmann and A. von Staden, 'A Room Full of "Views": Introducing a New Dataset to Explore Compliance with the Decisions of the UN Human Rights Treaty Bodies' Individual Complaints Procedures', *Journal of Conflict Resolution* 68 (2023): 534–561.

[93] See C. Giorgetti, 'What Happens After a Judgment Is Given? Judgment Compliance and the Performance of International Courts and Tribunals' in T. Squatrito, O. Young, A. Follesdal and G. Ulfstein (eds.), *The Performance of International Courts and Tribunals* (Cambridge: Cambridge University Press, 2024), pp. 324–350, 343; D. Hawkins and W. Jacoby, 'Partial Compliance: A Comparison of the European and Inter-American Courts for Human Rights', *Journal of International Law and International Relations* 6 (2010): 51-59. See also A. von Staden and A. J. Ullmann, 'Seeking Overlap and Redundancy in Human Rights Protection: Reputation, Consistency and the Acceptance of the UN Human Rights Treaties' Individual Communications Procedures', *The International Journal of Human Rights* 26 (2022): 1476–1502, 1478 ('it is at least partly driven by states' intention to maintain and consolidate a reputation as a sincere committer; abstaining from such commitment when it is expected may, by contrast, subject states to charges of inconsistency'). It is finally worth noting that in her comparative analysis of the degree of compliance which the judgments of the European and Inter-American Courts of Human Rights attracted, Dembour notes that the Inter-American Court is typically more demanding than the European Court in what it requires from states, in turn reducing Inter-American compliance rates: *When Humans Become Migrants: Study of the European Court with an Inter-American Counterpoint* (Oxford: Oxford University Press, 2015), 340–344.

[94] See M. Alexianu, 'Provisional, but Not (Always) Pointless: Compliance with ICJ Provisional Measures', *EJIL: Talk* (blogpost dated 3 November 2023). Regarding its final judgments, compliance appears to be much higher than 50 percent, with instances of non-compliance generally being the infrequent exception: H. L. Jones, 'Why Comply?

States have indicated that the quality, coherence, and correctness of human rights bodies' decisions are key factors in encouraging compliance.[95] Achieving rigorous standards in these respects is heavily reliant on access to reliable evidence. If the materials on which the Working Group must base its assessments are unreliable and lacking in probity, then it will be difficult to reach any firm factual conclusions on which to superimpose the legal standards governing arbitrary detention. For this reason, the Working Group has increasingly sought to tighten its approach to evidence, to ensure cogency and consistency in its findings. A similar rigour on the part of the UNTBs will assist in enhancing the legitimacy, acceptance and impact of their determinations.

5.5.2 *State Responses*

Another indicator from which to gauge the uptake of the Working Group's opinions, including reactions to its approach to evidence, is via state responses. On a number of occasions, the Working Group has been confronted with States questioning its determinations.

For example, in the context of the Working Group's 2002 country visit to Australia, disputed issues ranged from legal questions concerning the incorporation of international human rights law into Australian domestic law, to motivational questions concerning the purpose behind Australia's immigration policy,[96] to specific factual issues, such as whether detainees were generally handcuffed when leaving immigration facilities.[97] The Australian Government accused the Working Group of including 'inaccuracies' and 'incorrect' statements in its country visit report, making assumptions and inferences, and reporting unsubstantiated allegations.[98] The Working Group responded by noting that its information is received from a variety of sources and that it establishes

An Analysis of Trends in Compliance with Judgments of the International Court of Justice Since Nicaragua', *Chicago-Kent International and Comparative Law* 12 (2010): 58–98, Appendix C.

95 See N. Pillay, Strengthening the United Nations Human Rights Treaty Body System: A Report by the United Nations High Commissioner for Human Rights (OHCHR, June 2012), p. 8.

96 Australia took issue with the Working Group's observation that talks with Government officials indicated that one of the goals of the system of mandatory detention was to discourage would-be immigrants from entering without a visa.

97 UN Doc. E/CN.4/2003/G/22, 10 January 2003, Annex III ('Australian Objections'), pp. 7–8, 10–11.

98 Australian Objections; Viljoen, 'Fact-Finding', p. 55.

facts in 'as objective and impartial' a manner as possible in the limited time available.[99]

This exchange highlights the subtle but important difference between the Working Group's information-gathering function and its quasi-judicial individual complaint function. Information-gathering, such as through country visits, is an open and evolutive process which culminates in recommendations.[100] Conversely, the consideration of individual complaints has a more judicial character. The submissions of the parties are compared, before the Working Group ultimately sets out in its disposition whether violations of the relevant legal instruments have occurred. These approaches adhere to the Special Procedures Code of Conduct, which, as noted above, provides that in their fact-finding activities, Special Mandate holders should seek objective, reliable information from relevant credible sources and cross-check them as far as possible.[101] The Code of Conduct also specifies that Special Mandate holders' information-gathering functions have a distinct character from the quasi-judicial consideration of individual complaints, such as those conducted by the Working Group.[102]

In the context of the Working Group's individual complaints procedures, its approach to determining facts has also been challenged on occasion. For example, the United States of America accused the Working Group of reaching conclusions which were 'unsubstantiated', based on 'false facts' and a 'fundamental misunderstanding of our law',[103] in a 2002 case concerning the detention of two Indian nationals.[104] However, the United States Government had only provided general arguments which 'merely described the current procedure under

[99] UN Doc. E/CN.4/2003/G/22, 10 January 2003, Annex II ('Working Group Response'); Viljoen, 'Fact-Finding', p. 55.

[100] For example, the Working Group can re-visit a country and in doing so will seek to update the views and recommendations it presented in its earlier visit(s). This occurred in relation to Mexico, which the Working Group visited in 2002 and then in 2023; WGAD, Preliminary Findings from its visit to Mexico, 29 September 2003, p. 1.

[101] See fn. 77 above referring to Human Rights Council, *Code of Conduct for Special Procedures Mandate holders of the Human Rights Council*, 18 June 2007, Article 6(a).

[102] Human Rights Council, *Code of Conduct for Special Procedures Mandate holders of the Human Rights Council*, Article 8(c).

[103] Permanent Mission of the United States of America, Letter to the United Nations Office at Geneva addressed to the Secretariat of the Commission on Human Rights (E/CN.4/2003/G/72), 7 April 2003; Viljoen 'Fact-Finding', pp. 78–79.

[104] *Ayub Ali Khan and Azmath Jaweed* v. *United States of America*, WGAD opinion 21/2002, 3 December 2002, para. 1.

United States law without providing any information on the individuals in question'.[105] Ultimately, according to the Working Group, 'the misunderstanding seem[ed] to be rather on the American side',[106] as the State only presented specific and detailed information regarding the case after the deadline for its response had elapsed and after the Working Group had rendered its opinion. Through this adherence to a structured procedure, the Working Group insulates itself against inaccuracies and unfounded critiques. Both parties are given an opportunity to present their views in line with the principle of *audi alteram partem* (each side must be heard), but with time limits designed to facilitate the efficiency and finalisation of proceedings.

In an example illustrating the role of time limits, the Government of Cameroon expressed its dissatisfaction that the source's submissions were summarised in thirty-two paragraphs in a 2016 opinion, whereas the Government's submissions were limited to just one paragraph.[107] However, the Government overlooked that it had submitted its response one month late, thus violating the Working Group's adversarial procedure.[108] Nonetheless, the reference to the Government having 'duly' submitted its response may have caused confusion, and is not a term the Working Group would typically use in present times to describe a late-filed submission. Consequently, whereas the Working Group's adherence to its procedures helped to insulate it in this specific case, it highlights the need to ensure clear messaging in subsequent opinions, which has been the case.

Following the issuance of a Working Group opinion in 2019, finding that Rwanda had arbitrarily detained two women, the Government complained that the Working Group had reached erroneous conclusions and was 'fundamentally flawed'.[109] In this case as well, the Government failed to provide a timely response, meaning the Working Group could

[105] *Ayub Ali Khan and Azmath Jaweed,* (WGAD), para. 12; Viljoen, 'Fact-finding' (2004), pp. 78–79.

[106] Viljoen, 'Fact-Finding', pp. 78–79.

[107] OHCHR website, Cameroon, 'Government Response in Relation to Opinion 22/2016', 27 January 2017.

[108] See *Marafa Hamidou Yaya* v. *Cameroon*, WGAD opinion 22/2016, 1 July 2016, paras. 37–38. The government had asked for a 60-day extension but the Working Group was only able to grant it the maximum 30-day extension in line with its Methods of Work.

[109] Government response in relation to WGAD Opinion 24/2019 (Rwanda), 17 June 2019 (https://www.ohchr.org/sites/default/files/Documents/Issues/Detention/Opinions/Rwanda_reply__2019_06_19_14_29_44.pdf).

not place as much weight on the response as if it were timely filed,[110] in line with the established jurisprudence.[111] Nonetheless, the Working Group assessed the specific allegations and found some had been established and others not. In particular, the Working Group dismissed the claims of discrimination based on a pattern of harassment due to a lack of information indicating a connection with the State.[112] Again, this exchange highlights the importance of the Working Group's rigorous adherence to its adversarial procedures, particularly in relation to the receipt and weighing of evidence. The Working Group's adversarial procedure, in which both parties have the opportunity to submit their views, does not make it infallible but does insulate it against allegations of inaccuracy and lacking objectivity.

5.5.3 *Responses of UNTBs and Regional Human Rights Bodies*

A further means of assessing the Working Group's approach to evidence is via the response of external entities such as UNTBs and the regional human rights courts. Based on the Working Group's well-developed approaches to evidence, its views are cited by regional human rights courts. For example, the ECtHR has mentioned the Working Group's opinions or the reports of the country visit in many cases,[113] and considers the analysis of the Working Group when the same case is under the consideration of the Working Group.[114]A highly pertinent example is the ECtHR judgment in *Ibrahimov and Mammadov* v. *Azerbaijan.*[115] In this case, the Working Group had met the applicant in the Baku pre-trial detention facility on its country visit to Azerbaijan.

[110] See *Diane Shima Rwigara and Adeline Rwigara* v. *Rwanda*, WGAD opinion 24/2019, 2 May 2019, paras. 31, 36 ('the Government chose to submit its response late, knowing the consequences of such a late submission. In addition, the Government, in its late response, chose not to provide any supporting evidence.').

[111] See, e.g., *Do Nam Trung* v. *Viet Nam*, WGAD opinion 86/2022, 18 November 2022, para. 26.

[112] See, e.g., *Diane Shima Rwigara and Adeline Rwigara* (WGAD), para. 46.

[113] See, e.g., *Mohammadi* v. *Austria*, ECtHR, 71932/12, Judgment, 3 July 2014; *Rashad Hasanov and others* v. *Azerbaijan*, ECtHR, 2059/16, Judgment, 7 June 2018; *Abdolkhani and Karimina* v. *Turkey*, ECtHR, 30471/08, Judgment, 22 September 2009; *Aliyev* v. *Azerbaijan*, ECtHR, 68762/14 and 71200/14, Judgment, 20 September 2018.

[114] See, e.g., *Hilal Mammadov* v. *Azerbaijan*, ECtHR, 81553/12, Judgment, 4 February 2016; *Kavala* v. *Turkey*, ECtHR, 28749/18, Judgment, 10 December 2019.

[115] *Ibrahimov and Mammadov* v. *Azerbaijan*, ECtHR, 63571/16, 74143/16, 2883/17 et al., Judgment, 13 February 2020. See also *Ilnseher* v. *Germany*, ECtHR, 10211/12 and 27505/14, Judgment, 4 December 2018, para. 79.

The ECtHR quoted the statement of the Working Group that it 'observed what seemed to be physical sequels of such treatment'.[116] The ECtHR used this statement in consideration of the credibility of the applicant's claim. Noting that the claim was supported by the Working Group's report,[117] the ECtHR found that 'there is prima facie evidence in favour of the applicants' version of events and that the burden of proof shifts to the Government to provide a satisfactory and convincing explanation'.[118]

The above shines an important light on how the Working Group's approach to evidence affects its impact. This can provide insights for the UNTBs as well. Whereas compliance rates provide a form of quantitative indicia, States' responses provide a more qualitative explanation as to why certain determinations are well received, and whether the issues relate to procedure or substance or a mix of the two. The analysis demonstrates that the quality and consistency of fact-finding conducted by quasi-judicial human rights bodies such as the Working Group and the UNTBs is a major factor impacting on competent authorities' uptake of their determinations. Additionally, the use of UNTB and Working Group findings by regional human rights bodies is important for the cross-fertilisation of approaches to evidence, as the Working Group itself has not.[119]

5.6 Conclusions

Over the three phases of its operations, the Working Group has elaborated a clear but flexible approach to evidence and burdens. Since it explicitly spelled out its approach to burdens and evidence in its 2011 Annual Report, the Working Group's formulation has been increasingly repeated and refined to the point where it has become essentially a uniform component in its opinions. This contributes to the legal consistency and predictability of its opinions. Nonetheless, issues regarding the Working Group's approach in cases involving heightened review, digital evidence, materials from external sources and its own fact-finding are increasingly emerging as factors to address during this consolidation phase of its operations. Ensuring consistency is not just important for the coherence of the Working Group's jurisprudence, but also for the

[116] *Ibrahimov and Mammadov* v. *Azerbaijan*, ECtHR, para. 35.
[117] *Ibrahimov*, ECtHR, para. 92.
[118] *Ibrahimov*, ECtHR, para. 93.
[119] On cross-fertilization, see WGAD, Report 2011, para. 66.

uptake and implementation of its decisions and recommendations by governments which hold persons in detention. In line with Helfer and Slaughter's observations regarding the quality of legal reasoning as a controllable means of inducing adherence to human rights rulings, mechanisms established to provide quasi-judicial human rights determinations must accentuate the consistency and cogency of their outputs, including 'the legal language itself: the language of reasoned interpretation, logical deduction, systemic and temporal coherence'.[120]

In relation to adherence to its determinations and recommendations for redress, the Working Group faces considerable challenges. This is highlighted by comparison with other international bodies. For example, unlike the ICJ, the Working Group's jurisdiction is not based on the consent of the relevant government(s) to its proceedings, which generally can be expected to increase compliance rates.[121] Accordingly, compliance is far more dependent on the quality and persuasiveness of the Working Group's assessment and opinions and the perceived fairness of its procedures. Prior consent to the bodies' jurisdiction (as exists for the UNTBs) is a factor which should naturally lead to higher compliance rates. However, the quality of the body's issuances and the reasoning therein will be important factors for those advocating for greater uptake of the quasi-judicial human rights bodies' decisions. As Giorgetti has noted: 'If the losing party finds that the substantive part of the judgment is understandable and that the court listened to its arguments, it will make it easier to comply.'[122] The development of a consistent, coherent and predictable procedure during the three phases of the Working Group's existence enhances the persuasiveness of the position it arrives at in specific cases while at the same time raising the reputational costs inherent in ignoring its determinations.

This is particularly important for the Working Group's cases, where there is typically a vast power and resource gap between the government and the detained person. Adhering to the Working Group's calls to release the person and provide reparation will largely come down to the relevant government's acceptance of the validity of the reasoning

[120] Helfer and Slaughter 'Toward a Theory of Effective Supranational Adjudication', p. 318, referring to J. Weiler, 'A Quiet Revolution: The European Court of Justice and Its Interlocutors', *Comparative Political Studies* 26 (1994): 510–534, 521.

[121] See C. Schulte, *Compliance with Decisions of the International Court of Justice* (Oxford: Oxford University Press, 2004), pp. 403–410. C.f. Giorgetti, 'What Happens After a Judgment Is Given?', p. 343.

[122] Giorgetti, 'What Happens?', pp. 347–348.

behind the determination, along with individual factors regarding the detained person and the nature of the crimes for which they may have been arrested.

Moreover, like the UNTBs, the Working Group does not have a direct procedure enabling it to send cases to the United Nations Security Council (UNSC) for enforcement. Efforts to enforce ICJ judgments via the UNSC can be vetoed by any of the permanent five members, as occurred with the Court's judgments in the *Nicaragua* case, for example.[123] However, for the vast majority of States in the world, the mere possibility of being brought before the UNSC for not complying with an ICJ decision is a strong compliance pull factor. In theory, the Working Group could report a lack of compliance to the Human Rights Council, which in turn could report this to the United Nations General Assembly. In practice, though, this would rarely be done, particularly in light of debates over the bindingness of the Working Group's opinions.[124] This observation highlights the relevance of formal enforcement structures attached to human rights adjudicative bodies, as well as the impact of a rigorous approach to evidence and the law on improving implementation prospects.

Bearing in mind these external comparisons, the Working Group's operations can serve as a canary in the coal mine for emerging evidentiary issues which are increasingly becoming important for human rights litigation. As the Working Group continues to engage with the problem of arbitrary detention and build its credibility in the international human rights community, it may consider implementing the following recommendations:

1) First, the Working Group should consider a more explicit elucidation of the heightened review test and state whether this impacts factual determinations, particularly in category V (discrimination) cases, and particularly when intersectional issues arise.

123 Giorgetti, 'What Happens?'

124 See E. D. Redondo, 'Rethinking the Legal Foundations of Control in International Human Rights Law—The Case of Special Procedures', *Netherlands Quarterly of Human Rights* 29 (2011): 261–288, 283 and 286; J. M. Genser and M. K. Winterkorn-Meikle, 'The Intersection of Politics and International Law: The United Nations Working Group on Arbitrary Detention in Theory and in Practice' *Columbia Human Rights Law Review* 39 (2008): 687–756; A. Mazzinghy, 'Please, Set Me Free! The Right to Challenge an Unlawful Detention: Scrutinizing the Practice of the United Nations Working Group on Arbitrary Detention', *Perth International Law Journal* 5 (2020): 63–115, 84–85. See also Toomey, 'Detention on Discriminatory Grounds'.

2) Second, the Working Group should consider including a plain-language explanation of its approach to evidence and the standards and burdens it applies and should make this information available on its website and any other relevant official communications, as well as its model questionnaire. This will help individuals, NGOs, governments and other actors make the best use of the complaints and urgent appeals procedure. It may also clarify whether the Working Group applies the same test for fact-finding during country visits as it does during the assessment of individual complaints.
3) Third, the Working Group should explicitly set out the balance of probabilities standard as the approach it applies to individual cases and to its broader fact-finding functions, including during country visits.
4) Fourth, the Working Group should consider its specific approach to digital evidence, including what type of digital evidence the Working Group accepts, and how it evaluates and stores it. This should align with principles of data integrity, authenticity, confidentiality and quality, as well as the sources' privacy, where applicable.

Implementing these recommendations would allow the Working Group to gain an even greater acceptance as an authoritative international arbiter and make an even greater contribution to the global effort of protecting individuals from arbitrary detention.

Over four decades ago, renowned human rights expert Louis Henkin claimed that 'almost all nations observe almost all principles of international law and almost all of their obligations almost all of the time'.[125] While that was debatable at the time, it is clear that since then, compliance with international law has not become universal, and if anything, has deteriorated in many respects. Unfortunately, the field of human rights has not been spared this fate. Nonetheless, compliance can be achieved in many instances, making it all the more important that human rights bodies address the factors within their control. One of these is the rigour and consistency applied to assessing factual claims. In this respect, the Working Group's approach to evidence highlights a robust and dependable methodology, which is sufficiently flexible to account for the wide variety of cases it receives, while also being clear in its core parameters in most respects. However, a close examination of the Working Group's approach to evidence highlights areas in need of

[125] L. Henkin, *How Nations Behave* (New York: Columbia University Press, 1979), p. 47.

further clarification, as well as specific challenges on the horizon, regarding which adjustments have been suggested in this chapter. Through an ongoing assessment and refinement of its approach to evidence, the Working Group can provide a model for other human rights bodies, including UNTBs, to examine and potentially utilise in their own important efforts to universalise human rights compliance.

Select Bibliography

Connors, J. and S. Shah, 'United Nations' in D. Moeckli, S. Shah and S. Sivakumaran (eds.), *International Human Rights Law,* 4th edn. (Oxford: Oxford University Press, 2022), pp. 385–428.

Genser, J. *The UN Working Group on Arbitrary Detention: Commentary and Guide to Practice* (Cambridge: Cambridge University Press, 2019).

Gillett, M. and W. Fan, 'Expert Evidence and Digital Open Source Information: Bringing Online Evidence to the Courtroom', *Journal of International Criminal Justice* 21(4) (2023): 661–693.

Gillett, M., Y. Karukaya and M. Marzotto, 'Reconciling the Dual-Faceted Mandates of Quasi-Judicial Human Rights Bodies: The Working Group on Arbitrary Detention's *Prima Facie* Approach to Evidence', *Human Rights Law Review* 24(1) (2024): 1–25.

Giorgetti, C. 'What Happens After a Judgment Is Given? Judgment Compliance and the Performance of International Courts and Tribunals' in T. Squatrito, O. Young, A. Follesdal and G. Ulfstein (eds.), *The Performance of International Courts and Tribunals* (Cambridge: Cambridge University Press, 2024), pp. 324–350.

Schulte, C. *Compliance with Decisions of the International Court of Justice* (Oxford: Oxford University Press, 2004).

Toomey, L. 'Detention on Discriminatory Grounds: An Analysis of the Jurisprudence of the United Nations Working Group on Arbitrary Detention', *Columbia Human Rights Law Review* 50(1) (2018–2019): 185–282.

Ullmann, A. J. and von A. Staden, 'A Room Full of "Views": Introducing a New Dataset to Explore Compliance with the Decisions of the UN Human Rights Treaty Bodies' Individual Complaints Procedures', *Journal of Conflict Resolution* 68(2–3) (2024): 534–561.

Viljoen, F. 'Fact-Finding by UN Human Rights Complaints Bodies: Analysis and Suggested Reforms', *Max Planck Yearbook of United Nations Law* 8(1) (2004): 49–100.

Wilkinson, S. *Standards of Proof in International Humanitarian and Human Rights Fact-Finding and Inquiry Missions* (Geneva: Geneva Academy of International Humanitarian Law and Human Rights, 2014).

PART III

Developing Evidentiary Techniques Capable of Holding States Accountable

6

It's All Been Done?

Individual Communications, the Exhaustion Rule and a New Methodology Expanding and Evidencing Domestic Barriers to Justice

MEGHAN CAMPBELL*

6.1 Introduction

The application of admissibility criteria for the individual communication procedure of the UN treaty bodies (UNTBs) is not a topic that has received much attention. In 2021, however, international headlines did report on the inadmissibility of a communication which youth climate activists had lodged with the UN Committee on the Rights of the Child (CRC Committee). The authors had argued that by failing to address climate change, various states had breached their rights under the Convention on the Rights of the Child (CRC).[1] The CRC Committee was sympathetic to the merits of the claim,[2] but found the communication inadmissible for failure to exhaust domestic remedies. No domestic proceedings had been initiated. Why local actions had not been pursued is not entirely clear, but one may hypothesise on potential barriers to justice, as adolescents typically do not have the funds required to bring this expensive type of litigation. The youth climate activists argued before the CRC Committee that they should have been exempt from the requirement to exhaust as domestic remedies were too slow and ill-suited to the claim,

* This chapter could not have been done without the amazing research assistance from Apeksha Gandhi. Thank you to the editors Marie-Bénédicte Dembour, Deborah Casalin and Cornelia Klocker for all their brilliant insights and support.

[1] *Sacchi et al.* v. *Argentina*, CRC/C/88/D/104/2019, 22 September 2021.

[2] M. Wewerinke-Singh, 'Between Cross-Border Obligations and Domestic Remedies: CRC Committee Decision on *Sacchi v Argentina*', *Oxford Human Rights Hub* (blogpost dated 21 October 2021).

particularly the urgent need for international cooperation.[3] The CRC Committee disagreed. Its rejection of the communication brings to the fore overlooked tensions in the individual communications procedure. Which types of barriers to domestic justice should be considered when assessing whether the requirement to exhaust domestic remedies should be lifted? Should this assessment be sensitive to the circumstances of the individual and institutional structures, as well the political, economic and sociocultural realities that shape the ability to access domestic forums? How should authors evidence that they were prevented from obtaining domestic justice?

This chapter argues that the UNTBs must take a generous approach to the exhaustion rule both in determining whether an exemption is warranted and in how individuals evidence the futility of pursuing domestic remedies. To do otherwise would compound the failures of the domestic justice system at the international level. To achieve this normative aim, the chapter proposes an analytical frame for the exhaustion assessment that is grounded in authors' individual identities and experiences while being attentive to how these identities and experiences are connected to systemic inequality and broader political, economic, and sociocultural realities. The individual-centred and contextual nature of the assessment positively influences the proof required to demonstrate obstacles to domestic justice, by recognising that producing evidence can be shaped by an array of identities, factors and structures.

In adopting this generous approach to admissibility, the treaty bodies will be fulfilling not only the aims of the individual communication procedure but the very core purpose of the exhaustion rule. Individuals are required to pursue local remedies to respect state sovereignty and the subsidiary role of international justice. States must be given an opportunity to address the alleged violation of human rights before a UNTB weighs in.[4] There are, however, a wide range of obstacles that can prevent an individual from being able to access accountability at the national level, including financial costs, fears of reprisal, geographic remoteness, linguistic differences, lack of knowledge or discriminatory biases within the justice system. Gaps in the law may prevent individuals from

[3] *Sacchi* (CRC), paras 10.15–10.20.

[4] C. Romano, 'The Rule of Prior Exhaustion of Domestic Remedies: Theory and Practice in International Human Rights Procedures' in N. Boschiero, T. Scovazzi, C. Pitero and C. Ragni (eds), *International Courts and the Development of International Law: Essays in Honour of Trulio Treves* (Cham: Springer, 2013) 564; *M.A.* v. *Switzerland*, CEDAW/C/80/D/145/2019, 1 November 2021.

obtaining legal remedies, legal action may be painfully slow, or hostile lines of jurisprudence may make the pursuit of justice futile. Women, children, racial and ethnic groups, migrants, refugees, asylum-seekers and people living in poverty or in rural and remote places are more likely to be confronted with these barriers and denied access to domestic justice.[5] To navigate these tensions, there is a partial acknowledgement of the barriers to domestic justice in the admissibility criteria. Some treaties and optional protocols hold that there is no requirement to exhaust domestic remedies when it would be unreasonably prolonged.[6] Others go a step further and craft exemptions for when domestic remedies would be unlikely to bring effective relief.[7] The exemptions are silent on other barriers, such as costs or fear of retaliation. The proposed approach to the application of the requirement to exhaust in this chapter is consistent with the normative aims of the exhaustion rule as it ensures admissibility only when there is no potential for the domestic system to remedy the alleged violation while simultaneously enriching the application of the rule by heightened awareness of the intricacies of barriers to domestic justice.

Using the guidance from the treaty bodies, Section 6.2 identifies common barriers to domestic justice systems. Section 6.3 argues that the purposes of the individual communications procedures, the exhaustion rule and its exemption point towards a generous application of admissibility criteria. Section 6.4 is doctrinal and normative. It is ambitious in that it pulls together all of the admissibility decisions from the nine UNTBs from 2012 to 2022. Undertaking this mapping exercise

[5] See Section 6.2.

[6] Article 5, Optional Protocol to the International Convenant on Civil and Political Rights 999 UNTS 171, adopted 19 December 1966, in force 23 March 1976, 999 UNTS 171; Article 3(1), Optional Protocol to the International Convention on Economic, Social and Cultural Rights, adopted 10 December 2008, in force 5 May 2013, 2922 UNTS 29; Article 14, Convention on the Elimination of All Forms of Racial Discrimination, adopted 7 March 1966, in force 4 January 1969, 660 UNTS 195; Article 31, International Convention for the Protection of All Persons from Enforced Disappearance, adopted 20 December 2006, in force 23 December 2010, 2716 UNTS 3.

[7] Article 4, Optional Protocol to Convention on the Elimination of All Forms of Discrimination against Women, adopted 6 October 1999, in force 22 December 2000, 2131 UNTS 83; Article 7, Optional Protocol to the Convention on the Rights of the Child on a Communication Procedure, adopted 19 December 2011, in force 14 April 2014, 2983 UNTS 135; Article 2, Optional Protocol to Convention on the Rights of Persons with Disabilities, adopted 13 December 2006, in force 3 May 2008, 2518 UNTS 283; Article 20, Convention Against Torture and Other Cruel, Inhuman or Degrading Treatment or Punishment, adopted 10 December 1984, in force 26 June 1987, 1465 UNTS 85.

reveals how the treaty bodies are accounting for some barriers to justice, but others remain invisible and reveal how the treaty bodies continue to lapse into formalistic reasoning and unrealistic evidentiary requirements. To shift from this black-letter methodology, this chapter proposes an individual-centred, contextual approach to the exhaustion criteria and marks out how it can enrich the admissibility analysis. This approach takes seriously individuals' lived experiences, accounts for how identity characteristics are linked to systemic inequality and is cognisant of how realities on the ground interact with social norms and institutional structures. It weighs carefully how these combined forces shape domestic attempts to vindicate human rights and provides greater clarity on how individuals can evidence their inability to exhaust. An individual-centred, contextual application of the exhaustion rule will not address all the challenges that beleaguer the individual communications procedure, nor will it always guarantee the vindication of human rights, as many of the barriers to domestic justice are equally applicable to international justice. But greater attention to the relationship between individuals and the structures of domestic justice can ensure international justice does not ignore or silence the vulnerable, marginalised and oppressed.

6.2 Domestic Barriers to Justice

Access to justice is a process whereby individuals can turn to mechanisms to resolve allegations of rights violations.[8] This broad definition functions as a useful starting point for investigating common barriers to accessing mechanisms to resolve human rights complaints. The justice system is embedded in society and reflects its values.[9] The oppression, neglect and discrimination that permeate the state are replicated and reenforced in the domestic justice system.[10] Individuals do not have an equal ability to access justice in their domestic system nor consequentially an equal ability to meet the individual communications procedure admissibility criteria to exhaust domestic remedies. This section identifies

[8] F. Wilmot-Smith, *Equal Justice: Fair Legal Systems in an Unfair World* (Cambridge MA: Harvard University Press, 2019).

[9] UN Special Rapporteur on the rights of persons with disabilities, International Principles and Guidelines on Access to Justice for Persons with Disabilities (2020); V. Shikhelman, 'Access to Justice in the UN Human Rights Committee', *Michigan Journal of International Law* 39 (2018): 453–531, 457.

[10] European Agency for Fundamental Rights, Access to Justice in Cases of Discrimination in the EU – Steps to Further Equality (2012).

common domestic barriers to justice and reflects on what effective access to justice requires. It does so by borrowing from the General Recommendation on access to justice issued by the UN Committee on the Elimination of All Forms of Discrimination against Women (CEDAW Committee).[11] The necessary elements are justiciability, availability, accessibility, good quality, remedies and accountability. Each element is introduced before being utilised in Section 6.4 to develop the parameters of an individual-centred, contextual exhaustion assessment.

6.2.1 *Justiciability*

This element requires that individuals have 'unhindered access to justice' and recognises that not all 'rights and correlative legal protections are recognised and incorporated into the law'.[12] There are many examples of non-justiciability. Socioeconomic rights are still not consistently legally protected.[13] Racist hate speech is not prohibited in every state.[14] In these examples, individuals will not be able to remedy violations in domestic settings.

6.2.2 *Availability*

Availability requires the state to establish and maintain domestic accountability mechanisms.[15] This requires the building of the infrastructure needed for a functioning justice system. Geographic and ableist biases permeate the design of domestic justice. The clustering of courts in urban centres raises logistical and financial challenges for those living in rural or remote areas.[16] The facilities and services of the justice system also often fail to account for the needs of persons with disabilities.[17] Without

[11] CEDAW Committee, General Recommendation No. 33 on access to justice, CEDAW/C/GC/33, 3 August 2015.

[12] CEDAW Committee, General Recommendation No. 33, para. 15(a).

[13] UN Special Rapporteur on the right to food, Access to Justice and the Right to Food: The Way Forward, A/HRC/28/65, 12 January 2014, para. 28.

[14] CERD Committee, General Recommendation No. 31 on the prevention of racial discrimination in the administration and functioning of the criminal justice system, CERD/C/GC/31, 2005, para. 4(a).

[15] CERD Committee, General Recommendation No. 31, para. 15(b).

[16] UN Special Rapporteur on the right to food, Access to Justice and the Right to Food, para. 31; CEDAW Committee, General Recommendation No. 33, paras. 13–14; UN Development Programme, Access to Justice: Practice Note (2004).

[17] UN Special Rapporteur on the rights of persons with disabilities, International Principles and Guidelines on Access to Justice for Persons with Disabilities, p. 16.

ensuring justice mechanisms are available in a manner that is mindful of how and where people live their lives, domestic justice is not equally available.

6.2.3 *Accessibility*

Accessibility demands that all accountability mechanisms be economically, socially, culturally and physically accessible.[18] Individuals may be unaware that accountability mechanisms exist.[19] Linguistic barriers can deter individuals from claiming justice.[20] Sociocultural accessibility can take many forms, but treaty bodies are increasingly concerned about negative repercussions, including violence against individuals who pursue domestic accountability.[21]

Economic accessibility is of primary concern to multiple UN actors. Challenging breaches of human rights is expensive.[22] The biggest financial obstacle to accessing domestic justice is the cost of legal representation. States are repeatedly urged to fund legal aid.[23] Despite consensus on the value of legal aid, the treaty bodies have different recommendations on its scope but uniting them is a recognition that states must address economic barriers to justice.[24]

Little attention has been paid to developing global best practices standards with respect to eligibility criteria for legal aid. There are a handful of exceptions. The CEDAW Committee warns that due to the imbalance in control over family resources between women and men, eligibility criteria for women to access legal aid in cases of family conflicts

[18] CEDAW, General Recommendation No. 33, paras. 3, 15(c).

[19] CMW, General Comment No. 5 on migrants' rights to liberty and freedom from arbitrary detention, CMW/C/32/R.2, 14 August 2020, para. 79.

[20] CMW, General Comment No. 5, para. 79.

[21] CEDAW, General Recommendation No. 33, paras. 9–10; UN Special Rapporteur on the human rights of migrants, Access to Justice, A/73/178/Rev.1, 25 September 2018, para. 33.

[22] CEDAW, General Recommendation No. 33, para 17(a); HRC, General Comment No. 32, Right to equality before courts and tribunals and to fair trial, CCPR/C/GC/32, 23 August 2007, para. 10–11.

[23] CEDAW, General Recommendation No. 33, paras. 17(a), 36–37; CERD Committee, General Recommendation No. 31, para. 30.

[24] HRC, General Comment No. 32, para. 10; CERD, General Recommendation No. 31, para. 30; CRC, General Comment No. 24 on children's rights in the child justice system, CRC/C/GC/24, 18 September 2019, para. 51; CMW, General Comment No. 5, para. 79; CEDAW, General Recommendation No. 33, para. 36.

should take account of 'real income or disposable assets of women'.[25] The UN Office on Drugs and Crime also recognises the somewhat arbitrary nature of income thresholds. If an individual exceeds the means tests but still is not in a position to afford a lawyer, they should not be excluded from assistance when the 'urgency or complexity of the case or the severity of potential penalties'[26] demand legal aid.[27]

6.2.4 *Good Quality*

This element reflects on the competence, efficiency, independence and impartiality of the justice system.[28] There are multiple components to a well-functioning justice system. Human and financial resources are needed so human rights claims do not stagnate but are resolved in a timely manner.[29] Justice officials must have knowledge of human rights law.[30] Domestic justice systems must be impartial and free of myths and biases. The CEDAW Committee points out that 'often judges adopt rigid standards about what they consider to be appropriate behaviour for women and penalize those who do not conform to stereotypes'.[31] The CERD Committee observes the same with respect to racial discrimination.[32] The UN Special Rapporteur on the right to food highlights another threat to impartiality. She warns that close relations between the executive, legislative and judicial can undermine the independence of domestic accountability mechanisms.[33] The lack of good quality justice can make pursuing domestic remedies futile and should be accounted for when treaty bodies consider the exhaustion criteria. The treaty bodies have a long track record of assessing how the quality of the justice system

[25] CEDAW, General Recommendation No. 33, para. 37(e).
[26] UNODC, UN Principles and Guidelines on Access to Legal Aid in Criminal Justice Systems (2013), p. 13.
[27] A. Zysset and B. Cali, 'Exhausting Domestic Remedies or Exhausting the Rule of Law? Revisiting the Normative Basis of Procedural Subsidiarity in the European Human Rights System', *Transnational Legal Theory* 14 (2023) 157–177.
[28] CEDAW, General Recommendation No. 33, para. 19(b).
[29] UN Special Rapporteur on the right to food, Access to Justice and the Right to Food, para. 36; CRC, General Comment No. 24, paras. 54–55; CEDAW, General Recommendation No. 33, para. 33(a).
[30] UN Special Rapporteur on the right to food, Access to Justice and the Right to Food, para. 35.
[31] CEDAW, General Recommendation No 33, para. 26.
[32] CERD, General Recommendation No. 31, para. 31.
[33] UN Special Rapporteur on the right to food, Access to Justice and the Right to Food, para. 36.

impacts the admissibility to the individual communications procedure, particularly around issues of delay, a barrier that can be easily evidenced. There is less consideration of other aspects of quality, such as bias, which can be much more difficult to prove.

6.2.5 *Remedies*

Remedies for breaches of human rights are an element of access to justice. These must be effective, adequate and timely and holistically and proportionally redress the harm suffered.[34]

6.2.6 *Accountability*

Lastly, the justice system itself must be accountable and monitored.[35]

6.3 A Formal Accounting of Barriers to Justice

The UN individual communications procedure is, in part, designed to overcome the confluence of obstacles that prevents individuals from vindicating their rights. When justice is unattainable at the domestic level, individuals can turn to international mechanisms. The promise of international human rights accountability hinges, inter alia, on the exhaustion of domestic remedies. This section considers the purposes of the individual communication procedure, and the purpose of and formal exemptions to the exhaustion rule, providing the basis for arguing in Section 6.4 for an individual-centred, contextual application of this admissibility criterion.

6.3.1 *The Purpose of the Individual Communications Procedure*

An individual can lodge a communication with a treaty body alleging that the state has not fulfilled its human rights obligations under the respective treaty. If the communication meets the admissibility criteria, the treaty body will assess the communication on its merits and, if required, will recommend both individual and structural remedies to prevent future violations of human rights. The individual communications

[34] CERD, General Recommendation No. 31, para. 38(b); CMW, General Comment No. 5, para. 68; CEDAW, General Recommendation No. 33, para. 19(b).

[35] CEDAW, General Recommendation No. 33, para. 14(f).

procedure serves multiple purposes.[36] First, it seeks to secure individual relief.[37] Second, the individual communications procedure also aims to spark structural reforms to strengthen human rights not only in the state under review but around the world.[38] And lastly, the communications are an opportunity for the treaty body to develop treaty obligations at a more granular level.[39] The multiple functions of the individual communications procedure provide a strong foundation for a non-technical application of admissibility criteria. The purposes of the procedure would be hamstrung if individual communications are too readily deemed inadmissible for failing to exhaust.

6.3.2 *Purpose of the Exhaustion Rule*

A close examination of the function of the exhaustion rule makes it clear why the rule should not be rigidly enforced. The requirement to exhaust domestic remedies has a long history originating in diplomatic relations.[40] In the modern era, exhaustion is ubiquitous in international human rights adjudication. A majority of regional human rights instruments require individuals to pursue domestic claims before accessing international or regional courts.[41] Courts and scholars have identified a number of reasons for the exhaustion rule. Its primary purpose is to respect state sovereignty. The state should be given an opportunity to evaluate the claim before it is taken to the global stage. D'Ascoli and Scherr explain that the state should have a chance to 'discharge its

[36] A. Byrnes, 'An Effective Complaint Procedure in the Context of International Human Rights Law' in Anne Bayefsky (ed), *The UN Human Rights Treaty System in the 21st Century* (Leiden: Brill, 2000) p.139.

[37] Byrnes, 'An Effective Complaint Procedure'.

[38] G. Ulfstein, 'Individual Complaints' in H. Keller and G. Ulfstein (eds), *UN Human Rights Treaty Bodies: Law and Legitimacy* (Cambridge: Cambridge University Press, 2013), p. 75.

[39] M. Scheinin, 'International Mechanisms and Procedures for Monitoring' in C. Krause and M. Scheinin (eds), *International Protection of Human Rights* (Turku: Abo Akademi University Institute for Human Rights, 2009), p. 619.

[40] J. Crawford and T. Grant, 'Local Remedies, Exhaustion of' in *Max Planck Encyclopaedias of International Law* (Oxford: Oxford University Press, 2007).

[41] A. von Staden, 'Subsidiarity, Exhaustion of Domestic Remedies and the Margin of Appreciation in the Human Rights Jurisprudence of African Sub-regional Courts', *International Journal of Human Rights* 20 (2016): 1113–1131.

responsibility and to redress the wrong committed'.[42] Exhaustion is also a method for preserving a relationship of subsidiarity between domestic and international human rights law. Requiring individuals to pursue domestic remedies protects the primacy of domestic accountability and avoids 'domestic courts being replaced by international courts'.[43]

6.3.3 *Purpose of the Recognised Exemptions to Exhaustion*

The purpose of the individual communications procedure and the purpose of the exhaustion rule seem to pull in different directions, and as argued below the individual, contextual approach is a bridge between these competing imperatives. On the surface there appears to be a tension as, on one hand, a literal application of the exhaustion rule could frustrate the purpose of international human rights accountability and 'over-protect the interests of the state at the expense of the protection of the individual'.[44] Ignoring the exhaustion rule, on the other hand, could upend the carefully crafted relationship between domestic and international accountability. In the UN system, there is an incomplete bridge built between the need to fully protect human rights and the desire to protect subsidiarity through the recognition of exemptions to the exhaustion rule. An individual does not have to exhaust domestic remedies when the domestic justice process would be either unreasonably prolonged and/or unlikely to bring effective relief.[45] All treaty bodies can assess whether a remedy is unreasonably prolonged, but technically, only the CEDAW, CRC, Committee on the Rights of Persons with Disabilities and Committee against Torture (CRPD and CAT Committee, respectively) can assess whether the remedy is effective. Regarding unreasonable delay, if achieving domestic accountability will take an excessive amount of time, then there is no obligation on the individual to pursue it before accessing the individual communications procedure.[46] Regarding effective relief, an effective or available remedy is one which is 'in direct relation with the events that initially gave rise to the claimed violation and that ... may be reasonably considered as effective of remedying the

[42] S. D'Ascoli and K. Maria Scherr, 'The Rule of Prior Exhaustion of Legal Remedies in the International Law Doctrine and Its Application in the Specific Context of Human Rights Protection', *EUI Working Papers* 2 (2007) p.8.

[43] D'Ascoli and Scherr, 'The Rule of Prior Exhaustion'.

[44] D'Ascoli and Scherr, 'The Rule of Prior Exhaustion'.

[45] See (n 6) and (n 7).

[46] *Matson* v. *Canada*, CEDAW/C/81/D/68/2014, 14 February 2022, para. 17.5.

claimed violations'.[47] There is no requirement to pursue domestic remedies when there is no reasonable prospect of success.[48] Treaty bodies examine an array of factors when assessing effectiveness, including the procedural activity of the claim and the nature and seriousness of the alleged breach of human rights.[49] On a plain reading of the admissibility rules, there is an acknowledgement that insufficient quality and/or remedial power of the justice system can frustrate domestic accountability. International human rights law recognises that these difficulties, if sufficiently pronounced, alleviate the obligation to seek domestic relief. This, however, amounts to a partial accounting since only two of the six elements of access to justice as identified above are referred to, with the other elements – justiciability, availability, accessibility and accountability – not recognised exemptions from the requirement to exhaust. As the analysis below demonstrates, the treaty bodies are aware of the need for a generous application of the exhaustion rule and interpreting it to address other elements of access to justice,[50] but have yet to consistently and coherently achieve this aim.

6.4 A Dynamic Accounting of Barriers to Justice

The narrow textual exemptions to the exhaustion requirement have evolved to partially account for the confluence of obstacles that prevent individuals from claiming their human rights. Thus, it appears the treaty bodies are applying the exhaustion rule in a flexible and non-technical manner. This evolution, however, is nascent. The jurisprudence is riddled with contradictions. Sometimes the high costs are recognised as creating obstacles and sometimes they are not. There is deep uncertainty around proving how different barriers to justice make it impossible to give domestic forums an opportunity to address the alleged breach of human rights. While it has been clarified that individuals cannot argue for exemptions to exhaustion based on 'mere doubts' or 'assumptions',[51] it nonetheless remains unclear what can/should in practice constitute positive, compelling or persuasive evidence of obstacles to justice that

[47] *Arellano Medina* v. *Ecuador*, E/C.12/63/D/7/2015, 26 March 2018, para. 8.7.
[48] *Leo* v. *Australia*, CRPD/C/22/D/17/2013, 30 October 2019, para. 7.5.
[49] *Y.* v. *Tanzania*, CRPD/C/20/D/23/2014, 31 August 2018, para. 7.3.
[50] *S.S.R.* v. *Spain*, E/C.12/66/D/51/2018, 11 October 2019; *S.C. and G.P.* v. *Italy*, E/C.12/65/D/22/2017, 7 March 2019.
[51] *J.I.* v. *France*, CCPR/C/117/D/2154/2012, 4 July 2016, para. 6.5.

alleviate the need to exhaust. Analysing the admissibility jurisprudence of the treaty bodies over the past decade, this section identifies with greater precision where the inconsistencies lie and marks out how an individual-centred, contextual assessment can evolve the future relationship between domestic and international justice.

This section utilises the access to justice framework outlined in Section 6.3 to explore the dynamics of accounting for barriers to justice at the admissibility stage of the individual communications procedure. As mentioned in the introduction, this is a comprehensive review spanning across a decade. It argues that treaty bodies must account for a wide range of domestic barriers and examine multiple pieces of evidence – ranging from failed efforts at legislative reform to domestic criteria for legal aid, to the realities of poverty, gender stigmas and hostility towards refugees – when determining if the individual is required to pursue all available domestic remedies. The specific barrier and the evidentiary demands will be a function of the factual-legal matrix of the communication, but the guiding principle for the exhaustion assessment must be *individually and contextually centred.*

The assessment must understand how *individual* personal circumstances and identity characteristics, factors and experiences influence the ability to access domestic justice. The exhaustion assessment must be intersectional and account for how 'the dynamics of sameness and difference' across multiple and intersecting vectors shape access to justice.[52] The assessment should understand how the individual identity, factors and experience is connected to patterns of systemic inequality. Layered upon this, the exhaustion evaluation must also be *contextual*, taking account, at all levels, of the political, economic and sociocultural realities in which the individual is seeking accountability.[53] While the treaty bodies are dependent on the information provided by the parties, they can consider that evidence within its context – for example, understanding failure to exhaust in light of political inertia and animus, post-conflict tensions or community stigmas against sexual violence. Treaty bodies 'must be sensitive to the reality of the dilemma posed by the particular facts'.[54]

[52] S. Atrey, *Intersectional Discrimination* (Oxford: Oxford University Press, 2019), p. 37.

[53] C. Sheppard, *Inclusive Equality* (Montreal: McGill-Queen's University Press, 2010), Chapter 3.

[54] *Edmonton Journal* v. *Alberta (Attorney General)* [1989] 2 SCR 1326, para. 51 (Canadian Supreme Court).

These two elements of the proposed approach to exhaustion should not be conceptualised in isolation from each other but should reinforce and inform each other. The exhaustion evaluation must be holistic, seeking to understand who the person is and the realities they face in trying to vindicate breaches of human rights. An individual-centred, contextual assessment does not demand that the individual produces specific pieces of evidence. Rather, it recognises limits that individuals encounter when trying to identify domestic barriers and looks at all evidentiary sources with probative value for illuminating whether seeking domestic justice is actually futile.

In taking an individual-centred, contextual approach, the UNTBs are not undermining the purpose of the exhaustion rule but are fulfilling it by a thorough investigation into whether the domestic system is able to address the alleged breach of human rights. It more fully identifies instances where domestic justice will never have a chance to assess and remedy the wrong and thus does not undermine subsidiarity. Analysing the jurisprudence of the UNTBs, this section demonstrates how this approach can both enrich and provide greater consistency in the exhaustion assessment so that domestic barriers to justice do not frustrate access to international human rights forums.

6.4.1 *Justiciability*

The exemptions to exhaustion are being used to account for the justiciability dimension of access to justice, but there is evidentiary confusion on how to prove justiciability. There are relatively straightforward cases. For example, NB was subjected to corporal punishment at kindergarten.[55] The CRC Committee deemed the communication admissible despite the individual not seeking civil remedies, as the state did not recognise corporal punishment as grounding a cause of action.[56] This is an uncomplicated example where domestic law precludes human rights accountability, but this was not a barrier to accessing international accountability.

Challenges arise in more complex cases. Individuals routinely point to hostile lines of jurisprudence as evidence of non-justiciability. When there is 'established jurisprudence of the highest domestic tribunals' that would result in the claim 'inevitably be[ing] dismissed', the individual

[55] *N.B.* v. *Georgia*, CRC/C/90/D/84/2019, 1 June 2022.

[56] *N.B.* (CRC), paras 5.1, 6.3.

argues the communication should be deemed admissible.[57] States, however, hold that domestic courts can re-interpret, modify or even overturn law to ensure human rights compatibility. Drawing on the purpose of the exhaustion rule, the state can argue that the UNTBs should not admit communications that prevent the domestic system from redressing the claim. The treaty bodies must determine when the opportunity to internally reform the law is an illusion and identify when there is more than a mere doubt or assumption that a domestic claim will fail. Under the individual-centred, contextual assessment, the treaty bodies must expand beyond looking at domestic case law and examine multiple forms of evidence, such as legislative animus and lack of political will, to determine whether the claim is non-justiciable such that the individual should be exempt from pursuing domestic remedies.

6.4.1.1 Demanding Hostile Jurisprudence

The treaty bodies are more likely to conclude domestic remedies are inaccessible when the individual cites jurisprudence from apex courts that frustrate the ability to litigate the claim.[58] In *Gomaríz Valera* v. *Spain*, the Human Rights Committee (HRC) held 'when the highest domestic court has ruled on the matter … thereby eliminating any prospect that a remedy … may succeed, the author is not obliged to exhaust'.[59] Similarly, in *FKAG* v. *Australia*, the HRC held that it was not sufficient for the state to argue that there is a 'possibility' that the higher courts may 'someday' overrule a precedent.[60] Individuals should not have to expend time, energy and money merely because the state believes apex courts might uphold the individual's rights.

In *Ali* v. *Norway*, a father and a son did not appeal their immigration detention to the Supreme Court, as they argued that the Court had limited competence to review this decision.[61] The HRC, however, held that there was still a prospect. This conclusion was based on the lower courts expressing doubts on the individuals' detention. On the surface, *Ali* appeared to differ from *Gomaríz Valera* and *FKAG*, as the state could point to factors to prove that there was a prospect of success within the domestic system. However, applying an individual-centred, contextual

57 *D.C.* v. *Germany*, CRC/C/83/D/60/2018, 4 February 2020, para. 6.5.

58 *M.B.* v. *Czech Republic*, CCPR/C/106/D/1849/2008, 29 October 2012, para. 7.3.

59 *Gomaríz Valera* v. *Spain*, CCPR/C/84/D/1095/2002, 22 July 2005, para. 6.4.

60 *F.K.A.G. et al* v. *Australia*, CCPR/C/108/D/2094/2011, 26 July 2013.

61 *Ali* v. *Norway*, CCPR/C/135/D/2926/2017, 14 July 2022.

assessment destabilises this chance of success. None of the domestic courts gave serious weight to the fact that one of the individuals detained was a child, and the Supreme Court would not have jurisdiction to consider this crucial element of the claim. Moreover, as the dissenting members of the HRC pointed out, there were no positive facts that supported the conclusion that the Supreme Court would find the detention illegal. The Oslo District Court had repeatedly determined there was a factual basis to conclude that the individuals would abscond such that detention was the only option, and this finding was repeatedly upheld by the Borgarting High Court.[62] The state provided no positive evidence on why the Supreme Court would find differently. States must be given a chance to rectify human rights abuses, but that chance cannot rest on formalistic assessment of the jurisprudence; it must be deeply sensitive to the individual circumstances and the broader context of the jurisprudence.

In *DC* v. *Germany*, the CRC Committee also failed to examine the context of the hostile jurisprudence and did not account for insurmountable domestic barriers to children's access to justice. DC was a sixteen-year-old living in Germany who was prohibited from voting in local elections due to his age. The age limit was unsuccessfully challenged in the lower courts but not in the Constitutional Court of Saarland. DC argued that pursuing a constitutional remedy would be futile as the Constitution of Saarland only protects the right to vote for those over eighteen years old, and the Court would be bound to follow this provision. Moreover, he submitted that the Constitutional Court of Saarland would also rely on the Basic Law of Germany and on the jurisprudence of the Federal Constitutional Court, both of which prohibited those under eighteen from voting. The CRC Committee dismissed the claim, holding that 'a constitutional motion should not be considered bound to fail simply because of the current constitutional texts and a few general precedents'.[63] The Committee believed that the Constitutional Court of Saarland should be given a chance to bring domestic law in line with the CRC. The refusal to admit this communication goes to the heart of the purpose of the exhaustion requirement, that is giving the State an opportunity to resolve the alleged breach of human rights. However, the reasoning in DC implies that there is a degree of ambiguity in the

[62] *Ali* (HRC), dissenting opinion of Committee members Jose Manuel Santos Pais and Imeru Tamrat Yigezu.

[63] *D.C.* v. *Germany* (CRC), paras 6.5–6.6.

constitutional texts that could potentially be re-interpreted by apex courts. Article 38(A) of the Basic Law holds, on a plain reading, that only those eighteen years or older have the right to vote. The explicit limits on the right to vote for children would seem to be a textbook example of a non-justiciability argument and providing the Constitutional Court of Saarland with an opportunity to re-interpret voting laws in line with the CRC would be doomed. Failing to give serious weight to the context of non-justiciability results in the CRC Committee misapplying the burden of proof, undercutting the purpose of the exhaustion rule. DC was forced to pursue a domestic remedy where there was no reasonable likelihood of success and was procedurally prevented from accessing justice at the international level.

6.4.1.2 Contextualising Non-justiciability

A stronger approach is to use the individual-centred, contextual approach to examine multiple pieces of evidence when assessing whether justiciability frustrates domestic accountability as there may not be hostile jurisprudence to use as evidence.[64] Clearly worded statutes that bar action should be considered strong evidence that the claim will inevitably fail.[65] The cumulative effect of different sources of evidence for non-justiciability should also be taken into account, such as the failure of the state to implement recommendations from national human rights bodies or expert domestic legal advice that the 'case would have no reasonable prospect for success'.[66] The CRPD Committee did this in *Lockrey* v. *Australia*.[67] Michael Lockrey, who was deaf, was informed that steno-captioning would not be provided for jury selection processes and duty. He provided three types of evidence to support his contention that his claim would have a poor chance of success in the domestic courts. First, he cited numerous examples from the case law; second, he mapped out how the State would rebut the claims of disability discrimination in jury service; and third, he obtained legal advice that this rebuttal would likely be accepted by the domestic courts. In light of these detailed arguments, the CRPD Committee concluded there was no obligation to

[64] *D.R.* v. *Australia*, CPRD/C/17/D/14/2013, 24 March 2017, para 6.6; *Moylan* v. *Australia*, CERD/C/83/D/47/2010, 27 August 2013; *P.E.E.P.* v. *Estonia*, CCPR/C/128/D/2682/2015, 13 March 2020, para. 7.3.

[65] *Noble* v. *Australia*, CRPD/C/16/D/7/2012, 2 September 2016, para. 7.7.

[66] *Nasir* v. *Australia*, CCPR/C/116/D/2229/2012, 29 March 2016, para. 6.3; *A.S.* v. *Australia*, CCPR/C/132/D/2900/2016, 2 July 2021, para. 7.3.

[67] *Lockrey* v. *Australia*, CRPD/C/15/D/13/2013, 1 April 2016.

pursue these domestic remedies to access the individual communications procedure.[68]

Two communications are good examples of how to take account of the individual circumstances and macro-contextual factors that underpin non-justiciability. In *Ivanov* v. *Russian Federation*, the HRC exhaustion analysis was sensitive to the social and legal culture of homo- and transphobia. Ivanov was denied permission to hold a sexual orientation and gender identity pride parade in Moscow, and his various appeals failed.[69] In assessing whether the individual should have pursued a final avenue for appeal, the HRC observed that in a six-year period 'at least 252 public events on lesbian, gay, bisexual and transgender-related topics . . . could not be organized owing to persistent refusals by authorities'.[70] Referencing its own Concluding Observations on the Russian Federation, the HRC noted the laws that banned the promotion of non-traditional sexual activity were discriminatory and violated civil and political rights. The HRC concluded that 'the systematic application of this legislation to lesbian, gay, bisexual and transgender assemblies . . . and the support of this practice by the courts, in particular the Constitutional Court of the state party, render improbable a successful outcome' for any further appeals.[71] The animus to sexual orientation and gender identity equality was correctly used as contextual evidence of non-justiciability entitling the individual for an exemption from the requirement to exhaust.

The strengths of an individual-centred, contextual assessment were also evident in *Matson* v. *Canada*, as the CEDAW Committee took full account of the longstanding lack of political will to redress human rights violations.[72] Indigenous women in Canada were prohibited from passing their Indigenous status to their descendants when they married a non-Indigenous person.[73] Reforms from 1985, 2011 and 2019 failed to remedy this discrimination. Matson filed an individual communication, but the state responded that he should have pursued a domestic constitutional challenge to the law. A literal application of the exhaustion rule would have required deeming the communication inadmissible, as no

[68] *Lockrey* (CRPD), para. 7.3–7.4.
[69] *Vladimir Ivanov* v. *Russian Federation*, CCPR/C/131/D/2635/2015, 18 March 2021.
[70] *Vladimir Ivanov* (HRC), para. 6.5.
[71] *Vladimir Ivanov* (HRC), para. 6.5.
[72] *Matson* (CEDAW).
[73] *Matson* (CEDAW), paras 1–2.9.

domestic court had examined the law in question. However, an individual-centred, contextual assessment reveals the futility of pursuing domestic remedies for discrimination against Indigenous people. Lower courts had found that the previous reform efforts continued to perpetuate inequality, yet this had not prompted the state to fully remedy the wrong. The CEDAW Committee, in fact, observed 'that three constitutional claims on the same issue resulted in three sets of legislative reforms . . . that allegedly maintain the provisions that are discriminatory on the basis of gender'.[74] There was a sustained track record of failing to redress Indigenous women's inequality. The CEDAW Committee therefore concluded that the communication was admissible as a further constitutional claim would be unlikely to bring effective relief. An individual and contextual analysis highlighted how discrimination against Indigenous people and political inertia intersected with legal accountability. In taking this generous approach to admissibility, the CEDAW Committee did not transgress the purpose of the exhaustion rule, as discrimination in Indigenous status laws had been repeatedly drawn to the state's attention. When evaluating whether the individual has exhausted domestic remedies, treaty bodies should not only account for obvious black-letter dead ends. Rather, as in *Matson*, *Ivanov* and the dissenting opinion in *Ali*, they should examine the individual circumstances of claimants and the broader context – including the nuances of hostile jurisprudence and the intersection between legal accountability and political animus and inertia – so the exhaustion rule does not cement insurmountable hostility towards human rights accountability.

6.4.2 Availability

The availability element of access to justice has not been extensively examined by the treaty bodies at the exhaustion stage of the admissibility consideration. The one exception is the case of a member of the Tharu Indigenous community in Nepal who had been sexually assaulted. She had not filed a complaint within the statutory time limit because, inter alia, she 'lived in a rural area where most inhabitants were illiterate' and thus did not know how to navigate the justice system.[75] Taking an individual-centred, contextual approach highlights how a range of identity factors, such as race and gender, interact with the larger context of

[74] *Matson* (CEDAW), paras 1–2.9.

[75] *Maya* v. *Nepal*, CCPR/C/119/D/2245/2013, 17 March 2017, para. 6.4.

rural disadvantage to create obstacles that make domestic justice de facto unavailable. Inequalities in the state precluded domestic accountability mechanisms from having a chance to consider the claim. A technical application of the exhaustion rule would not fulfil the rule's purpose but only compound domestic inequalities. The HRC adopted this generous approach and concluded that domestic limitations meant domestic remedies were unavailable. This is an important recognition of both the practicalities of vindicating human rights and of how these practicalities connect to larger patterns of systemic inequality. The HRC's evidentiary demands furthered an individual-centred, contextual approach to exhaustion, as the individual did not have to provide concrete data on the distance to the police station, transport options or cost of travel, which may be difficult for a poor, rural, Indigenous woman to obtain. There was also no requirement to provide data on the links between literacy and knowledge of the justice system. The evidentiary burden regarding the availability of justice only required sensitivity to the relationship between access to justice, identity characteristics and geographic remoteness.

6.4.3 *Accessibility*

Under this element of access to justice, the treaty bodies are to assess when the individual is not required to exhaust domestic remedies due to ignorance of the latter's existence, language barriers, risk of backlash or costs. An individual-centred, contextual assessment gives the treaty bodies the tools to evaluate the accessibility of access to justice in a manner that ensures domestic barriers do not lock the individual out of international accountability.

6.4.3.1 Lack of Awareness

Lack of awareness of domestic remedies should not be automatically fatal to the communication. There are two examples from the jurisprudence where the UNTBs correctly applied an individual-centred, contextual approach to determining if lack of awareness precludes admissibility.

In *Suleymanova and Israfilova* v. *Azerbaijan*, when an individual was neither properly charged nor provided with a lawyer, the HRC held there was no obligation to challenge in domestic courts these breaches of his right to a fair trial.[76] The violations of his rights prevented him from

[76] CCPR/C/133/D/3061/2017, 3 February 2022 at para 6.3.

being aware of domestic remedies. Exempting him from pursuing the latter ensured that the exhaustion requirement was not used as a shield to hide the State from accountability when the failure to initiate domestic remedies flowed from the alleged breaches of human rights.

In the second case, Rosanna Flamer-Caldera did not bring a petition for pre-enactment review of reforms that criminalised same-sex sexual activity for women as she was not aware of this mechanism.[77] Far from blaming her for this, the CEDAW Committee critiqued the non-availability of information on pre-enactment review. Treaty bodies should not accept at face value the state's claims on the accessibility of domestic remedies. Rather, taking the individual-centred, contextual approach, they should assess how the mechanism operates in practice. Holding *Flamer-Caldera* v. *Sri Lanka* admissible was consistent with the purposes of the individual communications procedure, as it gave the CEDAW Committee an opportunity to condemn the criminalisation of same-sex sexual activity for women – a significant evolution in international human rights law for the recognition and protection of gender and sexual orientation equality. At the same time, admitting *Flamer-Caldera* also did not offend the exhaustion rule, as the Supreme Court of Sri Lanka was prohibited under the Constitution from reviewing enacted legislation, so there was no possibility for a court to assess the law after it was passed.[78] The only accessible mechanism was the obscure pre-enactment review: not using it did not preclude admissibility.

6.4.3.2 Linguistic Barriers

There is only one communication whose author raised linguistic barriers as an explanation for failing to exhaust. AP, a Russian national, was unable to appeal the State's decision to deport him to a country where he faced a risk of torture, as he did not have a lawyer and did not speak Finnish. Thus, he was unable to submit the necessary paperwork in the required language. The CAT Committee found that the inability to participate in the legal process due to linguistic barriers alleviated the need to pursue an appeal before the Supreme Administrative Court.[79] Future admissibility assessments regarding language and access to justice should follow in the path of *AP* v. *Finland*.

[77] *Flamer-Caldera* v. *Sri Lanka*, CEDAW/C/81/D/134/2018, 21 February 2022, para 8.3.

[78] *Flamer-Caldera* (CEDAW), para 5.1.

[79] *A.P.* v. *Finland*, CAT/C/60/D/465/2011, 10 May 2017, para. 8.3.

6.4.3.3 Backlash Risk

Seeking to vindicate human rights can expose individuals to severe social backlash, loss of employment, deportation, retaliation, criminal liability and even violence. For example, Maharjan was apprehended by the army and tortured. Upon release he did not make a claim within the statutory time limits as he went into hiding fearing reprisals. Using the individual-centred, contextual approach, he cited the CAT Committee's Concluding Observations against Nepal and several Amnesty International reports as evidence of the legitimacy of his fears of further state violence.[80] Given the danger in pursuing remedies, there was no obligation to exhaust. This is also a good example of how the treaty bodies' own work can provide the necessary context and evidence in which to assess exhaustion.

Backlash for championing human rights claims, however, does not always entail the high degree of severity seen in *Maharjan* v. *Nepal*. The treaty bodies must determine at what point backlash places the individual in a position of vulnerability that negates the obligation to seek domestic remedies. This subsection argues that the individual-centred, contextual assessment requires the treaty bodies to take account of either acute legal and sociocultural backlash or the risk of such backlash that the individual can prove beyond mere doubt or assumption.

This approach to the exhaustion analysis ensures that individuals do not have to pursue domestic remedies that will have negative legal repercussions.[81] An example can be seen in the HRC communication regarding Benattia Zerrougui, who was forcibly disappeared in 1995 by the Algerian state defence and security services. Anyone making an allegation against these actors was legally liable to prison and a substantial fine. The HRC concluded that Zerrougui's brother, who initiated the communication, did not have to undertake these risks to access the individual communications procedure.[82] In another communication against the Russian Federation, Kesmatulla Khakdar did not have a legal right to reside in the state but had married a citizen.[83] The State argued he should have pursued a legal right to reside on the basis of his marriage. This, however, would have required him to leave Russia and to return to his country of nationality, namely Afghanistan. There was no guarantee that he would be allowed back into the Russian Federation once he had

[80] *Maharjan* v. *Nepal*, CCPR/C/105/D/1863/2009, 19 July 2012, para. 7.6.
[81] *Cacho Ribeiro* v. *Mexico*, CCPR/C/123/D/2767/2016, 17 July 2018, para. 9.3.
[82] *Zerrougui* v. *Algeria*, CCPR/C/108/D/1796/2008, 25 July 2013, paras 4.5–4.6.
[83] *Khakdar* v. *Russian Federation*, CCPR/C/112/D/2126/2011, 17 October 2014, para. 10.6.

left it, and he would have been at risk of ill-treatment by the Taliban regime. The HRC held he was not required to pursue this remedy. In *Yaker* v. *France*, Yaker was convicted for wearing a 'garment [the niqab] to conceal her face in public'.[84] She only raised her human rights claims at the appeal stage. The state argued that to exhaust domestic remedies, she should have raised these claims in the first instance. Yaker pointed out that she tried to attend the initial proceedings but was arrested and fined again for refusing to remove her niqab for a security check. The HRC concluded that where it would be a criminal offense to pursue a domestic remedy, there is no requirement to exhaust.

In all of these communications, the individuals could refer to specific elements of the legal architecture of the state to substantiate the argument that backlash should exempt them from the requirement to exhaust. This deeply contextual understanding of the state's domestic system does not offend the exhaustion rule, as domestic law prevents state institutions from addressing the alleged breach of human rights. A strict requirement to exhaust would be useless and place the individual in a position of extreme vulnerability. *Zerrougui*, *Khakdar* and *Yaker* are the straightforward communications in this regard. *Nakawunde* v. *Canada*, a decision by the CAT Committee, is more challenging. This communication also highlights that an individual-centred, contextual analysis cannot examine the elements of access to justice in isolation from each other. Nakawunde, who was not represented by counsel, did not appeal the decision to deport her to Uganda as she was 'afraid of being detected by Canadian authorities'.[85] UN actors have warned that asylum-seekers are often afraid that state officials will deport them and are reluctant to engage in any part of the justice system.[86] The CAT Committee was unsympathetic to these fears. It held that the author had not exhausted domestic remedies as there was a scheme in the state which would defer the deportation while the appeal was pending. The treaty body failed to show awareness of how her identity characteristics, particularly her migration status, created availability and accessibility hurdles to justice. While the state may have mechanisms in place to mitigate legal backlash, making it seem feasible for the individual to pursue domestic remedies, this surface-level analysis fails to account for how backlash and lack of knowledge are connected to the individual's

[84] *Yaker* v. *France*, CCPR/C/123/D/2747/2016, 17 July 2018, para 2.1.

[85] *Nakawunde* v. *Canada*, CAT/C/64/D/615/2014 3 August 2018, paras 6.5–6.8.

[86] UN Special Rapporteur on the human rights of migrants, Access to Justice, para. 33.

status as an asylum-seeker. Nakawunde explained that she did not know of this deferral scheme. It is not difficult to surmise how an asylum-seeker, who is afraid of deportation and does not have a lawyer, is unaware of the complexities of the domestic legal system.[87] It is also incumbent on the treaty body to consider whether her lack of awareness was connected to her fears of backlash and her immigration status. The CAT Committee's assessment failed to grasp these lived realities. An individual-centred, contextual approach, however, brings to the fore these nuances and highlights how those with intersecting identity characteristics face multiple hurdles to accessing justice.

The proposed approach to the exhaustion rule would also account for other non-legal repercussions. The treaty bodies have not reflected on the degree of social or economic risk that should alleviate the need to exhaust, or how individuals can demonstrate these types of risks. A recent communication indicates how this could develop. In the context of a prolonged period of armed conflict, a Nepalese woman was unable to file a report of sexual assault within the statutory time frame. She did not seek justice as there was social stigma towards victims of sexual violence. She unsuccessfully appealed to have the time bar removed. Given the gravity of the alleged breaches of human rights, the HRC accepted, without requiring detailed evidence, that there was a practical limitation to pursuing domestic remedies.[88] This is a good example of an individual-centred, contextual assessment in practice. It establishes that other forms of backlash impact the ability to exhaust. The HRC did so by paying attention to the individual's identity characteristics, gender and the context of post-conflict and social stigma against sexual violence. Such a broad and holistic assessment of the relationship between backlash and exhaustion should be carried forward in the jurisprudence.

6.4.3.4 Costs

Legal proceedings invariably entail costs. As in cases of backlash, the treaty bodies must determine if there is a tipping point where costs preclude accessibility to the point of alleviating the exhaustion criteria. There is a line of decisions from the HRC, CEDAW, CRC and CERD Committees which have held that 'the author's weak financial situation in itself . . . does not absolve her from' challenging alleged violations of

[87] UN Special Rapporteur on the human rights of migrants, Access to Justice, para. 33.
[88] *Nyaya* v. *Nepal*, CCPR/C/125/D/2556/2015, 18 March 2019, para. 6.4.

human rights.[89] In *Sacchi*, the CRC Committee gave no real consideration to how young people could fund the costs of climate change litigation and just blithely assumed legal aid was available for this type of legal claim.[90] This stringent position, which is anathema to the individual-centred, contextual assessment, is oblivious to the relationship between socioeconomic status and access to justice. Failing to account for the economics of domestic accountability limits international justice to those who can afford to access domestic justice. This further marginalises low- and moderate-income individuals, who are often women, children, disabled persons and members of racial and ethnic groups. An individual-centred, contextual assessment, however, would pay close attention to how income poverty relates to identity characteristics and how that interacts with the structures of the justice system. The strict approach of the treaty bodies also does not further the core aims of the exhaustion rule. Domestic courts never have an opportunity to adjudicate on a claim when the domestic system places severe economic hurdles in the way of the individual. A rigid assessment of the relationship between costs and exhaustion will only entrench zones of impunity for human rights violations.

There is an emerging understanding of how costs can impede access to justice. The HRC, CEDAW, CERD and CAT Committees have hinted that if individuals explain why it would be unreasonable to expend resources to pursue domestic remedies, they could be absolved from fulfilling the exhaustion criteria.[91] There is jurisprudence fleshing out how to demonstrate financial unreasonableness, although it is inconsistent. The proof of the cost of pursuing proceedings – such as financial data on the de facto resources under the individual's control, the rates of legal fees and the availability and eligibility criteria for legal aid – should be satisfactory evidence, under an individual-centred, contextual

[89] *M.A.M.N.* v. *UK*, CEDAW/C/76/D/141/2019, 6 July 2020, para. 6.7; *Kell* v. *Canada*, CEDAW/C/51/D/19/2008, 28 February 2012, Individual Opinion of Committee member Patricia Shulz (dissenting), paras 2.1, 2.5, 2.6; *E.I.G.R.* v. *Spain*, CCPR/C/130/D/3639/2019, 6 November 2020, para. 7.4; *Moylan* (CERD), para 6.4; *Z.S. and A.S.* v. *Switzerland*, CRC/C/89/D/74/2019, 10 February 2022, para. 6.5; *J.S.* v. *Canada*, CAT/C/62/D/695/2015 28 November 2017, para. 6.5; *F.O.F.* v. *Brazil*, CRPD/C/23/D/40/2017, 2 September 2020, para 8.8; *J.B.* v. *Canada*, CAT/C/D/529/2012, 10 August 2016, para. 8.3.

[90] *Sacchi* (CRC) , para. 10.15.

[91] *Moylan* (CERD), para. 6.5; *E.I.G.R.* (HRC), para. 7.4; *J.S.* v. *UK*, CEDAW/C/53/D/38/2012, 12 October 2012, para. 6.3.

assessment, that costs block achieving domestic justice beyond a mere doubt or assumption.

Turning first to the cost of pursuing proceedings, MG's application for asylum in Switzerland was rejected. He was unable to pursue an appeal, and he filed a communication with the CAT Committee. MG, as an Eritrean asylum-seeker, was not permitted to work and relied exclusively on social welfare. The evidence indicated that during the relevant time, MG received between ten and fourteen francs per day. He did not have the resources to pay the fees of 600 francs to access the Federal Administrative Court. The CAT Committee concluded that since MG was 'destitute', it would be unfair and unreasonable to require him to pursue all domestic remedies.[92] Similarly, in *Abdulkarim* v. *Switzerland*, the CAT Committee held that it would be unfair for a Sudanese asylum-seeker to pay the legal application fee of 1,200 francs when the individual was not authorised to work and only received five francs per day from the State.[93] Given these dire financial circumstances, the CAT Committee held there was no obligation to appeal the deportation decision before the Federal Administrative Court. The evidence before the treaty body readily demonstrated that the mathematics of income and legal fees created insurmountable barriers to justice. Under an individual, contextual assessment, however, the treaty body could more fully engage with the economic accessibility. It is the intersection of poverty, race and migration status with the structures of the social welfare system and the justice system that denied MG and Abdulkarim access to domestic accountability. The exhaustion criteria should fully account for the totality of these obstacles.

An individual-centred, contextual assessment does not require that everyone who lives in poverty be able to provide sophisticated financial data. In a communication to the CRPD Committee, ANP argued he was entitled to a rebate on his municipal taxes as he was a disabled person on low to moderate income. He explained his income was 600 rand per month, while a South African lawyer charged between 2,000 and 3,000 rand per hour. The CRPD Committee characterised ANP's costs arguments as 'of a general nature'.[94] While this assessment of finances and costs was simple, it did reveal a significant obstacle. A more promising way forward comes from the HRC. A child was forced into domestic

[92] *M.G.* v. *Switzerland*, CAT/C/65/D/811/2017, 7 December 2018, paras 6.4–6.5.

[93] *Abdulkarim* v. *Switzerland*, CAT/C/62/D/710/2015, 6 November 2017, para 6.2.

[94] *A.N.P.* v. *South Africa*, CRPD/C/23/D/73/2019, 28 August 2020, para. 5.3.

work due to his family's financial precarity. His employers accused him of theft. He could not afford bail, was detained in an adult prison, where he was tortured, and ultimately, he was convicted. The HRC held that appealing the verdict would have been a 'significant financial burden he could not afford due to his economic status'.[95] The extent of the burden was not evidenced through financial statements but through the individual's identity characteristics as a young, convicted person who lived in poverty.

An individual-centred, contextual analysis also enriches the exhaustion analysis when access to legal aid is at stake. The CRPD Committee has criticised individuals for not taking any steps to obtain low-cost or free legal aid.[96] This assumes that the legal aid system is adequately funded. The CEDAW Committee in *Matson* v. *Canada* examined the funding model of legal aid programmes, as the state argued that the Indigenous low-income individual should have funded constitutional litigation through the various pro bono and legal aid schemes. It concluded that these schemes did not have sufficient funding.[97] Scrutinising the legal aid system revealed a chronic lack of funding, and as such, there was no requirement for the individual to secure it and pursue domestic remedies. This stands in contrast to *Sacchi* v. *Argentina* where, although it is not clear whether the individuals offered any explanation as to costs, the CRC Committee seems to have accepted at face value the sufficiency of legal aid. A more generous approach to costs, legal aid and the requirement to exhaust would identify how the design of legal aid can cement barriers to domestic justice, particularly for disadvantaged groups.[98] For example, NB and MWJ decided not to pursue domestic remedies on restrictions placed on the UK's disability support fund, arguing that the remedies were 'prohibitively expensive'.[99] At the admissibility stage before the CRPD Committee, the state argued NB and MWJ should have sought out legal aid. An individual, contextual assessment would bring to the fore gender and disability biases embedded in the structures of legal aid. MJW's husband's earnings would be included in the eligibility assessment, furthering assumptions on gendered economic

[95] *Pharaka* v. *Nepal*, CCPR/C/126/D/2773/2016, 15 July 2019, para. 6.5.
[96] *A.N.P.* (CRPD), para. 5.3.
[97] *Matson* (CEDAW), para. 17.6.
[98] Section 6.2; CPRD Committee, Concluding Observations: United Kingdom, CRPD/C/GBR/CO/1, 3 October 2017, para 33.
[99] *N.B.* and *M.W.J.* v. *UK*, CRPD/C/22/D/43/2017, 6 September 2019, para. 5.2.

dependency, and the assessment did not account for how much of their earnings were expended in relation to their respective disabilities. Various UN actors, as canvassed in Section 6.2, warned against this type of indirect discrimination in legal aid. The CRPD Committee applied a formalistic approach to the exhaustion requirement and deemed the communication inadmissible as NB and MWJ had not attempted to apply for legal aid.[100] A more sophisticated approach to exhaustion would identify how the individual circumstances of MWJ and NB interacted within a larger context of gender and disability inequality that had filtered into the design of the legal aid system. This would have revealed the significant economic barriers to accessing domestic justice. Udombana warns that the exhaustion rule should not focus on ticking boxes, as the ultimate point of the exhaustion rule is to ensure the most appropriate body redresses the 'wrong suffered'.[101] Forcing individuals to be rejected from legal aid so the treaty body can formally conclude remedies have been pursued loses sight of the '*raison d'être* of the rule'.[102]

In contrast to the CRPD Committee, a dissenting opinion from the HRC in *NE* v. *Denmark* and a majority opinion of the CRC Committee in *AS* v. *Denmark* placed the individual at the centre of the cost-exhaustion analysis. In both communications, the individual was rejected from legal aid schemes, but due to the high costs of legal proceedings, there was found to be no obligation to pursue remedies they could not afford.[103] Uniting these communications is a deep appreciation that the individuals were minors and thus less able to secure resources outside of the legal aid system. Using the individual-centred, contextual assessment, the UNTB should examine how the individual's circumstances – for example being a minor, disabled or from a racial minority – relate to contextual institutional structures, such as the design of legal aid and the costs of remedies.

[100] *N.B.* and *M.W.J. (CRPD)*, para. 6.6.

[101] N. Udombana, 'So Far, So Fair: The Local Remedies Rule in the Jurisprudence of the African Commission on Human and Peoples' Rights', (2003) *The American Journal of International Law* 97(1) (2003): 1–37, 1, 6.

[102] Udombana, 'So Far, So Fair', 6.

[103] *N.E.* v. *Denmark*, CCPR/C/133/D/3325/2019, 27 October 2021, para. 7.6; Joint Opinion by Committee Members Wafaa Ashraf Moharram Bassim and Jose Manuel Santos Pais (dissenting), para. 15; Individual Opinion by Committee Member Hélène Tigroudja (dissenting), para. 3; *A.S.* v. *Denmark*, CRC/C/82/D/36/2017, 26 September 2019, para. 9.2.

6.4.4 Good Quality

The final elements of access to justice – good quality and ineffective remedy – directly connect to the textual exemptions in the conventions and optional protocols and have been explored in various commentaries.[104] The first is an acknowledgement that the lack of quality of the domestic justice system can frustrate the individual's ability to meet the admissibility criteria. The most common quality issue is delay. This was unsuccessfully pleaded in *Sacchi* v. *Argentina*. However, despite the backlogs in courts, exacerbated by COVID-19, and the fact that novel and complex environmental claims can take decades to resolve, the CRC Committee held there was an effective remedy that the individuals should have pursued.[105] An individual-centred, contextual analysis can spotlight these larger contextual factors and ensure domestic delay does not preclude access to international accountability. As evidence of treaty body inconsistency, the CRC Committee, in relation to a different factual-legal matrix, was able to identify how individual identity characteristics and larger contexts should shape the exhaustion analysis. Within a two-year period, the state had not resolved disputes about a child's primary school registration. While on its face, two years is not an excessive period of time, it is significant in the context of a child's access to school, as the right to primary education for a minor must be realised immediately.[106] The CRC Committee therefore deemed the communication admissible. The larger political context was also relevant in *Abaida* v. *Libya,* a decision by the CEDAW Committee. Abaida had been repeatedly beaten, arrested and detained due to her campaigning for women's rights, but filing a complaint 'generated only an acknowledgement of receipt'.[107] The failure to investigate 'coincided with the breakdown of the rule of law in Libya'.[108] Despite there being no domestic investigation, the CEDAW Committee held, in light of these circumstances, that it was not precluded from considering the merits of the claim.

[104] M. Campbell and J. Connors, 'Optional Protocol' in P. Schulz and Others (eds), *CEDAW Commentary* (2nd edn.) (Oxford University Press: Oxford, 2022).

[105] D. Boyd and J. Knox, Amici Curiae Brief of Special Rapporteurs on Human Rights and Environment in Support of Admissibility (*C.S. et al.* v. *Argentina, Brazil, France, Germany and Turkey*) (2020).

[106] *A.E.A.* v. *Spain*, CRC/C/87/D/115/2020, 31 May 2021, para. 11.2.

[107] *Abaida* v. *Libya*, CEDAW/C/78/D/130/2018, 8 March 2017, para. 5.3.

[108] *Abaida* (CEDAW).

Individuals have also challenged the impartiality of the domestic justice system. Again, the treaty bodies adopted an individual-centred, contextual analysis, examining multiple pieces of evidence, to assess if the quality of the domestic remedies exempted the individual from pursuing them. For example, in one case, the HRC decided that international and civil society reports on the lack of independence of the Sri Lankan judiciary meant there was no requirement to pursue a remedy to the apex court.[109] In another communication against Cameroon, a journalist covering a South Cameroon separatist movement was arrested and tortured numerous times. He argued that the judiciary would not provide effective remedies to individuals involved in the independence movement. In this communication, the state brought evidence of separatists charged with similar offences who had had their charges dismissed by the courts.[110] Examining all of the evidence, the HRC concluded the accusations of bias were presumptive and unsubstantiated, and that the accusations of impartiality amounted to mere doubt or assumption. This communication is an important reminder that an individual-centred, contextual analysis does not inherently mean the communication is admissible, but it does provide the treaty bodies with a fuller, more detailed picture when coming to a determination on exhaustion.

6.4.5 *Ineffective Remedy*

The treaty bodies do assess whether the domestic remedy is effective. For example, when the accountability body does not have the competence to order a remedy that addresses the breach of human rights, there is no requirement to initiate any action before that body. The same applies if the remedy does not address the underlying breach of the right. In *Sacchi* v. *Argentina*, the individuals argued there were no domestic remedies that could effectively address the international elements of the climate crisis, but the CRC Committee disagreed that domestic remedies would be unable to address international cooperation.[111] A remedy is ineffective if the time limit for obtaining a remedy is too short. Although in theory, thirty-five days might be ample time to seek a remedy, an individual-centred, contextual assessment, as done by the HRC, revealed the individual could not use the remedy as they had been hospitalised for months

[109] *Samathanam* v. *Sri Lanka*, CCPR/C/118/D/2412/2014, 28 October 2016.
[110] *S.N.A.* v. *Cameroon*, CCPR/C/107/D/1962/2010, 25 March 2013, para. 4.2.
[111] *Sacchi* (CRC), para. 10.18.

after being tortured.[112] Determining whether a remedy is ineffective or not is enhanced through an individual-centred, contextual assessment, as the likelihood that the remedy will bring relief requires an understanding of on-the-ground realities that could help or hinder implementation of domestic remedies.

6.5 Conclusion

There is a plethora of reasons why individuals fail to bring their claims before domestic accountability bodies. Many of these reasons are rooted in systemic inequalities. Accountability via the individual communications procedure may be the only chance of vindicating grievous violations of human rights. Although little attention has been paid to the exhaustion criteria for admitting individual communications, the application of this rule can either compound the systemic failures of domestic justice, or it can acknowledge the lived experience of individuals. This chapter argues that a non-technical approach to exhaustion is required to both fulfil the purpose of the individual communications procedure and the goals of the exhaustion rule, and proposes an individual-centred, contextual approach be adopted. A generous approach should spillover into the evidencing of the domestic barriers to justice that frustrate the exhaustion rule. The UNTBs should not demand impossible proof from individuals but take into account how evidence can be shaped by identity characteristics, domestic structures and larger sociopolitical contexts.

Select Bibliography

Crawford, J. and Grant, T., 'Local Remedies, Exhaustion of' in *Max Plank Encyclopaedias of International Law* (Oxford: Oxford University Press, 2007).

D'Ascoli, S. and Scherr, K. M., The Rule of Prior Exhaustion of Legal Remedies in the International Law Doctrine and Its Application in the Specific Context of Human Rights Protection, *EUI Working Papers* (2007).

Romano, C. P. R., 'The Rule of Prior Exhaustion of Domestic Remedies: Theory and Practice in International Human Rights Procedures' in Boschiero, N., Scovazzi, T., Pitea, C. and Ragni, C. (eds.), *International Courts and the Development of International Law: Essays in Honour of Tullio Treves* (The Hague: Springer, 2013): 561-572.

[112] *Pandey* v. *Nepal*, CCPR/C/124/D/2413/2014, 30 October 2018, para 7.4.

Shikhelman, V., 'Access to Justice in the UN Human Rights Committee', *Michigan Journal of International Law* 39 (3) (2018): 453–531.

Udombana, N., 'So Far, So Fair: The Local Remedies Rule in the Jurisprudence of the African Commission on Human and Peoples' Rights', *The American Journal of International Law* 97 (1) (2003): 1–37.

von Staden, A., 'Subsidiarity, Exhaustion of Domestic Remedies and the Margin of Appreciation in the Human Rights Jurisprudence of African Sub-regional Courts', *International Journal of Human Rights* 20 (8) (2016): 1113–1131.

Zysset, A. and Çalı, B., 'Exhausting Domestic Remedies or Exhausting the Rule of Law? Revisiting the Normative Basis of Procedural Subsidiarity in the European Human Rights System', *Transnational Legal Theory* 14 (2) (2023): 157–177.

7

Reversing the Burden of Proof in Response to State Non-participation

Recent Evolutions in the Human Rights Committee's Examination of Individual Torture Claims

KASEY MCCALL-SMITH*

7.1 Introduction

In the earliest individual communications considered by the Human Rights Committee (HRC or Committee) in relation to breaches of the International Covenant on Civil and Political Rights (ICCPR),[1] there was little guidance on evidentiary burdens. Over the past four decades of reviewing individual communications, the HRC has developed greater consistency when allocating the burden of proof, particularly in relation to claims of torture. This development makes a unique case study for the consideration of evidence in torture claims, as these are rarely raised in isolation before the HRC. Unlike claims before the Committee against Torture (CAT), the HRC monitors a range of interrelated human rights that expand beyond the prohibition against torture. Allegations of breaches of other rights, such as the right to liberty and security of a person, often foreground torture allegations when raised before the HRC. In claims of torture while in the custody of the state, individual claimants, referred to as 'authors' in the treaty body system, and the state are generally on unequal footing in terms of accessing corroborative or exculpatory information. As such, the HRC tends to shift the burden of proof to the state as a means of addressing this asymmetry.

* With great appreciation to Isobel Burns, Marshall Putnam and Darcy Fahey for research assistance and thanks to the volume editors for their attention to detail.

[1] International Covenant on Civil and Political Rights, 16 December 1966, in force 23 March 1976, 999 UNTS 171 (ICCPR).

This chapter aims to assess whether the HRC's practice of shifting the evidentiary burden between the author and the state is consistent and traceable in the Committee's decisions on individual communications, known as 'final views'. The grounds on which this shift is made merit consideration: notably, the nature of the allegations, the evidence used to corroborate the allegations, and the extent to which the state engages with the process seem to impact the articulation of the shifted burden in certain cases. For example, in *Maya* v. *Nepal* (2017), a particularly egregious but not isolated case, the author alleged that she was beaten and gang raped by officers of the Royal Nepalese Army for being a suspected Maoist supporter.[2] Based on the alleged conduct by state actors, she claimed violations of multiple rights protected by the ICCPR, including breaches of the prohibition against torture or other cruel, inhuman or degrading treatment (CIDT) (Article 7), the right to liberty and security of person (Article 9) and the right to be free from inhuman treatment in detention (Article 10 (1)), among others. The core of Maya's claim was grounded in the state's failure to investigate her claims of torture while being held in an informal place of detention, despite her submission of supporting evidence to the local police. The evidence provided at the local level and to the HRC included detailed witness statements, medical records and legal documents.[3] In response to the claim before the HRC, Nepal indicated that 'the Royal Nepalese Army had no record of the author's detention'.[4] In its consideration of the merits, the HRC 'recall[ed] that the burden of proof cannot rest on the author of the communication alone, especially since the author and the State party do not always have equal access to the evidence and it is frequently the case that the State party alone has the relevant information'.[5] Following a finding that Nepal had breached the prohibition against torture, the HRC went on to discuss the breach of the right to liberty and security of a person. In response to the State's suggestion that the author failed to evidence her allegations relating to detention in the army barracks, which opened up the circumstances under which she was subsequently tortured, the Committee noted that 'requiring victims of arbitrary and illegal detention to provide records thereof would amount to a *probatio diabolica* [devil's proof]'.[6]

[2] *Maya* v. *Nepal*, CCPR/C/119/D/2245/2013, 17 March 2017.
[3] *Maya* (HRC), para. 7.
[4] *Maya* (HRC), para. 6.
[5] *Maya* (HRC), para. 12.2.
[6] *Maya* (HRC), para. 12.7.

In law, *probatio diabolica* denotes a proof which cannot possibly be achieved, meaning an impossible proof. In judicial proceedings, whenever such a proof is expected from a party, the latter will by definition not be in a position to bring it. The only remedy against this situation is for the adjudicatory body to shift the burden of proof onto the other party. In effect, if such a shift is operated, a presumption arises in favour of the party originally expected to prove their claim. This presumption will stand unless the party to which the burden has been shifted rebuts it with exculpatory proof. The framing of the burden of proof in the *Maya* case is interesting because the HRC's approach to establishing or balancing burdens of proof has not always been self-evident. The HRC has long recognised that the authors and states parties to the ICCPR will not always have equal access to evidence. However, there has been little attention paid to the base levels of evidence required to support a higher burden being placed on the state to disprove an alleged violation of the ICCPR. More reflection, too, is necessary on the ways in which a state's participation or non-participation in the individual communications process shapes any potential shift of the evidentiary burden.

The analysis presented below interrogates the types of evidence that are required from the author to shift the burden of proof to the state to disprove allegations of torture in violation of the ICCPR. As Joost Pauwelyn has explored previously, the 'burden of proof' can be separated in a number of ways, including by distinguishing between the burdens of, respectively, 'production' (referring to the evidence a party is expected to submit) and 'persuasion' (referring to the risk of losing the case for lack of having properly evidenced it).[7] While his work examines defences in more complex international claims, here the term 'burden of proof' absorbs both concepts for simplicity in the cases raised before a treaty body. A more complete understanding of the operation of the burden of proof in cases before the HRC is important, as treaty bodies shape the outer edges of human rights interpretations in response to the broad range of individual communications they review. In the context of what the HRC is doing in the cases examined, it appears to be developing a (increasingly) consistent practice of adjusting evidentiary burdens as a

[7] J. Pauwelyn, 'Defences and the Burden of Proof in International Law' in L. Bartels and F. Paddeu (eds.), *Exceptions in International Law* (Oxford: Oxford University Press, 2020), pp. 88–107. While not addressing human rights claims before treaty bodies, Pauwelyn's examination of burdens of proof in predominantly inter-state or investor-state claims offers an interesting counterpoint to the analysis offered here.

means of overcoming information asymmetries resulting from the inaccessibility of either inculpatory or exculpatory information. To effect this burden shift, the HRC appears to follow the following steps when assessing claims of a breach of the prohibition against torture or CIDT: (1) the allegations must be corroborated by some level of evidence; (2) the HRC applies a rebuttable presumption that the author's alleged facts are true; unless (3) the state offers evidence in direct response to the specific allegations of torture or CIDT. Tilmann Altwicker and Alexandra Hansen recently elaborated the main functions that presumptions serve in human rights adjudication, including: '(1) overcoming information asymmetries or the inaccessibility of information, (2) helping to bridge general facts and the legal assessment in individual cases, and (3) helping to avoid normative conflicts between legal regimes'.[8] The first of these functions, overcoming information asymmetries and inaccessibility of information, resonates with the practice of the HRC. Across the claims assessed by the HRC, the presumption is applied where the access to relevant inculpatory or exculpatory evidence is unequal and the state is in the stronger position to access such information. The presumption applied by the HRC also helps address the summary nature of the final views, where a complete account of the evidence presented is not available, but only summarised in the public decision. This reflects the second function of presumptions outlined by Altwicker and Hansen, as the presumption 'function[s] as a secondary rule on *secondary* rules of adjudication when they are applied in the context of uncertainties in fact-finding'.[9] It is suggested here that the presumption employed by the HRC aids in both overcoming information asymmetries and bridging general facts and the ultimate legal assessment.

This chapter will contextualise the situations of evidence burden shifting as they occur in torture claims before the HRC. First, Section 7.2 will briefly explain the individual communications underpinning this analysis. In Section 7.3, the burden of proof in the HRC individual communications procedure will be discussed in the context of (in)equality of access to information and how this sets the stage for the burden of

[8] T. Altwicker and A. E. Hansen, 'Presumptions as Secondary Rules in the Judicial Interpretation of International Human Rights' in G. Kajtár, B. Çali and M. Milanović (eds.), *Secondary Rules of Primary Importance in International Law* (Oxford: Oxford University Press, 2022), pp. 167–182, 182.

[9] Altwicker and Hansen, 'Presumptions', p. 180 (emphasis original). Their analysis focused predominantly on the European Court of Human Rights.

proof to be transferred from the author to the respondent state. It will outline how equality of access to information underpins the concept of equality of arms, which is defeated by state non-participation. Section 7.4 then traces the HRC's approach to burdens of proof and non-participation by states in cases where a breach of the prohibition against torture is alleged. The aim is to discern patterns in the allocation of evidentiary burdens, as indicated by a presumption being established in favour of the complainant. Section 7.5 offers some final reflections on the ways in which the practice of the HRC has coalesced when faced with information asymmetry and the need to bridge facts and legal assessment.

7.2 Brief Explanation of the Cases Sampled

Under the Optional Protocol to the ICCPR (OP-ICCPR) individuals may raise before the HRC a claim, in writing, that any right set out in the ICCPR has been violated as long as the individual has exhausted all domestic remedies and complies with other procedural requirements.[10] Notably, consent to the HRC's review of individual communications is an elective, additional obligation on the state that sits adjacent to obligations arising through the ICCPR. States parties to the OP-ICCPR have six months to explain or clarify the matters raised in a claim, including any remedies delivered at the domestic level, once the Committee has notified the state of the complaint.[11]

This chapter is based on a review of HRC decisions concerning alleged breaches of Article 7 of the ICCPR, which lays down the prohibition against torture or CIDT (the prohibition). Focusing on torture claims is interesting given the extensive codification[12] of the prohibition in international law, as well as its recognition as both a rule of customary international law and an inviolable peremptory norm.[13] Exploring the

[10] Optional Protocol to the ICCPR, New York, 16 December 1966, in force 23 March 1976, 999 UNTS 171 (OP-ICCPR), Art. 2; see further details in Human Rights Committee (HRC), Rules of Procedure, CCPR/C/3/Rev.12, 4 January 2021, Rules 90, 92.

[11] OP-ICCPR, Art. 4.

[12] E.g.: ICCPR, Art. 7; Convention against Torture and Other Cruel, Inhuman or Degrading Treatment, 10 December 1984, in force 26 June 1987, 1465 UNTS 85; Convention on the Rights of the Child, 20 November 1989, in force 2 September 1990, 1577 UNTS 3, Art. 37 (a).

[13] S. Greer, 'Is the Prohibition against Torture, Cruel, Inhuman and Degrading Treatment Really "Absolute" in International Human Rights Law', *Human Rights Law Review* 15

prohibition under the ICCPR, rather than the UN Convention against Torture and Other Cruel, Inhuman or Degrading Treatment, enables the breach of the prohibition to be understood in the context of other human rights violations addressed in the extensive jurisprudence of the HRC. Furthermore, within the ICCPR system, as explained below, torture is often the consequence that follows the breach of another civil and political right, such as interference with the right to liberty and security of person (Article 9 ICCPR). The content of the prohibition as a norm is constantly evolving in the distinctive treaty regimes. This evolution has the potential to influence the development of the prohibition's interpretation as both a treaty obligation and a customary rule of international law, which is generally assessed through state practice.[14] In light of the connective value between treaty interpretations and the progressive development of customary international law, the analysis below relies explicitly on the language deployed by the HRC to address evidentiary burdens in situations where the state does not participate, either fully or partially, in the individual communications process.

The cases underpinning the analysis provided in this chapter were selected using the following process. First, the Office of the High Commissioner for Human Rights (OHCHR) Juris Database was searched using the term 'forced confession' in conjunction with Article 7 (prohibition against torture), Article 9 (right to liberty and security of person) and Article 14 (right to fair trial) of the ICCPR (ninety-one results).[15] The process was repeated using 'solitary confinement' in conjunction with the same articles (forty-four results). These cases are premised upon the author being detained, legally or not, and the state using detention as an opportunity to force a confession or to punish the detainee.[16] As detention triggers an obligation for the state to keep records, these cases serve as a good basis for discussing the impact of the state's lack of participation in the individual communications process. This set of 135 cases was narrowed down through the elimination of cases that were either about *non-refoulement* or predominantly related to psychological suffering arising from the enforced disappearance of a family member.

(2015): 101–137, 108; D. Weissbrodt and C. Heilman, 'Defining Torture and Cruel, Inhuman, and Degrading Treatment', *Law and Inequality* 29 (2011): 343–394, 348.

[14] K. McCall-Smith, 'Treaty Bodies: Choreographing the Customary Prohibition against Torture', *International Community Law Review* 23 (2019): 344–368.

[15] JURIS database search results on 15 March 2024.

[16] Using torture to force a confession or to punish are both prohibited.

These would not have been helpful for examining the question addressed in this chapter, since non-refoulement cases are not claims of torture by the state that is party to the claim, but relate to the potential for torture if returned to another state. As such, the access to evidence about the detention or treatment of the individual author typically is not accessible by the defending state. Claims raised for psychological suffering arising from the enforced disappearance of a family member were excluded, also, because the psychological torture in these cases is an indirect effect of the state's alleged actions against another individual. Notably, however, some enforced disappearance cases are used to set out the original understanding of evidentiary burden shifting presented in Section 7.3. Narrowing the field to the two items of forced confessions and solitary confinement ensured that the research, although non-exhaustive, would be manageable, as well as broadly comparable in the forms of evidence that could be expected to be offered.

The set of cases was reduced yet further by only keeping decisions that included one (or more) of the following phrases, which indicated that the respondent state did not fully engage with the communications process: 'failure to refute allegations', 'absence of any convincing explanation', 'failure to contest', 'has not commented on allegations', 'absence of information', 'failure to provide information' and 'failure to provide a response'. This narrowed focus aids in tracing the shifting of the burden of proof in communications alleging a breach of the prohibition against torture. The result is that Section 7.4 is based on an analysis of twenty-six HRC final views.

7.3 The Burden of Proof in the Individual Communications Procedure

This chapter focuses on claims that have cleared the initial admissibility determination by the HRC. Among other information required to access the OP-ICCPR dispute settlement mechanism, communications must include '[t]he facts of the claim *and* evidence to substantiate them' (emphasis added).[17] This suggests that the HRC, like other dispute settlement bodies, requires more than a narrative of alleged facts. Typically, the extent to which the author must prove the alleged facts is referred to as the burden of proof. Notably, unlike traditional courts, the

[17] HRC, Rules of Procedure, Rule 90(1)(f).

publicly available decisions in the HRC individual communications procedure provide only a summary of the written exchanges between the individual and the state, which can obscure the evidentiary support for claims.

The burden of proving allegations links to the right to fair trial. In General Comment 32, the HRC explained that the right to fair trial (Article 14 ICCPR) requires that both sides of a dispute are 'given the opportunity to contest all arguments and evidence'.[18] It is a rights-protecting requirement to ensure equality of arms of the author and the respondent. As explored elsewhere, equality of arms in international law does not require 'mathematical equality', but rather a proportional opportunity to substantiate or rebut claims in order to uphold the substance of the right to fair trial as interpreted under the ICCPR.[19] Notably, most of the discussions relating to this aspect of fair trial play out in the context of international criminal law or regional human rights courts' analysis of domestic criminal prosecutions. The foundation for equality of arms is rooted in these examinations of what information the state might hold about a defendant in the criminal justice system. In such examinations, the defendant is being prosecuted for breaching the laws of the state. There is a concomitant obligation on the state to reveal any evidence in its possession that may exculpate the defendant.[20] The overarching aim is to ensure that the conditions relating to the presentation of the case, including any available evidence, do not place any party at a disadvantage vis-à-vis their opponent.[21]

As a preliminary matter, it is important to recognise that within the range of activities that give rise to a breach of the torture prohibition, some granularity is required in consideration of the specific actions alleged and the particular status of the victim. The analysis below will focus on two types of claims: forced confessions and torture as punishment of alleged criminals, including political dissidents and alleged terrorists. Some of the cases, unsurprisingly, will traverse both types of

[18] HRC, General Comment No. 32. Right to equality before courts and tribunals and to fair trial, CCPR/C/GC/32, 23 August 2007, para. 13.

[19] A. Clooney and P. Webb, *The Right to a Fair Trial in International Law* (Oxford: Oxford University Press, 2021), p. 753.

[20] D. Weissbrodt and K. K. Zinsmaster, 'Protecting the Fair Trial Rights of the Accused in International Criminal Law: Comparison of the International Criminal Court and the Military Commissions in Guantánamo' in B. S. Brown (ed.), *Research Handbook on International Criminal Law* (Cheltenham: Edward Elgar, 2011), pp. 261–283, 279.

[21] Clooney and Webb, *The Right to a Fair Trial*, p. 748.

claims. However, the analysis will focus on the key evidence features relevant to the HRC's decision on the merits. The different approaches to balancing burdens of proof in the two types of claims will be addressed in turn in Section 7.4. First, however, the sub-sections below will offer a brief explanation of the HRC's teleological treatment of evidence across the decades of its operation, as well as a comment on non-participation by states in the individual communications process.

7.3.1 Evidentiary Burdens in Cases of Torture Addressed by the HRC: Brief Teleological Review

In its early reviews of alleged violations of Article 7 (prohibition against torture), the HRC did not explain the process it used for weighing evidence. The Committee, however, noted that the victim's and the state's access to evidence substantiating or disproving a claim of torture was typically unequal. In the 1982 case of *Bleier* v. *Uruguay*, the HRC explained that this lack of equality necessitated shifting the burden of proof to the state:

> With regard to the burden of proof, this cannot rest alone on the author of the communication, especially considering that the author and the State party do not always have equal access to the evidence and that frequently the State party alone has access to relevant information.[22]

Two years later, in the case of *Weismann and Perdomo* v. *Uruguay*, Uruguay acknowledged that it had detained the complainants, but it dismissed the claims of torture as 'figments of the author's imagination'.[23] The HRC confirmed that it was up to the State to offer alternative explanations as a means of disproving the author's detailed allegations of torture while in detention – claims which were supported with medical documentation.[24] When Uruguay did not offer an alternative explanation, the HRC found a breach of the prohibition against torture and CIDT.

During the 1980s and 1990s, the HRC had the occasion to review many communications in relation to enforced disappearances, torture and other forms of prohibited treatment. Over the years, the Committee refined its evidentiary burden placement into a formula. This expressly

[22] *Bleierv. Uruguay*, CCPR/C/15/D/30/1978, para. 13.3.

[23] *Weismann and Perdomo* v. *Uruguay*, CCPR/C/OP/1, 3 April 1984, para. 8.

[24] *Weismann and Perdomo* (HRC), paras. 9, 11(c).

recognises that while the author holds the initial burden of proof, certain types of evidence – either implicatory or exculpatory in nature – will be held by the state. In such circumstances, the burden must shift to the state 'to provide a satisfactory and plausible explanation supported by evidence'.[25] While there has been no explicit guidance on what amounts to a 'satisfactory and plausible explanation', the HRC noted in *Khadzhiyev* v. *Turkmenistan* (2018) that '[i]f a death occurs in custody, it should be regarded prima facie as a summary or arbitrary execution, unless this presumption can be rebutted by a thorough, prompt and impartial investigation'.[26] In this particular case, the author had alleged that his sister, Ogulsapar Muradova, had died in state custody as a result of torture and ill-treatment, among other violations of the ICCPR. The evidence offered to the Committee included the personal, detailed observations of Muradova's body post-mortem, which strongly indicated torture and ill-treatment.[27] In its consideration of the merits, the HRC found that Turkmenistan's suggestion that Muradova committed suicide was not supported by any evidence. The State had also not presented any evidence of an investigation into her death that might have rebutted the allegations that she had died as a result of torture.[28]

As made clear by the HRC, the evidentiary shift stems from the onus on the state to take responsibility for the lives of individuals whom it takes into custody.[29] Part of the responsibility of the state when detaining individuals is the keeping of accurate records, including the legal basis for the original and ongoing detention, the treatment of the individual while in detention and the responses to any allegations of ill-treatment while in detention.[30] Withholding information about the individual during their time in the custody of the state deprives that individual of equality of arms with the state.[31] As noted in the *Maya* case introduced above, the HRC demands that when 'the author has presented a credible case as to

[25] *Khadzhiyev* v. *Turkmenistan*, CCPR/C/122/D/2252/2013, 24 May 2018, para. 5.2, citing *Bleier* (HRC), para. 13.3. See, also, *Pandey* v. *Nepal*, CCPR/C/124/D/2413/2014, 30 October 2018, para. 8.3; *Khoroshenko* v. *Russian Federation*, CCPR/C/101/D/1304/2004, 29 March 2011, para. 9.5.

[26] *Khadzhiyev* (HRC) , para. 5.2, citing *Eshonov* v. *Uzbekistan*, CCPR/C/99/D/1225/2003, 18 August 2010, para. 9.2.

[27] *Khadzhiyev* v. *Turkmenistan*, CCPR, paras. 2.14, 3.1, 5.3, 7.2.

[28] *Khadzhiyev* (HRC), paras. 7.2, 7.3, 7.4.

[29] *Khadzhiyev* (HRC), para. 7.3.

[30] HRC, General Comment No. 20: Article 7, CCPR/C/GC/20, 1992, para. 11; HRC, General Comment No. 35: Article 9, CCPR/C/GC/35, paras. 23, 58

[31] Weissbrodt and Zinsmaster, 'Protecting the Fair Trial Rights of the Accused', p. 279.

her detention … requiring victims of arbitrary and illegal arrest and detention to provide records thereof would amount to a *probatio diabolica*'.[32] The HRC's use of 'devil's proof' is a compelling framing of the evidentiary burden in the *Maya* case, where the author had presented detailed, multi-fold allegations of arbitrary detention and torture by members of the Royal Nepalese Army and Armed Police Force. The HRC's approach in *Maya* suggests that any burden amounting to 'devil's proof' should be examined carefully to ensure that no party bears an illogical burden. It is sufficient here to acknowledge that use of 'devil's proof' by the HRC in the context of burden shifting appears to resonate with other human rights bodies and warrants a closer examination to better understand such shifts.[33]

Across the different cases examined here, the Committee appears cognisant of the necessity for the teleological interpretation of the prohibition to draw a clear baseline for treatment that states parties should not cross. A question arises, however, in discerning where the facts actually lay in the context of proof of torture when the state fails to participate effectively in the proceedings. Section 7.3.2 considers non-participation in the context of individual communications procedures before the HRC.

7.3.2 Non-participation and Burdens of Proof in Final Views

Consent to the OP-ICCPR individual communications procedure is an additional, voluntary step that each state party must unilaterally elect to take. However, even though states choose to subject themselves to this procedure, this does not ensure that they will necessarily participate in actual proceedings. In claims of torture, decisions finding states in breach of the prohibition often result from the state's failure to participate in the proceedings. In such cases, states either fail to directly respond to the shifted evidentiary burden or do not participate at all in the proceedings, which permits the author's allegations to lay uncontested. Common

[32] *Maya* (HRC), para. 12.7. Repeated verbatim in *Nyaya* v. *Nepal*, CCPR/C/125/D/2556/2015, 18 March 2019, para. 7.7.

[33] See, e.g.: *Martinie* v. *France*, ECtHR, 58675/00, Judgment, 12 April 2006, compare the French and English versions of the joint partly dissenting opinion of Judges Costa, Caflisch and Jungwiert, para. 13; *Samüt Karabulut* v. *Turkey*, ECtHR, 16999/04, Judgment, 27 January 2009, paras. 43–44. For an example where the underpinning, non-human rights fact is contextualised using the term, see *Ova A.S.* v. *Slovakia*, ECtHR, 72493/10, Judgment, 9 June 2015, para. 22.

approaches in the deployment of secondary rules of law for non-participation in international dispute settlement proceedings recently were examined by Christopher Lentz, including in relation to the individual communications proceedings by the UN treaty bodies. In addition to the International Court of Justice (ICJ), the Permanent Court of Arbitration and the International Tribunal on the Law of the Sea, Lentz reviewed the HRC, the CAT and the Committee on the Elimination of Discrimination against Women and their approaches to non-participation in the course of assessing individual communications.[34] As explained by Lentz, the analysis was based on a non-exhaustive review of the three human rights treaty bodies as a means of discerning similarity or divergence in practice across the range of adjudicatory mechanisms. By contrast, this chapter narrows the focus to the HRC and explores whether there is a consistent pattern in the way this body determines claims of torture when the respondent state fails to participate in the proceedings or does not specifically rebut the facts underpinning the claim of torture.

In cases of non-participation, Lentz suggests that one must rely on the constitutive documents of a dispute settlement body to ascertain how far the adjudicator might go to determine a claim.[35] Similarly, relying on its competence-establishing document, the OP-ICCPR, the HRC must review 'all information made available to it' without setting a minimum threshold for what the state must present in response to an author's claim.[36] From the perspective of the state, participation affords the opportunity to defend itself against claims of human rights violations. Even if the state holds evidence confirming the facts alleged, opening discussions with the HRC about gaps in implementation or practice would direct the HRC's attention to the specific circumstances. This type of bilateral dialogue is a key purpose of the treaty bodies.[37] Provision of specific evidence could also guard against broader assumptions about the state's adherence to its treaty obligations or the state's general approach to implementation of the treaty.

[34] C. Lentz, 'The Evidentiary Implications of a Party's Non-participation in the Proceedings' in G. Kajtár, B. Çali and M. Milanović (eds.), *Secondary Rules of Primary Importance in International Law* (Oxford: Oxford University Press, 2022), pp. 202–218, 203.

[35] Lentz, 'Evidentiary Implications of a Party's Non-participation', p. 203.

[36] Art. 5, OP-ICCPR.

[37] See, e.g.: N. S. Rodley, 'UN Treaty Bodies and the Human Rights Council' in H. Keller and G. Ulfstein (eds.), *UN Human Rights Treaty Bodies: Law and Legitimacy* (Cambridge: Cambridge University Press, 2012), pp. 320–355.

7.4 Examining the Burden of Proof Across Two Foci

In the HRC's earliest reviews of individual communications, some states dismissed the efforts of the Committee in its quasi-judicial pursuits, deeming its requests for information on allegations of torture as 'not worthy of any further comment'.[38] Undeterred, the HRC set out that where a government refuses to furnish information in response to allegations under the OP-ICCPR, the HRC 'cannot but draw appropriate conclusions on the basis of information before it'.[39] There are countless examples within the treaty body jurisprudence database where the state does not directly respond to the explicit allegations raised. This makes it important to understand what initial burden of proof the HRC applies to the complaining author before shifting the burden of proof onto the state. Across the sample of communications reviewed here, the HRC's practice is charted chronologically to develop a preliminary picture of how the HRC is balancing evidentiary burdens in cases that involve claims of torture in detention. In this narrowed field of cases, there were only five examples where a state did not participate in the communications process at all. As such, the analysis weaves these cases of absolute non-participation with the cases where the state did not fully participate through a failure to respond directly to the author's claims. The following sub-sections consider two types of claims: forced confessions and torture as punishment of alleged criminals (including political dissidents and alleged terrorists).

7.4.1 Forced Confessions

The link between torture and forced confessions is a central motivation for the international prohibition against torture and one that is typically elaborated in national laws and rules of evidence.[40] Two 2004 decisions demonstrate the HRC's unequivocal practice in response to allegations of forced confessions. In *Singarasa* v. *Sri Lanka*, the HRC noted that it is not enough for an alleged victim to be required to meet a low burden of proof to substantiate a torture claim in the national criminal justice system, as

[38] *de Netto v. Uruguay*, CCPR/C/9/D/8/1977, 3 April 1980, paras. 8, 15.

[39] *de Netto* (HRC), para. 15.

[40] HRC, General Comment No. 20: Article 7, CCPR/C/GC/20, 1992, para. 12. This aspect also forms part of the definition of torture found in Art. 1, UN Convention against Torture.

was argued by Sri Lanka.[41] Instead, the HRC considered that the burden of proof to disprove torture resulting in admissions of guilt shifts completely to the State and requires that the State provide specific evidence to account for the treatment of the author during an interrogation resulting in a confession.[42] This shift is equally present, though less specific, in cases where the state fails to respond in any way to a forced confession claim. This was confirmed in *Khomidova* v. *Tajikistan*, where it was found that '[i]n the absence of a reply from the State party, due weight must be given to the author's allegations, to the extent that these have been properly substantiated'.[43] In this context, 'due weight' equates to the HRC's acceptance of the allegation of torture. 'Properly substantiated' initial allegations of fact appeared anchored in the detailed description of the alleged prohibited acts, including identification of the alleged perpetrators, coupled with the failure of the State to respond to the claim of a forced confession.[44]

The same phraseology was repeated in *Sultanova* v. *Uzbekistan* in 2006, where the allegations of torture to elicit a confession were presented in significant detail.[45] The State nevertheless failed to respond directly to Sultanova's claims.[46] Again, the Committee did not explain what is required to 'properly' substantiate a claim for the purposes of meeting the author's burden of proof. However, it appears to have treated the state authorities' failure to 'discharge their obligation effectively to investigate complaints about incidents of torture' as adding 'due weight' to the complainant's allegations.[47] In response to a similar complaint against Uzbekistan the following year, the HRC gave 'due weight' to the allegations of torture where the State failed to 'demonstrate that it conducted any inquiry' into allegations of a forced confession.[48] These cases suggest that the state's failure to carry out its positive obligation to investigate allegations of torture contributes to the weight with which the complaining author's version of the facts is received. It does appear, too,

41 *Singarasa v. Sri Lanka*, CCPR/C/81/D/1033/2001, 23 August 2004, para. 7.4.

42 *Singarasa* (HRC).

43 *Khomidova* v. *Tajikistan*, CCPR/C/81/D/1117/2002, 25 August 2004, para. 4.

44 *Khomidova* (HRC), para. 6.2.

45 (emphasis added) *Sultanova* v. *Uzbekistan*, CCPR/C/86/D/915/2000, 30 March 2006, para. 7.1.

46 *Sultanova* (HRC).

47 *Sultanova* (HRC), paras. 7.1, 7.2. The author had submitted almost 100 complaints requesting the local authorities investigate her allegations of torture, para. 2.4.

48 *Uteeva* v. *Uzbekistan*, CCPR/C/91/D/1150/2003, 13 November 2007, para. 7.2.

that some form of presumption is applied in order to counter the information asymmetry affecting evidence presented to the Committee. In both cases against Uzbekistan, the State failed to investigate the original claims of torture to extract confessions and also did not offer any information to directly rebut the claims of torture.

The presumption of factual validity in the absence of the state's response to allegations of forced confessions continued in *Rakhmatov et al* v. *Tajikistan* in 2008. The communication was submitted on behalf of five men, including two minors, who claimed to have been subjected to torture to elicit confessions.[49] However, it is notable that one of the Article 7 claims (in relation to Bobonyoz Safarov) was dismissed for failure to provide details or supporting documents. This confirms that there is a minimum standard to be met.[50] Tajikistan failed to engage with the Committee, and as a result, the HRC concluded that 'due weight must be given to the authors' allegations'.[51] Four of the five complainants provided extensive detail of their treatment, were able to identify the alleged perpetrators and provided evidence that they had raised the allegations with the prosecutor's office and in their first court appearances.[52] The HRC determined that, at the very least, Tajikistan had failed to fulfil its positive obligation to investigate the allegations of torture.

A similar 2011 decision against Tajikistan found the HRC determining that 'due weight' should be given to the detailed allegations of torture to force a confession in the face of the state's failure to respond.[53] Once again, the state's lack of participation led to a final view that Tajikistan had breached Article 7. In this instance, the victim's status as a prominent opposition politician meant that there was a great deal of open-source material available to support the allegations. The HRC repeated its formulation of 'due weight' in numerous subsequent cases of forced confessions where the state either failed to participate or failed to respond to the allegations of torture to elicit confessions.[54]

[49] *Rakhmatov et al.* v. *Tajikistan*, CCPR/C/92/D/1209/1231/2003 and 1241/2004, 24 August 2008, para. 5.7.

[50] *Rakhmatov et al.* (HRC), para. 5.3.

[51] *Rakhmatov et al.* (HRC), para. 6.2.

[52] *Rakhmatov et al.* (HRC).

[53] *Iskandarov* v. *Tajikstan*, CCPR/C/101/D/1499/2006, 30 March 2011, para. 6.2.

[54] E.g.: *Burdyko* v. *Belarus*, CCPR/C/114/D/2017/2010, 25 September 2015, para. 8.2; *Samathanam* v. *Sri Lanka*, CCPR/C/118/D/2412/2014, 28 October 2016, para. 6.; *Sannikov* v. *Belarus*, CCPR/C/122/D/2212/2012, 14 May 2018, para. 6.2.

Throughout the forced confession cases examined, the HRC has repeatedly reminded states that 'it is incumbent on the State party to produce evidence refuting the author's allegations'.[55] This position tracks the requirement in many common law systems that confessions be untainted. In cases of forced confessions, the non-participation of the state yields the same result whether the state fails to respond to the specific allegation or does not engage with the proceedings at all.

7.4.2 Punishment of Alleged Criminals

Allegations of the use of torture as a tool to punish alleged criminals and suppress political opposition, often under the guise of counter-terrorism, is a recurrent theme in the jurisprudence of the HRC. While the cases of forced confessions have a clear history of burden shifting, the use of torture as punishment is examined separately, as the HRC's approach to evidentiary burdens in this context took longer to emerge. In the 1984 *Weismann and Perdomo* case against Uruguay, discussed in Section 7.3, the HRC examined allegations of torture through the complainants' comprehensive narrative, accompanied by medical documentation and photographs.[56] The complaining authors offered extensive detail regarding which state authorities held them as 'subversives' in incommunicado detention and where the various forms of torture and ill-treatment took place.[57] Uruguay failed to offer any explanation or evidence to contradict the facts presented, other than to confirm that one of the authors had been detained, charged and tried in a military court.[58] No discussion of the corroborating evidence was presented. Ultimately, the HRC concluded that the 'present state of physical and mental ill-health for which no other explanation has been offered by the Uruguayan Government, confirms the allegations of ill-treatment which he suffered while under detention'.[59] The HRC's conclusion in *Weismann and Perdomo* laid out a presumption that is rebuttable, as the author's narrative and evidence were accepted in part due to the State's failure to offer a reasonable

55 *Kashtanova and Slukina* v. *Uzbekistan*, CCPR/C/118/D/2106/2011, *28 October* 2016, para. 8.2. See also, *Atachahua* v. *Peru*, CCPR/C/56/D/540/1993, 16 April 1996, para. 8.2; *Carranza* v. *Peru*, CCPR/C/85/D/1126/2002, 28 October 2005.

56 *Weismann and Perdomo* (HRC), paras. 9, 11(c). This claim subsumed a previous claim made by the authors' niece prior to their release by the state and expulsion.

57 *Weismann and Perdomo* (HRC), para. 9.

58 *Weismann and Perdomo* (HRC), para. 8.

59 *Weismann and Perdomo* (HRC), para. 14(1).

explanation to the contrary. The presumption seems to address information asymmetry between the parties as well as bridge the gap between the facts and the legal conclusion in this particular case, thus reflecting two of the three main functions that presumptions serve in law (as outlined in the introduction).[60] The level of detail offered by the author appears to be an important prelude to a complete shift of the burden of proof.

A decade later, in *Mukong* v. *Cameroon* (1994), the author offered extensive detail in support of his claims regarding the conditions suffered in incommunicado detention, including threats of torture and generally poor conditions of confinement.[61] As a journalist and outspoken advocate of political reform, Mukong was arrested on multiple occasions for peacefully expressing his opinions. In this instance, Cameroon engaged extensively with the Committee. In part, it defended the poor conditions as a reality of the developing social and economic status of the country, but did not offer any evidence to expressly refute the allegations of torture threats.[62] Notably, this demonstrated an effort on the part of the State to offer some degree of exculpatory evidence in terms of the environmental conditions that could lead to a breach of Article 7. However, the State also 'submit[ted] that the burden of proof for his allegations lies with the author'.[63] The author referred to reports by Amnesty International to reinforce the prevalence of torture in Cameroon, and the State submitted a report by the National Centre for Studies and Research about improvements to the prison system to support its defence.[64] The HRC considered all of the information made available but appears to have given greater weight to the detailed narrative offered by the complainant, using its previous phrasing that 'the author and the State party do not always have equal access to the evidence and that frequently the State party alone has access to the relevant information'.[65] Again, rather than concentrate on the author's burden, the Committee focused on the lack of detail

[60] See discussion in the introduction to this chapter on Altwicker and Hansen, 'Presumptions', p. 182.

[61] *Mukong* v. *Cameroon*, CCPR/C/51/D/458/1991, 10 August 1994, para. 6.2. This case unpicks some aspects of the prohibition of torture by clarifying that threats of torture also amount to a breach of Article 7, even if physical actions do not rise to the level of torture.

[62] *Mukong* (HRC), paras. 4.2, 6.3, 9.2, 9.4, citing *Bleierv. Uruguay*, CCPR, para. 13.3.

[63] *Mukong* (HRC), paras. 6.3, 9.1.

[64] *Mukong* (HRC), para. 6.3.

[65] *Mukong* (HRC), para. 9.2.

offered by Cameroon in direct response to the claims of torture, by which the State failed to adequately discharge the state's evidentiary burden.

Two years after *Mukong*, the HRC examined a claim addressing the torture and disappearance of a girl-child, following her detention by Peru for alleged terrorist activities.[66] While the State responded to the HRC, it did not provide any information on what happened to the victim prior to or following her pre-trial release, at which point she disappeared. In its decision, the HRC determined that where the State does not provide direct information on the substance of the claim, 'due weight must be given to the author's allegations, to the effect that they have been substantiated', but the Committee did not discuss what amounted to 'substantiated'.[67] This is the beginning of the use of 'substantiated' in connection with the complainant's level of proof in cases of torture as punishment. This was also deployed in cases of forced confessions, as seen in the cases against Uzbekistan discussed in Section 7.4.1. Even at this early stage it appears that the HRC was developing a practice of affording due weight to a 'substantiated' claim when the state failed to respond to the explicit allegations.

The following year, a similar case against Peru found the State countering the allegations of ill-treatment of an alleged terrorist by providing multiple medical reports about the victim's health and extensive information about detention conditions, including visits by the International Committee of the Red Cross (ICRC).[68] Unlike the previous case, the State provided much more formal evidence than the author, according to the information summarised in the decision. However, the State did not provide information specifically to rebut the allegations regarding incommunicado detention and torture prior to and immediately following the author's conviction. Some of Peru's arguments were rebutted by its own evidence and a letter from the ICRC.[69] Ultimately, the HRC found that although the State offered detailed information about the author's medical treatment, it failed to respond to specific torture claims, which resulted in a finding that the State breached Articles 7 and 10 of the ICCPR.[70]

[66] *Atachahua* (HRC).

[67] *Atachahua* (HRC), para. 8.2; see also, *Carranza* v. *Peru*, CCPR/C/85/D/1126/2002, 28 October 2005, para. 7.1.

[68] *Campos* v. *Peru*, CCPR/C/61/D/577/1994, 6 November 1997, paras. 7.2–7.7.

[69] *Campos* (HRC), paras. 8.3, 8.6.

[70] *Campos* (HRC), para. 8.7.

These cases against Peru demonstrate differing approaches to the state's provision of information vis-à-vis the allegations. The state's failure to respond specifically to detailed allegations of prohibited treatment across these cases suggests that the failure to respond weighs more heavily on the ultimate determination than the formal evidence supplied to corroborate the author's claims. This was confirmed in 2005 when the HRC examined *Carranza* v. *Peru*, another case regarding torture and ill-treatment of an alleged terrorist. The author provided an extensive account of the treatment suffered, while the State failed to provide any observations on the case. The HRC found a violation of Article 7, among other articles, noting that '[a]s the State party provides no information to contradict these allegations, due weight must be given to them and it must be taken that the events occurred as described by the author'.[71] When the state fails to engage effectively in the communications procedure, either through the lack of a direct response to the claim or by non-participation, the balance tips further in favour of the author.

A direct link between the evidence offered by the complainant and the state party's failure to respond to it was outlined in *Aber* v. *Algeria* in 2007. This is one of the first cases that provided unambiguous, succinct insight into the process followed by the HRC in terms of balancing evidence between the parties. As a starting point, the HRC recalled its long-standing principle that the burden of proof does not rest solely on the author of the communication and that a state party has an implicit good faith obligation to investigate allegations made against it and to provide the Committee with all information available.[72] The Committee then set out that when the alleged facts are 'corroborated by *credible* evidence' (emphasis added) and 'where further clarification depends on information exclusively in the hands of the State party', it may then consider the claims 'substantiated in the absence of satisfactory evidence or explanations to the contrary'.[73] The evidence provided in the *Aber* case included a detailed account of the applicant's treatment at various detention sites, which was uncontested by Algeria. There is no guidance as to what equates to 'credible' evidence or whether this is a standard similar to the 'proper' substantiation of evidence required in the cases against Uzbekistan, discussed above. The 'corroboration' appears grounded in the combination of evidence presented by the complainant

[71] *Carranza* (HRC), para. 7.2.

[72] *Aber* v. *Algeria*, CCPR/C/90/D/1439/2005, 16 August 2007, para. 7.2.

[73] *Aber* (HRC), para. 7.2 (emphasis added).

and the State's failure to provide exculpatory material.[74] *Aber* offers the clearest language indicating the direct relationship between the author's level of detail and the State's non-response being used as corroborating evidence. Algeria's failure to respond specifically using evidence that should have been in its possession meant that it did not meet its burden to disprove the allegations of torture. This resulted in the presumed factual validity of the claims and a finding that Algeria breached Article 7.

The subsequent case of *Almegaryaf and Matar* v. *Libya* (2014) reinforced the principle that the absence of the state's response leaves the evidence to stand for itself.[75] In this case, two political opposition leaders were kidnapped in Egypt and renditioned to Libya. Smuggled letters from one of the alleged victims delivered accounts of their whereabouts and their treatment, as outlined in the complaint. This information, coupled with UN reports on the inhuman conditions in the detention facility, information provided by a fellow inmate of one of the victims and the State's failure to respond, resulted in the finding of a breach of Article 7.[76] Here, we see the provision of variable forms of evidence by the complainants, coupled with the State's non-participation, underpinning the complete shift of the burden to the State to disprove the torture claim.

The HRC provided a further increment of guidance on what is required from the state when responding to allegations of torture in detention in *Tyan* v. *Kazakhstan* (2017). The author of the complaint offered extensive detail of his detention and treatment while in the custody of the State, as well as the discrepancies in the maintenance of procedure and paperwork that occurred at every stage of his detention, prosecution, conviction, and appeal.[77] Kazakhstan responded to the author's complaints on several very specific points relating to his written confessions, medical reports of his condition and evidence used in his trial for murder. However, none of the responses addressed the acts of torture. In its examination of the merits, the HRC determined that it was not enough that the State responded and offered documentation on the

[74] *Aber* (HRC), para. 7.4.

[75] *Almegaryaf and Matar* v. *Libya*, CCPR/C/110/D/2006/2010, 29 April 2014.

[76] *Almegaryaf and Matar* (HRC), para. 7.5. The UN Special Rapporteur on torture and other cruel, inhuman or degrading treatment or punishment and Amnesty International both were engaged in revealing the inhuman conditions of the Abu-Salim prison where the victims were held, see para. 2.10.

[77] *Tyan* v. *Kazakhstan*, CCPR/C/119/D/2125/2011, 16 May 2017.

decisions taken not to investigate the author's allegations. In finding a breach of Article 7, the HRC specified that the State must present documentation to support its arguments that torture has not taken place.[78] This suggests that the state's burden of proof to counter claims of torture may be higher than the complainant's burden in establishing a claim. In a number of the cases introduced, up to this point, the claims of torture were grounded entirely in the author's account of the circumstances underpinning the claim. Until the *Tyan* case, 'support' and 'corroboration' of the state's defences to the alleged breaches of Article 7 had not expressly required the production of exculpatory documentation by the state. With this line of cases, the HRC sets out a more demanding requirement on the state to defend itself against claims of torture as a way of addressing the asymmetry of access to information between the state and the victim.

Though a case of enforced disappearance, another 2017 communication against Nepal finally offered a concise articulation of the HRC's approach to assigning the burden of proof in cases of torture of an individual detained by the state. In this instance, the disappeared victim was a human rights defender and member of a political opposition group.[79] The author's claims were reinforced by further documentation provided to the Working Group on Enforced or Involuntary Disappearances and the ICRC, among others.[80] Nepal's response focused on a domestic Supreme Court *habeas corpus* proceeding, where it had denied detaining the author. It also highlighted the fact that Nepal was planning to establish a truth and reconciliation commission to address the widespread practice of disappearances.[81] Nepal did not, however, respond to the specific allegations of torture. As such, the HRC determined that:

> In cases where the author has submitted allegations to the State party that are corroborated by credible evidence, and where further clarification depends on information that is solely in the hands of the State party, the Committee may consider the author's allegations substantiated, in the absence of satisfactory or explanations to the contrary presented by the State party.[82]

[78] *Tyan* (HRC), para. 9.2.

[79] *Dhakal, Dhakal and Dhakal* v. *Nepal*, CCPR/C/119/D/2185/2012, 17 March 2017, para. 2.2. While the basis of this complaint is technically an enforced disappearance, the three authors also claimed breach of Art. 7, ICCPR.

[80] *Dhakal, Dhakal and Dhakal* (HRC), para. 2.8.

[81] *Dhakal, Dhakal and Dhakal* (HRC), paras. 4.2–4.4.

[82] *Dhakal, Dhakal and Dhakal* (HRC), para. 11.4.

This formulation was repeated almost verbatim in the subsequent case of *Pandey* v. *Nepal*[83] in 2018 and builds upon the cases discussed above that have been decided since 2007. The Committee's three-stage formulation of the provision of evidence in cases of alleged torture in state detention is as follows. First, the complaining author must provide 'credible evidence'. Second, the state must offer a response specifically to the evidence of the alleged torture supported by its own evidence. It is not sufficient for the state to offer general statements that laws exist to address the alleged infringements. There must be explicit responses to the facts alleged, supported by documentary evidence. Finally, in the absence of a satisfactory response, the presumption will be that the author's allegations are true.

Here, we return to the use of *probatio diabolica* by the HRC in the *Maya* case against Nepal, which prompted this chapter's exploration of evidentiary burdens by the HRC in the context of torture. The author in *Maya*, as well as the author in the subsequent case of *Nyaya* v. *Nepal*, submitted detailed witness statements, medical records and legal documents recounting failed attempts to get domestic justice following instances of gender-based violence amounting to torture.[84] Both women were arrested, raped and punished using various forms of gender-based violence due to their suspected association with Maoists.[85] A further dimension of vulnerability in *Nyaya* lies in the fact that the author was an indigenous fourteen-year-old girl-child at the time of the incidents recounted in her communication.[86] The failure of the domestic justice system to provide a viable means of redress, coupled with cascading breaches of the ICCPR resulting from Nyaya's initial detention, presented a complete failure by Nepal to comply with its international obligations. While Nepal extensively engaged with the proceedings, it responded that it had no records of the authors being detained, which is where the litany of ICCPR breaches began.[87] Rather than defend itself against the allegations specifically, Nepal instead demanded further proof of the alleged breaches from the victim. In assessing the capability of the parties to meet their burdens of proof, the HRC foreclosed the State's attempts to deprive

83 *Pandey* v. *Nepal* (HRC), para. 8.3.
84 *Maya* v. *Nepal* (HRC), para. 7; *Nyaya* (HRC), para. 2.9
85 *Maya* v. *Nepal* (HRC), para. 12.2; *Nyaya* (HRC), para. 2.2.
86 *Nyaya* v. *Nepal* (HRC), para. 2.2.
87 *Maya* v. *Nepal* (HRC), para. 6; *Nyaya* (HRC), para. 7.7.

the author of justice on the basis that the State claimed to have 'no record of the authors' arrest'.[88]

The HRC's response in framing the State's request as a demand that the complainant provide a *probatio diabolica* seems to solidify a complete shift of the burden of proof to the State. The complete shift requires the state to go much further to defend itself against claims by particularly vulnerable victims when the starting point is arbitrary arrest or detention.[89] In summary, in the confrontation between evidence that has been corroborated, sometimes by multiple sources, and the state's failure to respond directly to the factual claims, the HRC will presume that the state has breached its international obligation to prohibit torture or CIDT.

7.5 Final Reflections

In the cases examined above, the HRC appears to have developed an increasingly consistent practice of overcoming information asymmetries, by applying a presumption in favour of the author when the state fails to provide specific, exculpatory evidence negating claims of torture. To do so, the HRC: (1) looks for facts that are corroborated by some level of evidence; and (2) applies a rebuttable presumption that the author's alleged facts are true; unless (3) the state offers evidence in direct response to the specific allegations of torture or CIDT.

This leaves the question as to what types of evidence must the author present to corroborate the alleged facts. Due to the process and format of final views, it is not always clear what range of evidence had been offered to corroborate the allegations of torture. In some cases, the summary provided suggests the evidence was limited to a detailed account by the author. In other cases, there was not only expansive personal detail, but also extensive supplementary (and sometimes extraneous) evidence provided to corroborate the author's claims, such as reports by UN Special Procedures or international organisations such as the ICRC or Amnesty International,[90] medical reports or court documents that speak directly to

[88] *Nyaya* v. *Nepal* (HRC), para. 4.5.

[89] Compare with *Pharaka* v. *Nepal*, CCPR/C/126/D/2773/2016, 15 July 2019, where there were ample records of detention but a failure to investigate torture complaints.

[90] E.g.: *Samathanam* (HRC), paras. 2.7, 2.13; *Dhakal, Dhakal and Dhakal* (HRC); *Pandey* (HRC).

the indicia of torture.[91] This chapter's presentation of HRC's final views permits only a broad understanding of the range of evidence that might be presented to substantiate torture before the UN treaty bodies. The presumption that the state must overcome the author's evidence, on the other hand, seems to demand specific documentary evidence that is only available to the state. Both the broad and the specific evidentiary burdens increase understanding about how the HRC assesses alleged violations of the prohibition of torture.

This chapter aimed to examine whether the HRC is developing a consistent practice of overcoming information asymmetries in torture cases where the complaining author benefits from a presumption against the state due to the inaccessibility of evidence held by the state. From the analysis presented above, it is clear that cases raising allegations of forced confessions result in an automatic shifting of the full burden of proof to the state to disprove the claim. This stems from the long-standing view that confessions resulting from torture also interfere with the delivery of justice and an individual's fair trial rights. In comparison, cases where torture is used to punish alleged criminals, including members of political opposition groups or alleged terrorists, see a rebuttable presumption applied when there is evidence corroborating the author's allegations of torture. This presumption hinges on the extent to which the state participates in the proceedings. In either situation, if the claim is raised by an individual with distinctive vulnerabilities, there is a presumption that demands that the state bear the full burden of rebutting the facts alleged with specific, documentary evidence.

Ultimately, in all of these cases, where an author provides corroborated evidence of torture while detained by the state, there is ample practice to confirm that 'the burden of proof to rebut the author's evidence clearly lies with the State party'.[92] This not only demands that the state engage with the individual communications process, but that it takes care to provide exculpatory evidence that correlates expressly to the allegations made by the complaining author.

Select Bibliography

Altwicker, T. and Hansen, A. E., 'Presumptions as Secondary Rules in the Judicial Interpretation of International Human Rights' in Kajtár, G., Çali, B. and

[91] E.g.: *Pharaka* (HRC), para. 7.2; *Maya* (HRC).

[92] *Pharaka* (HRC), para. 7.7; *Maya* (HRC), para. 12.7.

Milanović, M. (eds.), *Secondary Rules of Primary Importance in International Law* (Oxford: Oxford University Press, 2022), pp. 167–182.

Clooney, A. and Webb, P., *The Right to a Fair Trial in International Law* (Oxford: Oxford University Press, 2021).

Lentz, C., 'The Evidentiary Implications of a Party's Non-Participation in the Proceedings' in Kajtár, G., Çali, B. and Milanović, M. (eds.), *Secondary Rules of Primary Importance in International Law* (Oxford: Oxford University Press, 2022), pp. 202–218.

McCall-Smith, K., 'Treaty Bodies: Choreographing the Customary Prohibition against Torture', *International Community Law Review*, 23 (2019): 344–368.

Pauwelyn, J., 'Defences and the Burden of Proof in International Law' in Bartels, L. and Paddeu, F. (eds.), *Exceptions in International Law* (Oxford: Oxford University Press, 2020), pp. 88–107.

Rodley, N. S., 'UN Treaty Bodies and the Human Rights Council' in Keller, H. and Ulfstein, G. (eds.), *UN Human Rights Treaty Bodies: Law and Legitimacy* (Cambridge: Cambridge University Press, 2012), pp. 320–355.

Weissbrodt, D. and Heilman, C., 'Defining Torture and Cruel, Inhuman, and Degrading Treatment', *Law and Inequality*, 29 (2011): 343–394.

Weissbrodt, D. and Zinsmaster, K. K., 'Protecting the Fair Trial Rights of the Accused in International Criminal Law: Comparison of the International Criminal Court and the Military Commissions in Guantánamo' in Brown, B. S. (ed.), *Research Handbook on International Criminal Law* (Cheltenham: Edward Elgar, 2011), pp. 261–283.

8

Not Just Single Events

Calling on UN Treaty Bodies to Expose Patterns or Practices of Violations

CHRISTOPHER ROBERTS*

8.1 Introduction

The process of transforming observations about the empirical world into claims of normative right and redress involves three steps: naming, blaming and claiming.[1] First, most challengingly and most significantly, wrongs must be recognised as such, and rendered visible and articulable. Over the past seventy-five years, the evolution of the international human rights system has advanced the potential for different forms of abusive action to be named. Often, however, international human rights advocacy has proceeded as if human rights violations are isolated events, deviations from a norm of rights respect. In reality, the vast majority of human rights violations are not unique, but rather part of one or more patterns or practices of violations.

Coming to see human rights violations not as isolated occurrences, but rather as part of patterns and practices of violations, where they are in fact such, is an important act of naming. It generates in those who undertake and encounter it a different view of the world. It is, in this sense, fundamentally an evidentiary issue, as adopting such an understanding alters baseline presumptions and impacts the sorts of evidence human rights bodies might consider and the conclusions they are likely to reach. Positively, United Nations human rights bodies have gradually

* The author would like to thank the entire DISSECT team, and the editorial team of Cornelia Klocker, Deborah Casalin and Marie-Bénédicte Dembour in particular, for all their thoughtful and insightful comments, engagement and support throughout the process of preparing this chapter.

[1] See W. L. F. Felstiner, R. L. Abel and A. Sarat, 'The Emergence and Transformation of Disputes: Naming, Blaming, Claiming …', *Law and Society Review* 15 (1981): 631–654.

come to possess increasingly sophisticated individual communication consideration functions. At the same time, while United Nations human rights treaty bodies (UNTBs) have on occasion recognised one or another pattern or practice of violations, they have done so inconsistently and haphazardly. Reflecting on human rights bodies with the aim of ensuring their ability to recognise and appropriately address patterns or practices of violations suggests the appropriateness of several sorts of approaches, some better and some less well recognised to date. This chapter considers various ways in which the processes undertaken by UNTBs should be shaped in order to better consider evidence of patterns or practices of violations as an input.

The manner in which United Nations human rights treaty bodies contemplate the evidence before them is only one aspect of the relationship between such bodies and evidence of human rights violations. This is because UNTBs are not only receivers of information relating to human rights, but also key sites for the generation of such information. As such, this chapter is not only concerned with how such bodies process evidence, but also with the information they create and disseminate, in recognition of the significance of such findings and their ability to generate positive (or negative) feedback loops.

This chapter has four parts. Section 8.2 reviews the different routes through which quasi-judicial bodies such as United Nations human rights treaty bodies receive information. The section highlights the multiple evidence-collecting functions engaged in by such bodies and their abilities to undertake their own investigations in certain cases, to consider amicus briefs and to introduce evidence proprio motu/sua sponte (i.e. on their own initiative). Section 8.2 also examines what sources such bodies have addressed and should consider appropriate to reference in their decisions. The more widespread one believes human rights violations to be, the more liberally evidence should be admitted. Positively, United Nations human rights treaty bodies have typically adopted fairly liberal approaches to date, though they might be more consistent in doing so.

Section 8.3 reviews two manners in which addressing patterns or practices of violations can impact on the manner in which cases are considered. Section 8.3.1 considers exhaustion of domestic remedies, examining the differently termed but similar manners in which the regional human rights systems have reflected on admissibility issues relative to patterns or practices of violations. Section 8.3.2 analyses whether and how addressing patterns or practices of violations might impact on the consideration of evidence and the burden of proof. In both cases, it is argued that UNTBs should adopt special approaches where patterns or practices of violations are encountered, including by emulating the practice of the regional systems relative to exhaustion in particular.

Section 8.4 considers how ensuring optimal openness to both the contemplation and finding of patterns or practices of violations militates in favour of particular approaches to case processing. Section 8.4.1 focuses on the input side, considering two modes of case processing that have been adopted in at least partial recognition of the existence of patterns or practices of violations, the repetitive cases procedure adopted by the Human Rights Committee (HRC) and the pilot judgment procedure employed by the European Court of Human Rights (ECtHR). Section 8.4.2 considers how human rights bodies may best recognise and underscore the existence of particular patterns or practices of violations in their findings. It argues that international human rights bodies should explicitly recognise patterns or practices of violations, and that they should clearly articulate 'general measures' or 'structural' remedies required in response.

Section 8.5 considers the manner in which information concerning patterns or practices of violations is publicly presented. As noted above, international human rights bodies are not only receivers and contemplators of human rights–related evidence and information, but also key nodes in its construction and dissemination. As such, the manner in which they present the information they produce is of great significance. While the information produced by United Nations human rights systems is already presented in several valuable ways, the dissemination of information concerning human rights violations would be enhanced, this chapter argues, by the clearer presentation of information concerning patterns or practices of violations as well. Taking this step would help to ensure a more readily accessible evidential record for future cases, and to produce greater pressure for such situations to be brought to an end.

8.2 Evidential Consideration by Quasi-Judicial Bodies

UNTBs are quasi-judicial bodies. That is to say, they combine court-like functions – considering state and individual communications – with other functions similar to those historically possessed by commissions of inquiry or the like. Typical functions of such bodies include consideration of state party reports and following up on concluding observations, special statements and general comments. In reality, such bodies receive information concerning human rights not only (or even primarily) from individual communications, but also from a wide variety of other sources. Sources of information include not only the formal channels of reports received in the context of state party review, but also the connections committee members and staff have to the wider world, including the broader system of human rights mechanisms based in Geneva.[2]

The Committee against Torture (CAT),[3] the Committee on the Elimination of Discrimination against Women (CEDAW),[4] the Committee on the Rights of Persons with Disabilities, the Committee on Enforced Disappearances, the Committee on Economic, Social and Cultural Rights (CESCR) and the Committee on the Rights of the Child (CRC)[5] have the ability to initiate inquiries on their own initiative where they have received information that serious or systematic violations of convention rights are taking place.[6] The existence of this expansive fact-finding power suggests general recognition of the appropriateness of

[2] The holistic manner in which such bodies receive and consider information is illustrated, e.g., by the references such bodies sometimes make to information received and concluding observations made as part of their periodic reporting work within their decisions on communications. See, e.g., *A.B.* v. *Finland*, CRC/C/86/D/51/2018, 4 February 2021, para. 8.6 fn. 23; *Abdel Jalil Laaroussi* v. *Morocco*, CAT/C/74/D/891/2018, 15 July 2022, paras 8.4–8.5; *S.R.* v. *Canada*, CAT/C/74/D/973/2019, 21 July 2022, para. 8.3; *A. and B.* v. *Azerbaijan*, CAT/C/74/D/905/2018, 27 July 2022, para. 8.6; *Lauren Henley* v. *Australia*, CRPD/C/27/D/56/2018, 26 August 2022, para. 10.10.

[3] The CAT had used this power on ten occasions as of the end of 2022. See OHCHR Website. UN Treaty Body Database, 'Confidential inquiries under Article 20 of the Convention against Torture'.

[4] The CEDAW had used this power on seven occasions as of the end of 2022. See OHCHR Website. UN Treaty Body Database, 'List of all CEDAW inquiry reports'.

[5] The CRC had used this power on one occasion as of the end of 2022. See OHCHR Website. UN Treaty Body Database, 'List of all CRC inquiry reports'.

[6] See Convention Against Torture and Other Cruel, Inhuman or Degrading Treatment or Punishment, New York, 10 December 1984, in force 26 June 1987, 1465 UNTS 85, Article 20; Optional Protocol to the Convention on the Elimination of All Forms of Discrimination Against Women, New York, 10 December 1999, in force 22 December 2000, 2131 UNTS 83, Article 8; Optional Protocol to the Convention on the Rights of Persons with Disabilities, New York, 30 March 2007, in force 3 May 2008, 2518 UNTS 283, Article 6; International Convention for the Protection of All Persons from Enforced Disappearance, New York, 6 February 2007, in force 23 December 2010, 2716 UNTS 3, Article 33; Optional Protocol to the International Covenant on Economic, Social and Cultural Rights, New York, 24 September 2009, in force 5 May 2013, 2922 UNTS 29, Article 11; Optional Protocol to the Convention on the Rights of the Child on a Communications Procedure, Geneva, 28 February 2012, in force 14 April 2014, 2983 UNTS 131, Article 13.

utilising all available avenues to obtain evidence where necessary. However, such investigations rarely prove a feasible tool in practice, as the ability of UNTBs to undertake them runs up against resource and practical constraints.

United Nations human rights treaty bodies have generally been open to third-party interventions, and the CAT, the CEDAW and the Committee on the Elimination of Racial Discrimination (CERD) have all recognised their contributions.[7] Rule 96 of the 2019 Rules of Procedure of the HRC indicates that the Committee 'may accept information and documentation submitted by third parties which may be relevant for the proper determination of the case'.[8] That information will be shared with the parties, who may respond if they so wish.[9] The Guidelines on third-party submissions adopted by the HRC at its 127th Session in October 2019 indicate that the HRC 'may on its own initiative request from an individual or entity a third-party submission (amicus curiae brief)'.[10] The openness UNTBs have shown to third-party interventions is especially positive relative to patterns or practices of human rights violations, as in such cases there are likely to be interested parties beyond those submitting the communication(s) in question.

In addition to their ability to consider and even request third-party interventions, UNTBs should be free to draw on other public information when considering cases as well. The Rules of Procedure of the HRC indicate that 'the Committee shall consider the communication in the light of all the information made available to it'.[11] The Rules of Procedure of the CESCR, in contrast, more clearly (but perhaps more limitingly) indicate:

> At any time after the receipt of a communication and before a determination on the merits has been reached, the Committee . . . may consult, as appropriate, relevant documentation emanating from other United Nations bodies, specialized agencies, funds, programmes and mechanisms, and other international organizations, including from regional

[7] *Slobodan Nikolic and Ljiljana Nikolic* v. *Serbia and Montenegro*, CAT/C/35/D/174/2000, 25 November 2005, para. 3.4; *Maria de Lourds da Silva Pimentel* v. *Brazil*, CEDAW/C/49/D/17/2008, 25 July 2011, para. 1; *T.P.F.* v. *Peru*, CEDAW/C/50/D/22/2009, 17 October 2011, para. 1; *TBB-Turkish Union in Berlin/Brandenburg* v. *Germany*, CERD/C/82/D/48/2010, 26 February 2013, para. 8.1.

[8] HRC, Rules of Procedure (CCPR/C/3/Rev.11), 9 January 2019.

[9] HRC, Rules of Procedure.

[10] HRC, Guidelines on Third-Party Submissions (CCPR/C/160), 3 September 2020, para. 3.

[11] HRC, Rules of Procedure, Rule 102 (1).

> human rights systems that may assist in the examination of the communication, provided that the Committee shall afford each party an opportunity to comment on such third party documentation or information within fixed time limits.[12]

A broad approach to the proprio motu consideration of information seems appropriate. First, a more limited approach would in many cases require a highly artificial pretence of ignorance, given committee members and staff will typically be aware of human rights information from many sources other than the communication in question. Second, such an approach would be impractical, requiring the duplication of the same information, often repeatedly, in the service of a formal limitation. Third, such an approach would be undesirable, asserting the primacy of compliance with narrow procedural rules over factual accuracy and human rights obligation enforcement.

In addition to how information is received, another issue pertains to the sources human rights bodies consider appropriate to reference in the context of case consideration. One particular question is whether human rights bodies may consult the work of prominent non-governmental organisations (NGOs), which provide much of the evidence of human rights violations in practice. Past practice here is mixed. Out of the total of one admissibility decision and seventy-six merits decisions issued by UNTBs in 2022,[13] Human Rights Watch or Amnesty International were referenced in thirteen cases – ten times by the CAT[14] and once each by the HRC,[15] the CEDAW[16] and the CRC.[17] In seven of those cases, the work of Human Rights Watch and Amnesty International was referenced

[12] Economic, Social and Cultural Rights Committee, Rules of Procedure (E/C.12/49/3), 15 January 2013, Rule 14 (1).

[13] This was the number of distinct cases shown by a search of 2022 decisions via OHCHR's Jurisprudence Database (accessed on 26 February 2023). One case, *A.Y.* v. *Switzerland*, showed up twice in the search, apparently in error.

[14] *D.S.* v. *Australia*, CAT/C/73/D/941/2019, 22 April 2022; *T.B.* v. *Switzerland*, CAT/C/73/D/862/2018, 22 April 2022; *T.A.* v. *Switzerland*, CAT/C/73/D/914/2019, 28 April 2022; *Yacob Berhane* v. *Switzerland*, CAT/C/73/D/872/2018, 28 April 2022; *Abdel Jalil Laaroussi* v. *Morocco* (CAT); *S.R.* v. *Canada* (CAT); *A.Y.* v. *Switzerland*, CAT/C/74/D/887/2018, 22 July 2022; *D.M.* v. *Switzerland*, CAT/C/74/D/880/2018, 22 July 2022; *A. and B.* v. *Azerbaijan* (CAT); *X. and Y.* v. *Switzerland*, CAT/C/75/D/1081/2021, 11 November 2022.

[15] *A.B. and B.D.* v. *Poland*, CCPR/C/135/D/3017/2017, 21 July 2022.

[16] *Jeremy Eugene Matson and others* v. *Canada*, CEDAW/C/81/D/68/2014, 14 February 2022.

[17] *S.K.* v. *Denmark*, CRC/C/90/D/99/2019, 1 June 2022.

only while considering complainants' arguments, rather than as an explicit basis for any of the findings made.[18] In six cases, the work of such organisations was referenced directly in the context of the committees' findings.[19]

In one of those cases, *A.Y.* v. *Switzerland*, the CAT directly addressed the relevant issues. In particular, the CAT took a moment to consider Switzerland's claim that the reports from human rights NGOs and a Special Rapporteur relied on by the claimant were 'intentionally selective'.[20] In response, the CAT observed that it 'ha[d] nothing before it to indicate that the State party's judicial authorities carried out a detailed assessment of the source material relied on by immigration authorities or the complainant at any stage'.[21] The CAT further reasonably concluded 'that, on balance, if a particular source were to be given less weight, it should be any that were to be assessed as having a clearly vested interest in the narrative provided' – meaning in particular 'information provided by government agents or sources within the country, who might face reprisals for any perceived criticism of the Government of Eritrea'.[22] The CAT further challenged Switzerland's suggestion 'that the refusal of a State to engage with or to accept a fact-finding visit is a reason to dismiss the findings of the report of that fact-finding mission, and that information from individuals who have fled persecution is less reliable'.[23] The CAT observed that adoption of such an approach 'would have a dissuasive effect on States engaging with human rights obligations and reduce transparency and accountability'.[24] On the particulars of the evidence, the CAT observed 'where sources are drawn widely from civil society and citizens in exile, the information provided is more likely on balance to represent reliable, uncensored first-hand accounts, as persons outside the country who have fled are arguably no longer living under censorship'.[25]

[18] See *T.B.* v. *Switzerland* (CAT), para. 3.2; *T.A.* v. *Switzerland* (CAT), para. 3.11; *Yacob Berhane* v. *Switzerland* (CAT), para. 3.1; *S.K.* v. *Denmark* (CRC), para. 3.3; *Abdel Jalil Laaroussi* v. *Morocco* (CAT), paras 2.12, 5.7; *A.B. and B.D.* v. *Poland* (HRC), para. 7.3; *D.M.* v. *Switzerland* (CAT), para. 3.2.

[19] *Jeremy Eugene Matson and others* v. *Canada* (CEDAW), paras 18.3, 18.9; *D.S.* v. *Australia* (CAT), para. 10.3; *S.R.* v. *Canada* (CAT), para. 8.3; *A.Y.* v. *Switzerland* (CAT), para. 8.10; *A. and B.* v. *Azerbaijan* (CAT), para. 8.9; *X. and Y.* v. *Switzerland* (CAT), para. 7.4.

[20] *A.Y.* v. *Switzerland* (CAT), para. 8.10.

[21] *A.Y.* v. *Switzerland* (CAT), para. 8.10.

[22] *A.Y.* v. *Switzerland* (CAT), para. 8.10.

[23] *A.Y.* v. *Switzerland* (CAT), para. 8.10.

[24] *A.Y.* v. *Switzerland* (CAT), para. 8.10.

[25] *A.Y.* v. *Switzerland* (CAT), para. 8.10.

The willingness of UNTBs to consult the work of human rights organisations in the cases considered above demonstrates that there is no legal rule prohibiting them from directly considering the work of human rights NGOs in the course of reaching their findings. At the same time, the relative paucity of references to the work of such organisations in UNTBs' decisions suggests that the latter exercise a degree of caution in referencing such sources. One reason for such potential caution is readily inferable: human rights bodies' members and staff are aware that states do not always look favourably on information concerning human rights violations made available through the work of such organisations, and hence seek to limit their references to that work in their decisions.

Several factors suggest UNTBs should consider evidence from human rights NGOs more freely than they have in the past. First, human rights NGOs play a key role in the global system of human rights enforcement, including by generating and making available information on human rights violations. Freely citing and relying on such information helps to support that vital work; refusing to do so limits it. Second, in contrast to UNTBs, numerous other United Nations bodies and mandates, including United Nations Special Rapporteurs, have been readily willing to explicitly cite to the work of such organisations.[26] There is no reason for human rights treaty bodies not to do the same. Third, if they want to obtain the broadest possible picture, UNTBs should be open to information from as many sources as possible. Instead of adopting a formalistic rule limiting certain sources of information, UNTBs should follow the CAT's reasoning in *A.Y.*, admitting information while assessing it in light of the potential bias of its sources. Fourth, as the CAT further observed in *A.Y.*, accepting evidence from human rights NGOS is important because failing to rely on such evidence would have a 'dissuasive effect on States engaging with human rights obligations'.[27]

In sum, this brief overview of UNTBs' approaches to evidence reveals most have been fairly liberal to date. This appears to have been facilitated by such bodies' quasi-judicial nature, as well as their recognition of the

[26] See, e.g., Human Rights Council, Report of the Special Rapporteur on the rights to freedom of peaceful assembly and of association, Exercise of the rights to freedom of peaceful assembly and of association as essential to advancing climate justice (A/76/222), 23 July 2021.

[27] *A.Y.* v. *Switzerland* (CAT) , para. 8.10.

challenges of gathering information concerning human rights violations. Recognising that many human rights violations constitute part of patterns or practices of violations provides further grounds for the adoption of maximally liberal approaches to the receipt of evidence. This is the case both because there will be multiple sources of information in such cases, and because instances of patterns or practices of violation cannot be recognised or properly understood unless multiple perspectives are taken into account.

8.3 Special Procedural Approaches

In addition to supporting United Nations human rights treaty bodies' adoption of a liberal approach to the receipt of evidence, recognition that human rights violations may form part of patterns or practices of violations suggests the need to adopt special approaches to certain procedural issues. This section argues that special approaches should be adopted in two areas: relative to admissibility and the burden of proof.

8.3.1 Admissibility

The rule of exhaustion requires that claimants 'exhaust' domestic remedies before having recourse to an international human rights body. The rule serves several purposes: placing states on notice; providing them with a first opportunity to remedy the situation in question; helping to ensure that international bodies can consider the issue after legal arguments and evidential submissions have been more fully developed; and promoting efficiency, by encouraging use of the lowest level remedial avenue available. Exhaustion is accomplished by bringing one's claim before national-level judicial bodies and, following a negative finding, taking advantage of judicial appellate procedures to the point that a final decision has been produced and no subsequent judicial appeal is possible.

In both general international law and before various international human rights bodies, several grounds for exception to the rule of exhaustion have been recognised over time. Most significantly for present purposes, European, Inter-American and African human rights bodies have all used different terminologies to find an exception to the rule of exhaustion in situations involving patterns or practices of violations. In Europe, the formerly operative European Commission of Human Rights found an exception applied in cases involving 'legislative measures and administrative practices'.[28] For its part, the ECtHR has similarly identified an exception in cases involving 'an administrative practice consisting of a repetition of [human rights violations]'.[29] The Inter-American Court has recognised an exception to the rule of exhaustion in situations involving 'a practice or policy ordered or tolerated by the government'.[30] The African Commission has established an exception where 'serious and massive violations of human rights' are taking place.[31] Elsewhere, in response to another situation involving widespread violations, the African Commission observed that:

> the Respondent State does not point to any legal procedure which makes it practicable for . . . a large number of victims to pursue local remedies, for example as a class. The upshot is that the procedure available to individuals cannot practically be utilized by numerous victims to secure redress of the alleged violations of a range of rights in the present case . . . (as such) the Commission finds it appropriate to exempt [certain claims] from the requirement to exhaust local remedies on the basis that it is practically impossible for the numerous victims to utilize whatever procedure is available to individuals at the domestic level.[32]

Broadly speaking, these precedents suggest an exception to the rule of exhaustion in cases of patterns or practices of violations is justified on several grounds. First, an exception is justified because the existence of a pattern or practice suggests the domestic remedial system is inaccessible or ineffective as such, as a well-functioning remedial system should be able to redress such issues before they rise to such a level. Second, where a

[28] *First Cyprus Case, Greece* v. *UK*, ECmHR, 176/1956, 2 June 1956.

[29] *Akdivar et al.* v. *Turkey*, ECtHR, 21893/93, Judgment, 16 September 1996, para. 67.

[30] See, e.g., *Velásquez Rodríguez* v. *Honduras*, IACtHR, 7920, Merits, 29 July 1988, para. 68.

[31] See, e.g., *Organisation Mondiale Contre la Torture and others* v. *Rwanda*, ACmHPR, 27/89, 46/91, 49/91 and 99/93, 31 October 1996, para. 17. See also *Free Legal Assistance Group et al.* v. *Zaire*, ACmHPR, 25/89, 47/90, 56/91 and 100/93, October 1995, para. 37; *Amnesty International et al.* v. *Sudan*, ACmHPR, 48/90, 50/91, 52/91 and 89/93, 15 November 1999, paras 30–33, 38–39; *Malawi African Association et al.* v. *Mauritania*, ACmHPR, 54/91, 11 May 2000, paras 81, 85; *Zimbabwe Human Rights NGO Forum* v. *Zimbabwe*, ACmHPR, 245/02, 15 May 2006, para. 71; *Haregewoin Gabre-Selassie and IHRDA* v. *Ethiopia*, ACmHPR, 301/05, 7 November 2011, para. 112. This formula should be understood as referring to patterns or practices of violations, as presumably the 'serious or massive violations' in question must be linked in order to be cognisable together. At the same time, the African system's criterion is potentially more restrictive, making reference to the extensiveness and gravity of the violations in question as well.

[32] *Ali Askouri and Abdel-Hakeem Nasr* v. *Sudan*, ACmHPR, 452/13, Admissibility, February 2016, paras 113f.

pattern or practice of violations exists, the concern with fairness to the state – which underpins the exhaustion rule – is lessened, as the state can be deemed to have already had a chance to redress the violation in question. Where the violations in question are of sufficient extent and/or severity, an exception is also justified by the fact that even if there is some potential to access remedies, those remedies are likely to be unduly delayed relative to the enhanced urgency involved.[33] It is not apparent that UNTBs have been specific as to the existence of a ground for exception to the rule of exhaustion in cases of patterns or practices of violations. Given the strong rationales for the existence of such an exception, they should follow the regional human rights bodies mentioned above by recognising it.

8.3.2 The Burden of Proof

In addition to recognising the need for an exception to the rule of exhaustion in cases of patterns or practices of violations, the Inter-American system has arguably recognised the appropriateness of a reversal of the burden of proof in such cases as well. In *Velásquez Rodríguez* v. *Honduras*, the Inter-American Court held that '[w]hen the existence of . . . a policy or practice has been shown, the disappearance of a particular individual may be proved through circumstantial or indirect evidence or by logical inference'.[34] The Inter-American Commission has similarly observed that 'when there is proof of the existence of a policy of disappearances sponsored or tolerated by the Government, it is possible, using circumstantial or indirect evidence, or through relevant logical inference, to prove the disappearance of a specific individual when that would otherwise be impossible given the link between that disappearance and the overall policy'.[35]

This jurisprudence suggests that claimants will succeed in their claims where: (1) a 'policy or practice'[36] of rights violations is shown to exist; and (2) a certain amount of evidence is presented that the person on

[33] For a similar point, see *Zimbabwe Human Rights NGO Forum* v. *Zimbabwe* (ACmHPR), para. 67.

[34] *Velásquez Rodríguez* v. *Honduras* (IACtHR), para. 124

[35] *Romer Morales Zegarra, Richard Morales Zigarra, Carmen Teresa Rojas Garcia and Carlos Vega Pizango* v. *Peru*, IACHR, Report No. 57/99, 13 April 1999, para. 50.

[36] This term is presumed equivalent to 'patterns or practices'. While arguments might be made on this point, they are omitted in the interests of space.

whose behalf the case is filed was a victim of that policy or practice. Relative to (1), a few open questions exist.

First, it is not clear where the burden of proof should lie. Given the structural nature of such claims, it is perhaps appropriate to say human rights bodies should adopt some independent initiative. At the same time, insofar as claimants will be interested in establishing the existence of patterns or practices of violations, the burden clearly also lies on claimants. This is all the more so since in many cases, claimants will fail should the 'policy or practice' in question not be recognised.

Second, it is not clear what standard of proof should apply. Those concerned with the seriousness of the charge against the state might suggest the matter should be proved beyond a reasonable doubt. This would import a standard developed to protect criminal defendants to the human rights sphere, however, and would impose a heavy burden on claimants. The standard of the balance of probabilities will, on the other hand, be challenged on the grounds that it is too light relative to so serious a finding. The standard of clear and convincing evidence represents a compromise between these positions. Ultimately, the question is a policy one, on which differences of perspective will doubtless persist.[37]

The burden of proving element (2) more clearly lies on claimants. A question exists here too, however, as to how much proof should be required: should the claimant be required only to make a prima facie case that the person on whose behalf the claim was filed was a victim of the policy or practice of violations in question, or should they have to show this on the balance of probabilities? The answer must be that only a prima facie case need be advanced, as to do otherwise would obviate the need for the first element (the proof of the pattern or practice of violations) to be shown at all.

While it is thus apparent that some details remain to be fleshed out, the Inter-American system has at least pointed the way towards a special approach to the burden of proof in cases in which a policy or practice of violations has been found. The Inter-American system's findings in this context were reached in the context of enforced disappearance, where the harm is particularly severe and claimants' access to information is especially limited, and hence application of a special approach is particularly compelling.

[37] If the suggestions in Section 8.5 of this chapter are followed, and a set of recognised patterns or practices of violations is established, the argument for application of a lower standard will weaken, as the relevant information will be more readily available.

Application of a similar approach in all cases of patterns or practices of violations is justifiable on a number of grounds. First, the approach employed may be understood, as the Inter-American system suggests through its reference to 'logical inference', as an application of common sense: where there is evidence of a pattern or practice of certain types of violations, and evidence of a particular violation fitting that general pattern or practice, the likelihood that the particular violation has taken place is enhanced by the information concerning the pattern or practice.

Second, adoption of a special approach may be understood as justified as a response to the pattern or practice of human rights violations in question, which enhances the pressure on concerned states to take steps to address that pattern or practice. To put this another way, broadly speaking, whether or not a human rights body adopts a special approach to cases involving patterns or practices of violations relates to its assessment of the relative risks of erroneous judgments. Failing to adopt such an approach will make it harder for claimants to succeed, and hence makes sense where one is more concerned with a wrongful judgment against the respondent than with the claimant failing to obtain justice. Adopting a special approach, in the alternative, makes sense if one is more concerned with rightful claimants failing to obtain justice than with wrongful decisions against respondents. In the context of patterns or practices of violations, the balance of these contemplations shifts in the direction of the latter – as to find against a rightful claimant would not only deprive that claimant of a remedy but also fail to exert pressure against the state to end the patterns or practices of violations in question. A wrongful judgment against a state, on the other hand, while it would not be just in the individual case, would still have merit in bringing such pressure to bear.[38]

Third, to the extent there are concerns with such a process, they will be heightened in the more formal context of a court than in a quasi-judicial body such as a UNTB. The Inter-American Court's willingness to adopt such an approach makes clear at least one leading international human rights court has no doubts as to the merits of such an approach, however. Quasi-judicial bodies such as the UNTBs should therefore also be willing to adopt such an approach. It is not apparent that UNTBs have adopted such a special approach to the burden of proof in cases involving patterns

[38] For similar observations, see C. Roberts, 'Reversing the Burden of Proof before Human Rights Bodies', *International Journal of Human Rights* 25 (2021): 1682–1703, 1693–1695.

or practices of violations. Given the strong rationales for such a reversal, they should follow the Inter-American Court in doing so.

8.4 Case Processing

This section considers another component of the UNTBs' work that might require adjustment if patterns or practices of violations are more regularly recognised: the manner in which cases are processed. From one perspective, human rights violations constitute individuated occurrences that should be considered in isolation from one another. From another perspective, the opposite is the case: most human rights violations are part of one or more patterns or practices of violations, and hence are best considered together with other violations that form part of the same pattern or practice.

In practice, many international human rights bodies have largely proceeded from the (generally unexamined) perspective that human rights violations, at least as and when brought forward by individuals rather than states, are individual occurrences. Interestingly, such approaches have come under challenge not on theoretical grounds, but rather due to the fact that situations involving patterns or practices of violations can generate multiple communications over time. While the issue has not become an urgent one in terms of institutional capacity at most UNTBs, it has been recognised at the HRC, as noted below. The potential for a large caseload to lead to new procedural approaches is demonstrated by the ECtHR, however, where the volume of cases received has prompted the adoption of a major new procedural approach – the pilot judgment procedure – specifically geared to address situations involving patterns or practices of violations.

From one perspective, the manner in which human rights bodies process cases concerns operational efficiency. From another perspective, the approaches adopted are closely related to evidential questions. This is true in the first place, on the input side, because the scope with which the matter before the human rights body in question is understood will impact on the evidence that may be considered. If the matter is considered to be a narrow one, evidence of the pattern or practice of which the matter forms a part may be excluded. If, by contrast, the matter is considered from a wider lens – including simply because multiple individual complaints are considered together – information concerning patterns or practices of violations will naturally arise, and it will be harder to exclude further information along such lines.

In addition, recognising that particular submissions constitute part of patterns or practices of violations also has implications on the output side. Such recognition will allow adjudicatory bodies to better ensure remedial consistency. It will also help them ensure remedies are comprehensive, addressing not only individuated harms but also the broader situation giving rise to the patterns or practices of violations in question. Finally, willingness to recognise patterns or practices of violations explicitly is significant in and of itself, as this recognition will then constitute part of the broader evidential record, enhancing the pressure on the state in question to bring the pattern or practice of violations in question to an end.

Section 8.4.1.) considers two different manners in which human rights bodies can structure individual communications. Section 8.4.1.1 considers the traditional model, under which each communication is considered as it is received. While many systems will likely not be comfortable going beyond this model, substantial variation is possible therein, as the subsection notes. These include streamlined procedures relative to repeat cases, as well as the potential joinder of communications by the human rights body in question. Section 8.4.1.2 considers a major alternative model of case processing, namely the pilot judgment procedure adopted by the ECtHR in 2004. The chapter reflects positively on this approach due to its tendency to make patterns or practices of violations visible.

Section 4.2. considers the findings human rights bodies reach, the orders they issue and the manner in which they engage in follow-up or enforcement of judgments.[39] Here, the chapter argues that UNTBs should adopt clearer findings relative to the existence of patterns or practices of violations as such, as well as concerning general measures or structural remedies that must be adopted in order to bring patterns or practices of violations to an end. Such findings, where made, should moreover be made readily publicly available, including through their incorporation within information presented by the Office of the High Commissioner for Human Rights (OHCHR) concerning particular patterns or practices of violations, as called for in Section 8.5.

[39] Thanks are due to Hanaa Hakiki for pointing the way to follow-up procedures, rather than case processing as such, as the key process through which pressure to address patterns or practices of violations might be most enhanced.

8.4.1 Case Structure

8.4.1.1 The Traditional Model

The traditional model of case processing sees *individual* cases submitted by lawyers or representatives of one or more victims, which are then processed by the human rights body in question. The speed with which cases are processed varies and appears somewhat flexible within and across human rights bodies. The human rights body considering the case may have a procedure for the issuance of interim orders and may take account of priority factors in relation to the speed of case processing, including, for instance, factors pertaining to the urgency, gravity and extent of the violations in question.[40] Once a decision is reached, that decision is final.

The traditional method can be stretched in various ways that render it a more suitable vehicle for the recognition of patterns or practices of violations. While cases may be submitted on behalf of solitary individuals, they may also be submitted on behalf of larger groups of individuals. While some systems apply tighter rules around standing and representation, others adopt more liberal approaches, which more readily allow claims to be advanced on behalf of groups as such.[41] In some instances, moreover, when human rights systems receive similar communications from different parties in close temporal proximity, they may choose to join them together for collective consideration. This too tends to make it easier to recognise patterns or practices of violations that may be involved in the various cases.[42]

The primary motivation for more liberal approaches to standing and representation historically appears to have been a desire to facilitate access to human rights systems. At the same time, consideration of cases that concern wider sets of victims and violations – regardless of the procedural technique applied to facilitate this – carries other benefits as well. In the first place, considering multiple cases together promotes

[40] The European Court of Human Rights has been comparatively clear on the issue of prioritization, having adopted a case priority policy in 2009, since updated in 2017. See ECtHR, The Court's Priority Policy.

[41] For example, it may be possible to engage in *actio popularis* actions in the interest of the public in general, a procedural potential that implicitly recognises the existence of patterns or practices of violation. For more, see W. J. Aceves, '*Actio popularis? The Class Action in International Law*', *University of Chicago Legal Forum* (2003): 353–402.

[42] Indeed, the act of joinder as such, premised as it may be on the recognition of certain similarities across cases, arguably constitutes a form of recognition of alleged patterns or practices of violations.

systemic efficiency. In addition, the consideration of cases through a wider-angled lens promotes the development of more expansive, innovative and assertive remedial orders, which are likely to be better designed to holistically address structural situations of violation, rather than to merely provide relief to individual claimants. In this context, the fact that the Inter-American regional system has been more willing to consider cases from a broader perspective may be understood as closely linked to that system's place at the forefront of remedial jurisprudence.[43]

In addition to employing a flexible approach to joinder, human rights bodies may adopt other procedures that enhance their ability to recognise patterns or practices of violations. This may carry other benefits of the sort described above, as well. The HRC, for instance, has adopted a procedural rule allowing for the appointment of special rapporteurs with responsibility for dealing with 'repetitive cases'.[44] In particular, the HRC has received large numbers of similar communications concerning the pattern and practice of forced disappearances in Algeria, to which it has responded with highly similar decisions.[45] Such a procedure constitutes another relatively straightforward way in which human rights bodies can devote more concerted attention to cases involving patterns or practices of violations.

8.4.1.2 The Pilot Judgment Procedure

The traditional approach has been challenged and complicated in the European human rights system. As noted above, the adoption of a new approach there was motivated in substantial part by the system's caseload crisis, resulting from the receipt of so large a number of cases that it was impossible to respond to all within a timely manner. A significant subset

[43] The Inter-American Court's ability to take such an approach has been facilitated by the fact cases there are generally initially considered by a Commission that has interpreted its mandate in a wide and flexible manner. For more on related themes, see T. Antkowiak, 'Remedial approaches to human rights violations: the Inter-American Court of Human Rights and beyond', *Columbia Journal of Transnational Law* 46 (2007): 351–419; C. M. Roberts, *Alternative Approaches to Human Rights: The Disparate Historical Paths of the European, Inter-American and African Regional Human Rights Systems* (Cambridge: Cambridge University Press, 2022).

[44] HRC Rules of Procedure, Rule 105.

[45] See, e.g., *Aicha Habouchi* v. *Algeria*, CCPR/C/128/D/2819/2016, 27 March 2020; *Djegdjigua Cherguit* v. *Algeria*, CCPR/C/128/D/2828/2016, 27 March 2020; *Malika Bendjael et al.* v. *Algeria*, CCPR/C/128/D/2893/2016, 27 March 2020; *Rachid Braih et al.* v. *Algeria*, CCPR/C/128/D/2924/2016, 27 March 2020; *Ahmed Souaiene and Aicha Souaiene* v. *Algeria*, CCPR/C/128/D/3082/2017, 27 March 2020.

of cases the system was receiving, moreover, were repetitive cases, namely applications concerning different claimants but concerning the same or highly similar factual situations and rights violation claims.[46]

The European human rights system responded by developing the pilot judgment procedure, often traced to an important resolution by the Committee of Ministers in 2004.[47] Essentially, the pilot judgment procedure allows the Court to freeze or adjourn repeat applications concerning certain situations, and instead consider a small subset of such cases as pilot judgments. In particular, Rule 61 of the Court's Rules of Procedure, adopted in 2011, specifies that recourse may be had to the pilot judgment procedure 'where the facts of an application reveal in the Contracting Party concerned the existence of a structural or systemic problem or other similar dysfunction which has given rise or may give rise to similar applications'.[48] While the ECtHR has been reluctant for much of its history to issue assertive remedial orders calling for structural reform or the like, these are considered not only possible but essentially required in the pilot judgment context. Here, the Court must order the state to adopt such measures as are necessary to amend the structural situation of violation, addressing not only the pilot case(s) but the situation of all the frozen cases as well. Should such measures not be adopted, the frozen cases may be resumed for consideration.[49]

Some open questions remain in relation to the pilot judgment procedure. Among other issues, the ECtHR has not developed very detailed criteria to ensure all relevant classes and interests of claimants are

[46] See ECtHR, Factsheet – Pilot judgments (November 2022), 1. www.echr.coe.int/documents/pilot_judgment_procedure_eng.pdf.

[47] See Committee of Ministers of the Council of Europe, Resolution Res(2004)3 on Judgments Revealing an Underlying Systemic Problem, 12 May 2004.

[48] ECtHR, Rules of Procedure, Rule 61(1).

[49] For more on the early use of the procedure, see L. Wildhaber, 'Pilot Judgments in Cases of Structural or Systematic Problems on the National Level', in R. Wolfrum and U. Deutsch (eds.), *The European Court of Human Rights Overwhelmed by Applications: Problems and Possible Solutions* (Heidelberg: Springer, 2009); P. Leach, H. Hardman, S. Stephenson and B. Blitz, *Responding to Systemic Human Rights Violations: An Analysis of Pilot Judgments of the European Court of Human Rights and Their Impact at National Level* (Cambridge: Intersentia, 2010); P. Leach, H. Hardman and S. Stephenson, 'Can the European Court's Pilot Judgment Procedure Help Resolve Systemic Human Rights Violations? Burdov and the Failure to Implement Domestic Court Decisions in Russia', *Human Rights Law Review* 10 (2010): 346–359; D. Haider, *The Pilot-Judgment Procedure of the European Court of Human Rights* (Leiden: Brill, 2013).

adequately considered.[50] In addition, the pilot judgment procedure has been challenged on the grounds that it allows the Court to foreclose claims and hence enable rights violations to go unaddressed in certain cases.[51] Despite such objections – which can and should be addressed – the pilot judgment procedure offers one effective, proven method through which patterns or practices of violations may be addressed. This can form a basis for other systems, including those at the United Nations level, to reflect on how optimally to process large numbers of similar cases.

8.4.2 Findings, Recommendations and Follow-Up

Recognition that the facts revealed in an individual case may constitute part of broader patterns and practices of violations should inform the manner in which UNTBs structure their decisions and follow-up procedures as well. First and foremost, human rights bodies should explicitly recognise, as clearly, honestly and accurately as possible, the systemic nature of those violations as such.[52] Simply recognising such situations will constitute a valuable first step towards exerting enhanced pressure for them to change.

Second, that recognition should inform the remedial measures that human rights bodies recommend. This means that those remedies should be oriented not only towards providing satisfaction or redress to the individual claimant or claimants, but also towards ensuring non-repetition. In the context of patterns or practices of violations, this entails the adoption of remedial measures aimed at reforming the aspects of law

[50] For some contemplations on this point, see T. Sainati, 'Human Rights Class Actions: Rethinking the Pilot-Judgment Procedure at the European Court of Human Rights', *Harvard International Law Journal* 56 (2015): 147–205; L. Glas, 'The Function of the Pilot-Judgment Procedure of the European Court of Human Rights in Practice', *Netherlands Quarterly of Human Rights* 34 (2016): 41–70.

[51] See D. Kurban, 'Forsaking Individual Justice: The Implications of the European Court of Human Rights' Pilot Judgment Procedure for Victims of Gross and Systematic Violations', *Human Rights Law Review*, 16 (2016): 731–769; E. Kindt, 'Giving up on individual justice? The effect of state non-execution of a pilot judgment on victims', *Netherlands Quarterly of Human Rights* 36 (2018): 173–188; E. Wagner, 'How Many Strikeouts Are Too Many? The ECtHR's Evolving Approach to Repetitive Cases and the Limits of Efficiency', in S. Schiedermair, A. Schwarz and D. Steiger (eds.), *Theory and Practice of the European Convention on Human Rights* (London: Bloomsbury, 2022).

[52] While this chapter has preferred the language of pattern or practices of violations, other similar terminologies have been and might be used, including references to structural, systemic, widespread, systematic, massive or gross violations.

and policy which allowed for the violations to take place. Among other terminologies, these sorts of remedies have been referred to as general measures and as structural remedies. In this, the UNTBs may look to the example set by the Inter-American, African and European human rights systems. The Inter-American and African systems have both demonstrated a longstanding willingness to issue structural orders. The European system has moved in a similar direction more recently, initially in the context of pilot judgments, and later more broadly.[53] The UNTBs might also consider adopting the Committee of Ministers of the Council of Europe's rule that indicates the need to oversee whether 'general measures have been adopted, preventing new violations similar to that or those found or putting an end to continuing violations'.[54]

A challenge may arise in the context of structural orders, however, insofar as they may take broad and vague forms.[55] General orders, calling, for instance, for states to take all measures necessary to remedy the situation in question, are a valuable addition to judgments that otherwise only require individual remedies. However, several scholars and practitioners have noted that specificity is highly desirable in human rights bodies' findings, especially relative to structural orders,[56] as this helps to make clear exactly what measures states should take to end the structural contexts of violation in question. UNTBs should hence work to ensure that the structural remedies they suggest are as clear as possible. Specific remedial recommendations are valuable not only insofar as they

[53] See H. Keller and C. Marti, 'Reconceptualizing Implementation: The Judicialization of the Execution of the European Court of Human Rights' Judgments', *European Journal of International Law* 26 (2016): 829–850, 838.

[54] See Rules of the Committee of Ministers for the Supervision of the Execution of Judgments and of the Terms of Friendly Settlements, 18 January 2017, Rule 6(2)(b)(ii); A. von Staden, 'Monitoring Second-order Compliance: The Follow-up Procedures of the UN Human Rights Treaty Bodies', *Czech Yearbook of International Law* 9 (2018): 329–356, 347.

[55] On the vagueness of many human rights bodies' follow-up reports regarding the steps required to comply with the judgment, see von Staden, 'Monitoring Second-Order Compliance'.

[56] See, e.g., T. Antkowiak, 'An Emerging Mandate for International Courts: Victim-centered Remedies and Restorative Justice', *Stanford Journal of International Law* 47 (2011): 279–332, 313; Keller and Marti, 'Reconceptualizing Implementation' 839f. For some nuanced reflections, that nonetheless support the view that 'intrusive[ness]' is more appropriate relative to 'guarantees of non-recurrence', see R. Murray and C. Sandoval, 'Balancing Specificity of Reparation Measures and States' Discretion to Enhance Implementation', *Journal of Human Rights Practice* 12 (2020): 101–124, 120.

enable stronger and more targeted pressure for compliance, but also because they establish a clearer basis for follow-up investigations.

In addition to more specific remedies, UNTBs should more clearly and accessibly publicise their findings regarding patterns or practices of violations. Pressure on states to comply with findings will be enhanced where those findings are made as publicly available as possible.[57] In this regard, information as to any findings requiring general measures, structural reforms or the like should be prominently included within any compilation or public presentation of information concerning patterns or practices of violations. This information could then be easily followed up on not only by the human rights body that reached the decision in question,[58] but also by all those working in and with OHCHR and affiliated mechanisms, as well as the human rights community at large.

8.5 The Public Presentation of Information Concerning Patterns or Practices of Violations

As emphasised in the introduction, it is important to recognise that there are two different angles from which one may consider evidentiary issues in relation to international human rights bodies. First, as explored in much of the above, there is the question of how these bodies receive and consider evidence. However, such bodies are not only receivers of evidence; they are also key actors in the production, shaping and global dissemination of evidence pertaining to human rights standards in theory and violations understood to have taken place in practice. Maximizing the accessibility, accuracy and impact of the information produced is hence of the greatest importance.

Currently, the work done by the United Nations' various human rights bodies is primarily presented in a functionally disaggregated manner:

[57] For a similar point, see A. Donald, D. Long and A.-K. Speck, 'Identifying and Assessing the Implementation of Human Rights Decisions', *Journal of Human Rights Practice* 12 (2020): 125–148, 143 ('[i]mplementation is hampered when information is outdated or not made public, precluding meaningful participation from all interested actors').

[58] UNTBs may also potentially enhance their follow-up on systemic issues by grouping similar cases together. In this, they may look to the example set by the regional systems: the Inter-American Court has held joint follow-up hearings where similar issues were at play, and the Council of Europe's Committee of Ministers has grouped similar cases together. See C. Sandoval, P. Leach and R. Murray, 'Monitoring, cajoling and promoting dialogue: what role for supranational human rights bodies in the implementation of individual decisions?', *Journal of Human Rights Practice* 12 (2020): 71–100, 77.

OHCHR statements (including certain outputs by Special Rapporteurs and others) may be found in one place;[59] the outcomes of the Human Rights Council's Universal Periodic Review (UPR) process, whereby states' compliance with their human rights obligations is regularly reviewed by other states, somewhere else;[60] human rights treaty bodies' work may be accessed via their individual pages,[61] or via a database;[62] each of the various Special Rapporteurs' different outputs is primarily accessible from their individual page;[63] and so on. The relevant information is also clustered and presented under particular unifying headings, including by country[64] and by type of violation.[65]

The organisation of human rights information per entity that has produced it, the state it concerns and the types of violation in question makes sense and should persist. However, relevant information may and should be clustered according to particular patterns or practices of violation as well. Such information could include any documentation produced concerning a particular pattern or practice of violations – be it a public statement, the outcome of UPR consideration, part of a Special Rapporteur's report or part of a country review or a case determination by any of the human rights bodies. Grouping together and presenting information in the context of the patterns or practices of which it forms a part would arguably promote efficiency (by preventing the same research work being done by multiple different parties when developing materials addressing that situation); promote consistency, by helping enable different organisations to respond to such situations in similar manners; make the nature, scope and gravity of such situations clearer; and generate more pressure for the violations in question to be addressed.

Ultimately, such an approach could lead to the consolidation of information under particular headings of (what would typically be ongoing but might also be past) patterns or practices of violations. In a particular state, for example, there might be information concerning patterns or practices of violations relative to: use of force by law enforcement; assembly rights; immigrants' rights; prison conditions; over-criminalisation;

59 See OHCHR website, 'Latest'.
60 See OHCHR website, 'Universal Periodic Review'.
61 See, e.g., OHCHR website, 'Human Rights Committee'.
62 See OHCHR website, 'UN Treaty Body Database'.
63 See, e.g., OHCHR website, 'Special Rapporteur on freedom of peaceful assembly and of association'.
64 See OHCHR website, 'Countries'.
65 See OHCHR website, 'Topics'.

due process violations; the right to health; surveillance; and so on. OHCHR's Universal Human Rights Index provides a valuable tool through which existing human rights findings relative to particular sorts of violations in different countries may be accessed.[66] However, recognising where the situation in question rises to one of patterns or practices of violations, and presenting that information directly as such, are steps that have not yet been taken.

With time, it will hopefully be possible to provide relatively comprehensive mapping (according to existing standards) of ongoing patterns or practices of violations in different substantive areas of rights concern across all states. The initial launch of such a mode of presenting information will perhaps pose a challenge, insofar as a great deal of novel informational processing will be necessary, and it may not be readily practicable to compile information on all ongoing patterns or practices of violations at the same time. One principled way in which to sequence attention would be through prioritisation criteria, in other words by beginning in those contexts in which violations are the most severe. Due to constraints of space, this chapter will not go further into that issue, but it is worth noting such issues have been dealt with, for example, by the Inter-American Commission in detailing the criteria it will consider when deciding whether or not to list a particular state in the portion of the Commission's Annual Reports that specifies where the most serious human rights violations are taking place (chapter IV.B).[67] Once information has been compiled on the most serious patterns or practices of violations, attention could be expanded to cover patterns or practices of violations which do not rise to the same level of gravity.

8.6 Conclusion

This chapter has argued that UNTBs should more clearly and consistently pay attention to and recognise the existence of patterns or practices of violations. It has considered what impacts this should have on UNTBs' receipt of information generally; their approaches to the exhaustion of domestic remedies, and the burden of proof; the manner in which cases are processed; and UNTBs' findings, remedial recommendations and follow-up practices. The chapter has also argued that OHCHR should

[66] See OHCHR, 'Universal Human Rights Index'.

[67] Inter-American Commission on Human Rights, Rules of Procedure, in force 1 August 2013, Rule 59 (6).

ensure information concerning patterns or practices of violations is specifically highlighted in their public dissemination of human rights information. Compliance with these recommendations will help to ensure patterns or practices of violation are more consistently recognised, that cases addressing such situations are appropriately handled, that a more readily accessible evidential record is available for future cases, and that information concerning patterns or practices of violations is more extensively publicly shared, resulting in greater pressure for such situations to be brought to an end.

Select Bibliography

Aceves, W. J., '*Actio Popularis? The Class Action in International Law*', University of Chicago Legal Forum *(2003): 353–402.*

Antkowiak, T., 'Remedial Approaches to Human Rights Violations: The Inter-American Court of Human Rights and Beyond', *Columbia Journal of Transnational Law* 46 (2007): 351–419.

'An Emerging Mandate for International Courts: Victim-Centered Remedies and Restorative Justice', *Stanford Journal of International Law* 47 (2011): 279–332.

Donald, A., Long, D. and Speck, A.-K., 'Identifying and Assessing the Implementation of Human Rights Decisions', *Journal of Human Rights Practice* 12 (2020): 125–148.

Glas, L., 'The Function of the Pilot-Judgment Procedure of the European Court of Human Rights in Practice', *Netherlands Quarterly of Human Rights* 34 (2016): 41–70.

Haider, D., *The Pilot-Judgment Procedure of the European Court of Human Rights* (Leiden: Brill, 2013).

Keller, H. and Marti, C., 'Reconceptualizing Implementation: The Judicialization of the Execution of the European Court of Human Rights' Judgments', *European Journal of International Law* 26 (2016): 829–850.

Leach, P., Hardman, H., Stephenson, S. and Blitz, B., *Responding to Systemic Human Rights Violations: An Analysis of Pilot Judgments of the European Court of Human Rights and Their Impact at National Level* (Cambridge: Intersentia, 2010).

Murray, R. and Sandoval, C., 'Balancing Specificity of Reparation Measures and States' Discretion to Enhance Implementation', *Journal of Human Rights Practice* 12 (2020): 101–124.

Sainati, T., 'Human Rights Class Actions: Rethinking the Pilot-Judgment Procedure at the European Court of Human Rights', *Harvard International Law Journal* 56 (2015): 147–205.

Sandoval, C., Leach, P. and Murray, R., 'Monitoring, Cajoling and Promoting Dialogue: What Role for Supranational Human Rights Bodies in the Implementation of Individual Decisions?', *Journal of Human Rights Practice* 12(2020): 71–100.

von Staden, A., 'Monitoring Second-Order Compliance: The Follow-Up Procedures of the UN Human Rights Treaty Bodies', *Czech Yearbook of International Law* 9 (2018): 329–356.

PART IV

What 'Evidence' May Leave Unseen

9

The Polluting Effect of Stereotypes on Evidence

CEDAW's Efforts to Address Gender-Based Discriminatory Narratives

ELENA GHIDONI*

9.1 Introduction

In legal literature, stereotypes are usually described as generalisations 'about the attributes or characteristics possessed by, or the role that is or should be performed by, members of a particular group'.[1] While stereotypes are often associated with inaccurate evaluations and misrepresentations of reality, their connection with evidentiary issues has not yet been fully explored in legal scholarship. Current research has especially focused on the impact of gender (and other) stereotypes on the adjudication of human rights more broadly, without attention being paid to evidence.[2] Yet, many judgments, from various regional courts and bodies, demonstrate that stereotypes can prevent proper ascertainment of the facts of a case. They may lead to

* I would like to express my deepest gratitude to all those who supported me throughout the process of writing this chapter. My sincere thanks to the editors, Deborah Casalin, Marie-Bénédicte Dembour and Cornelia Klocker, for their invaluable guidance, feedback and encouragement. I am also grateful to Dolores Morondo Taramundi, whose intellectual generosity and constructive critique enriched my work. The research for this chapter was conducted within the framework of the European Union's Horizon 2020 research and innovation programme under the Marie Sklowdoska-Curie grant agreement N° 665959.

[1] R. Cook and S. Cusack, *Gender Stereotyping: Transnational Legal Perspectives* (Philadelphia: University of Pennsylvania Press, 2010), p. 9.

[2] E. Brems and A. Timmer (eds.), *Stereotypes and Human Rights Law* (Cambridge: Intersentia, 2016); L. Clérico, 'Hacia un análisis integral de estereotipos: Desafiando la garantía estándar de imparcialidad', *Revista Derecho del Estado*, 41 (2018): 67–96; A. Timmer, 'Toward an anti-stereotyping approach for the European court of human rights', *Human Rights Law Review* 11 (2011): 707–738; I. Renzulli, 'Discrimination and gender stereotypes in judicial decisions: The jurisprudence of the European Court of Human Rights in light of JL v Italy: A retreat into the shadows?', *Netherlands Quarterly of Human Rights* 41 (2023): 155–173.

relevant pieces of evidence being ignored, irrelevant circumstances being given undue weight or higher standards of proof being imposed than would have otherwise been the case.

The Convention on the Elimination of Discrimination against Women (CEDAW), which was adopted in 1979,[3] has played a pivotal role in advancing women's human rights by addressing gender stereotypes as one of the manifestations of discrimination rooted in unequal power relations, particularly through Articles 2 (f) and 5 (a). Article 2 (f) requires states to modify or abolish laws, regulations and practices that constitute discrimination against women. Article 5 (a) makes explicit reference to the stereotyped roles of men and women and prejudices or practices based on the idea of the superiority of either of the sexes. It requires states to take all necessary steps 'to modify social and cultural patterns of conduct of men and women' with the aim of eradicating these discriminatory practices.

As illustrated below, the Committee tasked with the implementation of this Convention – namely the CEDAW Committee – has made it clear that gender-based stereotypes may not only be conveyed through individual acts but also in laws, social structures and institutions. The Committee has shown remarkable determination in actively using its mandate to interpret and develop legal obligations on states to combat gender stereotypes. Through its general recommendations, as well as its views on individual communications submitted under the Optional Protocol to CEDAW,[4] the CEDAW Committee is paving the way for a deeper understanding of stereotypes in law and shedding light on the interplay between gender stereotypes and access to justice.

This chapter engages with the CEDAW Committee's approach to stereotypes and evidence by providing an overview of the Committee's contribution to the definition of their interaction. It does so by reviewing selected views delivered on gender-based violence, a domain where the Committee itself has expressed concern about the pervasive negative impact of stereotypes in undermining women's access to justice.

Following this introduction (Section 9.1), a critical discussion of evidence law is first set out in Section 9.2. This aims to unpack the gendered

[3] Convention on the Elimination of All Forms of Discrimination against Women (CEDAW), 18 December 1979, in force 3 September 1981, 1249 UNTS 13.

[4] Optional Protocol to the Convention on the Elimination of All Forms of Discrimination against Women (OP-CEDAW), 6 October 1999, in force 22 December 2000, 2131 UNTS 83.

assumptions embedded in this field and sets the stage for an examination of how gender stereotypes connect to debates about factual construction and the rational evaluation of evidence. Section 9.3 goes on to provide an overview of CEDAW's framework for addressing gender stereotypes. It specifically focuses on the right to access to justice and how the CEDAW Committee's General Recommendation 33 enabled a better understanding of the interplay between stereotypes and evidence. The section then delves into the Committee's relevant jurisprudence. Section 9.4 offers an alternative approach to this interaction, which entails examining the impact of stereotypes through the concept of legal presumptions. This is followed by concluding thoughts and recommendations on the matter in Section 9.5.

9.2 Stereotypes and Evidence: An Emerging Issue

As the legal literature on stereotypes has consistently stressed, judgments should be based on law and facts, rather than myths, stereotypes and preconceived ideas.[5] Yet, is there a single, objective way to interpret law and facts? This question is far more complicated than the literature depicts it to be, evoking a classic debate in legal scholarship on how we conceive law, facts and the relationship between them as determinate categories. This debate assumes facts to be objective materials to be discovered and mechanically subsumed into a non-contested legal definition.

This section will delve into these ideas and their relevance for the study of stereotypes, with a twofold objective. First, it will expose how some tenets of evidence law systematically render women's accounts unsound. Second, it will introduce the issue of stereotyping into a broader discussion about factual construction and its challenges.

Theories of factual construction have problematised assumptions about how facts enter the judicial process: how they are perceived, selected for their relevance and evaluated, with this whole process affected by the socio-cultural background of the legal actors involved in the trial.[6] Beyond the application of rationalist criteria of logic, scientific

[5] S. Cusack, *Eliminating judicial stereotyping. Equal access to justice for women in gender-based violence cases* (Office of the High Commissioner for Human Rights, 2014); C. L'Hereux-Dubé, 'Beyond the myths; equality, impartiality, and justice', *Journal of Social Distress and the Homeless* 10 (2001): 87–104.

[6] The need to investigate facts was already signalled by Jerome Frank, and subsequently developed by W. Twining, *Rethinking Evidence: Exploratory Essays* (Cambridge: Cambridge University Press, 2006).

laws and maxims of experience, evaluating evidence is a process that involves a wide margin of discretion.[7]

While modern legal theory has tended to altogether ignore the *quaestio facti* (the issue of factual construction), legal hermeneutics has shed light on the intertwined relationship between law and facts, and the way they mutually influence each other's determination in the judicial process.[8] Causality, temporality, cultural dimensions and rules of language are shown to shape the interpretation of reality, thus undermining the pretence of an objective and unique factual account. The cultural dimension, in particular, concerns ethical and religious perspectives, social values, scripts and stereotypes that provide narrative frameworks to guide factual construction in a coherent way.[9] A narrative appraisal of the judicial process as composed of stories told by different parties is apt to reveal how factual components are likely to be selected and organised in accounts that are consistent with cultural frameworks, common sense, and regularities *(id quod plerumque accidit*, or common occurrences). This consistency makes the story appear plausible and coherent.

These theories have contributed to exposing the cultural contingency embedded in adjudication. Yet, they have not pushed their critique further and exposed how the rationalist tradition of evidence discourse and its assumptions about a universal and self-evident understanding of truth, rationality and justice, systematically erase the experiences of socially oppressed groups.[10]

Against this background, critical legal theories have exposed the false objectivity and neutrality of legal methods and the rules of evidence. They have examined adjudication not as mere perception of the facts as raw material, but as a process that 'purvey[s] truth'.[11] Feminist legal theorists, in particular, have unpacked the assumptions underlying the dichotomic framing of procedural and substantive law, with the former being conceived as the domain of pure logic and rationality, and the latter

[7] M. Paz Araya Novoa, 'Género y verdad: Valoración racional de la prueba en los delitos de violencia patriarcal', *Revista de Estudios de La Justicia* 32 (2020): 35–69.

[8] B. Pastore, *Interpreti e fonti nell'esperienza giuridica contemporanea* (Padova: CEDAM, 2014).

[9] F. Di Donato, *The Analysis of Legal Cases: A Narrative Approach* (New York: Routledge, 2020).

[10] D. Nicolson, 'Gender, epistemology and ethics: Feminist perspectives on evidence theory', in M. Childs and L. Ellison (eds.), *Feminist Perspectives on Evidence* (London: Routledge-Cavendish, 2000).

[11] Nicolson, 'Gender, epistemology and ethics', p. 16.

being the place where politics belong. In exposing how method shapes substance,[12] feminist theorists have questioned our 'ways of knowing' in law,[13] reformulating questions that bring original perspectives to the field. Instead of asking how value judgments exceptionally succeed in polluting law – portrayed as the realm of inherent objectivity – feminist discourse purports that power hierarchies are originally embedded in evidence law. This shift exposes a number of assumptions and mechanisms of the rules of evidence that systematically erase women's voices: the preference for physical over psychological evidence, direct over indirect evidence, presence over absence, continuity over discontinuity.[14] Moreover, evidence law builds on the assumption that truth is accessible to any unbiased observer who shares with the community a set of 'universally accepted generalisations about human behaviour'.[15] Thus, the idea of a 'universal competence' presents a hegemonic view of human behaviour as if it were universal, when in fact, women's experiences and those of other subordinated groups differ from the dominant view. These experiences are thus silenced, or viewed as irrational or illegible.[16]

In addition, the linear conception of truth as 'singular, immediately apparent, and permanent' has historically undermined the credibility of women's accounts of sexual violence.[17] Reliance on assumptions about internal consistency, narrative coherence, hard or physical evidence and the stability of storytelling over time has contributed to shaping a notion of truth detached from women's experiences of these violations.[18]

At the core of feminist and critical approaches lies a common understanding that law in general, and evidence law in particular, is built on

[12] K. T. Bartlett, 'Feminist legal methods', *Harvard Law Review* 103 (1989): 829–888.

[13] M. J. Mossman, 'Feminism and legal method: The difference it makes', *Wisconsin Women's Law Journal* 3 (1987): 147–168.

[14] R. Hunter, 'Gender in evidence: masculine norms vs. feminist reforms', *Harvard Women's Law Journal* 19 (1996): 127–167.

[15] D. Martinson, M. MacCrimmon, I. Grant and C. Boyle, 'A forum on Lavallee v. R: Women and self-defence', *University of British Columbia Law Review* 25 (1991): 23–68, 38.

[16] Recently, Gleeson pointed out that criteria like coherence, consistency and plausibility used in credibility assessment 'may mask discriminatory evidentiary hierarchies which privileges male experiences and 'credentialed knowledge' – M. Gleeson, 'Unlocking CEDAW's transformative potential: Asylum cases before the Committee on the Elimination of Discrimination against Women', *American Journal of International Law* 118 (2024): 41–97, 90.

[17] K. L. Scheppele, 'Just the facts, ma'am: Sexualized violence, evidentiary habits, and the revision of truth', *New York Law School Law Review* 37 (1992): 123–172, 127.

[18] S. Estrich, *Real Rape* (Cambridge MA: Harvard University Press, 1987).

pre-existing social inequalities.[19] Ignoring this premise makes it difficult to understand why human rights violations perpetrated against the oppressed often remain invisible. Instead, critical theorists advocate for alternative understandings of knowledge, rationality, and truth that allow the experiences of the oppressed to *make sense* and regain value.[20]

Debates about stereotypes and stereotyping resonate with those concerning factual construction and the assumptions underlying the ascertainment of factual truth during adjudication (and beyond). Following the seminal work of Cook and Cusack on stereotyping in international human rights law,[21] legal research has consistently referred to stereotypes as generalised views or preconceptions about the attributes, characteristics or roles that women and men should possess or perform.[22] Their harmfulness is usually associated with making assumptions about an individual simply based on their membership in a particular social group. While anti-stereotyping theories in law date back to the 1970s,[23] lawyers and theorists still struggle to identify the boundaries between stereotypes and other concepts such as stigma, prejudice and bias, and even generalisations, which are widely used in law.[24] In addition, much scholarly work is devoted to gender and intersecting stereotypes in international human rights adjudication,[25] while less research has focused on stereotypes based on other grounds of discrimination.[26]

[19] G. Minda, *Postmodern Legal Movements: Law and Jurisprudence at Century's End* (New York: New York University Press, 1995); Childs and Ellison, *Feminist Perspectives on Evidence*.

[20] The message is giving rationality new meanings, as in Bartlett, 'Feminist legal methods', p. 857.

[21] Cook and Cusack, *Gender Stereotyping*.

[22] Brems and Timmer, *Stereotyping in Human Rights Law*; L. Clérico, 'Estereotipos de género y violación de la imparcialidad judicial: Nuevos estándares interamericanos. El caso Manuela v El Salvador', *Revista de Derecho, Universidad y Justicia, SAIJ/ Universidad Nacional de Avellaneda* 1 (2022): 110–135; R. Holtmaat and J. Naber, *Women's Human Rights and Culture: From Deadlock to Dialogue* (Cambridge: Intersentia, 2011); Timmer, 'Towards an anti-stereotyping approach'.

[23] C. Franklin, 'The anti-stereotyping principle in constitutional sex discrimination law', *New York University Law Review* 85 (2010): 83–173.

[24] F. J. Arena, 'Los estereotipos normativos en la decisión judicial: Una exploración conceptual', *Revista de Derecho de la Universidad Austral de Chile* 29 (2016): 51–75.

[25] N. Bórquez and L. Clérico, 'Una vuelta de tuerca al análisis de estereotipo: estereotipo combinado', *Revista Electrónica. Instituto de Investigaciones Ambrosio L. Gioja*, 26 (2021): 1–28; L. N. Henningsen, 'The emerging anti-stereotyping principle under Article 14 ECHR', *European Convention on Human Rights Law Review* 3 (2022): 185–219.

[26] C. Hansen, 'Dismantling or perpetuating gender stereotypes: The case of trans rights in the European Court of Human Rights' jurisprudence', *The Age of Human Rights Journal* 18 (2022): 143–161.

Moreover, while stereotypes are often associated with misrepresentation of individual characteristics, and in general with inaccurate or false representations of reality, few contributions have paid attention to the specific impact of stereotyping on the assessment of facts and evidence in national and supranational jurisdictions.[27] The first study to provide an overview of the varied ways in which stereotypes may impact probative issues was commissioned by the Office of the High Commissioner for Human Rights in 2013.[28] The report focused on gender stereotypes and the adjudication of gender-based violence cases, pointing to how stereotypes affect the perception of facts. In particular, stereotypes impact perceptions of who is the victim and who is the aggressor, the culpability of the persons accused and the credibility of witnesses. They also affect the issues to be determined at trial, and may lead to the admission of irrelevant or highly prejudicial evidence, or to unjustified weight being attached to certain evidence.[29]

The need to improve gender-sensitive training for judges, prosecutors and other legal actors involved in the justice system has led to the development of protocols and professional manuals that provide more in-depth analysis of the interplay between stereotypes and evidence.[30] There have also been important developments in how international human rights bodies understand the impact of stereotypes on access to justice – and in particular, on evidentiary matters – that demand scholarly attention. In this light, the following sections explore developments at the CEDAW Committee with regard to gender stereotypes and their impact on evidence.

9.3 Lessons from the CEDAW Committee

Within international human rights law, CEDAW provides a legal framework to combat gender stereotyping in view of achieving substantive

[27] Exceptions include the contributions in F. J. Arena (ed.), *Manual sobre estereotipos en la impartición de la justicia* (Ciudad de México: Suprema Corte de Justicia de la Nación, 2022); F. J. Arena, *Los estereotipos detrás de las normas* (Córdoba AR: Toledo, 2022) and Clérico, 'Estereotipos de género y violación de la imparcialidad judicial'.

[28] Cusack, 'Eliminating judicial stereotyping'.

[29] Cusack, 'Eliminating judicial stereotyping', p. 20.

[30] Arena, *Manual sobre estereotipos en la impartición de la justicia*; M. Paz Araya Novoa, 'Acceso a la justicia, violencia de género y desigualdades invisibles al proceso penal', in P. Rovatti (ed.), *Manual sobre derechos humanos y prueba en el proceso penal* (México: Suprema Corte de Justicia de la Nación, 2021), pp. 188–228.

equality. Article 2 (f) and Article 5 (a) explicitly require states parties to modify or transform gender stereotypes and eliminate wrongful stereotyping.[31] These have been interpreted as freestanding provisions but also as sources of an overarching and cross-cutting obligation to be read in conjunction with other human rights.[32] The CEDAW Committee has specified that the elimination of discrimination is an obligation with three dimensions: (1) ensuring there is no direct and indirect discrimination in both public and private spheres; (2) improving women's de facto equality; and (3) addressing prevailing gender relations and the persistence of gender-based stereotypes.[33] According to the Committee, gender-based stereotypes 'affect women not only through individual acts by individuals but also in law, and legal and societal structures and institutions'. The obligation to address gender stereotypes binds the contracting state and its apparatus, including judges, prosecutors and law enforcement officials.[34] It also extends to taking positive action against stereotyping by non-state actors and individuals (Article 2 (e)).[35]

This obligation was applied in connection with the right to access to justice in the leading case *Vertido* v. *The Philippines*.[36] In this case, the Committee held the Philippines accountable for gender stereotyping by the judiciary, which affected the victim's access to a fair and just trial. The Committee observed that 'the judiciary must take caution not to create

[31] In general, it is assumed that stereotypes are not always wrongful, as they fulfil an important cognitive function and may also have a role in the construction of individual and group identities; see R. Holtmaat, 'Article 5 CEDAW', in M. A. Freeman, C. Chinkin and B. Rudolf (eds.), *The UN Convention on the Elimination of All Forms of Discrimination Against Women: A Commentary* (Oxford: Oxford University Press 2012), pp. 141–167, 148. For a critique, see E. Ghidoni and D. Morondo Taramundi, 'El papel de los estereotipos en las formas de la desigualdad compleja: Algunos apuntes desde la teoría feminista del derecho antidiscriminatorio', *Discusiones*, 28 (2022): 37–70.

[32] CEDAW Committee, General Recommendation No. 28, on the core obligations of states parties under Article 2 of the Convention on the Elimination of All Forms of Discrimination against Women, CEDAW/C/GC/28, 16 December 2010; Cook and Cusack, *Gender Stereotyping*, p. 75.

[33] CEDAW Committee, General Recommendation No. 25, on Article 4, paragraph 1, of the Convention on the Elimination of All Forms of Discrimination against Women, A/59/38, 18 August 2004, para. 7.

[34] CEDAW Committee, General Recommendation No. 33 (GR 33) on women's access to justice, CEDAW/C/GC/33, 3 August 2015, para. 27.

[35] See CEDAW Committee, General Recommendation No. 19 on violence against women, A/47/38, 30 January 1992, and General Recommendation No. 35 (GR 35) on gender-based violence against women, updating General Recommendation No. 19, CEDAW/C/GC/35, 24 July 2017.

[36] *Tayag Vertido* v. *The Philippines*, CEDAW/C/46/D/18/2008, 16 July 2010.

inflexible standards of what women or girls should be or what they should have done when confronted with a situation of rape based merely on preconceived notions of what defines a rape victim'.[37]

This principle has been repeatedly affirmed in subsequent views. It was also recalled in General Recommendation 33, which clarified the obligations to address gender stereotyping to guarantee the right to access to justice.[38] In this recommendation, the CEDAW Committee considered the right to access to justice to be a bridge between substantive and procedural law and an essential component for the realisation of all the rights enshrined in the Convention. Acknowledging that access to justice in its various dimensions is currently hampered by obstacles related to structural discrimination and inequality,[39] the Committee highlighted that gender stereotyping and procedural and evidentiary requirements are among the factors that constitute such obstacles.[40] It further held that reasoning based on gender stereotyping impairs the justice system, as it 'distorts perceptions and results in decisions based on preconceived beliefs and myths rather than relevant facts'.[41] Recalling the principle laid down in *Vertido* v. *The Philippines*, the Committee contended that by creating rigid standards of evaluation of human behaviour, gender stereotypes have a detrimental impact on the credibility given to women's accounts as parties and witnesses.[42] All these elements can cause judges to misinterpret or misapply laws and compromise the impartiality and integrity of the justice system, leading to miscarriages of justice.[43]

Since its adoption, this General Recommendation has become a useful tool to further substantiate the Committee's findings regarding gender stereotyping and elaborate specific recommendations to states parties. In subsequent communications, the Committee has interpreted the anti-stereotyping obligation in relation to other limbs of Article 2, which were

[37] *Tayag Vertido* (CEDAW), para. 8.4.

[38] CEDAW Committee, GR 33, paras. 3, 7, 8, 26–28. As in *Tayag Vertido*, the recommendation refers to 'rigid' or 'inflexible' standards of behaviour, and inflexible evidentiary requirements (paras. 26, 29.c.ii, 51.h).

[39] CEDAW Committee, GR 33, para. 14.

[40] CEDAW Committee, GR 33, paras. 3, 7, 8.

[41] CEDAW Committee, GR 33, para. 26.

[42] CEDAW Committee, GR 33, para. 26.

[43] A similar argument was developed in the recent case law of the Inter American Court of Human Rights – see Clérico, 'Estereotipos de género y violación de la imparcialidad judicial'.

invoked by the authors,[44] even without a specific mention of Article 5 (a) on some occasions.[45]

While CEDAW lays itself open to some criticisms with specific reference to stereotypes and stereotyping (e.g. the absence of definitions),[46] the Committee's work has provided greater visibility to the negative impact of stereotyping in women's rights adjudication. The Committee has also developed a more comprehensive approach to the issue in its recommendations.[47] However, there remains more to be done regarding the naming of the specific stereotypes at play, exposing the inferences they trigger, and articulating the specific harms they cause.[48] Despite this last limitation, CEDAW and the work of its Committee have deservedly become a reference in international human rights law for addressing gender stereotypes.[49]

This section will now discuss how the Committee has improved its reasoning on the impact of stereotypes on evidence. It does so by examining a set of individual communications which, submitted under the Optional Protocol, have resulted in a decision on the merits. Only communications where stereotypes were affecting the evidence *and* the Committee was seeing, naming and addressing this connection have been selected for analysis. In addition, only communications from the jurisprudence on gender-based violence[50] were sought, as this is the field

[44] For example, in *S.T.* v. *Russian Federation*, the author claimed a violation of Article 2 (c) for lack of effective legal protection, linked to gender-based misconceptions and myths: *S.T.* v. *Russian Federation*, CEDAW/C/72/D/65/2014, 25 February 2019, para. 3.3.

[45] *X.* v. *Timor-Leste*, CEDAW/C/69/D/88/2015, 26 February 2018, involving violations of Articles 2 (c) – (f) and 15; *J.I.* v. *Finland*, CEDAW/C/69/D/103/2016, 5 March 2018, involving violations of Articles 2 (a), (c), (d) and (f), 15 (a), 16 (1) d, f and Article 1. In both cases, the Committee nevertheless recalls the obligations under Articles 2 (f) and 5 (a), respectively, at paras. 6.8 and 8.9.

[46] CEDAW Committee, GR 33 addresses stereotypes with a focus on their effects, rather than defining what they are.

[47] S. Cusack, 'Building momentum towards change. How the UN's response to stereotyping is evolving', in Brems and Timmer, *Stereotypes and Human Rights Law*, pp. 11–38, 34.

[48] See, e.g., *S.L.* v. *Bulgaria*, CEDAW/C/73/D/99/2016, 19 July 2019, para. 7.9, where the Committee did not identify the stereotypes underlying the provocation argument brought forward by the domestic court.

[49] See, e.g., *Opuz* v. *Turkey*, ECtHR, 33401/02, Judgment, 9 June 2009, para. 164.

[50] Following the updated definition of the CEDAW Committee and in line with other international instruments (e.g. Istanbul Convention, Maputo Protocol), gender-based violence encompasses acts or omissions intended or likely to cause or result in death or physical, sexual, psychological or economic harm or suffering to women, threats of such acts, harassment, coercion and arbitrary deprivation of liberty (CEDAW Committee, GR 35, para. 14).

where the Committee has expressed most concerns in terms of the negative impact of gender stereotypes on access to justice.

These cases illustrate the polluting effect of gender stereotypes on evidence at various stages of the legal proceedings, from investigations to the trial phase. Stereotyped reasoning often results in incomplete and biased investigations, where relevant facts and evidence are not collected. This already puts victims of gender-based violence at great disadvantage in proving their cases and seeing their right to access to justice fulfilled. At trial, stereotypes may shape how the factual hypothesis is constructed, the weight given to certain facts and evidence, and the distribution of the burden of proof.

Shortcomings in the collection of evidence to substantiate the charges stand out as particularly problematic in gender-based violence cases. While the circumstances in which certain crimes are perpetrated (usually a private setting) might partially preclude the availability of witnesses, the prompt collection of other relevant pieces of evidence is also jeopardised by a stereotyped understanding of the facts. The Committee has adjudicated several communications that displayed these issues at the investigation stage, such as the failure of the police to record incidents of violence or collect witness statements, or denials or delays in opening investigations.[51] Although earlier views did not explicitly recognise how stereotypes would have created evidentiary hurdles, they recognised that discriminatory narratives distorted the perception of the circumstances that amount to gender-based violence, including the profiles of victim and aggressor.[52] Thus, stereotypes hampered the investigation and collection of evidence by law enforcement officials. This nexus was made explicit in *Vertido*, and later in *V.K.* v. *Bulgaria* (respectively, cases of sexual assault and domestic violence). In the latter case, the Committee pointed out that 'exclusive focus on physical violence and immediate threat to the life or health of the victim reflects a stereotyped and overly narrow concept of what constitutes domestic violence'.[53]

[51] *Isatou Jallow* v. *Bulgaria*, CEDAW/C/52/D/32/2011, 23 July 2012; *O.G.* v. *Russian Federation*, CEDAW/C/68/D/91/2015, 6 November 2017; *Reyna Trujillo Reyes and Pedro Arguello Morales* v. *Mexico*, CEDAW/C/67/D/75/2014, 21 July 2017, para. 9.6; *O.N. and D.P.* v. *Russian Federation*, CEDAW/C/75/D/119/2017, 24 February 2020, paras. 7.7f. See also *Valiulienė* v. *Lithuania*, ECtHR, 33234/07, Judgment, 26 March 2013.

[52] *The Vienna Intervention Centre against Domestic Violence and the Association for Women's Access to Justice on behalf of Banu Akbak, Gülen Khan, and Melissa Özdemir* v. *Austria* (*Fatma Yildirim* case), CEDAW/C/39/D/6/2005, 6 August 2007, paras. 8.4 and 8.14.

[53] *V.K.* v. *Bulgaria*, CEDAW/C/49/D/20/2008, 25 July 2011, para. 9.12.

Many individual communications before the Committee also point to a biased assessment of evidence during the trial phase of domestic proceedings. This has taken place through practices such as reliance on irrelevant facts over relevant ones based on stereotyped views; selective consideration of evidence based on whether it confirms or contradicts stereotyped hypotheses; and stereotyped assessments of the author's credibility.

The following paragraphs will examine the evolution of the Committee's case law on stereotyped evidence. Reviewing the cases chronologically, the analysis aims at assessing whether the Committee's reasoning has captured the impact of stereotypes on evidence in its various manifestations, and whether it has reached a rigorous and consolidated standard for its adjudication.

A first phase can be identified when the Committee was able to detect shortcomings in domestic authorities' consideration of available evidence, but could not connect these to hints of stereotyped reasoning. In *Goekce* v. *Austria*,[54] a case of domestic violence that ended in femicide, the Committee rightly pointed to the disconnect between abundant evidence of serious danger to the life of the author and the failure of the State to exercise due diligence to protect the victim.[55] However, the Committee did not consider that the submissions warranted further findings on Articles 1 (anti-discrimination provision) and 5 (anti-stereotyping provision). The fact that the public prosecutor withdrew the charges based on the assumption that threats were a regular feature of the couple's disputes, as well as the inability to ascertain which spouse started the violence, would have deserved additional analysis.[56] The normalisation of violence within a couple and the argument of mutual conflict are recurrent discriminatory narratives that serve to downplay the severity of the violence perpetrated against women and overshadow its roots in the gender roles that relegate women to inferior social status. Another case of domestic violence that ended in a fatal stabbing, *Yildirim* v. *Austria*, was adjudicated on the same day.[57] Similarly to *Goekce*, here

[54] *The Vienna Intervention Centre against Domestic Violence and the Association for Women's Access to Justice on behalf of Hakan Goekce, Handan Goekce, and Guelue Goekce (descendants of the deceased)* v. *Austria* (*Goekce* case), CEDAW/C/39/D/5/2005, 6 August 2007.

[55] *Goekce* (CEDAW), paras. 12.1.3 and 12.1.4 (here, the Committee provides an overview of such evidence).

[56] *Goekce* (CEDAW), paras. 4.8 and 8.8.

[57] *Fatma Yildirim* (CEDAW), paras. 8.4, 8.14.

the Committee noticed a contradiction between the dangerous situation the victim faced and the inaction of the local authorities that led to the femicide.[58] However, it did not explore whether this contradiction could have been motivated (and normalised) by a stereotyped understanding of violence.[59] The contradiction in the State's reasoning is apparent: while not disputing the death threats and the ineffectiveness of the police orders and interim injunction, the State still considered it disproportionate to issue an arrest warrant, since the aggressor 'had no criminal record and was socially integrated'.[60] At this early stage of the Committee's evolving approach towards stereotyped evidence, both the stereotypes of the 'ideal victim' in *Goekce* and the 'ideal perpetrator' in *Yildirim* went unnoticed, as the Committee explicitly refused to analyse the cases under Article 5.

Vertido v. *The Philippines* marked a shift in the Committee's anti-stereotyping analysis and signalled a more explicit understanding of the link between stereotypes and probative issues. As Cusack and Timmer have pointed out, part of this shift is attributable to the author's success in exposing the connection between stereotypes and the contradictions in the assessment of evidence carried out by the domestic court.[61] Following the author's narrative, the Committee was able to retrace the link between stereotypes and assumptions that undermine the author's credibility and impair the evidentiary process. Examples include assuming consent from lack of resistance to the assault or acquaintance with the aggressor; assuming rape accusations can be made with facility (the stereotype of *fabrication*); and giving less credibility to rape allegations based on the perpetrator's age.[62] In this case, the author was a female executive director at the local chamber of commerce who had been raped by the president of the chamber. Her testimony was not believed by the domestic criminal court because she did not comply with the behaviour of the 'ideal victim'. One year later, the Committee took this approach further in another key case, *V.K.* v. *Bulgaria*. Here, it explicitly found a link between gender stereotypes and the domestic court's narrow

[58] *Fatma Yildirim* (CEDAW) , paras. 12.1.4f.

[59] It found that the author's submissions on Article 1 and 5 did not warrant further findings: *Fatma Yildirim* (CEDAW), para. 12.2.

[60] *Fatma Yildirim* (CEDAW), para. 8.4.

[61] S. Cusack and A. Timmer, 'Gender stereotyping in rape cases: The CEDAW Committee's decision in *Tayag Vertido* v. *The Philippines*', *Human Rights Law Review* 11 (2011): 239–342, 336.

[62] *Tayag Vertido* (CEDAW), paras. 8.5f.

conception of domestic violence, which led the latter to apply a higher standard of proof and place an excessive burden upon the author.[63] In particular, the domestic court had refused to issue a permanent protection order against the author's husband, based on the assumption that striking someone may amount to violence 'only after breaking certain limits of abuse'.[64] According to the court, the author had not demonstrated that those limits were surpassed. The Committee found that this stereotyped understanding of domestic violence had led the court to neglect the history of verbal, economic and psychological abuse documented by the author.[65]

Compounded stereotypes might pose extra obstacles for assessing a victim's credibility. This is demonstrated in *R.P.B.* v. *the Philippines*, an individual communication submitted by a young girl who was deaf and mute. Her account had been assessed by domestic courts against the standard of an 'ordinary Filipina female rape victim'.[66] According to a 'reasonable standard of human conduct' proclaimed by the domestic court, such an ideal victim should have 'summon[ed] every ounce of her strength and courage to thwart any attempt to besmirch her honour and blemish her purity'.[67] Here, the Committee rightly pointed out that the guiding principles derived from judicial precedents in deciding rape cases amounted to gender stereotypes. In particular, the stereotype of the 'ideal victim' impaired the victim's credibility assessment and led the court to disregard her individual circumstances (i.e. disability and age).[68]

The Committee also found a connection between stereotypes and a biased assessment of facts and evidence by domestic authorities in *González Carreño* v. *Spain*. This was a case of domestic violence that resulted in the killing of a young girl by her father during court-authorised visitation. The domestic authorities had dismissed evidence of the danger posed by the father to the safety of his daughter and

[63] *V.K.* (CEDAW) , para. 9.12.

[64] *V.K.* (CEDAW) , para. 9.7.

[65] *V.K.* (CEDAW) , para. 9.9–9.12.

[66] *R.P.B.* v. *Philippines*, CEDAW/C/57/D/34/2011, 21 February 2014, paras. 2.5, 8.9.

[67] *R.P.B.* (CEDAW), para. 8.9. The Committee reiterated that there should be no assumption in law or in practice that lack of physical resistance implies consent, regardless of whether the victim was threatened (para. 8.10). See also the Joint General Recommendation No. 31 of the Committee on the Elimination of Discrimination against Women/General Comment No. 18 of the Committee on the Rights of the Child (2019) on harmful practices, CEDAW/C/GC/31-CRC/C/GC/18, 14 November 2019.

[68] *R.P.B.* (CEDAW), para. 8.9.

ex-partner, in favour of inconclusive reports submitted by social services.[69] The Committee found that domestic authorities' stereotyped conception of visitation rights 'gave clear advantages to the father despite his abusive conduct and minimized the situation of mother and daughter as victims of violence'.[70] This was also connected to the incoherence which the Committee observed between the authorities' actions and the evidence submitted.[71] Yet, the Committee did not point out specific gender stereotypes that could have motivated the authorities' inaction or the selective weighing of evidence, such as the stereotypes that violence is normal between (ex-)partners or that women fabricate accusations and their accounts are not reliable. This case certainly advances a welcome line of reasoning, but following *Vertido*, a more explicit and articulated discussion could have been expected.

These early cases planted the seeds of a better articulation of the stereotype-evidence link. However, the Committee's analytical approach in this regard is far from consolidated. An example of inconsistency can be seen in a case adjudicated only one year after *Carreño*. In *X. and Y.* v. *Georgia*,[72] the Committee did not delve into the stereotypes underlying the prosecutor's decision not to open a criminal investigation into domestic violence. These stereotypes could be seen in the emphasis placed on the good reputation of the aggressor, and on his social position as a student and businessman. Both elements distanced him from the 'ideal aggressor' standard. The violence was also viewed as a 'permanent conflict' that 'did not surpass the normal framework of attitude within the family'.[73] Moreover, the minor daughter – who was a victim of violence herself – gave statements confirming the beatings, but these were put into question by a psychological assessment (considered to be produced by an authoritative source). This finding reflects the stereotype that depicts both women and minors as inherently unreliable.[74] Additionally, the Committee remained silent on the State party's view that the author and the grandmother 'brainwashed' their children, 'causing them to testify against their father'.[75] This could be read in conjunction with the attempt to depict the author as mentally unstable, as both

[69] *Angela González Carreño* v. *Spain*, CEDAW/C/58/D/47/2012, 16 July 2014.
[70] *González Carreño* (CEDAW), para. 9.4.
[71] *González Carreño* (CEDAW), para. 9.4.
[72] *X. and Y.* v. *Georgia*, CEDAW/C/61/D/24/2009, 13 July 2015.
[73] *X. and Y.* (CEDAW) , paras. 2.11, 3.7.
[74] *X. and Y.* (CEDAW), para. 3.8.
[75] *X. and Y.* (CEDAW), para. 7.11.

elements concur in her negative credibility assessment. While the author explicitly denounced the existence of a socio-cultural pattern of conduct which 'accord[s] greater weight to the word of a man and accept[s] a level of physical violence and sexual touching as being within the realms of acceptable parenting for a man',[76] the Committee did not address the issue of selective weighing of evidence. Furthermore, it did not explicitly connect the lack of objective standards for assessing prima facie evidence, or the failure to gather and present evidence impartially, to underlying gender stereotypes about women's voices. It did, however, interpret several of these shortcomings as placing an extremely high burden of proof upon the author.[77] Nonetheless, the Committee in this case fell short of detecting and challenging a number of visible stereotypes, and missed the opportunity to discuss their effect on evidence, even though it had done so in previous views.

Just a month after *X. and Y.*, the Committee adopted its General Recommendation 33. It seems to be no coincidence that the views adopted afterwards mark an improvement in the analysis of the connection between gender stereotypes and evidentiary issues. This link is better delineated, for example, in *L.R.* v. *Republic of Moldova*, a case regarding the State's failure to carry out a prompt and effective investigation into domestic violence.[78] The author argued that the State had given insufficient weight to her statements and had not heard her witnesses or assessed her supporting documentary evidence. The Committee found that the domestic court's reasoning, which led to the denial of protection, had been biased. This was based on the Committee's consideration that the court had misinterpreted the violence as a civil dispute; given undue weight to the accused's good references; interpreted the contradiction between the parties' accounts with prejudice to the author; and disregarded medical and forensic evidence produced by her.[79] Furthermore, the author's attempts at seeking justice had resulted in a police officer reporting her as a family troublemaker, which undermined her credibility at trial. Moreover, prosecutorial authorities had focused on her mental state and even attempted to force her to undergo in-patient psychiatric testing – an additional sign of how women's accounts are not deemed credible.[80] Domestic authorities had

[76] *X. and Y.* (CEDAW), paras. 8.3, 8.7.
[77] *X. and Y.* (CEDAW), para. 9.5.
[78] *L.R.* v. *Republic of Moldova*, CEDAW/C/66/D/58/2013, 28 February 2017.
[79] *L.R.* (CEDAW) ., para. 13.8.
[80] *L.R.* (CEDAW) , para. 13.4.

also neglected relevant facts such as the protection order granted to the author, as well as witness statements and records of ambulance and police services which had responded when the accused attempted to strangle the author.[81] According to the Committee, all these elements – undisputed by the State – indicated that the decisions at domestic level had been based on stereotyped notions of domestic violence.[82] However, the Committee did not explicitly name the specific stereotypes underlying the case – such as the interpretation of women's reactions to domestic violence as irrational, or the assumption that their claims are fabricated.

The stereotype-evidence link was finally made fully explicit in two cases in 2018. *X.* v. *Timor-Leste* concerned the criminal trial of a victim of domestic violence who claimed to have acted against her abuser in self-defence.[83] The criminal proceedings had been fraught with serious negligence in the collection of evidence of domestic violence and its subsequent handling. The Committee explicitly pointed out that despite a retrial being granted to allow a due consideration of self-defence, '[judges] allowed gender stereotypes and bias to affect the weighing of evidence in the second trial, in particular by lending the author's voice less credence than that of her nephew, who had not been present at all relevant times'.[84] Similarly, in *J.I.* v. *Finland*, a case involving domestic violence and child custody proceedings, the Committee expressly pointed out how stereotypes pollute the rational assessment of evidence: by undermining the claims and evidence of the victim/survivor, while simultaneously supporting the defence arguments advanced by the alleged perpetrator.[85] Recurrent elements appeared in this case too: from the biased attitude towards the author and her statements (she was subjected to a psychiatric assessment and depicted as a hostile mother), to the neglect of evidence of violence, with prejudicial impact on custody arrangements.[86] In both cases, the Committee made extensive reference to General Recommendation 33 to support the stereotype-evidence link.

A preference for evidence submitted by the aggressor over that submitted by the victim was also at the core of *S.T.* v. *Russian Federation*.[87] Yet, the anti-stereotyping reasoning in this case was not entirely rigorous

81 *L.R.* (CEDAW), para. 13.8.
82 *L.R.* (CEDAW), para. 13.11.
83 *X.* (CEDAW).
84 *X.* (CEDAW), paras. 6.5, 6.9.
85 *J.I.* (CEDAW), para. 8.6.
86 *J.I.* (CEDAW), para. 8.9.
87 *S.T.* (CEDAW), paras. 9.6–9.9.

and left some problematic aspects untouched. While the Committee read the shortcomings in evidentiary evaluation as products of stereotyped reasoning, it missed the opportunity to challenge some specific arguments. For example, it remained silent on the prosecutor's request to mitigate the classification of the crime. This had been based on a psychiatric examination that excused the violent attack as an explosion of affect stemming from the loss of authority of the accused within the family.[88] This line was followed at trial by the court and led it to dismiss the victim's claim for compensation. Moreover, the court accused her of provoking and humiliating the aggressor through litigation and thus being responsible for the attack she suffered. In a narrative framework where hitting a woman with an axe was interpreted as a 'nervous breakdown',[89] a woman's attempts to seek justice were viewed as hints of 'systemic amoral behaviour' that worked to excuse the behaviour of the aggressor.[90] A more careful analysis would have been needed here to unpack the provocation argument, and to highlight the greater probative value attached to authoritative sources – in this case, the positive description of the aggressor by the mosque administration.

The unquestioned preference for evidence produced by authoritative parties (e.g. medical staff, social services, police officers) is another specific manifestation of the selective evaluation of evidence. These parties are generally assumed to be acting in the interests of the patient/client/victim, even when other evidence disproves this assumption. In *S.F.M.* v. *Spain*, a case of obstetric violence, the Committee acknowledged that stereotyped and thus discriminatory notions led the domestic authorities to assume that the doctor should decide whether or not to perform an episiotomy, despite lack of consent and evidence of non-compliance with *lex artis* (the current state of medical knowledge).[91] Regrettably, the Committee did not explicitly name this stereotype in its conclusion, although the author did mention that women are stereotyped as incapable of making their own choices and are treated as passive objects with a reproductive role.[92] The Committee further addressed the preference for evidence by authoritative parties in the recent case of *A.F.* v. *Italy*.[93] In this case, a woman alleged she was sexually

[88] *S.T.* (CEDAW), para. 2.15.
[89] *S.T.* (CEDAW), para. 2.17.
[90] *S.T.* (CEDAW), paras. 2.17, 3.9.
[91] *S.F.M.* v. *Spain*, CEDAW/C/75/D/138/2018, 28 February 2020, para. 7.5.
[92] *S.F.M.* (CEDAW), paras. 3.7f.
[93] *A.F.* v. *Italy*, CEDAW/C/82/D/148/2019, 20 June 2022.

assaulted by a police officer, to whom she had previously reported an assault by her ex-husband. The Committee acknowledged that the decision to overturn his conviction for lack of evidence could be explained by stereotypes that led the domestic court to give uncritical preference to the accused's evidence.[94] In particular, the court had re-interpreted the hospital report and the psychologist's diagnosis showing the possibility of rape as evidence of the accused's seductive ability. Conversely, the author's prompt reaction in collecting evidence after the assault was interpreted to suggest a fabricated accusation.[95] Importantly, the Committee noted the striking difference between the treatment of the author's evidence in contrast to that of the accused, as well as their contradictions. Indeed, while the author's revisions were interpreted as lies, 'the accused [could not] be blamed for his divergent explanations'.[96]

As emerges from this overview, the analysis of the stereotype-evidence link has not followed a linear or consistent path. Following the adoption of General Recommendation 33, this analysis has improved and the Committee's views have highlighted examples of selective weighing of evidence and preference for evidence submitted by the accused or produced by authoritative sources. In some cases, the link between these evidentiary hurdles and stereotypes is made explicit. In others, it emerged implicitly as a contradiction between facts presented and evidentiary findings at the domestic level. In other words, the Committee's approach in this regard requires further consolidation.

The extent to which the authors draw attention to stereotypes and their evidentiary effect may contribute to explaining the Committee's inconsistencies in its approach. Some submissions, like those in *Vertido*, *R.P.B.*, *S.F.M.*, and *A.F.*, see the authors meticulously exposing and analysing the stereotypes behind each biased assessment made by domestic authorities. In other instances, the authors leave the stereotypes at issue unnamed, but invoke general gender-related myths of how women must behave,[97] gender bias,[98] or the *Vertido* formula regarding judicial creation of inflexible standards of behaviour for victims.[99] While more articulated reasoning by authors on stereotype-related violations of

[94] *A.F.* (CEDAW), para. 7.16.
[95] *A.F.* (CEDAW), para. 7.11.
[96] *A.F.* (CEDAW), para. 7.15.
[97] *S.T.* (CEDAW), para. 3.9.
[98] *X.* v. *Timor-Leste* (CEDAW), para. 3.3.
[99] *J.I.* (CEDAW), para. 6.12. C.f. *Tayag Vertido* (CEDAW), para. 8.4.

CEDAW is welcome, this should not have to stand in for the Committee's ability to carry out its own anti-stereotyping analysis. The Committee should systematically name and contest stereotypes, as a necessary step before examining the impact of stereotypes on evidentiary findings.[100] Its present lack of systematicity is problematic, the more so as the Committee specialises in gender-based discrimination.[101] Clearer indications on its part as to what stereotypes are and the extent of the harm they produce would improve its own anti-stereotyping reasoning, as well as serving as guidance for other international bodies .

9.4 Exploring Stereotypes through Legal Presumptions

Given the widespread impact of stereotypes on the evidentiary domain, this final section seeks to explore how arguments and practices stemming from stereotypes might map onto legal mechanisms, which provide them with an appearance of soundness. Using the *González Carreño* communication before the CEDAW Committee as a case study, the analysis focuses on the hybrid mechanism of the legal presumption, which displays both evidentiary and substantive traits.[102] This comparison between stereotypes and legal presumptions illustrates the connections between stereotypes and evidentiary issues that the CEDAW Committee should be able to detect and challenge as forms of discrimination. In particular, the Committee should be aware that gender stereotypes may prevent the ascertainment of truth at trial by introducing ready-made narratives that resist contrary evidence, in a way similar to legal presumptions.

Presumptions are mechanisms deployed in judicial reasoning out of necessity, when it is not possible to ascertain a fact by direct evidence. De facto presumptions are mere inferences or arguments based on generalisations, usually drawn from empirical regularities or scientific knowledge. Legal presumptions, on the other hand, are characterised by foreclosing the ascertainment of truth, through substituting an unknown fact that should be ascertained with another (known) fact.[103]

[100] Timmer, 'Towards an anti-stereotyping approach'.

[101] See, e.g., *S.L.* v. *Bulgaria*, CEDAW/C/73/D/99/2016, 19 July 2019.

[102] For a broader discussion, see E. Ghidoni, 'Aproximación a los estereotipos como elementos del razonamiento judicial a través de las presunciones' in Arena, *Manual sobre los estereotipos en la impartición de la justicia.*

[103] R. Gama, 'Concepciones y tipología de las presunciones en el derecho continental', *Revista de Estudios de la Justicia*, 19 (2013): 65–89.

Rebuttable (or relative) presumptions establish a provisional truth, whereby the presumed fact is temporarily established, until contrary evidence is submitted. Such presumptions might be established by law or by the judiciary. They do not necessarily reflect a regularity or probability, but might rather stem from social and political reasons. For example, the presumption of paternity of children born in wedlock does not necessarily reflect empirical facts, but serves the social function of protecting children's interests. Notably, relative presumptions possess both constitutive and regulatory aspects: they contribute to shaping legal meanings or 'constituting the presumed fact into an institutional outcome'.[104] For example, the abovementioned presumption of paternity produces legal effects based on marriage between the parents without proof of paternity being required. Relative presumptions are also procedural rules which indicate the distribution of the burden of proof to the judge and the parties at trial.[105] In contrast, absolute presumptions establish an irrebuttable truth by requiring a fact to be viewed as corroborated on the basis of the mere occurrence of another fact. No effort is made to verify the actual situation, and there is no possibility to submit any contrary evidence.[106] Absolute presumptions do not fulfil any epistemic function and are more likely to shape legal categories and definitions.

Legal presumptions of both kinds share a constitutive feature, by which they can shape the elements of a legal definition. This highlights the pertinence of the interplay between evidence and substance. When gender stereotypes guide the selection of relevant facts, they also influence legal definitions of what amounts to, for example, violence and discrimination. The circular dynamic between the evidentiary and the substantive dimensions exposes how relevance itself is shaped by stereotyped frames, and how these frames might affect the boundaries and content of legal definitions. An analysis of the *González Carreño* case can be used to illustrate how stereotypes act as presumptions, with stereotypes also establishing provisional or even absolute truths, thereby allowing discriminatory views to hamper the rational evaluation of evidence.

González Carreño was one of the first cases adjudicated by the CEDAW Committee that problematised the treatment of violence in

104 J. Aguiló Regla, 'Las presunciones en el derecho', *Anuario de Filosofía del Derecho* (2018): 201–28, 221 (translation is mine).

105 Aguiló Regla, 'Las presunciones en el derecho', p. 220.

106 Aguiló Regla, 'Las presunciones en el derecho', p. 221.

custody proceedings and called into question the primacy given to a father's interests over the best interests of the child. As previously recounted, the case concerned the murder by a man of his daughter during an unsupervised visit authorised by the domestic court.[107] In the proceedings at domestic level, it appeared that national authorities had granted more weight to accounts from social services while completely neglecting the numerous domestic violence complaints filed by the author (the girl's mother).

This case illustrates how gender stereotypes may distort the evaluation of evidence, with evidence provided by the accused being privileged over that submitted by the victim, and inconclusive evidence being granted more weight than other consistent pieces of evidence. In *Carreño*, this was exemplified by the treatment of the reports from social services as opposed to the evidence provided by the author. The reports by social services contained a self-contradictory assessment of the father's parental capacity. For example, it was mentioned that he lacked empathy; had difficulty properly interacting with his daughter; used his child to transmit messages of animosity to the mother; and showed signs of an obsessive-compulsive disorder. Nevertheless, the social services, as well as the domestic court that relied on their assessment, seemed satisfied with a minimum display of affection from the father and dismissed other evidence to the contrary. The court thus concluded that there was a need to restore the relationship between father and daughter. Contrary evidence which was ignored included around thirty complaints filed by the mother, which had resulted in a conviction for harassment, as well as protection orders issued in favour of the mother and daughter.

Such an irrational assessment of evidence can only arise from the stereotype/presumption that women are untrustworthy, as they are considered more emotional and less rational than men. This stereotype usually underlies inferences that women tend to fabricate false allegations, that they create hostility or alienate their children from the father or that they are responsible for provoking violent attacks on themselves or their children. Originating from the idea of the inferiority of women, such narratives undermine the credibility of women and the relevance of the evidence they submit.

Closely linked to the public/private division, the stereotype of women as primary caretakers underpins the very different standards against

[107] *Gonzalez Carreño* v. *Spain* (CEDAW).

which mothers' and fathers' parenting capacity is measured, as also apparent in *González Carreño*. Mothers are subjected to pervasive scrutiny of their behaviour.[108] They are expected to be collaborative and facilitate the relationship between children and father, usually by sacrificing their own physical and psychological well-being. In contrast, fathers' behaviours are often not scrutinised. In some cases, they are not even held accountable for their negative actions, nor are they compelled to improve their parental abilities.[109] In the *González Carreño* case, the father did not comply with his maintenance obligations, nor with protection orders. He also engaged in behaviours which were detrimental to his underage daughter. However, none of these circumstances compelled the national authorities to take action, or at least consider them as relevant elements in their assessment.

As the Committee noted in *González Carreño*, national courts, social services and psychological experts were moved by the purpose of normalising the relationship between father and daughter, despite the reservations expressed about the behaviour of the father.[110] The CEDAW Committee identified this pattern of action as a 'stereotyped conception of visiting rights based on formal equality', which 'gave *advantages* to the father despite his abusive conduct and minimized the situation of mother and daughter as victims of violence, placing them in a vulnerable position'.[111] In other words, the domestic authorities used the principle of joint custody not in light of the best interests of the child, but to guarantee the privileges and entitlements of the (male) head of the family. This reaffirmed the gender hierarchy by which the father's superior role justified submission of and violence against mother and children.

Judicial practice may normalise these abusive behaviours by either neglecting or trivialising their importance, and leaving them without legal consequences. The effects are those of a legal presumption: on the level of evidence, the stereotyped reading of joint custody establishes that men – setting the standard of rationality – are presumed to be good parents. This truth is hard to rebut, since gender stereotypes usually lead to downplaying or discarding contrary evidence as irrelevant (even

108 A. Barnett, 'Contact at all costs? Domestic violence and children's welfare', *Child and Family Law Quarterly* 26 (2014): 439–462.

109 V. Elizabeth, N. Gavey and J. Tolmie, 'Between a rock and a hard place: Resident mothers and the moral dilemmas they face during custody disputes', *Feminist Legal Studies*, 18 (2010): 253–74.

110 *González Carreño* v. *Spain*, CEDAW, para. 9.4

111 *Gonzalez Carreño* v. *Spain* (CEDAW); italics are mine.

criminal convictions and restraining orders, as was the case in *González Carreño*).[112] Unless there is hard, physical evidence that domestic violence occurred, or that it affected the child directly, it is presumed that a father has a right to a relationship with his child that almost nothing can curtail.

On the level of substantive law, such judicial practice shapes the legal boundaries of desirable fatherhood by portraying violence, neglect or lack of affection as tolerable features of fathers' parenting.[113] Normalisation is reinforced by impunity and lack of consequences when parental obligations are not fulfilled, as happened in the *Carreño* case. This judicial presumption is so strong and pervasive that commentators have suggested that in order to counteract it, a legal presumption against contact should be instituted in cases of domestic violence.[114]

Gender stereotypes in child custody proceedings in situations of domestic violence work to downplay women's accounts of violence and their attempts at seeking protection. They filter and transform accounts of violence into irrational claims, through accusations of parental alienation and certain uses of joint custody that conceal male privileges. Either the credibility of allegations of violence is undermined, or the blame is shifted onto women. Overall, gender stereotypes work to protect gender norms and hierarchies within the family that relegate women to silence. This is achieved by systematically suppressing all attempts to ascertain the truth – a feature of absolute presumptions. Looking at gender stereotypes through legal presumptions sheds light on the issues of selective weighing of evidence, and might be helpful in detecting this specific feature of stereotypes. The CEDAW Committee should be more aware of these evidentiary issues, and adopt a more assertive role in examining the inconsistencies it finds and their connection to stereotyped understandings of gender roles.[115]

9.5 Conclusion

This chapter has shed light on the way gender stereotypes can negatively affect the rational evaluation of evidence and eventually compromise the

[112] *Gonzalez Carreño* v. *Spain* (CEDAW), para. 3.13.

[113] See also *X. and Y.* (CEDAW), para. 8.7.

[114] S. Choudhry, 'Domestic violence, contact, and the ECHR', in M. Freeman (ed.), *Law and Childhood Studies: Current Legal Issues Volume 14* (Oxford: Oxford University Press, 2012), pp. 339–356.

[115] Gleeson, 'Unlocking CEDAW's transformative potential', 87, 90–91.

adjudication of women's human rights. The analysis of individual communications has pinpointed different examples of how stereotypes lead to a systematic disregard of women's statements and evidence, which manifests through contradictions between the domestic courts' evaluation and the evidence produced. Engaging in more rigorous analysis of the factual construction (*quaestio facti*) is a crucial step towards ensuring that stereotyped arguments do not impair access to justice and to a fair trial.

The CEDAW Committee has made progress in its stereotype-evidence analysis, with some remarkable examples in its recent case law. That said, its anti-stereotyping reasoning needs to be further consolidated. Naming and contesting specific stereotypes is crucial to allow subsequent scrutiny of domestic judgments to ensure that any discrimination can be properly redressed.[116] This is still a pending task for the CEDAW Committee, which often seems to rely on the authors' work to identify the stereotypes underlying problematic arguments, without adding to or clarifying the content and inferences attached to them. While authors' activism is key to exposing the contradictions embedded in the evaluation of evidence, the Committee should strengthen its own independent ability to detect stereotypes and the circumstances when they pollute evidence, irrespective of the author's characterisation. This is paramount if the Committee seeks to develop a more solid anti-stereotyping approach in the future.

A more robust and consistent anti-stereotyping reasoning is also essential for the subsequent assessment of its evidentiary effects. The Committee is not alone in this endeavour – other regional bodies and judicial authorities should also be encouraged to make efforts to identify and challenge the stereotypes underlying all phases of the proceedings. The Committee – as a specialised body – could offer them guidance. A starting point could be to pay attention to selective weighing of evidence and preference for authoritative sources. These are two evidentiary issues that could be investigated in connection with other grounds of discrimination (e.g. race and ethnicity, disability, age), and in relation to human rights violations beyond gender-based violence.

In developing a stronger anti-stereotyping approach, it may be instructive for the Committee to more closely consider how stereotypes prevent the ascertainment of truth in a way that is similar to the functioning of (mostly) absolute presumptions. This kind of comparison

[116] Timmer, 'Toward an anti-stereotyping approach'.

can shed light on the full extent of the effects that stereotypes may have, particularly in the evidentiary domain. With a better understanding of their effects and harms, a more nuanced, articulated conceptualisation of stereotypes in law can be elaborated. Without this effort, courts and judicial bodies lack an important standard to examine discriminatory practices and their impact.

Select Bibliography

Arena, F. J., 'Los estereotipos normativos en la decisión judicial: Una exploración conceptual', *Revista de Derecho de la Universidad Austral de Chile*, 29 (2016): 51–75.

Bartlett, K. T., 'Feminist legal methods', *Harvard Law Review*, 113 (1989): 829–888.

Brems, E. and Timmer, A. (eds.), *Stereotypes and Human Rights Law* (Cambridge: Intersentia, 2016).

Childs, M. and Ellison, L. (eds.), *Feminist Perspectives on Evidence* (London: Routledge-Cavendish, 2000).

Clérico, L., 'Estereotipos de género y violación de la imparcialidad judicial: Nuevos estándares interamericanos. El caso Manuela v El Salvador', *Revista de Derecho, Universidad y Justicia, SAIJ/Universidad Nacional de Avellaneda*, 1 (2022): 110–135.

Cook, R. J. and Cusack, S., *Gender Stereotyping: Transnational Legal Perspectives* (Philadelphia: University of Pennsylvania Press, 2010).

Cusack, S., *Eliminating Judicial Stereotyping: Equal Access to Justice for Women in Gender-Based Violence Cases* (Office of the High Commissioner for Human Rights, 2014).

Ghidoni, E. and Morondo Taramundi, D., 'El papel de los estereotipos en las formas de la desigualdad compleja: Algunos apuntes desde la teoría feminista del derecho antidiscriminatorio', *Discusiones*, 28 (2022): 37–70.

Holtmaat, R. and Naber, J., *Women's Human Rights and Culture: From Deadlock to Dialogue* (Cambridge: Intersentia, 2011).

Timmer, A., 'Toward an anti-stereotyping approach for the European court of human rights', *Human Rights Law Review*, 11 (2011): 707–738.

10

The Dangers of Distant Evidence

The UN Human Rights Committee's Individual Communications, 512,000 Potential New Sámi Voters and Other 'Objective' Facts

MIIA HALME-TUOMISAARI AND REETTA TOIVANEN*

10.1 Introduction

In the absence of an international human rights court, the Human Rights Committee's (HRC or the Committee) monitoring state compliance with the International Covenant on Civil and Political Rights (ICCPR or the Covenant) is widely regarded as the United Nation's (UN) most authoritative and lawlike human rights monitoring mechanism.[1] Yet, surprisingly, little is known about how the Committee goes about creating its 'jurisprudence' on the communications that individuals initiate against states that have signed the ICCPR's Optional Protocol.[2] In particular, there is limited insight into how the Committee assesses the veracity of data submitted by the authors of communications, or how the Committee determines whether such data form reliable evidence.

This chapter sheds light on this issue by exploring how the Committee approached the evidence in two cases: *Näkkäläjärvi et al.* v. *Finland* (2018)[3] and *Sanila-Aikio* v. *Finland* (2018).[4] Both cases were ostensibly

* Miia.halme-tuomisaari@mrs.lu.se, reetta.toivanen@helsinki.fi. Warm thanks to Isabelle Schulte-Tenckhoff and this book's editors for helpful comments, and for diligent editorial assistance to Otso Metsola ja Tuija von der Pütten.

[1] M. Scheinin, *Towards a World Court of Human Rights*, research report within the framework of the Swiss Initiative to commemorate the 60th anniversary of the Universal Declaration of Human Rights, 2009, p. 4.

[2] Optional Protocol to the International Covenant on Civil and Political Rights, 16 December 1966, in force 23 March 1976, 999 UNTS 171.

[3] *Klemetti Näkkäläjärvi et al.* v. *Finland*, CCPR/C/124/D/2950/2017, 2 November 2018.

[4] *Tiina Sanila-Aikio* v. *Finland*, CCPR/C/124/D/2668/2015, 1 November 2018.

about the inclusion of new voters on the electoral roll of the Sámi Parliament, the highest political decision-making body on matters relating to the Sámi Indigenous people.[5] Underlying this issue were two more general questions: (1) Who is an Indigenous Sámi in Finland, and (2) in case of contestation, who has the authority to answer this question?

Two specific numbers – 93 and 512,000 – acquired special significance in the processing of the two communications. As for the first, ninety-three persons were added to the Sámi Parliament's electoral roll by the Finnish Supreme Administrative Court (SAC or the Court) in 2015. In other words, in the eyes of this Court, ninety-three persons had satisfactorily proven that they fulfilled the legal criteria of being Sámi. The authors of *Näkkäläjärvi et al.* and *Sanila-Aikio* contested this, which led them to lodge a complaint before the HRC. As for the second number, the authors of *Näkkäläjärvi et al.* argued that, were the SAC to continue with the interpretive line it had adopted in regard to the ninety-three persons referred to above, more than half a million Finnish persons, out of Finland's population of 5.5 million inhabitants, could be eligible to be included in the Sámi electoral roll, thereby significantly weakening Indigenous self-determination. The advanced figure of 512,000 new voters is as dramatic as it is inaccurate. In its examination of the two communications against Finland, the Committee nonetheless reproduced this figure without questioning its origin or reliability, thereby letting it acquire the status of an uncontested fact in the two communications' aftermath.

The two numbers 93 and 512,000 are used in this chapter as analytical entry points to reflect on the processes of translation that distance evidence from Committee members as they deliberate on individual communications, such that the second enormous and dubious figure is allowed to develop a life of its own in the Committee's proceedings. This leads us to raise broader questions regarding the evidentiary regimes of the HRC and the other UN treaty bodies (UNTBs), particularly their fact-checking abilities. The chapter also highlights the importance that intermediaries who act as counsel in communications hold for the Committee's deliberations. It finally reflects on how the evidentiary regime of the HRC produces and supports certain subjectivities while downplaying and eliminating others, simultaneously inflicting harm on the eliminated subjectivities.

[5] Law on the Sámi Parliament 974/1995.

Both *Sanila-Aikio* and *Näkkäläjärvi et al.* v. *Finland* are connected to long-standing and still ongoing controversies around the Sámi people in Finland. These cases are also only the latest in a long list of communications that the Sámi people have submitted against the State of Finland to different UN bodies.[6] One type of controversy underlying these communications is connected to how the State of Finland and the wider society treat – or, rather, continue to oppress – the Sámi.[7] The other type is related to internal contestations within the Sámi community over who is regarded as belonging to the Sámi community.[8] Importantly, the latter controversy exists mainly – but not exclusively – between registered and non-registered members of the Sámi community. As our case studies illustrate, these contestations are anchored in the question of who is allowed to join the Sámi Parliament's electoral roll, thereby being able to vote for and get elected to the Sámi Parliament.

We show how, in the Committee's argumentation, the first type of controversy – general treatment of the Sámi by Finland – becomes dominant, whereas the second type – relating to internal tensions and power struggles within the Sámi community – is erased from view, being only fleetingly referenced in the communication dossiers. The invisibility of these internal tensions is linked to the dominant assumption within the human rights field that Indigenous peoples are internally united, giving rise in turn to an assumption that it would be possible for Indigenous peoples to elect a small number of representatives who would harmoniously and homogeneously convey their (uniform) views and interests to different political entities and/or other bodies. As this chapter

[6] More on this later in this chapter, in Section 10.3. In addition, on the same electoral issue linked to SAC's decisions in 2015, a complaint was sent to CERD: *Anne Nuorgam et al.* v. *Finland*, CERD/C/106/D/59/2016, 22 April 2022. The same person, Martin Scheinin, acted as counsel in this case and in the *Sanila-Aikio* case.

[7] This oppression has included assimilationist educational and language policies and, most consistently, controversy over Sámi land rights. See L. E. Doran, '"For their own good": Examining "gentle" colonialism and Finnish exceptionalism within narratives of Finland's indigenous residential schools', *Scandinavian Journal of History*, 49 (2023): 172–195; O. Kortekangas, P. Keskitalo, J. Nyyssönen, A. Kotljarchuk, M. Paksuniemi and D. Sjögren (eds.), *Sámi Educational History in a Comparative International Perspective* (Cham: Palgrave Macmillan, 2019). Today, many practices are called green colonialism; see, e.g., E. M. Fjellheim, '"You can kill us with dialogue": Critical perspectives on wind energy development in a Nordic-Saami green colonial context', *Human Rights Review* 24 (2023): 25–51.

[8] See more in R. Toivanen, 'Protecting indigenous identities? An example of cultural expertise on Sámi identity', *Legal Pluralism and Critical Social Analysis* 54 (2019): 210–30.

shows, this is not the reality: the Sámi Parliament is full of differences in views, as is the case with any other people.

Basing our analysis on a close reading of the text of the views adopted by the Committee in the two cases, as well as indirectly drawing on Miia Halme-Tuomisaari's ethnography of the Committee[9] and Reetta Toivanen's ethnographic research with the Sámi,[10] we explain how the HRC reached outcomes that only considered and made visible the concerns of registered members of the Sámi people, thus leaving out those of non-registered Sámi. This is something that existing legal analyses of the two cases have not highlighted.[11] From a perspective that takes into account the complexities of social worlds, we attempt to decipher how the HRC may let itself be swayed by dubious *evidence*, producing unfortunate outcomes. This leads us to make some observations about the way the evidentiary regime of the HRC generally works.

To date, most scholarly contributions on UNTBs have been written by legal scholars, many of whom are former treaty body members.[12] This

[9] M. Halme-Tuomisaari, 'Meeting "the world" at the Palais Wilson: Embodied universalism at the UN Human Rights Committee', in. R. Niezen and M. Sapignoli (eds.), *Palaces of Hope: Anthropology of the United Nations* (Cambridge: Cambridge University Press, 2017), pp. 127–151; M. Halme-Tuomisaari, 'Methodologically blonde at the UN in a tactical quest for inclusion', *Social Anthropology/Anthropologie Sociale* 26 (2018): 456–70; M. Halme-Tuomisaari, 'Guarding utopia: Law, vulnerability and frustration at the UN Human Rights Committee', *Social Anthropology/Anthropologie Sociale* 28 (2020): 35–49.

[10] See projects funded by the Research Council of Finland, *On "glocal" governance: on the meanings and consequences of the "vernacularization" of human rights concepts*, decision nr 256143 and *Centre of Excellence in Law, Identity and the European Narratives*, decision nrs 312431 and 336678.

[11] C.J. Iorns Magallanes, 'Views adopted by the Committee under Article 5(4) of the Optional Protocol, concerning Sanila-Aikio v. Finland, Communication No. 2668/2015, and Klemetti Näkkäläjärvi et al., Communication No. 2950/2017 (H.R. Comm'n)', *International Legal Materials* 59 (2020): 302–332.

[12] Recent exceptions include D. Moeckli, H. Keller and C. Heri (eds.), *The Human Rights Covenants at 50: Their Past, Present, and Future* (Oxford: Oxford University Press, 2018); G. L. Neuman, 'Human rights, treaties, and international legitimacy', in S. Voeneky and G. L. Neuman (eds.), *Human Rights, Democracy, and Legitimacy in a World of Disorder* (Cambridge: Cambridge University Press, 2018), p. 51–72; L. Oette, 'The UN Human Rights Treaty Bodies: Impact and future', in G. Oberleitner (ed.), *International Human Rights Institutions, Tribunals, and Courts* (Leiden: Springer, 2018), p. 95–116; A. Seibert-Fohr, 'The UN Human Rights Committee', in G. Oberleitner (ed.), *International Human Rights Institutions, Tribunals, and Courts* (Leiden: Springer, 2018), p. 117–141. See also Halme-Tuomisaari, 'Embodied universalism'; 'Methodologically blonde'; 'Guarding utopia'.

has resulted in a strong legalistic emphasis and an absence of more holistic analyses that take into account the complexities of social worlds. A similar gap exists in regard to how individual communications are processed, including what data are accepted as evidence in the Committee's reflections. These observations also apply to our two selected case studies, which to date have been analysed from an exclusively legal angle. This chapter contributes to existing scholarship by building on the past two decades of anthropological work on international organisations and human rights.[13] Particularly important is existing – albeit limited – anthropological work on UNTBs, including the Committee on the Elimination of Discrimination against Women,[14] the Committee against Torture (CAT),[15] and the Committee on the Elimination of Racial Discrimination (CERD).[16] In addition, our chapter builds on the vast scholarship on the Sámi people,[17] as well as recent work on Indigenous peoples and their rights struggles.[18]

[13] See, e.g., J. Cowan, M-B. Dembour and R. Wilson (eds.), *Culture and Rights: Anthropological Perspectives* (Cambridge: Cambridge University Press, 2001); M. Goodale and S. Merry (eds.), *The Practice of Human Rights: Tracking the Law Between the Local and the Global* (Cambridge: Cambridge University Press, 2007); J. Clark and M. Halme-Tuomisaari (eds.), 'Virtual Edition: Human Rights', *PoLAR: Political and Legal Anthropology Review*, 2016; R. Niezen and M. Sapignoli, (eds.) *Palaces of Hope: The Anthropology of Global Organizations* (Cambridge: Cambridge University Press, 2017). See also, e.g., J. Billaud and J. Cowan, 'The bureaucratisation of utopia: Ethics, affects and subjectivities in international governance processes', *Social Anthropology/Anthropologie Sociale* 28 (2020): 6–16.

[14] S. Merry, *Human Rights and Gender Violence: Translating International Law into Local Justice* (Chicago: University of Chicago Press, 2006).

[15] T. Kelly, *This Side of Silence: Human Rights, Torture, and the Recognition of Cruelty* (Philadelphia: University of Pennsylvania Press, 2011); J. Clark, 'The global fight against racial discrimination: Human rights assessment and the making of obligation in Costa Rica and at the United Nations', PhD dissertation, University of California at Irvine (2016).

[16] Clark, 'The global fight against racial discrimination'.

[17] U. Mörkenstam, 'Organised hypocrisy? The implementation of the international indigenous rights regime in Sweden', *The International Journal of Human Rights* 23 (2019): 1718–41; R. Toivanen, 'European fantasy of the Arctic region and the rise of indigenous Sámi voices in the global arena', in N. Sellheim, Y. V. Zaika and I. Kelman (eds.), *Arctic Triumph: Northern Innovation and Persistence*, vol. 1 (Cham: Springer, 2019) pp. 23–40.

[18] D. Newman (ed.), *Edward Elgar Research Handbook on the International Law of Indigenous Rights* (Cheltenham: Edward Elgar Publishing, 2022); R. Toivanen and F. Stammler (eds.), *Young People, Wellbeing and Placemaking in the Arctic* (London: Routledge, 2021); D. C. Cambou, 'The UNDRIP and the legal significance of the right of indigenous peoples to self-determination: A human rights approach with a multidimensional perspective', *The International Journal of Human Rights* 23 (2019): 34–50.

Translation forms our broader theoretical lens for analysing the processes by means of which distinct pieces of information are accepted as forming facts in the HRC's proceedings.[19] One part of the translation process is figurative and aesthetic, including formatting documents to comply with the logic and structure of UN style, including the 'rubrics of classification and graphic elements such as paragraphs, tables, subtitles, fonts, margins, and bullets'.[20] These aesthetic elements form surface graphics that 'serve a range of semiotic functions',[21] conferring legitimacy on the data submitted to the Committee as providing reliable information.[22] Another part of the translation takes place when UN secretariat staff compress broader case material into synthesised summaries shared with Committee members, thereby removing the original material from the Committee members' reach when they are deliberating on the communications' merits.[23]

[19] On the multifaceted processes of policy translation, see S. Gal, 'Politics of translation', *Annual Review of Anthropology*, 44 (2015): 225–240; E. M. Babül, *Bureaucratic Intimacies: Translating Human Rights in Turkey* (Stanford: Stanford University Press, 2017); Kelly, *This Side of Silence*; N. Mathur, *Paper Tiger: Law, Bureaucracy and the Developmental State in Himalayan India* (Cambridge: Cambridge University Press, 2015); G. Sarfaty, *Values in Translation: Human Rights and the Culture of the World Bank* (Stanford: Stanford University Press, 2012); M. Halme-Tuomisaari, 'Contested representation: Exploring China's state report', *Journal of Legal Anthropology* 1 (2013): 333–359; A. Ballestro, 'What is in a percentage? Calculations as the poetic translation of human rights', *Indiana Journal of Global Legal Studies*, 24 (2014): 27–53.

[20] M. S. Hull, 'Documents and bureaucracy', *Annual Review of Anthropology*, 41 (2012): 251–67; see further A. Riles (ed.), *Documents: Artefacts of Modern Knowledge* (Michigan: University of Michigan Press, 2005); C. Moon, 'What one sees and how one files seeing: Human rights reporting, representation and action', *Sociology (Oxford)* 46 (5) (2012): 876–890.

[21] M. S. Hull, *Government of Paper: The Materiality of Bureaucracy in Urban Pakistan* (Berkeley: University of California Press, 2012), p. 44; see also A. Riles, 'Afterword: A method more than a subject', in D. Cowan and D. Wincott (eds.), *Exploring the 'Legal' in Socio-legal Studies* (London: Palgrave McMillan, 2015); H. Brown, A. Reed and T. Yarrow, 'Introduction: Towards an ethnography of meeting', *Journal of the Royal Anthropological Institute* 23 (2017): 10–27.

[22] Halme-Tuomisaari, 'Contested representation'.

[23] Secretariat staff work together with an assigned rapporteur among Committee members, who is designated to assist in the handling of communications (Human Rights Committee, Rules of Procedure, CCPR/C/3/Rev.12, 4 January 2021, Rule 98). The rapporteur attends to the following functions: (1) advising and finalising the draft decisions prepared by the secretariat; (2) presenting the draft decision in the working group and plenary; and (3) revising and finalising, with the support of the secretariat, the draft in light of the discussions in the working group and plenary. On a similar UN Human Rights Committee process relating to the Universal Periodic Review, see J. Billaud, 'Keepers of the truth: producing "transparent" documents for the UN

A pivotal part of translation regards actual linguistic translation from one language to another, a process that likewise distances original data from Committee members. The general language of operations for the HRC, as well as UN human rights monitoring bodies in general, is English.[24] This choice of language is neither always voluntary nor neutral: for example, NGO caucuses are typically held in English only because NGOs cannot afford translators. The shortage of resources reproduces the privileged position of the powerful English-speaking actors, emphasising their elite nature. Information provided by states parties to complement state reports in other languages may be overlooked, as resources do not permit the translation of all material. Thus, UN reality both reflects and strengthens the dominance of English as the lingua franca, reproducing the privileges and exclusions linked to its competence among different groups of actors participating in the sessions of the HRC and the other UNTBs. Yet, the original language of data and evidence that the Committee relies on is commonly in another language; in the cases at hand, it is Finnish. Only very few, or even none, of the relevant UN staff and HRC members likely have the necessary linguistic skills to examine documents in Finnish, which is neither an official UN language nor widely spoken worldwide. These observations raise the question: On the basis of what sources do Committee members receive information or form understandings on data that are not accessible to them, such as the ninety-three cases from the Finnish SAC that are at the core of the communications on *Näkkäläjärvi et al.* and *Sanila-Aikio*?

10.2 'The Closest to a Future World Court of Human Rights': Introducing the Human Rights Committee

The HRC was founded in 1976 when the ICCPR entered into force, after having been opened for signature in 1966.[25] The Committee has

Universal Periodic Review', in H. Charlesworth and E. Larking (eds.), *Assessing the Universal Periodic Review: Rights, Ritual, Ritualism* (Cambridge, UK: Cambridge University Press, 2015), pp. 63–83.

24 Merry has discussed how in CEDAW Committee proceedings, draft documents as well as suggested alternative wordings are presented in English. Thus, a person who has not mastered that language 'would have a great deal of difficulty assessing the implications and innuendos of different phrases and sentences' (Merry, *Human Rights and Gender Violence*, p. 44). The same applies to the Human Rights Committee's operations.

25 International Covenant on Civil and Political Rights (ICCPR), 16 December 1966, in force 23 March 1976, 999 UNTS 171.

stabilised its position as one of the UN's – and, by extension, the world's – most authoritative human rights bodies. The Committee, together with the other nine UNTBs monitoring the main UN human rights covenants, including the ICESCR, CRC, CAT and CEDAW, has established itself today as forming the steady pulse of UN human rights monitoring that brings abstract human rights ideals to life.

Submission of individual communications is stipulated in the ICCPR's first Optional Protocol, which has been ratified by 117 of the 173 states that have ratified the ICCPR.[26] The views that the Committee issues on the basis of its deliberations on the communications' merits are themselves legally non-binding on states.[27] The submission criteria for individual communications illustrate a complex relationship to the law that characterises the Committee's operations more generally.[28] As the website of the UN Office of the High Commissioner for Human Rights (OHCHR) outlines, the basic idea of the UN individual complaints mechanism is its openness to any layperson from a ratifying country.[29] In line with this idea, the formal submission guidelines stress that, in order to submit a communication, one need not be a lawyer or even be familiar with legal and technical terms. In practice, legal competence is paramount, both in order to get the communication deemed admissible and to get the Committee members to grasp the communication's merits. Translation acquires importance here also: in order to become visible and thus admissible to the HRC, an issue needs to be 'translated' into 'UN reality'.[30]

In regard to individual communications submitted to the Committee – as will be illustrated by our two case studies – this translation process entails identifying what kind of human rights violation has occurred specifically. It must also be identified how the individual rights of the applicant (denoted in Committee terms as the author) were violated under the ICCPR's provisions.[31] Translation also entails the use of

[26] OHCHR website. Status of Ratifications Interactive Dashboard – Optional Protocol to the International Covenant on Civil and Political Rights.

[27] OHCHR website. 'Individual Communications: Human Rights Treaty Bodies'.

[28] See Halme-Tuomisaari, 'Guarding utopia'.

[29] OHCHR, Individual Complaint Procedures under the United Nations Human Rights Treaties, Fact sheet No. 7/Rev.2 (2013), p. 1.

[30] Halme-Tuomisaari, 'Contested representation'.

[31] Another crucial criterion is the exhaustion of domestic remedies, meaning that all available domestic legal mechanisms, including the courts, have been resorted to before the communication has been brought to the Human Rights Committee. This requirement

correct bureaucratic discourse. This discourse is often 'impersonal and anonymous on the basis of lexical and semantic features: the prevalence of passive verbs, abstract nouns and the like'.[32] In our analysed cases, this translation process is significant for the authors' attempts to construct a 'collective agency from the agency of individuals'[33] by claiming to represent all Sámi people – claims that the Committee overlooks in its emphasis on individual Covenant violations. In utilising the right bureaucratic discourse, legal competence is often crucial. Consequently, in practice, many authors – including Tiina Sanila-Aikio – have legal counsel representing them. For her, this counsel was a former member of the HRC who, on this experiential basis, had insider knowledge on how to make a communication visible and admissible for the Committee.[34]

The HRC discusses individual communications in sessions that are closed to outside observers. The only people present at the hearings are members of the Committee, relevant UN secretariat staff, interpreters and possibly Committee members' interns. After deliberations, the Committee adopts *views* that are shared on the website of the OHCHR. To protect the authors, no exact transcripts of the Committee's deliberations are shared with outsiders.

10.3 The Sámi and the Sámi Parliament: A Complex Question of Inclusion

The cases of Näkkäläjärvi et al. and Sanila-Aikio are the latest in a long list of communications that the Sámi Indigenous peoples have sent to the HRC and other UN monitoring bodies, such as the CERD. Despite the fact that the Finnish Government has strengthened the rights of the Indigenous Sámi people in Finland through several laws, the exercise of these rights continues to be severely hampered in practice – notably when it comes to the right to take part in decision-making on local and

illustrates again the high level of legal competence that submitting a case to the Human Rights Committee requires. See Rules of Procedure, Rule 78/2 (a).

32 Hull, *Government of Paper*, p. 217.

33 Hull, *Government of Paper*, p. 22.

34 The counsel of Sanila-Aikio told Reetta Toivanen in personal communication how annoyed he was to discover there was another complaint about the same issue. He said that the members of the HRC had been confused: both complainants argued that they were representing themselves, the whole Sámi Parliament and all Sámi in Finland. It had been very difficult for him to explain to the HRC members why the two had not communicated before complaining (Toivanen's personal notes, 18.6.2019).

national levels.[35] International human rights treaties, especially those that deal with minority rights, have long been relied upon by Sámi activists.[36] Given that the European Court of Human Rights takes the view that the European Convention on Human Rights offers few legal bases to tackle cases concerning minority rights, European minorities – and Indigenous peoples especially – have put faith in the UN system. In terms of Article 27 of the ICCPR, the HRC has the legal grounds to receive Indigenous complaints in particular. The first decision by the HRC involving Sámi rights dates back to 1985 (*Kitok* v. *Sweden*)[37] and was followed by nine communications from persons identifying as Sámi from the three Nordic countries (Finland, Norway and Sweden).[38] Whereas none of these cases has been able to substantially promote self-determination, they have together contributed to strengthening recognition of the emerging rights of Indigenous peoples.

The Sámi are one of the peoples traditionally living in the Barents region in the Arctic. They share their living space with other local peoples who have lived in the territories for several generations and newcomers.[39] Politically, the Sámi have worked together since 1956 in the Sámiráđđi (Sámi Council, earlier the Nordic Sámi Council) to strengthen their voices vis-à-vis the majority states of Norway, Sweden and Finland[40] – and in recent decades, Russia as well – after a long period during which Sámi cultural rights and languages suffered under strong assimilation policies and practices.[41]

[35] L. Heinämäki and D. Cambou, 'New proposal for the Nordic Sámi Convention: an appraisal of the Sámi people's right to self-determination', *Retfærd: Nordisk juridisk tidsskrift* 41 (2018): 3–18; Mörkenstam, 'Organised hypocrisy?'.

[36] R. Toivanen, *Minderheitenrechte als Identitätsressource? Die Sorben in Deutschland und die Saamen in Finnland* (Münster, Berlin: LIT Verlag, 2001).

[37] *Kitok* v. *Sweden*, CCPR/C/33/D/197/1985, 27 July 1988.

[38] *Paadar* v. *Finland*, CCPR/C/110/D/2102/2011, 26 March 2014; *Länsman (Jouni) et al.* v. *Finland*, CCPR/C/58/D/671/1995, 30 October 1996; *Jonassen et al.* v. *Norway*, CCPR/C/76/D/942/2000, 25 October 2022; *Sara et al.* v. *Finland*, CCPR/C/50/D/431/1990, 23 March 1994; *Lansman (Ilmari) et al.* v. *Finland*, CCPR/C/52/D/511/1992, 26 October 1994; *Äärelä and Näkkäläjärvi* v. *Finland*, CCPR/C/73/D/779/1997, 24 October 2001; *Länsman (Jouni) et al. (2)* v. *Finland*, CCPR/C/83/D/1023/2001; *Sanila-Aikio* v. *Finland*, CCPR/C/124/D/2668/2015, 1 November 2018; *Näkkäläjärvi et al.* v. *Finland* CCPR/C/124/D/2950/2017, 2 November 2018.

[39] U-M. Kulonen, I. Seurujärvi-Kari and R. Pulkkinen (eds.), *The Saami: A Cultural Encyclopaedia* (Helsinki: SKS, 2005).

[40] R. Toivanen, 'Saami people and the Nordic civil societies', in N. Götz and J. Heckmann (eds.), *Civil Society in the Baltic Sea Region* (Aldershot: Ashgate, 2003), pp. 205–216.

[41] See A. Kotljarchuk, 'Indigenous people, vulnerability and the security dilemma: Sámi school education on the Kola Peninsula, 1917–1991', in O. Kortekangas, P. Keskitalo, J. Nyyssönen, A. Kotljarchuk, M. Paksuniemi and D. Sjögren (eds.), *Sámi Educational*

While the majority of Sámi today live in Norway, approximately 10,000 live in Finland.[42] From a legal perspective, the status of the Sámi as an Indigenous People was acknowledged in the Constitution of Finland in 1995 section 17.[43] In the same year, the Finnish Sámi Parliament was established by the Act on the Sámi Parliament.[44] The cultural self-government body of the Sámi in Finland, the Sámi Parliament, deals with the living Sámi languages and Sámi cultures in Finland (Skolt Sámi, Inari Sámi and Northern Sámi). The scope of cultural self-determination is limited to language as well as culture revitalisation and maintenance, and the views expressed by the Sámi Parliament do not bind the Finnish Parliament. The Act on the Sámi Parliament defines the functioning and powers of the Parliament. Pursuant to section 5(1), the task of the Sámi Parliament is to 'look after the Sámi language and culture, as well as to take care of matters relating to their status as an Indigenous People'. In matters pertaining to its tasks, the Sámi Parliament may take initiatives and make proposals to the authorities, as well as issue statements (section 5 (2)).

Ever since the Sámi Parliament was established, the question of who is entitled to vote in its elections – thereby raising the question of who is a Sámi – has remained the subject of fierce discussion and internal tensions.[45] The core of the disagreement, very much simplified here for the sake of making the point, is partly between reindeer-herding Sámi, who settled in what is today Finland around 1860 due to the closing of Swedish and Norwegian borders, and those who were by then already settled in the uppermost parts of Finland and had mostly adopted the Finnish language due to the strong assimilation policies of schools and the Church.[46]

This history has created an internal division within the Sámi community between those who are registered Sámi, and thus enjoy the right to vote and get elected to the Sámi Parliament, and those who are non-registered.[47]

History in a Comparative International Perspective (Cham: Palgrave Macmillan, 2019), pp. 63–82.

[42] Sámediggi 2020, www.samediggi.fi/sami-info/?lang=en.

[43] Constitution of Finland 731/1999.

[44] Act on Sámi Parliament in Finland 974/1995.

[45] J. Nyyssönen, '"Everybody recognized that we were not white": Sami identity politics in Finland, 1945–1990', PhD Dissertation, University of Tromsø (2007).

[46] J. Joona, *Ikimuistoinen oikeus: tutkimus Lapin alkuperäisistä maa – ja vesioikeuksista* [Immemorial right – Research on the original land and water rights in Lapland] Juridica Lapponica, PhD dissertation, University of Lapland (2019), p. 46.

[47] Obviously, the situation is much more complex. A more detailed discussion is outside the scope of the current chapter. A new law on the Sámi Parliament entered into force in summer 2025. The new law stipulates the following in Article 3: 'Right to be entered in

According to section 3 (a) of the Act on Sámi Parliament, 'Sámi' means a person who considers himself a Sámi, provided: (1) that he[48] himself or at least one of his parents or grandparents has learnt Sámi as his first language; or (2) that he is a descendent of a person who has been entered in a land, taxation or population register as a mountain, forest or fishing Lapp; or (3) that at least one of his parents has or could have been registered as an elector for an election to the Sámi delegation or the Sámi Parliament.

Every four years – just before new elections – hundreds of persons approach the Parliament's electoral committee (consisting of five Sámi with electoral rights) to apply for inclusion on the electoral roll. Each time, some applications succeed, while the majority are rejected. When an applicant is rejected by the Sámi Parliament, they can complain to the SAC, which serves as the appeals court with the authority to add applicants to the Sámi Parliament's electoral roll.

Whereas judicial appeal is generally considered an essential element of a democratic system, the role of the SAC has been criticised by some Sámi activists as threatening Sámi self-governance. Most elected Sámi parliamentarians are of the view that individuals whom they do not recognise as Sámi must be kept off the electoral roll in order to prevent further assimilation. However, some individuals recently added to the electoral roll clearly cannot be said to have weak links to the Sámi community. A striking example is that the candidate parliamentarian who attracted the most votes in both the 2015 and 2019 elections had been added to the register by the SAC only in 2011.[49] This illustrates that many Sámi voters strongly recognise as Sámi individuals whom the Parliament has refused to recognise and register.[50]

This state of affairs, which points to internal tensions within the Sámi community, forms the backdrop of the *Näkkäläjärvi et al.* and *Sanila-Aikio* cases. These cases arose from the Sámi Parliament's elections of

the electoral register belongs to a person who considers themself to be Sámi, provided that: 1) the person themself, or at least one of their parents, grandparents, or great-grandparents, learned a Sámi language as their first language; or 2) at least one of their parents is entered, or has been entered, as an eligible voter in elections to the Sámi Parliament held on 1 January 2027 or thereafter.'

[48] Finnish pronouns are gender-neutral but the unofficial translation of the Act uses the masculine forms 'he' and 'his'.

[49] In 2011, the SAC had added three persons to the electoral roll.

[50] Similar issues among other Indigenous Peoples have been discussed in A. Tsing, 'Indigenous voice', and J. Clifford, 'Varieties of indigenous experience: Diasporas, homelands, sovereignties', both in M. de la Cadena and O. Starn (eds.), *Indigenous Experience Today* (London: Routledge, 2007), pp. 33–67 and 197–223. We do not have space here to elaborate on this further.

2015, prior to which the SAC had added 93 persons (out of 181 appellants) to the Sámi electoral roll. An analysis of the argumentation used by the SAC in these decisions shows that there was a shift in reasoning in 2015: previous decisions by the Court had followed the Sámi Parliament's lead in emphasising 'group recognition'.[51] Accordingly, to be successful, an application needed to have the Sámi Parliament's full support. In 2015, however, the Court shifted to what it called a 'comprehensive' approach more 'sensitive to human rights'.[52] Under this approach, the Court assumed that the person appealing was a Sámi as long as one of the objective membership criteria laid down by law was fulfilled. If this was the case, the Court would accept the applicant's self-identification as Sámi, rather than placing evidentiary weight on the lack of recognition by the Sámi Parliament.

This new approach had been adopted as a follow-up to a negative assessment by UN human rights monitoring bodies such as CERD and the Council of Europe's Advisory Committee on the Framework Convention for the Protection of National Minorities.[53] While it was aligned with the views of these expert bodies, it did not please the Sámi Parliament. Later, it also failed to satisfy the HRC. In 2015, when the Court approved 93 applications that had been rejected by the Sámi Parliament, a crisis ensued. Ms Sanila-Aikio and Mr Näkkäläjärvi (then, respectively, sitting and former presidents of the Finnish Sámi Parliament) each submitted a communication to the HRC. They did so not only in their own names but also in the name of the Finnish Sámi Parliament and all Sámi in Finland. Although one would have expected these complaints to have been approved by the Parliament, data collected by Toivanen suggest that the parliamentarians were not aware that the complaints were being prepared and lodged. Moreover, it transpired that the two complaints had arrived at the HRC independently of each other, without one complainant being aware of the other complaint.[54]

[51] On 'group recognition' as a merit in defining Indigenous belonging, see the so-called Cobo definition in J. R. Martínez Cobo, Study of the Problem of Discrimination Against Indigenous Populations, Vol. 5, Conclusions, proposals and recommendations, UN Doc. E/CN.4/Sub.2/1986/7 (1987).

[52] In Finnish, *kokonaisharkinta*.

[53] Advisory Body of the CoE Framework Convention on National Minorities, Report on Finland 2019, para. 176.

[54] See Toivanen 'Protecting indigenous identities?'.

10.4 The SAC's Decisions: Not Necessarily Flawed

The decisions by the HRC in both *Näkkäläjärvi et al.* and *Sanila-Aikio* suggest that the Finnish SAC's argumentation was flawed, with the Court having relied on false evidence in its reasoning and demonstrated a lack of understanding of the Sámi culture and way of life. The views in *Näkkäläjärvi et al.* report that 'in a majority of those [93] decisions, the *Court stated explicitly that the person did not meet any of the objective criteria spelled out in section 3* of the Sámi Act]'.[55] It adds that '[t]he Court resorted to the overall consideration of the person's own "strong" *opinion* in considering himself or herself a Sámi and ignored the explicit requirement of meeting at least one of the objective criteria'.[56] It states that 'the Court accepted evidence that *relied entirely on the State party's public administration records*, such as those of church registry offices and the provincial archives of the State, and that those documents are unreliable'.[57] Further, it claims that the Court did not take 'into account the international obligations of Finland, especially those under the Covenant', also ignoring relevant observations by CERD.[58]

Echoing this description, the Committee's view on *Sanila-Aikio* argues that 'the Court failed to require satisfaction of at least one of the objective criteria in the majority of cases, instead applying an "overall consideration" and examining whether a person's *own opinion* about considering themselves a Sámi was "strong"'.[59] It continues by suggesting that the Court thereby 'infringed on the capacity of the Sámi people to exercise, through the Sámi Parliament, a key dimension of Sámi self-determination in determining who is a Sámi'.[60] It assesses that the Court based its views on an 'expansive application' of section 3 of the Act on the Sámi Parliament, which resulted in 'arbitrariness and lawlessness'.[61]

[55] *Näkkäläjärvi et al.* (HRC), para. 2.10.
[56] *Näkkäläjärvi et al.* (HRC) , para. 2.10.
[57] *Näkkäläjärvi et al.* (HRC) , para. 7.6.
[58] *Näkkäläjärvi et al.* (HRC), para. 7.5: 'Although the Court based its findings on the recommendations of the Committee on the Elimination of Racial Discrimination contained in the concluding observations on the tenth and seventeenth to nineteenth reports of the State, it ignored those contained in the concluding observations on the twentieth to twenty-second periodic reports, in which the Committee criticised the Court's interpretation of section 3 of the Act on the Sámi Parliament.'
[59] *Sanila-Aikio* (HRC), para. 6.11.
[60] *Sanila-Aikio* (HRC), para. 6.11. See the decision on admissibility at paras. 2.8–2.10.
[61] *Sanila-Aikio* (HRC), para. 3.6.

Finland's responses to these observations suggest that the latter were based on significant inaccuracies. According to Finland, the Court had 'thoroughly assessed the special status and rights of the Sámi people, also taking into account the obligations of Finland under the Covenant'.[62] In Finland's opinion, 't]he SAC ha[d], in its case law, paid attention to the safeguarding of the rights of the Sámi Indigenous people and its obligations under the Covenant', consulting the board of the Sámi Parliament as well as, 'inter alia, articles 1, 2 (1), 25, 26 and 27 of the Covenant, and the UN Declaration on the Rights of Indigenous Peoples'.[63] Finland also summarised how the Court had considered CERD's concluding observations on Finland's ninth, tenth, and seventeenth to nineteenth periodic reports.[64]

An analysis of the SAC's ninety-three cases supports Finland's defence, thus showing *Näkkäläjärvi et al.* and *Sanila-Aikio* to have been misguided in having found the Court's rulings arbitrary and overlooking relevant criteria of Article 3 of the Sámi Act. The appellants had always provided the Court with proof of at least one objective fact required by Article 3 of the Sámi Act. Often, this fact was an archival statement about their Sámi ancestry.[65] Additionally, in most cases, the appellants could show that they satisfied the linguistic criteria of the Sámi Act (para 3.1).[66]

Thus, contrary to what *Näkkäläjärvi et al.* and *Sanila-Aikio* claim and the HRC concluded, the Court *did* consider the history of the Sámi

[62] The citation is bolded in the original; that is removed here for stylistic reasons. In these concluding observations, Finland was instructed 'to better take into account the individual's self-identification within Sámi definition' (*Näkkäläjärvi et al.* (HRC), at para. 4.7, bold in original). Finland further emphasised that 'It is not for the Committee to re-evaluate the facts that have led a national court to adopt one decision rather than another, or to question the findings and conclusions of national courts' (*Näkkäläjärvi et al.* (HRC), para. 4.7, bold in original).

[63] *Näkkäläjärvi et al.* (HRC), para. 4.7.

[64] *Näkkäläjärvi et al.* (HRC), para. 6.3 (referring to CERD A/45/18, para. 91, CERD/C/63/CO/5, para. 11, and CERD/C/FIN/CO/19, para. 13).

[65] The diligence exercised by the Court is captured by a study of the Arctic Centre at the University of Lapland. See L. L. Heinämäki, C. Allard, S. Kirchner, A. Xanthaki, S. Valkonen, U. Mörkenstam, N. Bankes, J. Ruru, J. Gilbert, P. Selle, A. Simpson and L. Olsén, 'Actualizing Sámi Rights: International Comparative Research', Publications of the Government´s analysis, assessment and research activities 4/2017. (Valtioneuvoston kanslia, 25.1.2017). See also Toivanen, 'Protecting indigenous identities?'. The SAC begins all decisions from the application round of 2015 with the following statement: 'the applicant identifies herself/himself as a Sámi'. The decisions then state: 'The appellant has presented a certificate from the archive authority stating that they are a descendant of a person listed among the Lapps in the land register of [the year].'

[66] R. Toivanen, 'Protecting indigenous identities?'.

people in these ninety-three cases.[67] This consideration includes the historical reasons why people may have been removed from the relevant personnel registries, such as moving to another Nordic country or having been prevented by the Finnish authorities from using Sámi as their first language.[68] Importantly, in a strong statement for Sámi self-determination, the SAC argued that the consequences of such assimilationist history should not be allowed to affect present-day decision-making.

In sum, *Näkkäläjärvi et al.* and *Sanila-Aikio* contain misleading information about the SAC's decisions.[69] All of the ninety-three persons accepted by the SAC had not only been able to produce proof of their descendancy as Sámi, but actually enjoyed group recognition. In the elections that followed in 2015 and 2019, several of them were elected as members of the Sámi Parliament.[70] What the ninety-three cases poignantly demonstrate is the extent of the internal tensions within the Sámi community about who is considered a Sámi and who is not.

10.5 The Extravagant Number of 512,000 New Voters: Getting the Facts Wrong

> The Committee notes the authors' contention that the application of the principle of self-identification could, at least theoretically, lead to the inclusion of 512,000 non-Sámi persons on the electoral roll of the Sámi Parliament. The

[67] Kristina Björkvall closely followed as part of her studies the work of the SAC during the autumn of 2015, when the Court knew that it might receive up to 200 appeals addressing access to the electoral roll of the Sámi Parliament. She provides evidence on how the Court prepared for the work and internalised a positive 'human rights friendly' approach to minorities that would understand assimilation histories. K. Björkvall, Saamelaiskäräjävaaliasiat 2015 – projektityöskentely korkeimmassa hallinto-oikeudessa [Sámi Parliament Election Matters 2015 – Project Work in the Supreme Administrative Court] (University of Eastern Finland, Department for legal sciences, 2015).

[68] The history of the Sámi people includes strong assimilationist policies, such as forbidding use of the Sámi language and forceful removal of Sámi children from their parents. See Heinämäki *et al.*, 'Actualizing Sámi Rights'; V.-P. Lehtola, *Entiset Elävät Meissä. Saamelaisten Historiat ja Suomi [Those before Us live in Us]* (Helsinki: Gaudeamus, 2022).

[69] See also Heinämäki *et al.*, 'Actualizing Sámi rights', and Toivanen, 'Protecting indigenous identities?', for more analysis of this.

[70] Among the ninety-three individuals added to the Sámi Parliament's electoral roll by the SAC, there are no persons who would be classified as complete 'outsiders'. All of them had Sámi relatives, and most lived from Sámi livelihoods. See Finnish SAC rulings No.2621; No. 2624; No. 2671.

> Committee also notes the disturbing submission, which was not contradicted by the State party, that anti-Sámi organisations are campaigning and assisting non-Sámi persons to apply for recognition as Sámi persons and inclusion in the electoral roll, because of underlying economic interests.[71]

These words are part of the individual opinion expressed by HRC member Olivier de Frouville in *Sanila-Aikio*.[72] De Frouville concurred with the Committee's view that Finland had violated Article 25, read alone and in conjunction with Article 27 of the ICCPR. The purpose of his opinion was to explain why the complaint had been declared admissible, despite its author not having been personally involved in any of the ninety-three cases ruled upon by the SAC – a reasoning which also applied in *Näkkäläjärvi et al.*, where the authors had also had no personal involvement in the court cases.

Against this background, it was unexpected that these communications would be considered admissible: usually the author of a complaint before the HRC has been a party to the domestic case which they challenge before the HRC for having failed to respect their rights under the ICCPR. *Sanila-Aikio*'s and *Näkkäläjärvi et al.*'s communications were differently anchored: their authors argued that the outcome of the cases through which ninety-three persons were added to the electoral roll of the Finnish Sámi Parliament amounted to a violation of their rights as Sámi. De Frouville's quoted statement suggests that this mechanism could be reproduced over and over again, potentially resulting in over half a million non-Sámi people motivated by anti-Sámi economic interests being given access to the Sámi Parliament. The question arises: What is the source of this statement?

The figure '512,000' is first mentioned by *Näkkäläjärvi et al.*'s authors in submissions summarised by the Committee as follows:

> Once a person is included in the electoral roll, all descendants can be included in it. This can lead to a snowball effect where persons who do not lead a Sámi way of life and do not share the Sámi identity can take part in the elections. ... *According to the authors, a study by a mathematician* has found that there are around 512,000 living descendants of Lapp taxpayers. According to the new interpretation applied by the Court they could potentially apply to be included in the electoral roll.[73]

[71] *Näkkäläjärvi et al.* (HRC), Individual opinion (concurring) of Olivier de Frouville, para. 4.

[72] *Näkkäläjärvi et al.* (HRC), para. 2.14.

[73] *Näkkäläjärvi et al.* (HRC), para. 2.14.

The figure is then repeated in de Frouville's view to illustrate the threat of forced assimilation that new members of the electoral roll pose for the Sámi:

> The inclusion of non-Sámi individuals in the electoral roll of the Sámi Parliament could set a precedent that could, at least theoretically, lead to 512,000 non-Sámi persons being included in that electoral roll. The Sámi Parliament would thus gradually represent the interests of non-Sámi persons and would no longer ensure the preservation of Sámi linguistic and cultural heritage, amounting to a gradual forced assimilation of the Sámi people in Finland.[74]

The figure re-appears a third time as the Committee summarises the merits of the communication, stating that the SAC's decisions to include new people in the electoral roll could, 'at least theoretically, lead to the inclusion of 512,000 non-Sámi persons on the electoral roll of the Sámi Parliament'.[75] This is connected to the alleged existence of '*many anti-Sámi organizations*' which are said to be 'offering to assist ethnic Finns with applying and eventually appealing to the SAC', which is in turn explained by a possible 'economic interest in including a high number of non-Sámi individuals on the electoral roll to ensure the Sámi Parliament's acceptance of large-scale projects in the areas of mining, mass tourism and infrastructure'.[76]

As already noted, Olivier de Frouville also relies on the potential 512,000 new voters in his individual opinion in *Näkkäläjärvi et al.* to clarify why the case deserved to be declared admissible. To him, this figure is the primary reason why the authors' rights could be considered to be potentially violated at admissibility stage, despite the absence of a direct infringement of their rights.[77] De Frouville appended a similar individual opinion in *Sanila-Aikio*, thus repeating the figure, even though it had not been mentioned by either Ms Sanila-Aikio or her counsel.

It is as if the figure of 512,000 acquires solidity in the life of these two communications through being repeated as a litany. Noteworthily, however, the original source for this number is nowhere to be found in the text of the Committee's views. The reference to a 'study by a mathematician' is not accompanied by any further information as to where this

[74] *Näkkäläjärvi et al.* (HRC), para. 7.3.
[75] *Näkkäläjärvi et al.* (HRC), para. 8.9.
[76] *Näkkäläjärvi et al.* (HRC), para. 8.9.
[77] *Näkkäläjärvi et al.* (HRC), Individual opinion (concurring) of Olivier de Frouville, para. 4.

study was published or conducted, nor by whom exactly – the mathematician remains unnamed. Nowhere in their texts do the views suggest that the Committee entertained any doubt regarding the veracity of this figure, despite it being extremely large, given that Finland counts no more than circa 5.5 million inhabitants. It remains entirely unclear what this figure in the Committee's view is based on, even when it is repeated in the documents as if representing an unquestioned, objective fact.

In fact, the figure appears to be a gross exaggeration also with reference to the number of people who have actually applied to be added to the electoral roll in the last twenty-five years. The very first elections of the Finnish Sámi Parliament took place in 1999. At that time, the electoral roll had counted 5,121 Sámi persons.[78] When their children became adults, they were automatically added to the roll, representing an increase of 436. The same year, another 1,128 people applied for inclusion in the Sámi electoral roll. The Sámi Parliament's electoral committee accepted 100 of these applications. Of the 1,028 rejected, 765 applied for a review, which resulted in twenty-five being granted enrolment. Of the 740 rejected at the review stage, 726 appealed to the government of the Sámi Parliament, which accepted one application. Then 712 people appealed to the Sámi Parliament's general meeting, which granted enrolment to twenty-six applicants. Finally, 656 complained to the SAC.

The SAC granted enrolment to seven applicants because of evidence that one of their grandparents had spoken Sámi as their first language. In sum, out of the 1,128 applications for electoral enrolment prior to the 1999 elections, 159 eventually were accepted and 969 rejected.[79] Numbers remained small in subsequent years. In 2011, the SAC requested the Sámi Parliament to add four applicants who had previously been refused. In 2015, 800 persons applied to be added to the electoral roll, of whom 483 were accepted, mostly because they were adult children of persons who were already members. The 201 persons who applied to the Sámi Parliament for a review were all rejected, mostly on the grounds that the Sámi community did not recognise any of the individual

[78] For the study on which the numbers are based, see E.J. Aarnio, Saamelaiskäräjien toimintakertomus vuodelta 1999 [Annual Report of the Sámi Parliament for the Year 1999], pp. 11f, 16.

[79] See Heinämäki *et al.*, 2017. 'Actualizing Sámi Rights'; see also the governmental bill to the Parliament to laws to change the law on Sámi Parliament and Criminal Code 40 section 11§, HE 274/2022 vp.

applicants to be Sámi. Of these, 182 persons appealed to the SAC, which added 93 of them to the electoral roll.

This overview of the reality of people seeking to be added to the electoral roll of the Finnish Sámi Parliament shows no signs of either the potential snowball effect mentioned repeatedly in *Näkkäläjärvi et al.* and *Sanila-Aikio*, or a sudden rise in the number of applicants. The numbers given above indicate that hundreds of people – not thousands, let alone hundreds of thousands – have sought inclusion in the Sámi electoral registry. From this perspective, it appears *Näkkäläjärvi et al.*'s authors may have used the striking figure of 512,000 new potential voters as a scare tactic, which would have served to capture the Committee members' attention, but without it being properly anchored in empirical reality or substantiated by evidence.

Näkkäläjärvi et al. and *Sanila-Aikio* misrepresent the basis on which the SAC accepted the applications of ninety-three persons in 2015, including the level of detail into which the Court went in its consideration of Sámi identity. The Committee's views in these two cases also downplay how the Court considered the ICCPR and other relevant international covenants and standards related to Indigenous rights. In addition, our discussion above makes it clear that the HRC either did not get the correct information or did not notice the red flags that marred the whole process, starting with the fact that each applicant said they were acting in the name of the Sámi Parliament and Sámi peoples in general, but did not know about the other's complaint.

The figure 512,000 further illustrates problems with the factual basis upon which these communications were decided. Neither view has an appendix listing the evidence that was submitted. In *Näkkäläjärvi et al.*, the Committee simply states: 'The Committee has considered the communication in the light of all the information made available to it by the parties, in accordance with article 5(1) of the Optional Protocol.'[80] The result is that, despite the number 512,000 finding no support upon empirical inquiry, the Committee ends up reproducing it as an uncontested fact, without questioning it or seeking evidence to substantiate it. By repeating the figure in both communications, the Committee increases the figure's weight as an objective fact. This outcome gives rise to the impression that once material enters the Committee's system and is accepted as part of the proceedings, there is no further discussion on

[80] *Näkkäläjärvi et al.* (HRC), para. 6.1.

the reliability of evidence. Any assessment as to the reliability of a particular piece of evidence is conducted at an early stage in a communication's life cycle, which explains how the idea of 512,000 potential new Sámi voters was able to become *a fact* without any grounding.

10.6 Translating into Distance

How can the Committee have got the facts so wrong in these two cases? We would suggest the answer to this question must be found in processes of translation, understood both in its literal sense and more metaphorically. First, it must be noted that the ninety-three court cases from the SAC were not available for inspection by the Committee members, as the Finnish-language decisions have not been officially translated into English. What one finds instead is a summary of three of the ninety-three cases in the Committee's views on *Sanila-Aikio*. Thus, when the Committee deliberated on its views, it did so without direct access to the cases as primary sources. Subsequently, in its deliberations, the Committee was reliant on how the SAC cases were summarised for the Committee by the authors of *Näkkäläjärvi et al.* and *Sanila-Aikio*. Further, the Committee members had to depend on the summaries of the communications prepared by UN secretariat staff and had no means of looking *behind* what is included in the background dossier.

These cases reveal that in its argumentation, the Committee places familiar emphasis on the prevailing narrative within the human rights field of states attempting to restrict the rights of Indigenous peoples while simultaneously diminishing their autonomy and possibly pushing for forced assimilation.[81] The Committee also builds on a familiar narrative of the internal unity and harmony of Indigenous communities, which are connected to nature but outside politics.[82] By extension, the tensions that these communications capture are cast as existing solely between the unified Sámi peoples and the dominant population as represented by the State, and internal controversies within the Sámi community are erased from view.[83]

[81] See R. Hanski and M. Scheinin, *Leading Cases of the Human Rights Committee* (Turku: Institute for Human Rights, Åbo Akademi University, 2007).

[82] R. Toivanen and N. Fabritius, 'Arctic youth transcending notions of "culture" and "nature": Emancipative discourses of place for cultural sustainability', *Current Opinion in Environmental Sustainability* 43 (2020): 58–64.

[83] The analysis in Magallanes, 'Views adopted by the Committee', reproduces this argument.

This outcome legitimises the power of those segments of the Sámi people which have the majority in such institutions as the Sámi Parliament, and by extension have the authority to decide who is included in the Sámi electoral roll and who is excluded. This result distorts reality and further marginalises those Sámi people who are already marginalised, due to having been denied the status of registered Sámi by those members of the Sámi people who have the power to make these decisions within the Sámi Parliament.[84] These two communications are deeply detrimental to those Sámi who are marginalised in internal power struggles due to having been denied the status of registered Sámi voters.[85]

The relevant question for our argument is: How is it possible that the HRC took so many misleading arguments as legal facts and was not in a position to verify the information received? One of the biggest reasons is that in the HRC, there are only two parties: the individual and the member state. In the cases of *Näkkäläjärvi et al.* and *Sanila-Aikio*, the ninety-three Sámi whose electoral rights both communications were complaining about could not submit any communication of their own, not having any recognisable legal status or ongoing controversy vis-à-vis the State of Finland. In principle, before the results of these two communications were published, they did not even know that their voting rights were being disputed at the HRC,[86] and were not able to correct flawed information shared by the authors of *Näkkäläjärvi et al.* and *Sanila-Aikio*.

Translating felt injustices into the language of international human rights shifts their meaning.[87] As was already noted, such monitoring mechanisms as individual complaints have 'the capacity "to make things come into being"'.[88] Yet, as our case studies have illustrated, such processes also 'hide as much as [they] reveal'.[89] In translating *real life events*

[84] J. Ridanpää, 'Conceptualizing the North: Orientalism in the Arctic', *Arctic and Antarctic: International Journal of Circumpolar Sociocultural Issues* 1 (1) (2007): 11–38.

[85] This is not the focus of this chapter, however.

[86] See Toivanen, 'Protecting indigenous identities?'.

[87] R. Toivanen, 'Localizing the global in the superdiverse municipalities of the Arctic: The case of Inari', in R. Toivanen and J. Saarikivi (eds.), *Linguistic Genocide or Superdiversity? New and Old Language Diversities* (Bristol: Multilingual Matters, 2016), pp. 221–246.

[88] B. Frohmann, 'Documentary ethics, ontology, and politics', in *Archival Science* 8 (2008): 165–180; Hull, 'Documents and bureaucracy', p. 259.

[89] T. Kelly, 'The UN Committee against Torture: Human rights monitoring and the legal recognition of cruelty', *Human Rights Quarterly* 31 (2009): 777–800.

into *human rights violations* recognised as falling within the scope of the ICCPR, intermediaries acquire an important role. Intermediaries can be the claimants themselves, but more importantly, they are often individuals who know the Committee's jurisprudence well, such as former Committee members, as was the case in *Sanila-Aikio*. This raises the question of whether this complaint mechanism is open to everyone, or whether, due to its *evidentiary regime*, it ends up only being genuinely accessible for those who are skilled in translation.

A close reading of these communications illustrates how the accompanying translation processes can translate an argument, or a number, into an uncontested fact. Yet, these translation processes are not neutral, but instead assume a decisive role in creating narratives about contested situations while simultaneously seeking to legitimise these narratives.[90] Strikingly, the communications contain information that is presented as uncontested *fact* but without substantiating the information in any way, such as offering a source to assess its veracity. A perfect illustration of this is the repeated mention of 512,000 new voters which the SAC rulings could have possibly made a reality.

The consequences of the HRC's views regarding these two cases were devastating for the ninety-three persons, their children and future generations. This is illustrated by the aftermath of the communications: following the HRC's views, the Sámi Parliament in the elections of 2023 unilaterally decided to exclude these people from the electoral register. The Finnish SAC had to once again decide on complaints by these persons. Accordingly, the timetable became too tight for these persons, including the top candidate of the two last elections, to run for election.[91]

These events reveal how assessments of what constitutes a fact acquire important consequences in real life, even if the Committee's views are not legally binding. This is communicated by a letter dated 21 February 2023 that the Sámi Parliament sent to all those persons who had been added to the electoral roll by the SAC: 'In the view of the decisions and views by the UN committees on Human Rights and CERD, the electoral body of the parliament cannot consider that the decisions by the Finnish SAC are still valid for the elections 2023. The persons listed in the annex (not public) can, in case they wish, appeal this decision to the Sámi

[90] For a discussion on contestation over facts, see Halme-Tuomisaari, 'Contested representation'.

[91] The elections ran during the period of 3 September to 4 October 2023.

Parliament. The electoral committee of the Sámi Parliament promises to review the appeals objectively and lawfully.'[92]

10.7 Conclusion

In this chapter, we have combined two different kinds of ethnographic research – research on the HRC and research on Sámi rights struggles – with the aim of explaining what kind of information may be considered as fact in the HRC's individual communications procedure. Both *Näkkäläjärvi et al.* and *Sanila-Aikio* deal with the same issue – namely the self-determination of the Finnish Sámi to decide upon their membership through the involvement of an appeals court, the SAC. After struggling with the issue of admissibility, the HRC still found the existence of a Covenant violation. In doing so, the Committee relied on evidence that our analysis shows mischaracterised the actions of SAC. The Committee further went on to cite the dubious figure of 512,000 possible new voters as substantiation for individual violations, even though this figure has no concrete basis in reality.

Together, our case studies raise numerous compelling questions that call for further inquiry. What happened behind the scenes in these communications, which resulted in these outcomes? What roles were played by the authors' representatives, one of whom was a former Committee member and thus an insider to the Committee's operations? On the basis of these two case studies, what kind of broader conclusions can be drawn regarding the Committee's evidentiary regime?

It should also be noted that conducting rigorous analysis on such complex communications requires vast and specific expertise. In the present case, this has not only included ethnographic knowledge of the Committee's operations and Sámi rights struggles, but also the competence that we – this chapter's authors – have in the Finnish language. Only this combination of expertise has enabled us to look behind the written materials of these two communications, going all the way back to the original ninety-three court cases, which were distanced from the Committee members in the cases' written dossiers. Individual members of the HRC, primarily being experts in international human rights law in general and the ICCPR more specifically, understandably cannot have similar expertise for every communication that they process. Also,

[92] Sámi Parliament, minutes of the meeting in 4/2023, 21.2.2023, D nro. 486.

realistically, both Committee members and UN secretariat staff work under severe time constraints. This is an additional reason why data, such as ninety-three court cases, can become distanced; there is simply not enough time to read vast amounts of data, even if the individuals possessed the needed linguistic skills to do so.

Of necessity, Committee members have to rely on distinct techniques for assessing the veracity of data and arriving at their final conclusions. In doing so, they need to assess the reliability of the authors, as well as the comprehensiveness with which the UN secretariat has prepared the background dossiers. As these case studies illustrate, this approach may lead to outcomes that erase internal tensions from view. The same applies to such marginalised subjectivities as non-registered Sámi, as seen in our case studies. These outcomes may result in different kinds of human rights violations that the current monitoring framework focusing only on the relationship of states and communication authors – in this case, registered members of the Sámi people – is ill-equipped to address. We hope that our case studies and analysis may contribute to a nuanced debate on the evidentiary regimes of the HRC, as well as other international monitoring mechanisms, by generating new kinds of insights concerning their blind spots and unexpected consequences.

Select Bibliography

Billaud, J., 'Keepers of the Truth: Producing "Transparent" Documents for the UN Universal Periodic Review', in Charlesworth, H. and Larking, E. (eds.), *Assessing the Universal Periodic Review: Rights, Ritual, Ritualism* (Cambridge, UK: Cambridge University Press, 2015), pp. 63–83.

Brown, H., Reed, A. and Yarrow, T., 'Introduction: Towards an ethnography of meeting', *Journal of the Royal Anthropological Institute* 23(1) (2017): 10–27.

Cowan, J., Dembour, M.-B. and Wilson, R. (eds.), *Culture and Rights: Anthropological Perspectives* (Cambridge: Cambridge University Press, 2001).

Goodale, M. and Merry, S. (eds.), *The Practice of Human Rights: Tracking the Law Between the Local and the Global* (Cambridge: Cambridge University Press, 2007).

Halme-Tuomisaari, M., 'Guarding utopia: Law, vulnerability and frustration at the UN Human Rights Committee', *Social Anthropology/Anthropologie Sociale* 28(1) (2020): 35–49.

Hull, M. S., *Government of Paper: The Materiality of Bureaucracy in Urban Pakistan* (Berkeley: University of California Press, 2012).

Merry, S., *Human Rights and Gender Violence: Translating International Law into Local Justice* (Chicago: University of Chicago Press, 2006).

Moeckli, D., Keller, H. and Heri, C. (eds.), *The Human Rights Covenants at 50: Their Past, Present, and Future* (Oxford: Oxford University Press, 2018).

Niezen, R. and Sapignoli, M. (eds.), *Palaces of Hope: The Anthropology of Global Organizations* (Cambridge: Cambridge University Press, 2017).

Riles, A. (ed.), *Documents: Artefacts of Modern Knowledge* (Michigan: University of Michigan Press, 2005).

Toivanen, R., 'European fantasy of the Arctic Region and the rise of Indigenous Sámi voices in the global arena', in N. Sellheim, Y. V. Zaika and I. Kelman (eds.), *Arctic Triumph: Northern Innovation and Persistence,* vol. 1 (Cham: Springer International Publishing, 2019), pp. 23–40.

Toivanen, R., 'Protecting Indigenous identities? An example of cultural expertise on Sámi identity', *Legal Pluralism and Critical Social Analysis* 54 (2–3) (2019): 210–230.

PART V

Going Forward: Practical Recommendations

11

Practical Recommendations for Greater Fairness, Accessibility and Transparency in the UN Treaty Bodies' Evidentiary Norms and Practices

LISA REINSBERG, HANAA HAKIKI AND VINCENT PLOTON*

11.1 Introduction

The procedural steps through which the United Nations Human Rights Treaty Bodies (UNTBs) resolve individual communications are often broadly similar, if not identical. This broad commonality holds in particular for the ways in which the treaty bodies go about establishing the facts underpinning the individual communications they receive. As such, UNTBs' evidentiary principles and practices share common features. They also suffer from similar gaps and flaws, namely lack of consistency, legal clarity, visibility and fairness (including due to the inequality of evidentiary arms between individuals and states being insufficiently redressed).

This chapter is our response to these problems. It identifies practical recommendations for the consideration of every treaty body authorised to decide individual complaints,[1] thereby complementing reforms previously suggested by academics and practitioners.[2] Although this chapter

* The authors thank the DISSECT team, contributors to this volume and others who provided input and feedback toward the development of these recommendations.

[1] For their names and acronyms, see Table 1.1.

[2] Among the thoughtful recommendations made by scholars and practitioners with a wealth of knowledge on UNTB functioning, see I. Jelić and L. Mührel, 'The Human Rights Committee: Challenges and Prospects for Enhanced Effectiveness and Integration', *Journal of Human Rights Practice* 14 (2022): 17–43; B. Çalı and A. Skander Galand, Strengthening and Enhancing the Effective Functioning of the UN Human Rights Treaty Body System Individual Complaint Mechanisms: Recommendations from Members of Academia and Civil Society in View of the 2020 UN Human Rights Treaty Body Review (Centre for Fundamental Rights, Hertie School, 2020); C. Callejon, K. Kemileva and F. Kirchmeier, Treaty Bodies' Individual Communication Procedures:

has been written by its three indicated authors, the recommendations it offers have been endorsed by all the contributors to this volume – bar one who feels constrained by a conflict of interest.[3] Our collective sense is that the implementation of the advocated normative changes and transparency efforts would put future parties in a better position to understand and fulfil what is evidentiarily required of them, at the same time as enhancing the UNTB system's public legitimacy and efficiency.

The text is divided into two parts. The first part addresses evidence-specific matters. The second discusses general issues of access and information within the UNTB individual communications' procedure, as they relate to evidence.

11.2 Evidentiary Legal Principles

Fact-finding in general, and evidentiary principles in particular, are hardly addressed in the UNTBs' founding instruments. The facts of a complaint are generally expected to have been determined by the national judge before recourse to the communication procedure, which itself does not include a phase for discovery or investigation. Yet, rare are the cases where a UNTB can afford not to be concerned with reviewing the facts at all: domestic fact-finding may have been limited or flawed, if not inexistent; a committee may have to establish the relevant factual basis of its jurisdiction and determine the legal significance of the factual allegations, applying standards that differ from those of national jurisdictions; and a factual examination is in order if the complaint may be part of a wider state pattern or practice of human rights violations. Notwithstanding all this, UNTBs are not constrained by specific evidentiary rules, and those they have devised in practice may lack specificity or consistent interpretation. Our view is that this flexibility needs to be reined in. We propose that the standards of proof applicable through the various stages of the proceedings should be identified (Section 11.2.1); that the broad principles governing the burden of proof should

Providing Redress and Reparation to Victims of Human Rights Violations (Geneva Academy, 2019), Part 4; K. Kemileva, 'UN Inefficiencies Undermine Effective Handling of Individual Petitions', *OpenGlobalRights* (blogpost dated 29 October 2019); F. Viljoen, 'Fact-Finding by UN Human Rights Complaints Bodies: Analysis and Suggested Reforms', *Max Planck Yearbook of United Nations Law* 8 (2005): 49–100.

[3] Due to his current active membership of the Working Group on Arbitrary Detention, Matthew Gillett abstained from endorsing the recommendations offered in this chapter.

be clarified (Section 11.2.2); and that so should evidentiary forms and formats (Section 11.2.3).

11.2.1 Standards of Proof

The individual complaint procedure involves three decision points: registration, admissibility and merits. Each of these three decisions tends to involve an assessment of factual claims. However, neither the UNTBs' founding instruments nor their rules of procedure[4] address the relevant standards of proof. We believe that a uniform and clearly defined standard of proof should be adopted in respect of each procedural stage of the procedure, as follows: for registration, a complainant's factual allegation should be considered to have been sufficiently proven when it is *possible*; for admissibility, when it is *plausible*; for the merits to be upheld, when it is *probable*. These standards should be subject to certain exceptions when the complainant could not possibly have accessed relevant evidence or when the respondent state refrains from (fully) participating in the proceedings. Below we detail our proposals in respect to each main stage of the procedure.

11.2.1.1 Registration

Supposedly an initial, quick and simple stage, registration is clearly not so straightforward in practice, at least not from a complainant's perspective: more than 80 per cent of individual communications are rejected at this stage.[5] The reasons for non-registration are not detailed in a written decision, nor are they shared with individual complainants or reported externally in statistical form. Accordingly, the public has insight into neither the common nor the individualised reasons for non-registration in actual cases.

Interestingly, none of the treaty texts explicitly mentions 'registration'. Rather, they indicate that communications will be 'received' if they are submitted by individuals claiming to be victims of a violation of a treaty right by a statetate that has accepted the individual complaint procedure. Other textual conditions for a communication to be received include, for

[4] An overview of existing UNTB rules of procedures on registration and admissibility criteria is available in Table 11.3

[5] See, e.g., OHCHR website, UN Human Rights Report 2021, p. 441. Of the 2,867 new communications received by the treaty bodies in 2021, 399 were registered.

example, that the communication is not anonymous. Table 11.1 compiles the relevant treaty provisions.

UNTBs' rules of procedure, by contrast, refer – variably and inconsistently – to the steps and requirements to 'receive', 'transmit' to the UNTB or 'register' communications.[6] Rules typically delegate decisions on registration to one or several committee members or to the UN Secretary-General (in practice, staff in the Office of the High Commissioner for Human Rights, OHCHR).[7] Nothing is said about delegating decisions on admissibility, which therefore must be understood to be for the committees to take.

Despite registration and admissibility clearly being conceived as two different procedural stages, OHCHR guidance and some UNTBs' rules strangely suggest that communications should satisfy admissibility requirements – including substantiation – to be registered. One guidance note indicates that '[l]ack of sufficient substantiation of facts and allegations may result in the rejection of the registration of a communication'.[8] The OHCHR webpage states that 'the Committee will decide whether the case should be registered, that is to say formally listed as a case for consideration' ... ' [b]ased on the above mentioned requirements', in reference to explanation of criteria including timely submission, a complete and chronological recitation of the facts, an explanation as to exhaustion of domestic remedies, and basic personal information.[9] Similarly, the CERD's new Rules of Procedure allow for the Secretary-General to 'request clarification' concerning the elements of the communication, including 'information to substantiate the allegations', prior to its transmission to the Committee for a decision on registration;[10] and the Committee on the Rights of the Child (CRC)'s rules prohibit the receipt (registration) of any communication that fails to satisfy the admissibility criteria, including substantiation.[11]

[6] See, e.g., HRC, Rules of Procedure, Rule 92: 'As soon as possible after the communication has been received, the Committee, through its special rapporteur ... shall decide whether the communication brought to its attention should be registered.'

[7] See, e.g., CAT, Rules of Procedure, Rule 104.1: 'Complaints may be registered by the Secretary-General or by decision of the Committee or by the Rapporteur on new complaints and interim measures.'

[8] OHCHR website, Guidance for Submitting an Individual Communication to the UN Treaty Bodies, Part. 14.

[9] OHCHR website, Individual Communications, text under 'The Complaint Procedure' heading.

[10] CERD, Rules of Procedure (2025), Rule 95 regarding the information to be contained in a communication.

[11] CRC, Rules of Procedure, Rule 16(3).

Elsewhere, the OHCHR and UNTBs have referred to registration as a prima facie assessment of (all) admissibility requirements.[12] They have not publicly defined this legal standard (which can have different meanings in different legal systems) nor explained why admissibility would be assessed at this stage. This, however, is the actual practice: each individual complaint that is submitted gets reviewed by a member of the OHCHR's Petitions Section, who filters out communications deemed 'clearly inadmissible',[13] before conveying the remainder to the relevant treaty body's designated rapporteur or working group responsible for registration. In other words, only those complaints that appear, at first look, to satisfy all admissibility requirements, on the basis of the complainant's submissions, will be registered.

The UNTBs' regional counterparts provide instructive – if limited – examples of how the registration requirements may be assessed without imposing a higher burden on complainants than what is required by their founding instruments and rules.[14] The African Commission on Human and Peoples' Rights (ACHPR) and Inter-American Commission on Human Rights (IACHR), for example, make registration decisions based on whether the complainant's allegations *might* constitute a right's

[12] See, e.g., OHCHR website, Information note by the OHCHR Human Rights Treaty Body Branch: Achievements of the Human Rights Treaty Bodies in 2022, 3 January 2023: '320 new individual communication cases met prima facie admissibility requirements and were registered by the treaty bodies between 1 January and 1 December 2022'; OHCHR website, UN Human Rights Report 2021, p. 441: OHCHR 'received 2,867 new communications that were subject to prima facie admissibility analyses in its screening process, resulting in 399 new cases registered, as they appeared to fulfil the prima facie admissibility requirements'. See also *Stitou and Ben Hmdou* v. *Spain*, E/C.12/72/D/86/2018, 10 October 2022, para. 6.5: 'The Committee recalls that, even where a communication appears prima facie to be admissible because the initial submission is sufficiently substantiated for purposes of registration, nothing prevents the Committee from concluding, after further examination and on the basis of the information on admissibility provided by both parties, that the communication is inadmissible for want of sufficient substantiation.'

[13] Information conveyed to the authors by an insider to the UNTB system.

[14] The regional human rights bodies provide no explanation as to the reasoning behind their (mostly negative) registration decisions, leaving this process as opaque as in the UNTBs system, as well as exclusionary. See, e.g., M. A. Jimoh, 'A Critique of the Seizure of the African Commission on Human and Peoples' Rights', *African Human Rights Law Journal* 22 (2002): 362–378; J. Gerards, 'Inadmissibility Decisions of the European Court of Human Rights: A Critique of the Lack of Reasoning', *Human Rights Law Review* 14 (2014): 148–158; H. Keller, A. Fischer and D. Kühne, 'Debating the Future of the European Court of Human Rights after the Interlaken Conference: Two Innovative Proposals', *European Journal of International Law* 21 (2010): 1025–1048.

violation.[15] The IACHR terms this a 'colourable claim' standard, requiring it to determine whether the facts alleged, if proven to be true, could constitute a violation of a protected right.[16] As such, the IACHR is not assessing the evidentiary support, but rather whether the factual allegations – if substantiated – would allow the possible legal conclusion that the state violated its obligations. For its part, the European Court of Human Rights (ECtHR) requires that applicants fully complete and sign the application form and attach supporting documentation in order for their applications to be lodged (received).[17] As in the UNTB system, the regional bodies (with the exception of the ECtHR) may, or must, request additional information from the petitioner if compliance with the registration criteria is unclear.[18]

Taking into account the UN human rights treaty texts' limited registration criteria (most often, simply that an individual claim be a victim of a violation of a treaty right by a State Party that has accepted the complaint procedure), the broader and more stringent criteria currently applied in practice (namely prima facie admissibility), the lack of clear guidance to complainants, the high proportion of communications rejected at registration and the fact that filtering and registration decisions are often made with only minimal UNTB member involvement while admissibility decisions are theoretically the sole prerogative of the treaty bodies themselves, the following recommendations should be considered:

1) Implement a truly *prima facie*[19] or 'colourable claim' standard of proof for registration, based on the common requirement that individual complainants claim to be victims of a treaty violation by a State Party.[20] This means that when what a communication asserts, if taken

[15] ACmHPR, Rules of Procedure (2020), Rule 115.

[16] See, e.g., IACmHR website, Digest of the IACHR on its Admissibility and Competence Criteria (2020), para. 282.

[17] See, e.g., ECtHR, Rules of Procedure, Rule 47; ECtHR, Analysis of statistics 2024 (2025), indicating that 8,650 applications were disposed of administratively (not lodged) in 2024, compared to 28,784 applications allocated to a judicial formation; ECtHR, Report on the implementation of the revised rule on the lodging of new applications (2015), indicating that 23% of complaints were rejected in 2014 for failure to meet these requirements.

[18] See, e.g., HRC, Rules of Procedure, Rule 90; IACHR, Rules of Procedure, Rule 26.2; ACHPR, Rules of Procedure, Rule 115.4.

[19] On how prima facie should be legally understood, see Chapter 3, this volume.

[20] This standard is frequently described as a requirement to present a prima facie allegation of a violation. See, e.g., IACmHR website, Digest of the IACHR, para. 2; ACmHPR

to be true, could constitute a violation of the relevant treaty by a State Party, the communication will be registered. Registration should take place even if the factual allegations and supporting documentation are incomplete, so long as they are not clearly false and could make out a legally cognisable claim, and any other treaty/rule-specific registration requirements (such as that the communication is in writing and not anonymous) are met.

2) When a particular text imposes additional registration requirements, ensure that these requirements are clearly explained in the public guidance to complainants.
3) For any communication, only assess the registration requirements that apply to communications brought under that particular treaty.
4) Refrain from evaluating admissibility requirements at the registration stage, unless the relevant rules make them applicable at registration.
5) Reconcile actual practice and the rules of procedure, such that, for example, if a UNTB is not willing to register communications that do not appear to satisfy all admissibility criteria, this condition is clearly indicated as a registration requirement, at least in the relevant guidance to complainants to begin with and as soon as possible afterwards in an amendment to the rules of procedure.

11.2.1.2 Admissibility

Admissibility requirements are much more clearly set out in the UNTBs' founding instruments. They typically include the requirements applicable to registration, plus the following: that domestic remedies have been exhausted; that the claim be sufficiently substantiated or not manifestly unfounded; that it is compatible with the treaty; that it has not been lodged elsewhere (non-duplication); and that it does not constitute an abuse of the right of submission (including by being untimely).[21]

However, the standard of proof to be applied when assessing whether they are met remains opaque. For instance, in regard to the sufficiently substantiated/not manifestly unfounded requirement, UNTB decisions

website, Information Sheet No. 4: Communication Procedure: 'The Commission shall decide whether to be seized of the communication by determining whether it alleges any prima facie violation of the Charter.'

[21] On the latter requirement, see for example, *Alzery* v. *Sweden*, CCPR/C/88/D/1416/2005, 25 October 2006, para. 8.2.

and guidance frequently reference a prima facie threshold, but as Reinsberg has shown in Chapter 3, this standard is inconsistently interpreted, with its common legal understanding distorted in various ways that result in it being taken to imply a higher standard of proof than is normatively appropriate.[22] In addition, the exhaustion rule brings a lot of difficulties.

We therefore offer a number of recommendations.

1) Regarding the rule of the exhaustion of domestic remedies:

  1.1) When the complainant presents a prima facie argument that they have exhausted domestic remedies, and the state disputes this argument, shift the burden of proof onto the state and require it to provide a convincing and substantiated (thus well above prima facie) explanation that the exhaustion requirement has not been met.[23]

  1.2) Recognise an exception to the exhaustion rule when information available to the treaty body, even from sources beyond the parties' submissions, such as its own case law, information it has gathered in the exercise of its other functions or findings emanating from other human rights mechanisms or organisations, demonstrates the existence of a pattern or practice of violations relevant to the submitted complaint, which makes clear that local remedies are unavailable, ineffective or insufficient.[24]

  1.3) Extend the exceptions to the exhaustion rule to all situations where the complainant was, in practice, facing obstacles that prevented them from accessing domestic remedies.[25]

2) Regarding the 'sufficiently substantiated' requirement:

  2.1) Apply a prima facie (i.e., plausibility) standard of proof, whereby if the complainant's allegations and arguments *could* be true and possible, the complaint is admissible.

  2.2) Apply this standard *without* consideration for the Sstate's submissions.[26]

[22] See Chapter 3, this volume.
[23] See Chapter 7, this volume.
[24] See Chapter 8, this volume.
[25] See Chapter 7, this volume.
[26] As to why this consideration is important, see Chapter 3, this volume.

2.3) Whatever doubt arises due to missing or conflicting evidence, consider the allegations sufficiently substantiated/not manifestly unfounded (for admissibility purposes) as long as they are plausible.

2.4) In assessing plausibility, consider the complainant's circumstances, including: their difficulties/inability to access justice or legal representation; their proven presence (or absence) in the location mentioned in the complaint; their membership in a vulnerable or marginalised group; the state's conduct in clarifying and responding to the alleged facts at the national level; and the way the trauma of the alleged violation would have affected their ability to provide evidence or explanations, etc.[27]

2.5) In assessing plausibility, take into account relevant findings from within the UN system, including those developed internally by the UNTB or its counterparts in the course of all their functions, concerning, for example, similar alleged violations, state policies and practices and the background to the situation complained of.

2.6) Explicitly examine the factual allegations disputed by the parties by reference to the prima facie standard for purposes of admissibility. In other words, do not amalgamate the admissibility and merits stages. If appropriate, indicate that the facts are proven to a standard of proof which is higher than prima facie, and specifically name this higher standard of proof.[28]

2.7) As appropriate, fully and consistently exercise the power granted to UNTBs to request additional information necessary to the determination of admissibility, including by inviting parties to oral hearings where possible and relevant.[29]

[27] See, e.g., *F. and G.* v. *Denmark*, CCPR/C/119/D/2530/2015, 16 March 2017, para. 7.5: 'The Committee also takes note of the authors' assertion that these inconsistencies were due in part to the trauma that they had endured. The Committee considers that the authors have provided sufficient explanations as to the reasons for which they fear that forcible return to Egypt would result in a risk of treatment incompatible with article 7 of the Covenant. They have also argued that the Board denied them the opportunity to provide medical evidence to substantiate their claims regarding the torture that F endured in detention. The Committee therefore considers that, for the purposes of admissibility, the authors have sufficiently substantiated their allegations.' See also Chapter 2, this volume.

[28] On the importance of this point, see Chapter 2, this volume.

[29] See, e.g., CRC, Guidelines for oral hearings in the context of the Committee's consideration of communications under the Optional Protocol on a communications procedure, CRC/C/157, 26 October 2021; HRC, Guidelines on making oral comments concerning communications, CCPR/C/159/Rev.1, 26 March 2019.

11.2.1.3 Merits

The merits stage calls for a higher standard to be applied than at admissibility. However, this standard should not be so high as to defeat the purpose and possibility of accepting individual complaints. There is broad agreement in human rights scholarship that the appropriate standard of proof for the merits stage in human rights complaint proceedings should generally be the 'balance of probabilities',[30] also known as the 'preponderance of evidence' or 'more probable than not' standard. However, there are circumstances when the standard should be either lowered or heightened, as we shall indicate below.

The fundamental problem here is that UNTBs, like other human rights bodies such as the regional courts, rarely specify the standard of proof they are applying. A fortiori, their decisions fail to observe when the factual basis of a complaint is proven in practice to a higher standard than legally required. This risks resulting in an inadvertent upscaling of the applicable standard, due to the level of proof achieved in some cases, unconsciously setting the bar to be met by subsequent complainants.

Vagueness regarding standards of proof is problematic.[31] Not only does it inevitably produce inconsistencies, but it also keeps decision-makers from resolving the crucial issue of defining the level of evidence sufficient to confirm a complaint's factual allegations. This lack of clarity affects all other stakeholders, including the complainants who are left without guidance as to what evidence they need to submit.

We recommend the following:

1) UNTBs should declare the balance of probabilities to be the standard of proof generally applicable for confirming disputed factual allegations at the merits stage.
2) The complainant's factual allegations are to be presumed true when the state does not contest them and other evidence does not negate them.[32]

[30] Chapters 2 and 8, this volume.

[31] As to why the undifferentiated 'intime conviction' standard adopted in the Civil Law tradition is sub-optimal in human rights adjudication, see Chapter 2, this volume.

[32] See, e.g., *Katwal* v. *Nepal*, CCPR/C/113/D/2000/2010, 1 April 2015, para. 11.1: 'The Committee takes note of the author's unrefuted allegations . . . In the absence of any other relevant information on file, the Committee considers" the allegations substantiated.'

3) When considering whether the balance of probabilities standard of proof is met, UNTBs should consider not only the submissions before it, but also:

   3.1) limitations on the complainant's ability to submit additional evidence, for example due to their limited ability to access justice or legal representation, or disability, trauma, membership in a vulnerable or marginalised group, etc.[33]

   3.2) what information the state was or should have been in a good position to submit, but did not submit, drawing adverse inferences from this as appropriate;[34]

   3.3) information generated through their other functions.

4) When the complainant alleges that a particular violation is part of a systematic pattern or administrative practice, the standard of proof should be heightened to 'clear and compelling' regarding the context (existence of the pattern/practice), but lowered to prima facie regarding the link between the context and the individual violation claimed.[35]
5) A similar heightening and lowering of the standard of proof should take place when the claim arises in a context such that it is reasonable to presume that the state has acted in the way alleged by the complainant.[36]
6) Final views should specifically indicate when a standard of proof higher than the balance of probabilities has actually been met in a particular case, so as to avoid the level of evidence met in that case becoming the standard expected to be met in subsequent cases.

11.2.2 Burden of Proof

As a general rule, in legal proceedings, the party making allegations bears the burden of proving them to the relevant standard of proof.[37] UNTBs have nonetheless recognised that variations to this default may be necessary

[33] See Chapter 2, this volume.

[34] See Chapter 6, this volume.

[35] See Chapter 8, this volume.

[36] See Chapters 2 and 6, this volume.

[37] See, e.g., *Case Concerning Pulp Mills on the River Uruguay (Argentina* v. *Uruguay)*, ICJ, 20 April 2010, para. 162: '[T]he Court considers that, in accordance with the well-established principle of *onus probandi incumbit actori*, it is the duty of the party which asserts certain facts to establish the existence of such facts.'

when the parties do not enjoy equal access to information and evidence.[38] This is especially so when violations of human rights take place covertly, such as in cases of incommunicado detention, enforced disappearance, extraordinary rendition and pushbacks of people on the move.[39]

The Human Rights Committee (HRC) has observed that the 'burden cannot rest alone on the author of a communication, especially if one considers that the author and the State Party do not always have equal access to the evidence, and that frequently the State Party alone is in possession of the relevant information', in part because of the state's 'duty to investigate in good faith all allegations of violations' of a human rights treaty.[40] The CRC has similarly recognised that 'the burden of proof does not rest solely on the author of the communication, especially considering that the author and the State Party do not always have equal access to the evidence and that frequently the State Party alone has access to the relevant information'.[41] Coming from a different angle, the Committee against Torture (CAT) has stated that 'when the complainant cannot elaborate on his or her case, for instance when the complainant … is deprived of his or her liberty, the burden of proof is reversed and it is up to the State Party concerned to investigate the allegations and verify the information on which the complaint is based'.[42] Additionally, treaty bodies have recognised states' duty to cooperate with individual complaint procedures they have accepted.[43]

[38] As documented in Chapters 2,5, 6 and 8, this volume.

[39] Apart from the relevant chapters in this volume, see CAT, General Comment No. 4 on the implementation of article 3 of the Convention in the context of article 22, CAT/C/GC/4, 4 September 2018, para. 38; *Bleier* v. *Uruguay*, CCPR/C/15/D/30/1978, 29 March 1982, para. 13.3; *Al Khazmi* v. *Libya*, CCPR/C/108/D/1832/2008, 18 July 2013, para. 8.2; *Almegaryaf and Matar* v. *Libya*, CCPR/C/110/D/2006/2010, 29 April 2014, paras. 7.2 and 7.4; *Al Daquel and others* v. *Libya*, CCPR/C/111/D/1882/2009, 21 July 2014, para. 6.3; *Hidalgo Rea* v. *Mexico*, CCPR/C/131/D/3259/2018, 25 March 2021, para. 9.3. See also *Velásquez Rodríguez* v. *Honduras*, IACtHR, 7920, Merits, 29 July 1988, para. 131; *Morales Zegarra et al.* (Peru), IACmHR, Report No. 57/99, 13 April 1999, paras. 47-9; *Egyptian Initiative for Personal Rights and Interights* v. *Egypt*, ACmHPR, Comm. No. 334/06, 3 March 2011, para. 142; *Al-Nashiri* v. *Poland*, ECtHR, 28761/11, Judgment, 24 July 2014, para. 400; *Onyachi and Anor* v. *Tanzania*, ACmHPR, 003/2015, 28 September 2017, para. 169; *Nguza Viking (Babu Seya) and Johnson Nguza (Papi Kocha)* v. *Tanzania*, ACmHPR, 006/2015, 23 March 2018, para. 71.

[40] See, e.g., *Bleier* (HRC), para. 13.3; see also Chapter 6, this volume.

[41] *D.D.* v. *Spain*, CRC/C/80/D/4/2016, 1 February 2019, para. 13.3. For a critique of this formulation, see Chapter 2, this volume.

[42] *A.J.E.* v. *Sweden*, CAT/C/71/D/874/2018, 22 July 2021, para. 8.5. See also CAT, General Comment No. 4, para. 38.

[43] HRC, General Comment No. 33 on the Obligations of States Parties under the Optional Protocol to the International Covenant on Civil and Political Rights, CCPR/C/GC/33,

Despite these general recognitions, the UNTBs have not always clearly and consistently allocated the burden of proof in their consideration of the merits of individual complaints. This is true both with respect to the burden of production (which goes to the issue of which party is responsible for furnishing which kinds of evidence) and the burden of persuasion (which goes to the issue of which party is responsible for meeting the relevant standard of proof).

With regard to the burden of proof, UNTBs should consider the following recommendations:

1) The state should bear the burden of proof relative to information to which the state has superior access. Inter alia, this includes:
   - 1.1) producing evidence concerning persons in the custody of the state, including their fate after detention, and whether they have been appropriately treated;[44]
   - 1.2) proving the existence and adequacy of procedural guarantees relative to detention;[45]
   - 1.3) proving the conventionality of decisions to use allegedly excessive force,[46] as well as other key decisions taken by authorities;
   - 1.4) producing records in the hands of the authorities, including those pertaining to nationality;[47]
   - 1.5) producing information concerning the potential risk of being subjected to torture if expelled, returned or extradited;[48]

5 November 2008, para. 15: 'A duty to cooperate with the Committee arises from an application of the principle of good faith to the observance of all treaty obligations'.

44 See Chapter 5, this volume.

45 See WGAD, Report of the Working Group on Arbitrary Detention 2011, para. 68: 'Where it is alleged that a person has not been afforded, by a public authority, certain procedural guarantees to which he or she was entitled, it may be difficult to establish the negative fact that is asserted. A public authority is generally able to demonstrate that it has followed the appropriate procedures and applied the guarantees required by law – if such was the case – by producing documentary evidence of the actions that were carried out. In general, the burden rests with the Government: it is for the Government to produce the necessary proof'.

46 See *Soare and Others* v. *Romania*, ECtHR, 24329/02, Judgment, 22 February 2011, para. 139; *Ataykaya* v. *Turkey*, ECtHR, 50275/08, Judgment, 22 July 2014, para. 46.

47 See *Wetsh'okonda Koso and Others* v. *Democratic Republic of Congo*, ACmHPR, 281/03, 24 November 2008, para. 90; *Gihana and Others* v. *Rwanda*, ACtHPR, 017/2015, 28 November 2019, paras. 84–85; see also *Penessis* v. *Tanzania*, ACtHPR, 013/2015, 28 November 2019, paras 92, 96–97.

48 See CAT, General Comment No. 4, para. 38; *X. and Y.* v. *Switzerland*, CAT/C/75/D/1081/2021, 11 November 2022, para. 7.3; *Berhane* v. *Switzerland*, CAT/C/73/D/872/2018, 28 April 2022, para. 7.4

1.6) proving compliance with the relevant treaty in situations in which investigations or court proceedings have been delayed;[49]

1.7) proving a non-discriminatory justification for differences in treatment in cases of alleged discrimination, where the complainant has made a plausible claim.[50]

2) When information available to a treaty body indicates a pattern or practice of violations has occurred or is occurring,[51] and the applicant has made a plausible case that they were subject to a violation or violations constituting part of that pattern or practice, the state should bear the burden of proof of showing it is more likely than not that the violation alleged did not in fact occur.

3) As appropriate, fully and consistently exercise UNTBs' authority to request additional information necessary to the determination of the merits, including by inviting parties to oral hearings where possible and relevant.

11.2.3 Forms and Formats of Evidence

The UNTBs, like other human rights mechanisms, have taken a free approach to the evaluation of evidence.[52] This means that they are not constrained by rules requiring certain forms or sources of evidence to be afforded particular weight, and can consider the probative value of the

[49] See *Desmond Williams* v. *Jamaica*, CCPR/C/59/D/561/1993, 8 April 1997, para. 9.4. See also *Briggs* (Trinidad and Tobago), IACmHR, Report No. 44/99, 15 April 1999, para 53; *Giménez* (Argentina), IACHR, Report No. 12/96, 1 March 1996, para 101; *Lamey et al.* (Jamaica), IACmHR, Report No. 49/01, 4 April 2001, para. 183; *Canese v. Paraguay*, IACtHR, 12.032, Merits, 31 August 2004, para. 142.

[50] See *V.P.* v. *Belarus*, CEDAW/C/79/D/131/2018, 28 June 2021, para. 7.10: 'The Committee considers that, when relevant information is presented in a communication indicating, prima facie, the existence of a legal provision that, although formulated neutrally, might in fact affect a much higher percentage of women than men, it is for the State Party to show that such a situation does not constitute indirect discrimination on the grounds of gender.' See also *Hoogendijk* v. *Netherlands*, ECtHR, 58641/00, Judgment, 6 January 2005, paras 21–22; *D.H. and Others* v. *Czech Republic*, ECtHR, 57325/00, Judgment, 13 November 2007, para. 3; *Dorzema et al.* v. *Dominican Republic*, IACtHR, 12.688, Merits, 24 October 2012, para. 229; *Open Society Justice Initiative (on behalf of Noumeni)* v. *Cameroon*, ACmHPR, 290/04, 18 September 2018, para. 189; *Cînta* v. *Romania*, ECtHR, 3891/19, Judgment, 18 June 2020, para. 79.

[51] This context should be established to an appropriately high standard of proof. On how high this standard should be, compare the views of Dembour and Hakiki (Chapter 2, this volume) and Roberts (Chapter 8, this volume).

[52] See, e.g., CAT, General Comment No. 1: Implementation of Article 3 of the Convention in the context of Article 22 (refoulement and communications), A/53/44, 16 September 1998, Annex IX, para. 9.

information before them on a case-by-case basis. While the individual complaint proceedings are primarily written proceedings, some UNTBs have also opted to allow, at least in principle, the submission of evidence through oral hearings,[53] although to date this has seldom been used. Nonetheless, important gaps in policy and practice remain, which may result in incomplete or inconsistent consideration of complainants' evidence. For example, the OHCHR instructs complainants not to send audiovisual or 'electronic' content,[54] and provides no guidance on the inclusion of, or reference to, digital materials such as webpages. The public guidance does not advise complainants on how to submit forms of evidence that are not written documents, nor are there publicly identified channels for doing so. Beyond the possible inconsistencies that this may engender, lack of clarity in this area also means complainants cannot be assured that OHCHR or UNTBs will actually review the links, videos, photographs or other content they submit. When so much relevant information is audiovisual or digital, including open-source evidence, treaty bodies ought to confirm that they will receive and evaluate these various forms of evidence.[55]

Additionally, and despite the UN's extensive system of fact-finding mechanisms, UNTBs have not clarified whether, when and to what extent they will consider evidence already collected and analysed either by the UNTBs – including through the individual complaint, state review, and inquiry procedures – or by other international investigative mechanisms. Adopting the following changes would increase the consistency, comprehensiveness and clarity of UNTBs' evidentiary standards:

1) Adopt consistent standards of acceptance regarding types and formats of evidence across UNTBs, with a view to maintaining the accessibility of the complaint procedure to individuals and ensuring an open, consistent, and comprehensive approach to fact-finding.

[53] See, e.g., CRC, Guidelines for oral hearings; HRC, Guidelines on making oral comments; *Abdussamatov* v. *Kazakhstan*, CAT/C/48/D/444/2010, 1 June 2012.

[54] See, e.g., OHCHR website, 23 Frequently Asked Questions about Treaty Body Complaint Procedures (2007): '[D]o not send tapes, videos, CDs or other electronic information, unless expressly asked'.

[55] See, e.g., OHCHR and Human Rights Center at the University of California, Berkeley, Berkeley Protocol on Digital Open Source Investigations (2022), paras. 7–8. To be noted that open-source evidence is also relevant to treaty bodies' own fact-finding efforts: D. Murray, Y. McDermott and K.A. Koenig, 'Mapping the Use of Open Source Research in UN Human Rights Investigations,' *Journal of Human Rights Practice* 14 (2022): 554–581.

2) Expressly permit the submission of audiovisual and digital forms of evidence, in recognition of the important factual evidence they provide.
3) Modify the individual complaint form to indicate the accepted forms of evidence and provide submission instructions.
4) Allow complainants to present evidence in oral hearings,[56] which may be held virtually, and establish a clear process for requesting, granting and holding hearings, in line with the existing policies on oral comments from the CRC[57] and HRC.[58]
5) Take official notice *motu proprio* of UN documents, including treaty body decisions and communications and reports from Special Procedures and UN fact-finding and investigative bodies, that are relevant to the credibility of the alleged violations or the complainant's ability to satisfy admissibility criteria (e.g., exhaust domestic remedies), and reference them in views adopted.
6) Formalise and implement the practice of explaining, in writing, the reasons for which a third-party submission is rejected, and communicate these to the submitting entity and to the parties to the complaint.
7) Develop clear norms through jurisprudence and public guidance concerning the UNTBs' approach to:

    7.1) taking official notice of widely accepted or widely reported facts;
    7.2) testimonial evidence, including through hearings;
    7.3) digital evidence;
    7.4) expert opinion evidence;
    7.5) third-party submissions.[59]

11.3 Procedural Transparency and Accessibility

Consistency and transparency of UNTB practice, as well as express acknowledgment and explanation in instances when a UNTB comes to diverge

[56] See F. Viljoen, 'Fact-Finding by UN Human Rights Complaint Bodies – Analysis and Suggested Reforms', *Max Planck Yearbook of United Nations Law* 8 (2005): 49–100, 90–93.
[57] CRC, Guidelines for oral hearings.
[58] HRC, Guidelines on making oral comments.
[59] See, e.g., CAT, Guidelines on third-party submissions under article 22 of the Convention (2023); CRC, Guidelines on Third-Party Interventions under the Optional Protocol to the Convention on the Rights of the Child on a Communications Procedure (OPIC) (2020); HRC, Guidelines on Third-Party Submissions (2019); CESCR, Guidance on Third-Party Interventions (2016). See also International Service for Human Rights, Guide for Third Party Interventions before UN Human Rights Treaty Bodies (2022).

from prior practice, are important for the coherent functioning, legitimacy and fairness of the UNTB complaint procedures.[60] This chapter has highlighted several areas in which UNTB practice may be unclear or inconsistent with regard to evidentiary standards and the handling of evidence in individual complaint proceedings. For example, some treaty bodies' instruments or rules include an admissibility requirement that individual complaints be 'sufficiently substantiated' or 'not manifestly ill-founded', but not all do.[61] Similarly, UNTBs sometimes announce their conclusions concerning these differing substantiation requirements in individual cases without referencing to or sharing their analysis of the relevant evidence.[62] Nonetheless, and despite the fact that not all UNTBs apply the same requirement, the OHCHR advises all complainants that a communication may be rejected at registration or be considered inadmissible if it is not 'sufficiently substantiated'.[63] These statements fail to distinguish between the UNTBs' different requirements, and also provide little meaningful guidance to complainants. Additionally, the public guidance to complainants appears to have been written for an audience with legal training, and is dispersed in multiple, lengthy, sometimes inconsistent documents.[64]

The public guidance provided by the OHCHR is critically important for both experienced and novice users of the complaint procedure. If clearly and accurately written, this guidance can save complainants time and effort and make the complaint procedure more accessible to its intended beneficiaries. Of course, the UNTBs themselves also stand to

[60] See, e.g., *Ziablitsev* v. *France*, E/C.12/71/D/176/2020, 2 March 2022, individual opinion of Committee member Rodrigo Uprimny (concurring).

[61] See Chapter 3, this volume.

[62] See, e.g., *S.M.* v. *Bosnia and Herzegovina*, CCPR/C/135/D/3154/2018, 8 July 2022, para. 6.6; *Mohammdi Bandboni et al.* v. *Switzerland*, CEDAW/C/85/D/173/2021, 15 May 2023, para. 6.7.

[63] OHCHR website, 'Guidance for Submitting an Individual Communication to the UN Treaty Bodies', section 14: 'Lack of sufficient substantiation of facts and allegations may result in the rejection of the registration of a communication.'

[64] OHCHR, Individual Complaint Procedure under the United Nations Human Rights Treaties, Fact Sheet No. 7/Rev. 2 (2013), p. 8: 'Is the complaint sufficiently substantiated? If the relevant Committee considers, in the light of the information before it, that the complainant has not sufficiently presented/ described the facts and arguments for a violation of the Covenant, it may reject the case as insufficiently substantiated, and thus inadmissible'; OHCHR website, 'Individual Communications: Human Rights Committee': 'Complaints under the Optional Protocol to the Covenant that contain the necessary prima facie elements are referred to the Committee's Special Rapporteur on New Communications and Interim Measures, who decides whether the case should be registered and transmitted to the State Party for the observations.'

benefit from increased public understanding of their law and procedure, including to the extent that access to relevant information helps individuals assess the appropriateness of submitting a complaint and meet the evidentiary requirements.

11.3.1 Clarity of Guidance

In order to increase the consistency of UNTB decision-making concerning evidence, as well as allow individual complainants and the public to accurately understand the relevant requirements and procedures, UNTBs, with the support of the OHCHR, should:

1) Revise the OHCHR guidance to complainants to be more accessible to the general public, including with regard to substantiation as an admissibility requirement
2) Expressly define any legal terms used as a standard in the context of, respectively, registration, admissibility, and merits decisions
3) Modify the individual complaint form as necessary to request, and provide space for, information related to complainants' difficulties obtaining evidence
4) Synthesise and consolidate public guidance to individual complainants, with a view to eliminating duplicative and contradictory content and ensuring its accuracy and consistency
5) Explicitly state the burden(s) and standard(s) of proof at each stage of the proceedings, and make clear any variations among treaty bodies in documents made publicly available, such as OHCHR factsheets and guidance on individual communications
6) Explicitly state in the OHCHR guidance to complainants when (how and in which circumstances) the burden of proof is shifted or the standard of proof is lowered
7) Where appropriate, modify rules of procedure to clearly reflect the principles and standards applied in practice with regard to burden and standard of proof and acceptable forms of evidence
8) Identify and clearly explain differences in practice where those exist, in publicly available guidance to complainants

11.3.2 Clarity in Practice

1) Clearly explain the evaluation of evidence in admissibility and merits decisions, with reference to the relevant pieces of information in

treaty body views. More detailed explanation could be accommodated by condensing the summaries of the parties' arguments and incorporating the evidentiary details into treaty bodies' analyses.

2) Consider eliminating the (unofficial) limit on the length of adopted views.
3) Consistently apply principles concerning the burden and standard of proof and evaluation of evidence.
4) Seek to harmonise UNTB practice regarding evidentiary standards and the handling of evidence in individual complaint proceedings, to the maximum extent allowable under their respective founding instruments.[65]

11.3.3 Effective and Equal Participation

In order for individual complainants to submit relevant evidence and for UNTBs to be able to review material information, complainants must be able to effectively and fully participate in the complaint process. This includes ensuring accommodation and assistance for persons with disabilities, minimising the barriers imposed by language requirements, protecting complainants and their representatives from the risks of non-secure communication channels, enabling parties' access to case files and processing information, and providing individualised support as necessary to overcome technological and other challenges. Currently, the OHCHR website and guidance documents contain no information regarding accommodation or assistance. In light of these needs, UNTBs should consider the following recommendations:

1) Actively involve users of the system, including treaty body petitioners, in the process of developing tools, procedures and guidelines which affect individual communications, including but not limited to evidentiary regimes.[66]
2) Provide assistance and accommodation for persons with disabilities in presenting their complaints if and when required, and clearly explain the process and any requirements for requesting assistance or accommodation in the OHCHR guidance to complainants.

65 Such efforts could build on the recent establishment of an advisory mechanism on the harmonisation of working methods across UNTBs. See Report of the Chairs of the Human Rights Treaty Bodies on their 36th annual meeting, A/79/292, 6 August 2024, para. 70.

66 See, e.g., International Service for Human Rights website, Joint NGO Statement to the 2023 Meeting of Treaty Body Chairpersons.

3) Abstain from requiring that complainants translate their submissions or evidence when presented in an official UN language, even if this is not the State Party's language.[67]
4) Building on positive precedents of OHCHR support to individual petitioners at risk,[68] establish a User Support Section or Victim/Witness Unit to provide support to complainants and witnesses, as well as protection if and when required, including in hearings, and to address, among other issues, their privacy and digital security needs.

11.3.4 Transparency and Accessibility of Information

Individual complainants' ability to understand and comply with evidentiary standards depends, in large part, on their access to timely and relevant information on UN human rights treaties' substantive protections and UNTBs' procedural rules and practices. UNTBs have fleshed out the interpretation of their founding instruments and rules through concluding observations, individual cases, amendments to their rules of procedure and, to a lesser extent, in general comments or general recommendations. Current and future parties to a complaint proceeding must be able to locate and search these documents in order to craft and support their own legal arguments and anticipate how a UNTB will likely resolve factual and legal questions.

Other actors also depend on access to UNTB information. Third-party intervenors can identify opportunities to contribute to a UNTB's consideration of a communication only when they have adequate notice of the existence and substance of pending complaints.[69] Scholars and

[67] This translation requirement is addressed in a joint private NGO letter to the UNTBs and Secretariat dated 26 June 2017 and endorsed by 14 international NGOs which engage with the UNTBs on individual communications. The letter argues that the practice of requesting petitioners to submit translations of documents should be abandoned on the following grounds: it does not have a legal basis in any of the UN treaties and their rules of procedure; it is detrimental to the victims' basic right of access to justice; it is incompatible with a victim-centred approach and the *pro homine* or *pro personae* principle; and it is not reflected in the practice of other international complaint bodies.

[68] See International Service for Human Rights website, Treaty Body Protection Measures in Cases of Reprisals and Intimidations against Treaty Body Petitioners, Letter to OHCHR Petitions Unit, 27 June 2017. See also CAT letters to Morocco regarding reprisals against the petitioner and his wife in relation to communication No. 606/2014 (OHCHR website, 'UN Treaty Body Database', Document Type: Reprisal Letter, Treaty: CAT, Country: Morocco).

[69] V. Ploton and J. Urizar, 'Friends of the Court: Making the most of Amicus Curiae with UN Treaty Bodies', *EJIL Talk!* (blogpost dated 18 April 2022): 'The most obvious limitation to the submission of TPIs to UNTBs is lack transparency (*sic*) and publicly accessible information about cases pending review. Quite clearly, if information about

researchers require access to decisions in order to effectively analyse and explain the UNTBs' substantive and procedural functioning.

However, while the UNTBs and OHCHR have made enormous strides toward making information accessible in recent years, important gaps remain. For example, the JURIS database of UNTB decisions is often out of date and can produce incomplete or irrelevant search results.[70] Translations of decisions and guidance are not available in all six official UN languages.

Many of the current gaps likely stem from insufficient resources, which leave the treaty body system with too few people and too little money to ensure optimal access to information.[71] A vital, shared goal for all those invested in human rights protection must be the allocation of adequate resources to the UNTB system.

Resources aside, however, adoption of the following key principles and specific changes could result in significantly improved access to information:

1) Regularly update and publish lists of registered communications pending review by individual treaty bodies,[72] ideally indicating the

what cases are pending review before the Committees is not made available, it is factually impossible for third parties to intervene.'

[70] For example, a search of the database conducted on 16 November 2023 indicated CERD's most recent decision to be from April 2023, whereas CERD's webpage devoted to Session 110 includes a decision adopted in August 2023. A JURIS Database search for the word 'sterilized' returns two CEDAW Committee inadmissibility decisions, but does not include the CEDAW Committee's decision on the merits in *A.S.* v. *Hungary*, CEDAW/C/36/D/4/2004, 29 August 2006, which concerns forced sterilisation and uses the word 'sterilized' four times.

[71] On the system's lack of resources, see, e.g., A. Skander Galand and B. Çalı, 'Human Rights Victims' Complaints to UN Not Treated Effectively', *Open Global Rights* (blogpost dated 20 March 2020), Recommendation 7.

[72] HRC's and CESCR's rules of procedure already expressly require the preparation and publication of a list of registered communications, which is a practice these committees fulfil. See HRC, Rules of Procedure, Rule 89.2: 'The Secretary-General shall prepare a list of the communications registered by the Committee, together with a brief summary of their contents, and will make it public while keeping the author's name confidential'; CESCR, Rules of Procedure, Rule 2.2. The rules of procedure of some UNTBs require the Secretary-General to keep a record and summary of registered communications, but do not address the publication or confidentiality of this list. See, e.g., CAT, Rules of Procedure, Rule 106. CAT does not currently publish a list of pending communications. The OHCHR webpage on CAT's individual communications states, under the heading 'Recent Complaints': 'The Committee publishes a list of all complaints that have been received on an annual basis. This list is not comprehensive.' This links to the JURIS database, which only contains *adopted* decisions and reports. Some rules of procedure prohibit publication of the list of registered cases, although the relevant treaties and optional protocols do not include this prohibition. See, e.g., CEDAW, Rules of Procedure, Rule 57.2: 'The Secretary-General shall prepare lists of the communications submitted to

relevant keywords and list of articles allegedly violated.[73] If necessary, consider amending the rules of procedure to allow for publication of the list of registered communications.

2) Ensure that all adopted decisions, as well as relevant reports such as follow-up reports on views, are made publicly available in the JURIS Database in a timely manner.
3) Improve access to decisions through timely communication to the parties.
4) Consider publishing parties' submissions, subject to complainants' consent and the relevant UNTB treaty requirements and with appropriate redactions to respect confidentiality and data privacy. Where current UNTB rules prohibit publication of complaints or submissions, consider revising those rules in line with treaty requirements and in the interest of transparency.

Improve searchability of decisions in the JURIS database, through:

5) improved accuracy of the full-text functionality
   expansion of the list of keywords
   showing snippets or previews in results view, and
   enabling users to search views by treaty articles which the UNTB has found to have been violated, rather than merely alleged to have been violated.
6) Ensure that all functions of the JURIS database are available in the six UN languages.
7) Implement a system for tagging or identifying lead cases or views that UNTBs frequently refer to or that establish important or precedential principles.
8) Consistently publish annual data and statistics on petitions, including those rejected in the registration phase,[74] such as in the OHCHR annual report.[75]

the Committee, together with a brief summary of their contents'; Rule 74.3: 'The Committee, working group or rapporteur shall not make public any communication, submissions or information relating to a communication prior to the date on which its views are issued.' See also CRC, Rules of Procedure, Rule 29.3; CRPD, Rules of Procedure, Rules 76.2, 76.3; CED, Rules of Procedure, Rule 80.3.

[73] International Service for Human Rights, Submission to OHCHR Questionnaire in relation to General Assembly Resolution 68/268 (2019).

[74] Regional human rights mechanisms publish such statistics annually.

[75] See, e.g., OHCHR, UN Human Rights Report 2021, p. 441.

Annexes

Table 11.1 *Receivability requirements as per the texts of the UNTBs' foundational instruments*

ICERD	Art. 14	The Committee has competence to 'receive and consider communications from individuals . . . claiming to be victims of a violation by [a] State Party of any of the rights' in the CERD, so long as that state has accepted the individual complaint procedure, but that it 'shall not receive anonymous communications'.
ICCPR-OP1	Arts. 1–4	The Committee shall not receive a communication 'if it concerns a State . . . which is not a Party' to the Optional Protocol and, additionally, that communications may be submitted by 'individuals who claim that any of their rights enumerated in the Covenant have been violated and who have exhausted all available domestic remedies', but that communications that are anonymous, an abuse of the right of submission, or incompatible with the provisions of the Covenant 'shall be consider[ed] inadmissible' and not communicated to the state.
CAT	Art. 22	'[N]o communication shall be received . . . if it concerns a State Party' that has not accepted the individual complaint procedure and a communication will be submitted to the state unless it is inadmissible by virtue of being anonymous, an abuse of the right of submission, or incompatible with the Convention).

Table 11.1 (*cont.*)

ICESCR-OP	Arts. 1–2	The Committee shall not receive a communication 'if it concerns a State . . . which is not a Party' to the Optional Protocol, and, additionally, that communications may be submitted by, or on behalf of, individuals 'claiming to be victims of a violation' of Covenant rights and the Committee may 'decline to consider a communication where it does not reveal that the author has suffered a clear disadvantage, unless the Committee considers that the communication raises a serious issue of general importance').
CEDAW-OP	Arts. 1–4	'[C]ommunications may be submitted by or on behalf of individuals or groups of individuals, under the jurisdiction of a State Party, claiming to be victims of a violation' of Convention rights by a State Party' and that '[c]ommunications shall be in writing and shall not be anonymous').
CRC-OP	Arts. 1–5	The Committee shall not receive any communication concerning a state that is not party to the optional protocol or concerning an instrument to which it is not a party; '[c]ommunications may be submitted by or on behalf of an individual or group of individuals, within the jurisdiction of a State Party, claiming to be victims of a violation by that State party' of the CRC or its two substantive optional protocols.
ICRMW	Art. 77	'[N]o communication shall be received by the Committee if it concerns a Party that has not' accepted the individual complaint procedure; a communication shall be considered inadmissible – without being communicated to the state – if it is anonymous, an abuse of the right of submission, or incompatible with the Convention.
CRDP-OP	Art. 1–3	The Committee shall not receive any communication concerning a state that is not a party to the Optional Protocol; a communication will be considered inadmissible without being transmitted to the state if it is anonymous, an abuse of the right of petition or incompatible with the Convention, does not meet the requirements of non-duplication

Table 11.1 (*cont.*)

		and exhaustion of domestic remedies, is 'manifestly ill-founded or not sufficiently substantiated', or concerns facts that occurred prior to the entry into force of the Optional Protocol for the State Party).
CED	Art. 31	The Committee has competence to 'receive and consider communications from or on behalf of individuals subject to its jurisdiction claiming to be victims of a violation by this State Party of provisions of this Convention'; the 'Committee shall consider a communication inadmissible' without submitting it to the state if it is anonymous, an abuse of the right of submission or incompatible with the Convention, or does not meet the requirements of non-duplication and exhaustion of domestic remedies).

Table 11.2 *Comparison of treaty texts' receivability (registration) and admissibility requirements*[a]

		Submitted by individual claiming to be a victim	Against a State Party to complaint procedure	Not anonymous	Exhaustion of domestic remedies	Not abusing the right of petition	Compatible with convention	Not submitted to another forum	Sufficiently substantiated and/or not manifestly ill-founded
ICERD									
Receivability	Art. 14(6)(a)	x	x	x					
Admissibility	Art. 14(7)(a)				x				
ICCPR									
Receivability	OP1, Arts. 1, 2	x	x		x				
Admissibility	OP1, Arts. 3, 5			x	x	x	x	x	
CAT									
Receivability	Art. 22(1)	x	x						
Admissibility	Arts. 22(2), 22(5)			x	x	x	x	x	
CMW									
Receivability	Art. 77(1)	x	x						
Admissibility	Arts. 77(2), 77(3)			x	x	x	x	x	

		Submitted by individual claiming to be a victim	Against a state party to complaint procedure	Not anonymous	Exhaustion of domestic remedies	Not abusing the right of petition	Compatible with convention	Not submitted to another forum	Sufficiently substantiated and/or not manifestly ill-founded
CEDAW									
Receivability	OP, Arts. 2, 3	x	x	x					
Admissibility	OP, Art. 4				x	x	x	x	x
CED									
Receivability	Art. 31(1)	x	x						
Admissibility	Art. 31(2)			x	x	x	x	x	
CRPD									
Receivability	OP, Art. 1	x	x						
Admissibility	OP, Art. 2			x	x	x	x	x	x
ICESCR									
Receivability	OP, Arts. 1, 2	x	x						
Admissibility	OP, Art. 3			x	x	x	x	x	x
CRC									
Receivability	OP3, Art. 5	x	x						
Admissibility	OP3, Art. 7			x	x	x	x	x	x

[a] Many treaty texts or optional protocols also require that the facts alleged occurred prior to the entry into force of the complaint mechanism for the State Party concerned. In addition, the optional protocols to the ICESCR and CRC include the admissibility requirement of timely submission (within one year of exhaustion of domestic remedies), and the ICESCR may decline to consider a complaint unless it reveals a 'clear disadvantage' to the author. The relevant optional protocols to CEDAW, ICESCR, and the CRC require consent (or explanation of the lack thereof) for submission of a communication on behalf of individuals or groups.

Table 11.3 *Provisions in UNTB rules of procedure on registration and admissibility criteria*

	Specific rule(s) on registration	Separate rule(s) on admissibility	Decision on registration by a rapporteur	Decision on registration by working group	Decision on registration by Secretary-General	Decision on registration by Committee
CERD	Rules 91–96, 100	Rule 106		x		
HRC	Rules 91, 92	Rule 99	x			
CAT	Rule 104	Rule 113	x		x	x
CESCR	Rule 5	Rule 12	x	x		
CEDAW	Rule 56	Rule 67			x	
CRC	Rule 16	-[a]			x	
CRMW	-	-	-	-	-	-
CRPD	Rules 55, 68	Rule 69	x	x		
CED	Rule 67	Rule 73		x		s

[a] While the CRC's Rules of Procedure describe the process for determining admissibility, they do not identify the requirements that must be satisfied. See CRC, Rules of procedure under the Optional Protocol to the Convention on the Rights of the Child on a communications procedure, Rules 18–22.

INDEX